Birth of The Byzantine Army 476–641 CE

Volume 2: Watch them Fight!

Philippe Richardot

Helion & Company Limited
Unit 8 Amherst Business Centre
Budbrooke Road
Warwick
CV34 5WE
England
Tel. 01926 499 619
Email: info@helion.co.uk
Website: www.helion.co.uk
X, formerly Twitter: @helionbooks
Facebook: @HelionBooks
Visit our blog https://helionbooks.wordpress.com/

Published by Helion & Company 2025
Designed and typeset by Mary Woolley, Battlefield Design (www.battlefield-design.co.uk)
Cover designed by Paul Hewitt, Battlefield Design (www.battlefield-design.co.uk)

Text © Philippe Richardot 2025
Maps by George Anderson © Helion & Company 2025
Illustrations © Philippe Richardot unless otherwise credited

Every reasonable effort has been made to trace copyright holders and to obtain their permission for the use of copyright material. The author and publisher apologise for any errors or omissions in this work and would be grateful if notified of any corrections that should be incorporated in future reprints or editions of this book.

ISBN 978-1-804518-48-9

British Library Cataloguing-in-Publication Data.
A catalogue record for this book is available from the British Library.

All rights reserved. No part of this publication may be reproduced, stored in a retrieval system, or transmitted, in any form, or by any means, electronic, mechanical, photocopying, recording or otherwise, without the express written consent of Helion & Company Limited.

For details of other military history titles published by Helion & Company Limited contact the above address or visit our website: http://www.helion.co.uk.

We always welcome receiving book proposals from prospective authors.

Publisher's Note
All dates, unless specifically specified otherwise, are CE

Contents

Acknowledgements		v
Chronology		vi
Introduction		xvii
8	The Army Watches over the Borders	19
9	Preparing for a Campaign	88
10	The Fleet Sets Sail for a Distant Shore	108
11	The Enemy is Spotted!	127
12	Catapults Versus Ramparts	133
13	Elite Cavalry and Second-Class Infantry?	172
14	The Pitched Battle: Tactics and Practice	210
15	The Battle of the Yarmuk, the End of the Late Antique World	243
Conclusion: A New Model Army		266
Colour Plate Commentaries		273
Bibliography		276

Publisher's note: The chapter numbers for this volume run on sequentially from those in Volume 1.

Acknowledgements

I want to express my friendly gratitude to David Wilson and to the Numerus Invictorum Reenactment Group for their respective help, and to my old and trusted friend Etienne Le Baube.

Chronology

476 Romulus Augustulus, last Emperor of the West, overthrown by Odoacer *Generalissimo* and Patrician, then new King of Italy. Siege of Constantinople and restoration of Emperor Zeno by Isaurian troops. Elimination of the usurper Basiliscus.

478 Mutiny of Theodoric Strabo, Ostrogothic King settled in Thrace, against Eastern Roman Empire.

479 Usurpation of Marcian, son of the Western Emperor Anthemius, in Byzantium, put down by Illus the Patrician, Emperor Zeno restored again. Thrace, Rhodope, Macedonia and New Epirus raided by Ostrogothic Prince Theodoric the Amal. Siege and fall of Epidamnos/Dyrrachium (today Durrës in Albania) by Theodoric the Amal.

480 Ostrogothic King Theodoric Strabo attacked by Bulgars, at the request of Emperor Zeno.

481 Byzantium spared by Theodoric Strabo in exchange for ransom. Dalmatia conquered by Odoacer.

482 Siege and fall amd then fired of Larissa in Thessaly by Theodoric the Amal.

484 Theodoric Strabo assassinated near Philippi in Thrace; Theodoric the Amal new King of the Ostrogoths. Samaritan revolt put down by Emperor Zeno.

485 War and truce concluded between Emperor Zeno and King Vakhtan I Gorgasali of Georgia. Construction of a Romano-Byzantine fortress on Tzanic territory by Longinus, Emperor's Zeno brother.

487 Moesia raided by Theodoric the Amal.

488 Theodoric the Amal sent by Emperor Zeno to Italy against the usurper Odoacer.

491–518 Anastasius I Emperor.

492–497 Rebelled Isaurians pacified by Romano-Byzantines.

492 Battle of Kotyaion won by Masters of Soldiers, John Gibbo 'the Hunchback' and John the Scythian, over Isaurian rebels.

493 Odoacer killed by Theodoric the Amal (later 'the Great'), becomes new King of Italy.

493 or 494 Unlocated battle in Thrace won by Bulgars over Julian, Master of the Soldiers to Illyricum who is killed in battle. Heruls driven out of Moravia by Lombards.

CHRONOLOGY

498 Euphratensis raided by Lakhmid Bedouins and Palestine raided by Ghassanids. Both repelled by Eugenios, Duke of Euphratensis or Osrhoene, and Romanus, Duke of Palestine.

499 Battle of the River Tzurta won by Bulgars over Aristus, Master of the Soldiers to Illyricum.

502–532 Thirty Years' War between Romano-Byzantines and Sassanid Persians. War is considered split into two phases: the Anastasian War 502–506 and the Justinian War 526–532.

502 Iberian Kingdom (modern eastern Georgia) invaded and King Vakhtang I Gorgasali killed by Persians.[1] Siege and capture of Theodosiopolis of Armenia and Martyropolis (today Erzurum and Silvan in Turkey) by the Sassanid Persian King Kavadh I. Battle of Bismideon, (today Tell-Besmai west of Mardin in Turkey) won the Persians over Olympios, Duke of Mesopotamia. Carrhae's region in Osrhoene raided by Lakhmid Bedouins. Thrace raided by Bulgars.

502–503 Siege, and fall, of Amida by the Persian King Kavadh I.

503 Siege of Amida by Masters of the Soldiers Present Patricius and Hypatius. Siege and battle of Nisibis (today Nusaybin in Turkey) on the Persian border by Flavius Areobindus Dagalaifus, Master of the Soldiers to the East; Persian relief army routed but Nisbis remained in Persian hands. Battle of Apadna won by King Kavadh I over Patricius and Hypatius. Sieges of Constantina/Constantia of Osrhoene and of Edessa, present-day Viranşehir in Turkey and Şanlıurfa in Turkey, by Persians. Northern Persia threatened by Huns at the request of Anastasius I. Arabia Petraea, Palestine and eastern Egypt raided by Lakhmid Bedouins.

504 Arzanene in Persarmenia and Jebel Sinjar raided by Flavius Areobindus Dagalaifus Master of the Soldiers to the East. Amida regained by Romano-Byzantines after negotiations.

505 Siege of Sirmium (today Sremska Mitrovica in Serbia) taken by Ostrogothic General Pitzia from Gepids, a Germanic tribe. Battle of Horreum Margi or Margoplanum (Ćuprija in Serbia) won by Ostrogoth Count Pitzia and Gepid "cattle thieves'" leader Mundo over Sabinian the Younger, Master of the Soldiers to Illyricum and his Bulgar *foederati*. Construction of the Dara fortress on the border with Persia by Romano-Byzantines. Lazica raided by Tzani.

508 Frankish King Clovis honoured with the title of Consul by Anastasius I. Romano-Byzantine naval expedition against Taranto held by Ostrogoths.

512 Heruls settled as *foederati* in Singidunum (today Belgrade in Serbia) by Anastasius I.

513 Armenian rebellion.

---

1 At this period, Spain was called in Latin Hispania, Iberia was the Roman and Early Byzantine name for present-day Georgia.

513–518 Rebellion led by Vitalian Count of the *Foederati* against Anastasius I.

515 Naval Battle of Bytharia won over rebel Vitalian the Thracian by the Praetorian Prefect Marinus of Syria. Armenia, Cappadocia and Lycaonia raided by Sabir Huns.

517 Balkans raided by Slavs. Long Walls erected by Anastasius I in order to protect Byzantium suburbs.

518–527 Justin I Emperor.

518 Vitalian the Thracian reconciled with the new Emperor.

520 Vitalian the Thracian assassinated shortly after being appointed Consul.

524–525 King Tzath I of Lazica and King Gourgen of Iberia revolt against Persians with the help of Hun mercenaries paid by Justin I.

526–532 Iberian War between Romano-Byzantines and Persians.

526 Persarmenia raided by Masters of the Soldiers Sittas and Belisarius. Syria raided by Lakhmid Bedouin King, al-Mundir III ibn al-Nu'man.

527 Unlocated battle in Persarmenia won by Persarmenian Generals and brothers Narses and Aratius Kamsarakan over Sittas and Belisarius. Siege of Nisibis and sudden retreat by Libelarius who was then replaced as Master of the Soldiers to the East by Belisarius.

527–565 Justinian I Emperor.

528 Ghassanid pro-Roman Bedouin tribe attacked by Lakhmid Bedouin King al-Mundir III ibn al-Nu'man, Romano-Byzantine reprisals. Unlocated battle won over Persian-allied Huns by Boa, Queen of the Sabir Huns. Scythia, Moesia and Thrace raided by Bulgar Huns. Two battles won over Justin Master of the Soldiers to Moesia who is killed in battle, then Masters of the Soldiers to Moesia and to Illyricum, Constantiolus and Askum the Hun, captured by Bulgars. Battles of Thannuris (today Tell Tunainir in Syria) and of Mindouos (the modern hamlet of Kasriahmethayro) won by Persian General Xerxes over Belisarius.

529 Region of Antioch (today Antakya in Turkey) raided by Lakhmid King al-Mundir III ibn al-Nu'man. Bulgar Hunnic raid repulsed by Mundo, Master of the Soldiers to Illyricum.

530 Battle of Dara won by Belisarius, Master of the Soldiers to the East over Persian General Perozes. Battles of Theodosiopolis and of Satala won by Sittas, Master of the Soldiers Present, over Persian General Mermeroes/Mihr-Mihroe. Slavic raid in Illyricum and Bulgar raid in Thrace both repelled by Mundo, Master of the Soldiers to Illyricum.

531 First Battle of Callinicum won by Persian General Azarethes over Belisarius. Siege and fall of Abgersaton fortress in Osrhoene by Persians. Romano-Byzantine Lazica and Anatolia raided by Sabir Huns. Two failed sieges of Martyropolis by Persians.

531–533 Slavic raids from Antes and Sklavenes repelled by Chilbudius, Master of the Soldiers to the Thraces.

532 'Eternal Peace' concluded between Persians and Romano-Byzantines. Nika revolt against Justinian I in Byzantium suppressed by Belisarius.

CHRONOLOGY

533–534 Vandal War, destruction of the Vandal Kingdom of Africa by Belisarius.

533 Battles of Ad Decimum and Trikamaron won by Belisarius, Master of the Soldiers to the East, over Vandal King Gelimer.

534–535 Moors revolt.

534 Battle of Mammes won by Solomon, Master of the Soldiers to Africa, over Moors. Unlocated battle north of the Danube won by Sklavenes over Chilbudius, Master of the Soldiers to the Thraces.

535–562 Gothic War in Italy between Romano-Byzantines and Ostrogoths.

535 Battle of Mount Bourgaon won by Solomon, Master of the Soldiers to Africa, over Moors. Sicily invaded by Belisarius. Siege and fall of Panormus (modern Palermo) by Belisarius. Dalmatia conquered from Ostrogoths by Mundo Master of the Soldiers to Illyricum. Battle of the River Iatrus in Moesia, now River Yantra, Bulgaria, won over Bulgar raiders by Sittas, Master of the Soldiers to the Thraces.

536 Romano-Byzantine troops mutiny in Byzantine Province of Africa (roughly today's Libya) led by Stotzas, a 'common soldier'. Siege and fall of Naples, then occupation of Rome by Belisarius. Eastern borders of Egypt and province of Euphratensis in Northern Syria raided by Saracens from the Arabian Peninsula. Dalmatia invaded by Ostrogoths. Battle of Salona won over them by Mundo who was killed in the battle. Dalmatia reconquered by Constantianus Patrician, Count of the Stable, and new Master of the Soldiers to Illyricum.

537 Battle of Skalai Beteres won over Stotzas' mutineers in Africa by Germanus cousin of Justinian I. John Cottistis mutiny at Dara. Battle of Scardon won over the Ostrogothic General Uligisal by Constantianus, Patrician and Count of the Stable. Siege of Salona by Uligisal and Asinarius.

537–538 Siege of Rome victoriously defended by Belisarius against Ostrogoth King Vitiges.

538 Narses the Eunuch sent with reinforcements to Belisarius in Italy. Ariminium (today Rimini) occupied by Romano-Byzantines. Siege of Rimini by Vitiges. Battle of Ticinum (present-day Pavia) won over Ostrogoths by Mundilas, Romano-Byzantine commander. Liguria and Mediolanum (today Milan) occupied by Romano-Byzantines. Sieges and fall of Urbinum and Urbs Vetus (today Urbino and Orvetio in central Italy) by Belisarius. Frankish King Theudebert I's intervenes in Italy but forced to retreat by outbreak of dysentery. Battle of Oinochalakon won by Armenian rebels over Sittas, Master of the Soldiers Present.

538–539 Siege and destruction of Milan by Ostrogoths and Burgundians.

539 Romano-Byzantines defeated by the Gepids on the Danube. Double Battle of Tortona won over Ostrogoths then Romano-Byzantines by Franks. Battle won by the Gepids over Calluc, Master of the Soldiers to Illyricum who was killed in battle. Siege and fall of Faesulae (today Fiesole in Tuscany) by Cyprian and Justin. Siege and fall of Auximum (today Osimo) by Belisarius.

540 'Eternal Peace' breached by the Persian Sassanid King Khosrow I, invasion of Mesopotamia, siege and destruction of Sura, ransoming of Hierapolis of Syria, capture of Beroea of Syria (today Aleppo) and sacking of Antioch. Siege and fall of Ravenna, capture of King Vitiges by Belisarius. Belisarius recalled from Italy to fight the Persians. Illyricum and Thrace raided by Kutrigur Huns without any opposition. Solomon campaigns against the Moors in the Aures Mountains.

540–562 Romano-Byzantine-Persian War.

541–557 Lazic War between Romano-Byzantines and Persians.

541 Battle of Treviso won by the ephemeral Ostrogoth King Ildibad over Vitalius, Master of the Soldiers to Illyricum, and Heruls. King Gubazes II of Lazica defects to the Persians when Khosrow I invaded his country. Siege and fall of Petra fortress in Lazica (today Tsikhisdziri in Georgia) by Persians. Siege and fall of Verona to Romano-Byzantines then successfully counter-attacked by Totila, new Ostrogothic King. Siege and fall of Sisauranon to Belisarius.

542 Battles of Faventia and of Mucellium (modern Faenza and Mugello valley) won by Totila over Romano-Byzantines. Siege and fall of Callinicum, razed to the ground and its population deported by Persian King Khosrow I.

542–543 Siege and fall of Naples by Totila.

543 Battle of Anglon (near modern Dvin in Armenia) won by Persians over Martin, Master of the Soldiers to the East.

543–547 Desert Moors revolt against Romano-Byzantines.

544 Battles of Theveste and Cillium won by the Moors over Solomon, Master of the Soldiers to Africa, who is killed in battle. Belisarius sent to Italy against Ostrogoths. Thrace raided by Antes. Siege of Edessa by Persian King Khosrow I.

545 Battle of Thacia in Africa won by John the Son Sisiniolus' loyal troops over over the rebel Stotzas, whos is killed in battle. Five-year Peace concluded with Persians by Justinian I.

545–546 Siege of Rome by Totila who partly destroyed the city walls. Thrace raided by Sklavenes.

546 Assassination of Areobindus, Governor of the Province of Africa Proconsularis by secessionist Guntharith, Duke of Numidia, whi was himself subsequently murdered.

546–547 Moors pacified by John Troglita, Duke of Libya.

546–562 War between Ghassanids and Lakhmids.

547 Battle of Marta won by Syrtes tribes led by Carcasan over John Troglita, Duke of Libya. Battle of the Fields of Cato won by Troglia over Syrtes tribes. Rome reoccupied by Belisarius. Campania reconquered by Totila. Rebellious Gepids and Heruls pacified by Romano-Byzantines.

548 Siege and fall of Ruscianum (today Rossano, in Calabria) by Totila. Belisarius blockaded in south of the Italian peninsula. Veneto invaded by Franks. Battle in Veneto won by Lombard Prince Ildiges over Lazarus, Master of the Soldiers. Illyricum raided by Sklavenes. King Gubazes II of Lazica's demand for help against Persians. Siege of

Persian-held Petra fortress in Lazica by Dagistaheus, Master of the Soldiers to Armenia.

548–549 Siege and fall of Perusia (today Perugia in Umbria) by Totila.

549 Belisarius recalled to Constantinople. Battle of Laureate in Dalmatia won by Ostrogoth General Indulf over Romano-Byzantines. Illyricum, and Thrace raided by Sklavenes. Battle of the River Phasis, Persian General Phabrizus defeated by Dagisthaeus and Gubazes II.

549–550 Siege and fall of Rome by Totila.

550 Illyricum, Dalmatia and Thrace raided by Sklavenes. Battle of Adrianople, Scholasticus the Eunuch defeated by Sklavenes. Illyricum raided by Kutrigur Huns. Battle of Tanais (present-day River Don) won by Utigur Huns and Tetraxite Goths sent by Justinian I over Kutrigurs. Battle of the River Hippis or Mucheirisis or Mocheresis won by Dagisthaeus and Gubazes II over Persian General Chorianes, who was killed in the battle. Rome and Sicily reconquered by Totila. Renewal of the Five-Year Peace with Persians, in exchange for 2,600 pounds of gold.

550–551 Siege and fall of Petra fortress in Lazica, destroyed by Bessas, master of the soldiers to Armenia.

551 Truce between Romano-Byzantines and Persians. Ostrogothic naval operations south of the Adriatic and sacking of Corfu. Naval Battle of Sena Gallica (today Senigallia) won by John, the nephew of Vitalian, and Valerian, Master of the Soldiers, over the Ostrogothic Generals Indulf and Gibal. Sicily reconquered by Romano-Byzantines. Corsica and Sardinia invaded by Ostrogoths. Illyricum raided by Sklavenes. Third war between Lombards and Gepids. Athanagild rebelled against Visigothic King Agila and called on Byzantium for help.

552 Battle of Taginae/Tadinae or Busta Gallorum (today Gualdo Tadino and Sassoferrato) won by Narses the Eunuch over Totila, who died from wounds received. Siege and fall of Rome to Narses the Eunuch. Late 552/early 553, Battle of Mons Lactarius (today Monti Lattari south of Naples) won by Narses the Eunuch over Teias the last Ostrogoth King. Romano-Byzantine landings in Malaga and at other Spanish coastal towns.

553 Italy invaded by Franks. Battle of Rimini won by Narses the Eunuch over the Franks. Siege and fall of the Telephis Fortress in Lazica by Persian General Mermeroes.

554 Battle of the Volturnus or of Casilinum (current River Volturno in Capua), won over Franks and Alemanni by Narses the Eunuch. Battle of Yawm Halima near Chalcis (today Qinnasrin) won over Lakhmid King al-Mundhir III ibn al-Nu'man, who was killed in action, by Ghassanid King al-Harith ibn Jabalah. Siege and fall of Nesos fortress in Lazica by Persian General Mermeroes. Small Romano-Byzantine expeditionary force landed in Spain.

554–555 Siege and fall of Compsa (today Conza della Campania) by Narses the Eunuch.

554–567 Sporadic war between the Visigothic King of Spain Athanagild and Romano-Byzantine coastal cities.

555 Narses the Eunuch campaign south of the Po. Lazic War, siege and Battle of Onoguris won by Persian General Nachoragan over Martin, Master of the soldiers to Armenia, and Bouzes.

556 Siege and Battle of Phasis in Lazica (today Poti in Georgia) won over Persian General Nachoragan by Martin, Master of the Soldiers to Armenia.

557 Lazic War, truce between Romano-Byzantines and Persians.

556–557 Misimian revolted against Romano-Byzantines.

558 Revolt of Tzani, subsequently put down by Romano-Byzantines.

559 Greece and Chersonese of Thrace raided by Kutrigur Huns, led by Zabergan, and Sklavenes. Siege of Byzantium by Zabergan. Battle of Melanthius (modern Hoşköy Belediyesi) won over Zabergan by Belisarius who then retired.

562 Last Ostrogothic resistance north of the Po crushed by Narses the Eunuch. 'Fifty-Year Peace' or Treaty of Dara concluded with Persians: Lazica returned to Romano-Byzantine rule. Obaisipolis (Odyssus?) and Anastasiopolis in Thrace raided by Huns.

563–565 Moors revolt against Romano-Byzantines.

565–578 Justin II Emperor.

567 Battle of the Field of Asfeld won by the Lombards and Avars over the Gepids.

568 Veneto conquered by Lombards.

569 Liguria conquered by Lombards.

569–579 Moorish rebellion against Romano-Byzantines.

570 Baza region and the city of Malaga reconquered from Romano-Byzantines by Visigothic King of Spain Leovigild. Thrace raided by Avars then repulsed by Count Tiberius. Siege and fall of Benevento by Lombard Duke Zotto.

570–571 Three battles won over Praetorian of Africa Theodore, Masters of the Soldiers Theoctistus then Amabilis – all killed in action – by Moorish King Garmul.

571 Siege and fall of Sidonia in Spain, reconquered from Romano-Byzantines by Visigothic King of Spain Leovigild.

572–591 War between Romano-Byzantines and Persians initiated by Justin II.

572 Persian province of Arzanene raided by Romano-Byzantine. Battle of Sarmathon/Sargathon (present-day Qasr Serijihan) in Syria won over Persian General Varaman by Marcian the Patrician, Master of the Soldiers to the East.

573 Failed campaign of Marcian the Patrician, Master of the Soldiers to the East. Siege of Nisibis by Marcian the Patrician. Siege and fall of Dara, Ghassanids submit to Persian King Khosrow I.

574–575 War in Mesopotamia between Persians and Romano-Byzantines.

574 Battle of Khalamakhik won over Persians by rebellious Persarmenians. Truce concluded between Romano-Byzantines and Persians.

576 Unlocated battle in Italy won over Baduarius, Master of the Soldiers, by Lombards. Caucasian tribe Suans pacified by Romano-Byzantines. Thrace raided by Sklavenes. Battle of Melitene won over Persian King Khosrow I by Justinian, Master of the Soldiers to the East.
577 Unlocated battle in Armenia won over Justinian, Master of the Soldiers to the East, by Persian General Tamkhosrow.
577–579 Campaign against rebel Moors by Gennadius, Master of the Soldiers to Africa.
578 Unlocated battle in Italy won over Romano-Byzantines by Lombards. Thrace and Greece raided by Sklavenes. Sklavene lands raided by Avars at the request of Justin II. Coastal cities of Betica reconquered from Romano-Byzantines by Visigothic King of Spain Leovigild.
578–582 Tiberius II Constantine Emperor.
578–580 War between Persians and Romano-Byzantines in Mesopotamia.
578–579 Siege of Rome by Lombards finally paid to abandon siege by Pope Pelagius II.
579 Pacification of Moors and King Garmul killed by Gennadius, Master of the Soldiers to Africa.
580–603 War interspersed with truces between Romano-Byzantines and Avars.
580–582 Siege and fall of Sirmium by the Avars, after a two-year blockade.
581 Campaign in Mesopotamia of Maurice Master of the Soldiers to the East and Ghassanid King al-Mundir III ibn al-Harith. Second Battle of Callinicum won over Maurice, Master of the Soldiers to the East, by Persians. Siege of Naples by Lombard Duke Zotto.
581–583 Ghassanid revolt against Byzantine rule after unfair arrest of al-Mundir III ibn al-Harith.
582 Battle of Constantina in Osrhoene won over Persian Generals Adarman and Tamkhosrow (latter killed) by Maurice, Master of the Soldiers to the East.
582–602 Maurice Emperor.
583 Northern Illyricum and Thrace raided by Avars.
584 Balkans raided by Sklavenes. Battle of the River Erginia won by Comentiolus the Master of the Soldiers to the Thraces, over Sklavenes.
585–590 War between Persians and Romano-Byzantines.
585 Persian Arzanene province raided by Philippicus, Master of the Soldiers to the East. Thrace raided by Sklavenes. Battle of Ansinon won against them by Comentiolus the Thracian.
586–588 War between Romano-Byzantines and Avars in the Balkans.
586 Istria raided by Lombards. Enclave at the island of Como conquered from Romano-Byzantines by Lombard King Authari. Northern Balkans raided and siege of Thessaloniki by Sklavenes and Avars. Battle of Solachon in Mesopotamia won over Persian General Kardarigan by Philippicus, Master of the Soldiers to the East. Persian province of Arzanene raided by Philippicus. Siege of Tigranocerta (also called Chlomaron or Cholimma) by Philippicus relieved by a Persian Army.
587–588 Siege of Rome by the Lombards.

587　Balkans raided by Avars then repulsed by Comentiolus the Thracian. Avars taught by a Byzantine prisoner how to construct siege machines. Persian territory raided by Heraclius the Elder, second in command to the master of the soldiers to the East.

588　Easter mutiny at Monocarton over pay. Battle of Heraclea won by Avars over Priscus, military pay master to the Thraces. Rebellious Moors pacified again by Gennadius. Battle of Martyropolis in Armenia won by Germanus, Duke of Phoenice Libanensis against Persian General Marouzas, killed in action.

589　Balkans raided by Sklavenes. Eastern Army mutinies but pacified by Philippicus, Master of the Soldiers to the East. Battle of Sisauranon won against Persians by Comentiolus the Thracian, appointed during the autumn new Master of the Soldiers to the East.

590　Siege and fall of Benevento and of Reggio by Lombard King Authari. Peace concluded between Romano-Byzantines and Persians. New Sassanid Persian King Khosrow II political refugee in Syria. Dara fortress returned to Emperor Maurice by the King of the Persians in order to get his help against usurper Bahram VI Chobim.

591　Battle of Blarathon, near Lake Urmia in Iran, won by Khosrow II over Persian rebels. Peace concluded between Romano-Byzantines and Persians.

593–596　War between Romano-Byzantines and Sklavenes.

593　Central Italy partly reconquered from Lombards by Romanus Patrician and *Exarch* of Ravenna. Siege and fall of Perugia by Lombard King Agilulf; Maurice, Lombard Duke of Perugia allied with the Empire, killed. Thrace raided by Sklavenes then liberated by Peter the Kouropalates, Master of the Soldiers. Campaign against Sklavenes by Priscus, Master of the Soldiers to the Thraces.

594　Campaign of Peter the Kouropalates against Sklavenes along Middle Danube.

595–602　War between Romano-Byzantines and Avars.

595　Siege and fall of Singidunum by Avars then liberated by a Romano-Byzantine amphibious operation led by Godwin. Dalmatia raided by Avars.

597　Moesia raided by Avars. Siege of Thessaloniki by the Sklavenes.

598　Siege of Tomi (now Constanța in Romania) by Avars. Battle of Shipka Pass won against Avars by Romano-Byzantines. Truce concluded between Romano-Byzantines and Avars.

599　Istria raided by Sklavenes. Priscus's and Comentiolus the Thracian's joint campaign against Avars, Gepids and Sklavenes along Middle Danube.

600　Thrace raided by Avars. Daughter of Lombard King Agilulf captured by the *Exarch* of Ravenna. Istria raided by Sklavenes.

601　Siege and fall of Padua razed to the ground by Lombard King Agilulf.

602　'Eternal Peace' concluded between Romano-Byzantines and Persians. Istria raided by Lombards and Sklavenes. Siege and fall of Monselice by Lombards. Romano-Byzantine Danube army mutiny. Emperor Maurice beheaded.

602–610 Phocas Emperor.

603–630 Last war between Romano-Byzantines and Persians.

603 Siege and fall of Cremona and of Mantua by Lombards, helped by Sklavenes sent by the Khan of Avars. Rebellon of Narses Strategos, ex-Master of the Soldiers to the East. Battle of Edessa won over Germanus, Master of the Soldiers to the East, by Persian King Khosrow II and Narses Strategos.

604 Siege of Thessaloniki by Sklavenes. Battle of Constantina won by Persians over Germanus, Master of the Soldiers to the East, who died from wounds.

604–605 Siege and fall of Dara fortress by Khosrow II.

605 Siege and fall of Bagnoregio and of Orvieto by Lombards. Truce concluded between Romano-Byzantines and Lombards. Edessa reconquered from Narses Strategos by Domentziolus the Younger, Master of the Soldiers to the East. Battle of Arzamon (today the River Gümüş Çay, Turkey-Syria) won by Persian King Khosrow II against Leontius the Syrian, Master of the Soldiers to the East,.

606 Truce between Romano-Byzantines and Lombards renewed.

607 Battle of Theodosiopolis of Armenia won over Domentziolus the Younger by Persians.

608 Rebellion of Heraclius the Elder, *exarch* of Africa.

609 Egypt conquered by Niketas, general of Heraclius the Elder. Unlocated battle in Cappadocia won by Persians over Sergius, Master of the Soldiers to the East, who was killed in battle.

610 Syria invaded. Sieges and fall of Emesa, current Homs in Syria and of Antioch by Persians. Phocas deposed and executed after Heraclius the Younger landing in Byzantium with the African army.

610–641 Heraclius I Emperor.

611–612 Ill-fated campaign of Priscus, Master of the Soldiers to the East, against Persians.

611 Istria raided by Sklavenes. Siege and fall of Caesarea of Cappadocia, modern Kayseri in Turkey, by Persian General Shahín. Battle of the River Halys (today Kızılırmak in Turkey) won over Romano-Byzantines by Persians.

612 Priscus recalled to Constantinople and replaced with Philippicus as Master of the Soldiers to the East. Syrian border raided by Saracens. Battle of Caesarea won over Persian General Kesruan by the Master of the Soldiers to the East Niketas the son of Gregory.

613 Battles of Damascus and Antioch won over Heraclius by Persian Generals Shahrbaraz and Shahín.

614 Siege and fall of Jerusalem by Persian General Shahrbaraz. True Cross sent to Ctesiphon. Shore of the Bosphorus temporary reached at Chalcedon by Persian General Shahín.

615 Siege and fall of Salona by Avars. Northern Greece raided and siege of Thessaloniki by Sklavenes. Palestine raided by Arab tribes. Two

- battles won over Romano-Byzantine troops in Spain and loss of cities to Visigothic King Sisebuth.
- 616 Peace concluded in Byzantium with Visigoths of Spain.
- 617 Siege of Thessaloniki by Avars and Sklavenes.
- 619 Siege and fall of Alexandria of Egypt to Persians.
- 621–631 Last Byzantine cities in Spain retaken by the Visigothic King Svinthila.
- 622–625 First campaign of Heraclius against Persians.
- 622 Siege and fall of Ganzak, destroyed along with the Zoroastrian Temple of Fire Adhur Gushnasp, by Heraclius.
- 623 Byzantium suburb raided by Avars.
- 624 Rhodes raided by Persians.
- 626 Siege of Byzantium by Avars, Sklavenes and by a Persian fleet. Battle of Satala won over Persian General Shahín by Theodore Trithyrios the Sakellarios.
- 626–627 Surprise winter attack on Sharbaraz's headquarters in Persarmenia by Heraclius, balance of morale changed in favour of Romano-Byzantines.
- 627–629 Heraclius' second campaign against Persians.
- 627 Battle of Nineveh won by Heraclius against Persian General Rahzadh.
- 628 Persian King Khosrow II overthrown and executed by his son Siroes.
- 629 Siege and fall of Jerusalem retaken from Persians by Heraclius. Peace between Romano-Byzantines and Persians.
- 630 Battle of Mothous/Mouta/Mu'ta won over Muslim Arabs by Romano-Byzantines. Siege and fall of Singidunum by Sklavenes, then siege of Thessaloniki.
- 634–640/642 Palestine and Syria conquered by Islamic Arabs.
- 634 Battles of Dâthín, Ajnadayn and Fahl in Palestine and Syria won over Romano-Byzantines by Muslim Arabs.
- 635 Siege and fall Damascus by Muslim Arabs.
- 635–636 Mesopotamia conquered by Muslim Arabs.
- 636 Battle then siege of Emesa won over Romano-Byzantines by Muslim Arabs.
- 637 Battle of the Yarmuk won over Romano-Byzantines by Muslim Arabs.
- 637–652 Persia invaded by Muslim Arabs.
- 638 Siege and fall of Jerusalem by Muslim Arabs. Siege of Emesa by Romano-Byzantines. Siege and fall of Antioch by Muslim Arabs.
- 639–646 Egypt conquered by Muslim Arabs.
- 639 Siege of Salona razed to ground by Sklavenes. Armenia raided by Muslim Arabs.
- 641 Death of Heraclius, then Alexandria taken by Muslim Arabs.

Introduction

The Byzantine army of the sixth and seventh centuries inherited from the Roman period a solid logistical organisation mainly based on civil administration, its ability to levy taxes, recruit, produce weapons, requisition wheat, wagons and pack animals, boats and sailors. Launching a sea invasion of Northern Africa or invading Northern Mesopotamia was only a matter of a two or three-months in time of logistical preparation. No logistics without money, without a lot of money, especially since the proto-Byzantine state, like the Roman Empire, retained the model of a costly professional army. It was a costly but effective army but also a two tier army, with low quality hardly payed border troops and fighting crack units well equipped and better remunerated if not on a regular basis. The question of the navy must also be addressed and seen from the angle of Roman heritage. Nevertheless, the traces of this legacy are rather vague. Of course, Byzantium inherited from Late Roman period some types of imperial warships or couriers. But as with the armament of soldiers, there has been an evolution of ships. The idea of an all-powerful thalassocracy must be nuanced and balanced; as Byzantium of the 600s–700s was neither Athens nor the British Empire. Assembling a troop transport fleet required improvisation, as did sometimes assembling ships for combat at sea. A Romano-Byzantine fleet was never at full capacity unless ground forces were mobilised. The army also inherited from the Roman times a vast network of border outposts, fortified towns, and the powerful land and naval hub formed by the City of Byzantium itself, the New Rome of the East. Nevertheless, this outpost screen was not impassable, and even during Justinian's glorious reign the gates of Byzantium itself had to face the Huns with just an insufficient and quite heteroclite garrison, while the manoeuvre Byzantine army was nearly engulfed in Italy. The worse came in 626 when the city was besieged by the dreadful Avars with their iron-clads heavy cavalrymen and a complete array of siege machines, then Heraclius had to face the invading Persians in Asia Minor… It was also times of miracles in this very Christian Empire. However, Persians, Avars, Slavs, Goths and other Lombards knew how to take Roman walls, but it is worth to remind that Byzantium's army had to take Roman cities from the grasp of Barbarians, Rome itself when "reconquering" or merely conquering of Ostrogothic Italy. Romano-Byzantine soldiers and even civilians had the knowledge and sometimes the war machines to defend a walled city but impregnable fortresses of that time were like unsinkable the Titanic later was. We must confess the Romano-Byzantine army was not invincible and suffered several defeats, as did the Romans, but it took only 30 years for Justinian's generals to take Italy from the Ostrogoths, while 300 years were necessary for Rome to subjugate the whole Peninsula… So, the army of Justinian was efficient as later the army of Heraclius who brought fire and havoc to the heart of the Persian Empire like no Roman Emperor before. The account of the battles by a historian like Procopius or by a poet like Corripus is astounding. Tactics were not the Roman or even Late Roman tactics. They were more elaborated and versatile, adapted to the different types of enemies of the Empire, Slavs of the marshes and forests, Hunnic or Arabic horsemen of the Steppes and deserts, mountain men from Caucasus or the Atlas and disciplined and adaptive Persians. Ethos of combat also was different. The Muslim conquest of Romano-Byzantine Near-East is a major question in History, shaping until today the geopolitics of this ever troubled region. Closing this book, the battle of the Yarmuk was a decisive an unclear event where the tide has irremediably turned against Byzantium. All contradictory sources will be presented and confronted here to give a realistic picture of this battle and its campaign avoiding oversimplification. As you will see, an army can never remain the same over two to three centuries, even if technology evolves slowly. Geopolitical challenges always are faster, more changeable and more pressing, so they were during these times of turmoil.

8

The Army Watches over the Borders

> Forts must be built near the border and must not be far from the road the enemy is supposed to take, so that no invasion can be undetected from the garrison.
>
> *Peri Strategikes*, 8, 9–11

In the early sixth century, the Byzantine borders corresponded roughly to the Danube and Eastern limits of the later Roman Empire, and the Byzantine Empire inherited the forts and the camps, the towns and the roads. It restored the old forts, sometimes built new ones, and eventually by the 530s expanded the frontiers into North Africa and Italy. The key idea was to deploy a chain of fortresses along a border – ideally one located on a river like the Danube or a road as in the Syrian Desert – and to control the valleys that penetrated into the hinterland. Under the reign of Justinian I many fortifications were restored or built, but one can question their effectiveness; After having lavishly praised Justinian in his work *On Buildings*, Procopius was more reserved in his *Wars* but bitterly complained about the Emperor in *The Secret History*.

The Danube, the Most Fortified Border in the Empire

A cavalryman lowers his lance to pass under the arch of the gate in the shadow of two towers. He enters a narrow vestibule which leads to another arch, a sort of 'airlock' which traps the potential attacker. Long before him, legionaries from the *V Macedonica* and the *1 Iovia Scythica* and even sailors from the riverine fleet of Moesia had preceded him into this stone enclosure which would resemble a shapeless rectangle if it did not have *six* irregular sides. Eleven small horseshoe shaped towers protrude on either side of the gate and from the enclosure walls. Three large ones, all fan-shaped, defend the most exposed angles, namely the wall of the main entrance to the south-east and the north-west enclosure. After saying a short prayer in the small *basilica* built immediately to the left upon entering, the rider comes along the *via principalis*, which is neither very straight nor very wide. From left to right he sees a maze of recent, shabby, clay-built barracks before arriving at the *praetorium* (headquarters) built in stone, a work from the old days, like the house which adjoins it on the right – the Governor's residence. Thus, might appear in the mid-sixth-century the fortress of Dinogetia, on the left bank of the Danube, on the level plain of Romanian Dobruja. This outpost of the Empire will suffer greatly with the arrival of the Kutrigurs, then the Sklavenes and later the Bulgars.[1] We are on the Danubian border, the most fortified in the Empire. Procopius was quite critical of the work done there by the ancient Romans:

> Previous Emperors had built forts and towns to prevent the barbarians who lived on the other side from crossing the Danube. But these towns and forts served more to show that the shore was not completely uninhabited, than to defend it because, at that time, the barbarians did not know how to carry out sieges. In fact, most of these fortifications consisted of only a simple tower, called a monotower, where there were a small number of soldiers. This was then enough to stop them. But later, Attila came with a formidable army, destroyed these forts easily, no one could stop him and he plundered a large part of the Roman Empire. Justinian raised them not as they were but made them more solid.[2]

The Balkan border was bounded to the north by the Lower Danube, to the west by one of its tributaries of the Veliki Morava, formerly Margus, and to the east by the Black Sea. The two cities at the eastern and western ends of Danube border were Odyssus, today Varna in Bulgaria and Viminacium (near the now village of Kostolac in Serbia), 560km distant from each other in a straight line. Odyssus reported to the master of the soldiers to the Thraces and Viminiacum was attached to Illyricum. The Lower Danube bordering Thrace was backed by the Haemus Mons, now the Balkan Mountains. It formed an internal barrier thinly split in the centre by the Shipka Pass. This defile, called *kleisourai* in Greek or *clausurae* in Latin, led south to the Maritsa Valley, a river born in the Rila Mountains the Thracian plain crossing to the east before turning south at Adrianople (now Edirne in Turkey) and plunging into the Aegean Sea. To the west of the River Maritsa, Eastern Thrace was (and still is) a peeled brownish region defended by the fortresses of Adrianople and Tzurullum. Thrace confined to the Bosphorus Strait between the Black Sea and the Sea of Marmara. On an inlet of the Bosphorus Strait, called the Golden Horn, lay Byzantium.

---

1   I. Barnea, 'Dinogetia – ville Byzantine du Bas-Danube, sec. IV-XII', *Byzantina*, 10 (1980), pp.237–287.
2   Procopius, *Aed.*, IV, 5, 2–7.

THE ARMY WATCHES OVER THE BORDERS

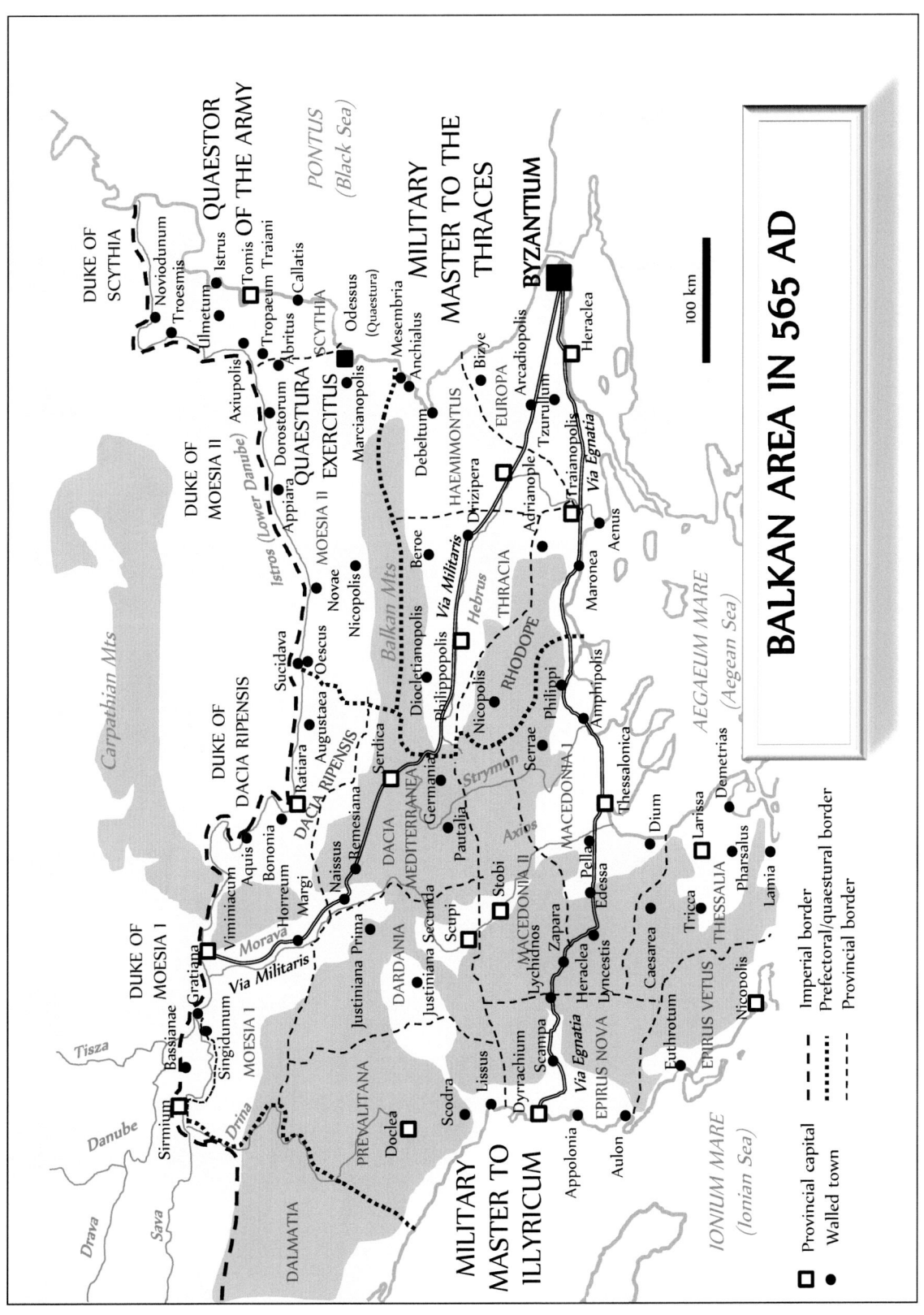

The Thracian Black Sea coastline was the shorter route from Danube to Byzantium, 260km in a straight line separated Odyssus from Byzantium, but along an irregular coastline the distance was roughly 460km. It was the highway for Huns Kutrigurs invaders. The two main fortified ports were Odyssus with imposing its thermal baths, a very Roman atmosphere and sheltered by high walls and Anchialos.

Borders were not as clear as those of today. Procopius stated that Serdica was a town from Illyricum but *c.* 550 Germanus appointed Master of the Soldiers to the Thraces had established his headquarters there.[3] North of Serdica, the 100 kilometres wide Danube area along the Iron Gate Gorge was defended by 15 forts restored or built by Justinian. Old Roman forts received the Byzantine touch – a chapel. They were mainly square forts with round towers, of the *quadriburgium* type. The size of the garrison varied – the smallest had only 19 men, the largest had 3,650.[4] Life in these forts appears to have been rough and monotonous. The *Peri Strategikes* recommended frequently relieving the garrisons and not housing families in forts where they were endangered and could cause a problem of food supply.[5] It also advised supplying guard posts with wood and dry grass to send signals signalling the approach of the enemy and their numbers and also alerting residents to prepare to flee.[6] Justinian put bridgeheads north of the Danube by reoccupying Literata and Recidiva.[7] The most heavily fortified sector under Justinian according to Procopius was Thrace: 'He fortified the rest of Thrace and the country called Haeminontus [the Balkans]. He repaired all the places in Philippopolis and Plotinopolis [Plovdiv in Bulgaria and Didymoteicho in Greece] which were in danger of ruin or which were weak and unable to withstand the shock of the enemies. He built countless forts in Thrace, and while it was previously subject to raids and ravages, he preserved it entirely.'[8] Most of these constructions were located north of the 1,120km long Via Egnatia between Byzantium and the Adriatic at Dyrrachium; the old route to Rome linking Thrace to Illyricum. The Greek provinces were not neglected by Justinian's rebuilding programme including: Cassandrea in Macedonia, Thebes, Pharsalus, Demetrias, Larissa, Diocletianopolis, Metropolis, Gomphi, Tricca, Caesarea, Centauriopolis in Thessaly, Athens, Plataea, cities of Boeotia and Corinth in central Greece.[9]

---

3   Procopius, *BG*, VII, 40, 1 (Serdica) and 6 (Germanus).
4   F. Curta, (2001), pp.182–184.
5   *Peri Strategikes*, 9, 24–33.
6   *Peri Strategikes*, 8, 1–32.
7   Nov. J., XI, 13–14. M. Pillon, 'Armée et défense de l'Illyricum Byzantin de Justinien à Héraclius (527–641). De la réorganisation justinienne à l'émergence des 'armées de cité', *Erytheia*, 26 (2005), p.19.
8   Procopius, *Aed.*, IV, 11, 5.
9   J. B. Bury, *A History of the Later Roman Empire from the Death of Theodosius I to the Death of Justinian (AD 395 to AD 565)*, vol. 2 (New York: Dover Publications, 1958), p.310. Procopius, *Aed.*, IV, 2, 23–24 (Greece).

THE ARMY WATCHES OVER THE BORDERS

Table 12 - Forts Built or Restored by Justinian in the Danube and Balkan area

Province	Location	Forts built	Restored
Procopius, *De Aedificiis*, IV, 4, 3			
Epirus Nova (Greek Illyricum)	From the River Drina to the Ceraunian Mountains (Albania)	32	26
Epirus Vetus	Epirus region in present-day Greece	12	12 plus a cistern
Near Justinianopolis* and Photiki	*Former Adrianople, modern Edirne in European Turkey	-	11
Macedonia	Present-day Macedonia		46
Thessaly	Present-day Thessaly	-	7
Dardania	Present-day Kosovo	8	61
Near Serdica-Sardica (Sardikē)	Dacia mediterranea, Present-day Sofia, Bulgaria	-	9
Cabetzus District	Albania?	1	16
?	?	5	23
Near Germena	Strymon Valley (Struma)?	1	6
Near Pauta(lia)	Kyustendil, Bulgaria	-	5
Skassetana District	?	-	5
Near Naissus	Niš, Serbia	32	7
Remisianisia/ Remoesiana District	Bela Palanka, Serbia	-	30
Aquenisium/ Ad Aquas Disctrict	Prahovo, Serbia	1	37
SUB-TOTAL			393
Procopius, Aedificiis, IV, 11, 20			
Europe	Byzantium outskirts	2	-
Rhodopē	Thrace, Rhodopes Mountain Present-day Bulgaria and Macedonia	12	-
Thrace	Bulgaria and Europen Turkey	35	-
Haerminontum	Balkan area (Mons Haemus)	53	-
Thrace near Euxine Sea, Ister and Moesia	Black Sea western coastline, Danube Delta,	26	-
Thrace, interior	Tomi, present-day Constanta Roumania, Romanian Dobruja, Northern Bulgaria	26	-
SUB-TOTAL		154	-
TOTAL			547

Between the Danube and the Adriatic Sea, Illyricum

The north-western flank of Byzantium's Empire was the most exposed. During the later Roman era, the prefecture of Illyricum, which traditionally focused on the western Adriatic, included Crete, Greece, Illyricum and stretched as far as the Upper Danube at Vindobona (now Vienna, Austria). The original Pannonia, where Vienna is located, was definitively lost in 441 and Dalmatia was lost around 481. According to the work of Hierocles, written *c.* 526, Illyricum still included: Crete (main city Gortyne), Achaia or Helladia (Corinth), Thessaly (Larissa), the old Epirus (Nicopolis) and new Epirus (Dyrrachium), the First Macedonia (Thessaloniki) and the Second Macedonia (Stobi), Prevalitania (Doclea), Dardania (Scupi), the Mediterranean Dacia (Sardica/Serdica) and Riverine Dacia (Ratiaria), the First Moesia (Viminacium) and the Second Pannonia (Sirmium).[10] Only the last section of the Middle Danube and the Lower Basin were left to Byzantine rule. It was an area covering today the Iron Gate Gorge on the frontier between Serbia and Romania and the mountains and plains bordering Bulgaria and Romania up to the delta. For the sixth and seventh century Byzantine authors, Illyricum's boundaries were unclear. For example John Malalas, *Evagrius Scholasticus,* and the anonymous author of the *Paschal Chronicle* referred to Justin I and his nephew Justinian as Thracians from Bederiana, which Agathias referred to it as an Illyrian city.[11]

The Northern Danubian stronghold of Illyricum was Viminacium, ex-capital of Moesia Superior and the main anchorage of the Danube fleet, a 450-hectare legionary town destroyed by the Huns in 441 that was poorly garrisoned.[12] By the 490s, Illyricum was under heavy pressure by the Bulgars and portion of the Danube east of Viminacium was strengthened by Anastasius I. Town walls such as those of Ratiara (today Arzar Palanka in Bulgaria) were repaired and new forts were built.[13] Although restored by Justinian I, Viminacium never regained its Roman period prosperity – the road from Byzantium to Viminiacum was 960km long.[14] Viminacium

---

10 Hierocles, *Le Synecdèmos d'Hiéroklès et l'opuscule géographique de George de Cyprus*, 1939, p.14–21. M. Pillon, 'Armée et défense de l'Illyricum', p.12.
11 V. Ivanišević, 'Une capitale revisitée: Caričin Grad (Justiniana Prima)', *Comptes rendus des séances de l'Académie des Inscriptions et Belles-Lettres*, 161–1, 2017, p.95.
12 *Notitia Dignitatum*, OR.XI.20.38 (*praefectus classis Histricae*). Vl. Kondić, 'Les formes des fortifications protobyzantines dans la région des Portes de Fer' in Collectif, *Villes et peuplement dans l'Illyricum protobyzantin. Actes du colloque de Rome (12–14 mai 1982),* (Rome: PEFR, 77, 1984), p.134. V. Ivanišević, M. Kazanski, A. Mastykova (eds), *Les nécropoles de Viminacium à l'époque des grandes migrations* (Paris: Collège de France-CNRS, Centre de Recherche d'Histoire et Civilisation de Byzance, Monographies, 22, Association des amis du Centre d'histoire et civilisation de Byzance, 2006), p.129 (Viminiacum).
13 S. Williams & G. Friell, *The Rome That Did Not Fall*, p.116.
14 V. Ivanišević, M. Kazanski, A. Mastykova (eds), *Les nécropoles de Viminacium*, pp.7–8 (site), pp.131–132 (restoration).

was some 20km east of Veliki Morava in the mountainous region of the Iron Gates, where today the Danube separates Romania from Serbia. The Viminacium heights dominate the Danube to the north and their western flank is bordered by the narrow valley of the Mlava. From Viminacium, the Roman road along the Lower Danube ran to the Black Sea. From there it was easy to go north-west to Illyricum marching on the old Via Militaris in a straight line to Naissus (present-day Niš, Serbia). From Naissus, following the Veliki Morava valley to the north, Viminacium was reached.

To the west of the River Veliki, Morava stretched into some sort of desolate zone with few towns which corresponded to the lost part of the Dacia diocese in Dinaric Alps.[15] To the north of this zone, two ex-Roman cities had been held since 441 by barbarians but still retained some Roman population, Singidunum on the Danube (now Belgrade) and Sirmium on the River Sava (present-day Sremska Mitrovica). Procopius unenthusiastically described the 50km distance between the two towns as: 'a vast area entirely deserted except for a few places where barbarian populations lead a beastly and repulsive existence.'[16] These two fortified river towns controlled the passage south, so, the Drina-Morava gap was the main avenue for Bulgars, Avars and especially the Sklavenes. A few centuries later, the entire area came to be called Sklavinia, and is now Serbia.[17] Reoccupying all of this area was more or less carried out by Anastasian for the Singidunum area and by Justinian who drove back Ostrogothic influence in Sirmium from 535. Both Emperors settled *foederati* here, Heruls and Gepids. The new western border of Byzantine Illyricum was then set on the Drinus, today the River Drina and the natural frontier between Serbia and Bosnia-Herzegovina. The southern part of this area remained under Romano-Byzantine hands and was called Dardania. It covered Kosovo, the southern tip of Serbia and northern Macedonia blocking the road to Greece where the first main city was Thessaloniki. The capital of Dardania was Ulpiana (now Lipljan 8km south of Pristina in Kosovo). It controlled the strategic road between Byzantium and the Adriatic via Naissus plus the one that descended towards Thessaloniki. Thus, *c.* 400 Ulpiana was a garrisoned and walled city falling under the diocese of Illyricum. In 518, over a length of 45km a terrible earthquake destroyed 24 castles in Dardania. Scupi, near modern Skopje in Macedonia, was completely wiped out.[18]

---

15   V. Ivanišević, 'Une capitale revisitée', p.93.
16   Procopius, *Aed.*, IV, 5, 19–22.
17   F. Curta, *The Making of the Slavs. History and Archælogy of the Lower Danube c.500–700* (Cambridge: Cambridge University Press, 2001), pp.120–189.
18   *Notitia Dignitatum*, OR.IX.44 (troop of *Ulpians, Ulpienses*, garrisoned at Ulpiana, under the authority of master of the soldiers to Illyricum). Marcellinus Comes, *Chr.*, a.518 (30 Roman paces; 24 *castella*, Scupi). Chr. J. Goddard and *alii*, 'D'Ulpiana à Iustiniana Secunda, d'une cité à l'autre dans l'Antiquité tardive (prospection géophysique 2019–2020)', *Revue archéologique. Bulletin de la société française d'Archéologie classique*, 73 (2022), pp.153–162.

Justinian although he often repaired works done by Anastasius I, restored or built nearly 600 small forts or fortresses in Dardania, Macedonia, Epirus and Greece, roughly Northern Illyricum.[19] Iustiniana Prima (today the site of Caričin Grad in Serbia) was identified by John of Antioch with Bederiana, the birthplace of Justin I then renamed by Justinian,[20] and here Justinian established the archdiocese of all Illyricum in April 535. Nevertheless, it was only a small, ten-hectare fortified town city built on a rocky plateau reaching 395m at its highest. The place stretched along a 50m wide and 400m high hill standing at the confluence of the two rivers, Caričinska and Svinjarička. It was a defensive site far from major roads and located 45km south-east of Naissus. Separated by a wall, an acropolis stood to the north with episcopal basilica and baptistery in a narrow street. A gate with two pentagonal towers was opening on a lower town surrounded by a 27 towers enclosure with north and east gates. This less than eight-hectare complex formed neither a large city nor an impressive fortress, but a 21km aqueduct has been built with it.[21]

Ulpiania had lost its military value until its restoration under the name of Iustiniana Secunda. As the site occupies a plain, Justinian's fortifications were substantial to compensate the lack of natural defences. The new wall was a quadrilateral with four gates, flanked by 44 semi-circular or triangular towers spaced every 45m. Four suburbs with successive enclosures without towers show the city's extension to more than double its area. A four-tower fort, known as St Elias, was located on a mound to the east above a mini-dam lake.[22] East of Dardania, the 200km Veliki Morava line was firmly held by Naissus and Horreum Margi (today Ćuprija in Serbia). All of these towns were part of the diocese of Dacia and strengthened by Justinian as was Serdica located on the Via Militaris.

Thrace and Illyricum Under Constant Pressure

After the Ostrogoths' departure for Italy in 488, the Illyrian border was threatened on a regular basis by Bulgars, Slavs, proto-Turkish Huns and then Avars. According to Jordanes, the Bulgars were from north of the

---

19   J. B. Bury, *A History of the Later Roman Empire*, p.308.
20   V. Ivanišević, 'Une capitale revisitée', pp.95–96.
21   B. Bavant, 'La ville dans le Nord de l'Illyricum (Pannonie, Mésie I, Dacie et Dardanie)', *PEFR*, 77 (1984), pp.272–284. Nov. J., XI (archbishopric). Procopius, *Aed.*, IV, 1. L. Maksimović, 'L'administration de l'*Illyricum* septentrional à l'époque de Justinien', in H. Ahrweiler, *Philadelphie et autres études* (Paris: Éditions de la Sorbonne, Byzantina Sorboniensa, 1984), pp.143–157. Iustiniana Prima reconstructed in 3D video: Römisch-Germanisches Zentralmuseum and ARC digital production, (2011), www.youtube.com/watch?v=WhUkp0JtHqw.
22   Procopius, *Aed.*, IV, 28–29. Chr. J. Goddard and *alii*, 'D'Ulpiana à Iustiniana Secunda', p.155.

Black Sea.[23] At the very end of the fifth century, the Bulgars not only became aggressive but they seemed to be unstoppable. In 493, they killed the Master of the Soldiers Julian who tried to intercept them. Six years later, the Bulgars annihilated the *Militia Illyriciana* (Army of Illyricum) and its commander Aristus on the River Tzurta (unidentified). In 502, they completely devastated the region but 'no Roman soldier resisted' according to Count Marcellinus.[24] Nevertheless in 505 at the Battle of Horreum Margi, the Bulgars were *foederati* in Sabinian the Younger's army which was defeated by Ostrogothic and Gepid troops of Pitzia and Mundo.[25] In 515, the Bulgars and the Huns served in the army of Sabinian who was probably Master of the Soldiers to the Thraces or a senior officer.[26] After Vitalian's defeat few was recorded about Bulgars for one century and a half. But it is a problem to decide between the Huns and the Bulgars in most Byzantine sources. In 517, the Sklavenes raided Macedonia, Thessaly up to Thermopylae and then Epirus, all without opposition. Anastasius had to pay a ransom to get rid of them.[27]

Then the Slavs became the most restless enemies in the Danube area. The Slavs were divided into two peoples speaking the same language and having the same customs: Antes lived between the mouth of the Danube and the Dnieper on the Black Sea (an area corresponding roughly to Romania); the Sklavenes, settled north of the Danube (roughly in present-day Wallachia) were a direct threat to the Diocese of Thrace.[28] From 530 to 531, while the bulk of the field army was fighting the Persians the entire Danube border became porous. In 530, Mundo Master of the Soldiers to Illyricum had to repel a (probably) Sklavene raid in Illyricum and a Bulgar one in Thrace.[29] It should be noted that Thrace was not the area of operation of Mundo and the 500 Bulgars he killed made his victory resemble much more of a large skirmish than a pitched battle. The Empire did not have enough troops to counter even an enemy that did not seem particularly numerous.

In the short interval from 531 to 534 Chilbudius, Master of the Soldiers to the Thraces, defended the border by an offence, crossing the river to slaughter and enslave the barbarians. In 534, as he customarily led a small force north of the Danube, the Sklavenes ambushed him with all their strength and killed him. Procopius stated that Danube was again open to

---

23 Jordanes, *Getica*, V, 36.
24 Zonaras, *Ep.H*, III, 137 (Julian). Marcellinus Comes, *Chr.*, a. 499 and a. 502 (Tzurta and new invasion).
25 Ennodius of Pavia, *Panegyricus dictus regi Theoderico* (1882) p.278, v. 16–22.
26 John Malalas, *Chrgr.*, XVI, 16.
27 Marcellinus Comes, *Chr.*, a. 517 (Getae name for Sklavenes). Theophylact Simocatta, *HU*, III, 4, 7 ('As for the Getaen that is to say the herds of Skavenes').
28 Jordanes, *Getica*, V, 34. B. Ferjančić, 'Invasions et installation des Slaves dans les Balkans' in *Villes et peuplement dans l'Illyricum protobyzantin. Actes du colloque de Rome (12-14 mai 1982)*, (Rome: PEFR, 1984), pp.85–109.
29 Marcellinus Comes, *Chr.*, a.530.

the barbarians, without providing any chronological data.[30] During this rather dark period, the Antes and Sklavenes fought each other, but this did not lead to peace on Danubian border. Meanwhile in 535 Bulgar raiders were defeated in Moesia in a battle near the River Iatrus (now Yantra in Bulgaria).[31] After the River Iatrus battle no more is recorded about the Bulgars for more than 100 years. Once their war with the Sklavenes was over, the Antes again plundered Thrace and enslaved numbers of people. The year could be guessed at to *c.* 536.[32] As may be understood, the ruined provinces of Moesia Second and Scythia could no longer provide for the needs of the garrisons. So, in 536 Justinian created the questorship of the army for supplying these regions by sea from Caria, a region of Asia Minor opposite the island of Rhodes: a vast distance on interior naval lines which led up to the Danube.[33]

Count Marcellinus reported for the year 539 the death and defeat by the Gepids of the Master of the Soldiers to Illyricum Calluc, probably near to Sirmium.[34] Chilbudius was killed in 534, Mundo two years later and then Calluc. By then Thrace and Illyricum had lost their commanders and their most able leaders were involved in the conquest of Italy or the pacification of Africa. A crisis of leadership left the Danubian border open to invasion. In 540, the Huns Kutrigurs crossed the Eastern Danube and utterly ravaged a wide area from the Ionian Gulf (Gulf of Corinth) to the outskirts of Byzantium, took 32 strongholds in Illyricum and the city of Potidia (today Cassandria) without ever having attacked fortified walls before. They captured 120,000 prisoners and returned home unopposed. According to Procopius, it was the worst invasion Europe had ever known.[35] Afterwards the Kutrigurs launched a series of raids in the Balkans. Procopius placed all these raids between the appearance of a comet and before the resumption of the war with the Persians, two events usually dated to 540; however that seems too much for one year. Although dating in Procopius is quite fuzzy, it is not unrealistic to think these incursions took over several years. So, the Kutrigurs penetrated the Anastasian Long Walls in Chersonese, slaughtering and enslaving all the Romano-Byzantines they encountered, Procopius judged this area as badly fortified. From there the Kutrigurs crossed the Dardanelles to plunder Abydos (now Çanakkale in Turkey). The next time they raided Illyricum and Thessaly, and reached the Pass of Thermopylae. Stopped by the walls and the garrison, the Kutrigurs repeated Xerxes' feat by turning the Pass of Thermopylae; then they overcame all the Greek defenders. Then they retreated after this bloody success, probably for

---

30   Procopius, *BG*, VII, 14, 1–6.
31   Marcellinus Comes, *Chr.*, *Addimentum* a. 535.
32   Procopius, *BG*, VII, 14, 7 (Antes and Skavenes at war); 11 (Thrace).
33   J. F. Haldon, *The Byzantine Wars*, p.44.
34   Marcellinus Comes, *Chr. Addimentum*, a. 539.
35   Procopius, *BP*, II, 4, 5–9.

THE ARMY WATCHES OVER THE BORDERS

fear of a contingent of Peloponnesians.[36] Later, Justinian strengthened the Thermopylae Pass, raising and doubling the walls of the old fortress that was there, installing a cistern to store rainwater, walling the accesses to the mountains. He installed a permanent garrison of 2,000 men, instead of the inexperienced peasants who became improvised soldiers in the time of an invasion. He also strengthened the surrounding localities.[37]

The years 548 to 551 were years of massacres and looting. The Sklavenes invaded Illyricum and reached Dyrrachium, plundering and enslaving the adult population. Procopius specified that the military leaders of Illyricum were content to follow the enemy who had seized impregnable but undefended forts.[38] Apparently regional commanders, unable to choose between defending places and counter-attacking the invaders, decided to do nothing. In 549, two groups of 1,800 and 1,500 Sklavenes separately invaded Illyricum and Thrace, successively defeating more numerous Romano-Byzantine troops. Elite cavalry was stationed at Tzurullum/Tzourullon (now Çorlu) located halfway between Edirne and Byzantium, exactly 159km from Byzantium. This place was the last outpost before the Anastasian Long Walls and was held by two forts – Ludikai and Elaiai,[39] but the garrisons were massacred and their commander Asbad was tortured and then burnt alive. Turning west, the Sklavenes stormed Topeiros near the Aegean Sea at the foot of the Rhodope Mountains, around 12 days' march from Byzantium (today the ruins of Topeiros lie south of the modern village of Paradeisos). The Sklavenes savagely exterminated the 1,500-male population of this city, impaling them, beating them to death, or burning them alive. In 550, the Sklavenes invaded Moesia Superior as far as Naissus, but prisoners taken by the Romano-Byzantines revealed that the main objective was Thessaloniki. Learning that the Patrician Germanus was at Serdica, the Sklavenes set sail towards Dalmatia. But Germanus, responsible for gathering the troops from Thrace and Illyricum to leave for Italy, stubbornly sticking to the orders he had received did not pursue them and died unexpectedly in the autumn.

Subsequently, a second group of Sklavenes, perhaps bribed by the Ostrogothic King Totila to pin down Imperial troops in the Balkans, crossed the Danube River and joined up with the first, reaching Adrianople, a five-day march from Byzantium. There the Eunuch Scholasticus awaited them with a large army but the battle, rushed by an impatient army, went unfavourably for him. So, the Sklavenes reached the Long Walls just a day away from Byzantium. A new Romano-Byzantine force caught some of the

---

36   Procopius, *BP*, II, 4, 4–11 (raids); *Aed.*, IV, 10, 1–9 (inadequate defence of Dardanelles). E. Kislinger, 'Ein Angriff zu viel: zur Verteidigung der Thermopylen in justinianischen Zeit', *BZ*, 91 (1998), pp.45–58 (raid of 540).
37   Procopius, *Aed.*, IV, 2, 1–16 (Thermopylae).
38   Procopius, *BG*, VII, 29, 1–4 (invasion of 548).
39   Procopius, *Aed.*, IV, 11 (Ludikai, Elaiai). A. Pralong, 'Remarques sur les fortifications Byzantines de Thrace orientale' in H. Ahrweiler, *Géographie historique du monde méditerranéen* (Paris: Éditions de la Sorbonne, 1988), pp.179–181.

Sklavenes by surprise, killing them and retaking the captives and plunder. The second group was able to return with and their loot and their prisoners.[40]

In 551, there was further Sklavene plundering, slaughtering and enslaving raid towards Illyricum: they were helped to cross the Danube, and protected in doing so, by the Gepids for the sum of one gold *stater* per head. The Imperial army sent against them, commanded by the sons of Germanus, was outnumbered and could only attack the stragglers. The Sklavenes again returned home undefeated with their spoils.[41] With the siphoning of its best troops for Italy the main problem to defend the Danube during these years seemed to be the lack of competent leaders, as shown by the desperate appointment of Scholasticus, a palace official without any military background. Additionally, John of Ephesus stated that the Slavs were better at fighting than the Romans.[42] Procopius has painted a disastrous picture of the Balkan peninsula during Justinian's reign:

> Illyricum and the whole of Thrace, that is to say the region stretching from the Gulf of Ionia to the outskirts of Byzantium, which includes Greece and the Chersonese, were invaded almost every year by the Huns, the Sklavenes and the Antes, from the time Justinian received the government from the Romans, and they inflicted horrible suffering on the people of these regions. I think that during each of these invasions, more than 200,000 Romans were killed or enslaved. As a result, a veritable Scythian desert stretched across this country.[43]

Total losses from the beginning of Justinian's reign to the writing of *The Secret History* by years 527 to 550s, are quite difficult to estimate. Surprisingly Theophanes did not mention any Sklavene invasion during this period. The strategic solution to the Sklavene threat was temporarily found in 552, when Justinian sent an army to help the Lombards, at their request, in order to fight the Gepids whom they defeated.[44] Therefore, with the Gepids beaten the Sklavenes had lost their Danubian boatmen rendering any raid south quite hazardous. Coincidentally, their regular raids ceased when the Ostrogothic Kingdom, the possible string puller of these actions, collapsed. The Antes probably came to an agreement with Byzantium as they were uninvolved in the latest raids and afterwards were mentioned only as allies.

It is now time for some thoughts about the forgotten Dalmatia. Illyricum bordered Dalmatia to the northwest and in 535 Justinian ordered the seizure back of this province from Ostrogothic grasp. Dalmatia offered the opportunity for a pincer movement against the Ostrogothic Kingdom while

---

40 Procopius, *BG*, VII, 38, 9–23 (invasion of 549; Topiros); 40, 1–8 (invasion of 550); 31–45 (invasion of 551).
41 Procopius, *BG*, VIII, 25, 1–6.
42 John of Ephesus, *HE*, III, 6, 25.
43 Procopius, *Anecdota*, XVIII, 19–21.
44 Procopius, BG, VIII, 25, 10–14.

Belisarius was landing in Sicily: a great strategic vision. Once reconquered, Dalmatia was put under command of the master of the soldiers to Illyricum. Dalmatia also offered a land route north of the Adriatic providing a direct line of operations between Italy and Byzantium despite the mountainous terrain. In 551, Narses the Eunuch led his army through Dalmatia towards Ravenna, the Ostrogothic capital.[45] Needless to say Dalmatia did not retain much attention either in historical sources nor in Imperial Government.

The Crisis of 559

In 557, the so-called Long Walls were severely damaged by an earthquake and Justinian had to repair them, but two years later this work was still incomplete. Agathias harshly pointed out the weakness of the Danubian defences during the invasion of the Huns Kutrigurs into Thrace in 559. Nothing opposed the invasion except the walls of Byzantium and some cities:

> Such was the situation of the Romans that they suffered such horrors in the very vicinity of the Imperial city, and at the hands of a very small number of barbarians. Their audacity did not stop there, but they had penetrated without difficulty inside what we call the Long Walls and were approaching the interior fortifications. In several places, this large rampart had fallen or been damaged by time and lack of maintenance. The barbarians themselves had demolished parts of it, without fear or scruple, as if they had demolished their property. There was nothing to hinder them, because no military post was established there, neither defensive machines nor those who know how to use them; we did not even hear – if it is not too laughable to say so – the barking of a dog, and not a noise also in pigsties and stables. This is because the armies of the Romans were not as numerous as under the ancient Emperors.[46]

Zabergan, Khan of the Kutrigurs, first sent a horde to ravage the Thracian Chersonese (today the Gallipoli peninsula) and a second one to Greece, while he himself headed to Byzantium with 7,000 horsemen. The first horde was defeated when assaulting the walls of Chersonese of Thrace, valiantly defended by Germanus, son of Dorotheos. Then Kutrigurs tried to bypass the wall on rafts made of bundles which were destroyed by the Romano-Byzantines who gathered about 20 boats to counter this attack. The second

---

45   M. P. S. Gomez, 'The Byzantine Balkan Path in the Gothic Campaigns of 536 and 551', Universidad Catolica San Antonio, Murcia, España, (2014), Online edition at Academia.edu.
46   Agathias, *Hist.*, V, 5, 5–7.

horde, halted by the Thermopylae garrison, withdrew to Thrace. The Huns had already failed there in 540. For his part, Zabergan's 2,000 cavalry vanguard reached the outskirts of Byzantium. All of the *Scholae Palatinae* were mobilised to defend the walls of the city, where the population panicked. The old, retired and brilliant Belisarius sallied out to set an ambush in a wooded valley not far from the village of Melantias, (modern Hoşköy Belediyesi) around 20km west of Byzantium, where the Huns had their camp. After an inspiring speech a mob of peasants made a noise to frighten the Kutrigurs then only some 300 elite soldiers attacked. Up to 400 Huns perished while the Romano-Byzantines sustained only a few wounded. The so-called Battle of Melantias was only an ambush. Nevertheless, Zabergan was not ready for a formal siege, agreeing to withdraw and free his prisoners in exchange for gold from Justinian.[47]

John Malalas gave an account slightly different from Agathias. The Huns Kutrigurs began the siege in March 559, supported by the Sklavenes who had invaded Thrace. Master of the Soldiers Sergius was even captured during an unlocated battle. As part of the Long Walls that border the Bosphorus peninsula had breaches, the barbarians penetrated as far as St Stratonikos. The population of the suburbs fled to Byzantium. A battle took place near the Long Walls where the *Scholarioi* suffered heavy losses. Justinian had the *ciborium* and silver altars removed from the outlying churches. The garrison on the Theodosian rampart was formed by the *Scholae Palatinae*, the *Protectores*, unspecified units (*arithmoi*) and all the senators, probably with their bodyguards. As the barbarians did not dare to go any further, Justinian commissioned Belisarius to counter-attack them with some senators; mobilising all available horses, including those of the Imperial stables and the hippodrome, from priests and from private individuals. Leaving for the village of Chiton (Chettos in Agathias), Belisarius set up an entrenched camp and launched raids against any isolated barbarians. Then he simulated the approach of a large army by creating a cloud of dust, pushing the Kutrigurs to retreat towards Decaton in the district of St Stratonikos. Upon hearing of reinforcements arriving in Byzantium, the Kutrigurs retreated towards Arcadiopolis (present-day Lüleburgaz, Turkey). The Emperor hastily had the Long Walls rebuilt and remained there until August. Meanwhile, the Kutrigurs raided until Justinian had double-prowed ships built to cut off their retreat on the Danube. Worried by this unpleasant news, Kutrigurs negotiated their departure and the Emperor delegated his nephew Justin to lead them back.[48] Michael the Syrian, who

---

47 Agathias, *Hist.*, V, 12, 6 (7,000 Hun horsemen in Chersonese); 15, 1–2 (*scholae* defending circuit-wall); 6 (unfit to war); 7 (Belisarius); 16, 2 (300 elite infantrymen plus an inexperienced and unarmed mob); 3 (numerous peasants); 19, 1–20, 8 (ambush battle); 20, 3 (Huns departing from their camp at Melantias); 21 and 22 plus 23, 1–4 (Huns defeated at Gallipoli) 23, 6 (Thermopylae and retreat); 23, 8 (tribute).
48 Jean Malalas, *Chrgr.*, XVIII, 129, partly confirmed by Theophanes Confessor, *Chrgr.*, AM 6051 (double-prowed boats and negotiations not mentioned).

wrongly placed the siege earlier (in the 27th year of Justinian's reign, 554), declared the Long Walls were breached, the suburbs pillaged and burnt, and that Huns and Sklavenes came back twice more. He probably conflated several events into one to shorten the narrative.[49]

This aborted siege of 559 was the action of Steppe barbarians, strong in a formal battle, incapable of complex politics, but it demonstrated that only the walls of Byzantium held firm and that Danubian border was nothing more than a torn curtain. The fact that only 7,000 horsemen laid siege to the Empire's capital says much about the army's weakness at the end of Justinian's reign, and the fortifications did not have sufficient men to guard them. By spending fortunes building or restoring almost 550 forts and fortresses, Justinian dispersed his efforts and squandered the Empire's finances.

In March and April 562, the Huns took the Thracian cities of Obaisipolis (unidentified) and Anastasiapolis (today only an archaeological site in northern Greece on Lake Vistonida). However the military situation had improved since the Ostrogoths had been defeated in Italy, Justinian now had enough troops, and sent a large army under the command of his nephew, the Master of the Soldiers Marcellus.[50] From 572 to 591, the bulk of Imperial Army was engaged against the Persians and accordingly the Danubian frontier lay almost defenceless, it had an attraction effect on the invasions. In 576, according to a Spanish chronicler, the Sklavenes depopulated some cities in Thrace. Five years later, they devastated Illyricum and Thrace again.[51]

The Empire's defensive strategy was to sacrifice agricultural lands, fighting the Persians first and relying on Byzantium's walls – a calculated risk.

Still Standing

In order to repulse Sklavene hordes, Tiberius II concluded a reverse alliance. He sent John, Praetorian Prefect of Illyricum, to negotiate with Baian, Khan of the Avars, the new regional power since they had conquered the Carpathian Basin in 568. Leaving garrisons in Pannonia among subjugated Romanised and Germanic peoples they settled along the Tisza in the Alföld, the Great Hungarian Plain so favourable to horse breeding. This proto-Mongol tribe established a khanate up to the Azov Sea ruling Slavs, Germans and Bulgars.[52] From there, probably across the Sava, the Avars were transported

---

49 Michael the Syrian, *HU*, IX, 33, t. 2 (1963), p.269 (he was the only one to involve the Sklavenes in the raid of 583 or 584, whether it dates from AG 894 or 582). John of Biclaro, *Chr.VT*, 46 (erroneously dating this siege in 577).
50 Theophanes Confessor, *Chrgr.*, AM 6054.
51 John of Biclaro, *Chr.VT*, 41 (576); 60 (581).
52 T. Vida, 'Conflict and coexistence: the local population of the Carpathian Basin

in 'big ships' to Illyricum by the Romano-Byzantine riverine fleet, and then along the Danube to attack the Sklavenes 'in Scythia'.[53] Roman Scythia was the present-day Dobruja plain in Romania, south of the Danube Delta but geography was a nebulous notion in Byzantine chronicles. After that the Empire sought to bribe the Avars with an annual tribute but the idea was bad even in the short term, since in a barbarian mind-set those who paid to be protected were rich but weak, and easy prey. After receiving the annual tribute of 80,000 gold coins, *c.* 580 the Avars forced some Romano-Byzantine engineers to build two bridges across the Sava in order to cut off the supplies and to starve Sirmium. The Khan even tried to fool Tiberius II in arguing these bridges were built to destroy the Sklavenes.

Notwithstanding this story the Emperor clearly understood the real purpose, and he had nothing to oppose the Avars since the Imperial field army was fighting the Persians in Armenia and Mesopotamia. Then he tried to worry the Khan by telling him that the Turks were on the verge of attacking him, but it was the Khan's turn not to be deceived. The Emperor reinforced the Sirmium garrison with officers and border troops sent from Illyricum and Dalmatia. In vain he tried to bribe the Lombards for military help and from the Turks sending them Narses the Sakellarios.[54] The Avars were able to blockade Sirmium which fell to them. According to John of Ephesus, upon entering the town, the Avars had 'compassion upon the starving inhabitants, and gave them bread to eat and wine to drink' but told them to quickly depart from the city which was accidentally burnt one year later.[55] In 583, as their request for an increase in tribute was refused by Emperor Maurice, the Avars took Singidunum after heavy losses, ravaged Viminacium and went along the Danube to the Black Sea to the port of Anchialos, 200km north of Byzantium and the Empire had to pay again.[56] In 584, the Sklavenes arrived at the Long Walls in the suburbs of Byzantium before being defeated by Comentiolus the Thracian on the River Erginia

---

under Avar rule (sixth to seventh century)' in 'Avar Chronology Revisited, and the Question of Ethnicity in the Avar Qaganate' in F. Curta & R. Kovalev (eds), *The Other Europe in the Middle Ages. Avars, Bulgars, Khazars and Cumans, East Central and Eastern Europe in the Middle Ages, 450–1450*, vol. 2 (Leiden: Brill, 2009), pp.13–17, (location). P. Stadler, 'Avar Chronology Revisited, and the Question of Ethnicity in the Avar Qaganate' in F. Curta & R. Kovalev (eds), *The Other Europe in the Middle Ages*, p.47, (sudden conquest of 568).

53   Menander Protector, *Fragm.*, 21.
54   A. H. M. Jones, J. R. Martindale, J. Morris, *PLRE*, 3a (1992), pp.930–931 (Narses 4).
55   Menander Protector, *Fragm.*, 25, 1 (one bridge on the Save between Sirmium and Singidunum in order to attack the Sklavenes; Maurice unnamed; errors of Tiberius); 2 (Persians; Turkish threat). John of Ephesus, *HE*, VI, 30 (Roman engineers). Theophylact Simocatta, *HU*, I, 2, 4 (dated by the very beginning of Maurice reign); 3, 7 (tribute). John of Ephesus, *HE*, VI, 30 (two bridges built; Tiberius embassy to Lombards and other tribes); 31 (failed embassy of Narses the Spatharius across Pontus to the Turks,); 32 (two-year blockade; compassion; dehousing); 33 (accidental burning of Sirmium).
56   Theophylact Simocatta, *HU*, I, 4, 1–3 (Singidunum), 4 (Viminacium, Anchialos).

(now Ergene a Maritsa tributary in eastern Turkish Thrace). The Sklavenes suffered another setback near Adrianople.[57] Two years later, Maurice sent the Antes to devastate Sklavene lands, located in present-day Wallachia. This strategy proved unsuccessful as the latter did not stop their raids.[58] The same year the Avars sacked some cities.[59]

So, in spring 587, Comentiolus the Thracian led a pre-emptive attack into Avar territory, with the only disappointing result being that the Avars invaded northern Thrace during the summer. Their route suggests that they came down the Danube through the Balkans via the Shipka Pass. The Avars besieged numerous cities without managing to take them despite the fact that they now had Roman-style siege machines at their disposal: Beroea of Thrace (Stara Zagora, Bulgaria), Diocletianopolis (Hisarya, Bulgaria), Philippopolis (Plovdiv, Bulgaria) then Adrianople (current Edirne in European Turkey). By 378, this place was already able to resist, even after the destruction of the Eastern Roman mobile army by the Goths. It was renamed Justinianopolis by Justinian who reinforced the fort of St Donatus. There the Avars retreated after being defeated by a Germanic officer called Droctulf, Drokton using his Greek name. The Avars only success in this campaign was to be bribed for abandoning the siege of Beroea of Thrace.[60]

In spring 588, the Avars demanded a large increase in annual tribute from the Emperor, but it was merely a pretext and a deceptive manoeuvre in preparation for a new invasion. Maurice refused again as he had done the previous year. The Avars with their Sklavene allies, failed against the walls of Singidunum but they extorted 2,000 *darics* gold coins to leave. The Khan went east to the Black Sea at Anchialos, but was repulsed from walls of the city without gaining any ransom. Then he tried his chance more to the south besieging Priscus' army in Tzurullon and left only after having been given a tribute.[61] The Avars had nevertheless arrived 120km from Byzantium without having fought a battle and decided to rest. In 589, the Sklavenes devastated Thrace.[62]

In the summer of 593, Priscus led a campaign on the Danube to prevent a Sklavene offensive. This did not prevent a band of 600 Sklavenes the following year sacking Zadalpa (Krushari, Bulgaria), Aquis (Prahovo, Serbia?) and Scopi (current Skopje, Macedonia). In 595, the Avars destroyed Singidunum's walls, deporting the inhabitants as slave subjects to their homeland. Priscus arrived with riverine *dromones* and tried to negotiate

---

57 Theophylact Simocatta, *HU*, I, 7, 1–4.
58 Michael the Syrian, *HU*, X, 21, t. 2 (1963), p.362.
59 Theophylact Simocatta, *HU*, I, 8 1–11.
60 Theophylact Simocatta, *HU*, II, 10, 8–15; 11–16 (Comentiolus the Thracian); II, 16, 12. 1–4 (Avars conducted unsuccessful sieges; Beroa was also the ancient Greek name for Aleppo, Syria); 17, 1–13 (Drocton).
61 Theophylact Simocatta, *HU*, VI, 3, 9–4 (demand an increase in tribute; refusal by the Emperor); 4, 1–3 (Singidunum), 4–5 (Sirmium); 5, 1–2 (Anchialos); 10 (Tzurullon); 16 (tribute). Evagrius Scholasticus, *HE*, VI, 10.
62 Theophylact Simocatta, *HU*, III, 4, 7.

with the Khan. When the latter angrily interrupted the discussion, Priscus sent Godwin with ships to quickly free Singidunum. Caught by surprise the Avars chose to flee. Blocked by Priscus in Northern Illyricum, they went west to ravage the poorly protected Dalmatia.[63]

Under these repeated blows, the Illyricum *limes* collapsed in the Iron Gates area between 593 and 596, as suggested by the find of numerous monetary deposits and the long interruption of money flow after this date.[64] However, *c.* 599 one last time Comentiolus the Thracian and Priscus assembled their forces at Singidunum, then established an operational base near to, or in, Viminacium. Comentiolus prudently being sick let Priscus venture north of the Danube up to the Tisza achieving dashing successes against the surprised Sklavenes, Gepids and Avars. This operation, as in 595, would not have been possible without the Danubian fleet, a Roman heritage.[65] The other condition for victory was a defenceless Sklavene land as two letters from Pope Gregory the Great in May 599 and July 600 mentioned Sklavene raids on Istria.[66] It is presumed that the Skavene began a process of moving from Vallachia to the River Drina, a task easier due to the loss of Sirmium. In 601, from this foothold and in conjunction with the Avars and Lombards they pillaged Istria, an operation they repeated on their own 10 years later.[67]

In summer 602, the Khan of the Avars sent his General Apsich to fight the Antes who were allied to the Romano-Byzantines. It was a retaliatory action because the territory of his allies, the Sklavenes, had been despoiled by a surprise incursion that the Emperor Maurice had ordered. As a result of these actions, large numbers of Sklavenes defected from the Avars and joined the Emperor.[68] Numismatic data suggests that Naissus in Upper Moesia fell to the Sklavenes around 615, as did Narona near the Dalmatian coast.[69] This corresponds, with the exception of imprecise geographical details, to the date given by Isidore of Seville when he wrote: 'Heraclius entered the fifth year of his reign [begun in 610], at the beginning of which the Sklavenes took Greece from the Romans.'[70] Greece in this context was intended to mean the Balkan area. Sklavenes, Avars and Huns Kutrigurs were settling south of the Sava and the Danube as revealed by archaeology.[71]

---

63   Theophylact Simocatta, *HU*, VI, 6, 2–9, 15 (Priscus' campaign); VII, 2, 2 (Slkavenes); 10, 1–11, 8 (Singidunum); 12, 1–9 (Dalmatia).

64   Kondić Vl. (1984, p.160.

65   Theophylact Simocatta, *HU*, VIII, 1, 11 (Singidunum); 2, 2 and 5 (Viminiacum); 2, 8–9 (ships on Danube); 3, 11–15 (success).

66   Gregory the Great, *Ep.*, IX, 154; X, 15.

67   Paul the Deacon, *HL*, IV, 24 and 40 (Istrie).

68   Theophylact Simocatta, *HU*, VIII, 5, 13 (Apsich); 14 (defectors).

69   Vl. Popović, 'Les témoins archéologiques des invasions avaro-slaves dans l'Illyricum byzantin', *MEFR*, 87–1 (1975), p.502.

70   Isidore of Seville, *Hist.*, 120. Confirmed by *Chr.* 754, 7 (Greece).

71   Vl. Popović, 'La descente des Koutrigurs, des Slaves et des Avars vers la mer Égée: le témoignage de l'archéologie', *Comptes rendus des séances de l'Académie des*

In Dardania, Iustiniana Prima declined towards the late sixth century, ceasing to be occupied in the first decades of the following century. The city of Iustiniana Secunda held out against earthquakes, floods and barbarians until the late seventh century.[72]

Justinian's work on the fortifications in Illyricum is sometimes considered ineffective, since the Avars and Sklavenes were able to besiege Byzantium in 626. This did not mean that all the forts and cities were swept away. Many of them were still standing in the enemy's rear, and it was on these fortifications, restored or built by Justinian, that the *themata* militias from the Balkans still relied upon effectively up to the Eighth and Ninth centuries.[73] Sardica, for example, did not fall to the Bulgarians until 809.

The Gepids Occupy the Sirmium Region

From a military point of view, the Danube no longer formed the barrier it was until 376, the date of the introduction of the Visigothic *foederati* into the Balkans. The Eastern Danube border was the first to collapse and drive a wedge into the Empire, but it was later reformed. After being encouraged to emigrate westward in 402, the Huns established themselves south of the Middle Danube in Valerie and Pannonia around 433. In the following years, they were a constant threat to the Empire of the East and in 441 took Sirmium, a fortified city located on the left bank of the Sava. This former capital of Roman Pannonia was still a beautiful fortified city of 100 hectares in the early fifth century, a rectangle with a projection formed by the hippodrome.[74]

After their vassal peoples shook off their yoke in 454, the Huns left Roman Pannonia and settled north of the Danube, then vanished into the steppes from whence they came. The Ostrogoths replaced them in the Sirmium region, named Pannonia Sirmiensis in Theodoric the Great's official letters.[75] Originally from the northern Germanic forests, the Gepids settled here in 473 or 474 after the departure of the Ostrogoths. They left necropolises there containing belt buckles typical of their culture and decorated with eagle heads.[76]

During the War of 505, Count Pitzia, sent by Theodoric the Great, drove out the Gepids from Sirmium. Then he went on as far as Horreum Margi or Margoplanum (present-day Ćuprija in the Great Moravian Valley in

---

Inscriptions et Belles-Lettres, 122–3 (1978), pp.596–648.
72   V. Ivanišević, 'Une capitale revisitée', p.114 (prima). Chr. J. Goddard and *alii*, 'D'Ulpiana à Iustiniana Secunda', p.157 (secunda).
73   M. Pillon, 'Armée et défense de l'Illyricum', pp.7–85.
74   A. Poulter, 'The Use and Abuse of urbanism in the Danubian Provinces during the Later Roman Empire' in J. Rich (ed.), *The City in Late Antiquity* (London, New York: Routledge, 2002), pp.106–109.
75   Cassiodorus, *VE*, III, 23, 2.
76   V. Ivanišević, M. Kazanski, (2014), p.145.

Serbia). There he crushed Sabinian the Younger Master of the Soldiers to Illyricum who came with a small police contingent to neutralise the bandits of Mundo, the future Romano-Byzantine general under the Greek name of Moundos.[77] The Ostrogoths in *c.* 528 again attacked Gepid settlements and also the city of Gratiana on the Illyrican border. This action would tend to show that to the Ostrogoths mind, the Gepids and the Romano-Byzantines were allies against them.

In 535 according to Procopius the Gepids took Sirmium when Justinian drove the Goths away.[78] Twenty years later, he painted a grim picture: 'As for the Gepids, they occupy Sirmium and the surrounding areas, all areas which, in a word, are completely empty of inhabitants.'[79] Although *foederati*, the Gepids behaved quite ungratefully:

> [The Gepids] in turn plunder the population of Dalmatia and Illyricum as far as the suburbs of Epidamnos, taking prisoners. and when prisoners manage to escape and return home, these barbarians, arguing that they were at peace with the Romans, they came to Roman territory, and when they recognised some of their former captives, they took them away as if they had been fleeing slaves, and snatched them from their parents, brought them back with them without anyone opposing them.[80]

While Procopius wrote that the Gepids controlled Singidunum and were also settled on both sides of the Danube, he later contradicted himself by stating that certain towns in Dacia and Singidunum had been given by the Emperor, in 527, to the Heruls as *foederati*, adding that Heruls plundered Illyricum and Thrace many times.[81] For a Roman-Greek all these Gepid or Herul barbarians looked alike. The equally ungrateful Gepids were also plundering and enslaving Dalmatian and Illyrican inhabitants as far as Dyrrachium on Adriatic Sea. To counter them Justinian had settled Lombards in Noricum, a former Roman territory next to the Gepids. But in 547 the Lombards requested a military alliance with Justinian against the much to numerous Gepids. The Emperor agreed and sent a 10,000-strong army to help the Lombards. In retaliation the majority of the Heruls were incited by Gepids to rebel against the Empire, but they were utterly routed

---

77   Jordanes, *Getica*, LVIII, 300 (Count Pitzia *at* Sirmium and Margoplanum).
78   Procopius, *BG*, V, 3, 15 (war between Ostrogoths and Gepids); VII, 33, 8 (Sirmium occupied by the Ostrogoths). A. Sarantis, 'War and diplomacy in Pannonia and the north-west Balkans during the reign of Justinian: The Gepid threat and imperial responses', *DOP*, 63 (2009), pp.15–40.
79   Procopius, *Anecdota*, XVIII, 18.
80   Procopius, *BG*, VII, 33, 12.
81   Procopius, *BV*, III, 2, 6 (Sirmium and Singidunum to Gepids); *BG*, VII, 33, 8 (Justinian); 34, 17 and 34, 35 (Sirmium to Gepids); 33, 13 (Singidunum to Heruls).

by vanguard of this Romano-Byzantine Army. This bloody warning induced the Gepids to swiftly conclude a truce with Lombards thwarting Justinian's great expectations.[82]

Between 549 and 567, the Gepids were at war with the Lombards no less than six times, undoubtedly for the control of southern Pannonia.[83] Dark Ages historians are no help in discovering the truth but leave us to discover the answer if we can. In 566 according to Theophylact Simocatta, King Alboin of the Lombards seriously offended the Gepid King Cunimund by raping his daughter.[84] The conflict broke into open conflict in 567 when Cunimund attacked Alboin 'to avenge old insults', according to Paul the Deacon the pro-Lombard historian. However Menander Protector had another version of the story in which the Lombards were the aggressors: 'Alboin, the King of the Lombards, could not forget his hatred for Cunimund but wished by all means to destroy the power of the Gepids.'[85] In any case, the Gepids were utterly defeated because the Lombards had allied themselves with the powerful Khan of the Avars. The latter, however, was not keen on accepting this Lombard alliance and had imposed very harsh conditions on them: a tenth of the Lombards' livestock and half of their booty and territorial conquests. The Gepids and the Lombards asked for help from Justin II, but in vain. Once defeated, the Gepids became vassals of the Lombards and Alboin took as his wife Rosamund, daughter of Gepid King (no story of rape this time).[86]

In 568 when invading Italy, 'Alboin had brought with him to Italy much of the different peoples whom he or other Kings had submitted to. From this it comes that even today it is designated as Gepids, Bulgars, Sarmatians, Pannonians, Sueves, Noriques or other appellations of the same type the places where they settled.'[87] Justin II took the city of Sirmium back from the declining Gepids who left little of themselves trace thereafter. C. 572, Reptila the nephew of King Cunimund and Trasaric Arian Bishop of the Gepids went to Byzantium with all the treasures of their people.[88] This quite

---

82 Procopius, *BG*, VII, 33, 12 (Dalmatia, Illyricum); 34, 1–46 (Lombards; Justinian; Heruls; truce).
83 H. Gračanin, 'The Gepids and Southern Pannonia in the Age of Justinian I' in T. Vida, D. Quast, Z. Racz, I. Koncz (ed.), *Kollaps – Neuordnung – Kontinuität. Gepiden nach dem Ungtergang des Hunnenreiches. Tagung der Internationalen Konferenz and der Eötvös Lorand Universität, Budapest (14–15 Dezember 2015* (Mainz, Budapest: Institut für Archäologiewissenschaften, Eötvös Lorand Universität, Budapest Institut für Archäologie des Forschungszentrums für Humanwissenschaftender Ungarischen Akademie der Wissenschaften, Leibniz-Forschungsinstitut für Archäologie, Römisch-Germanisches Zentralmuseum, 2019), p.254.
84 Theophylact Simocatta, *HU*, VI, 10, 7–13.
85 Menander Protector, *Fragm.*, 12, 1 (Alboin). Paul the Deacon, *HL*, I, 27.
86 Menander Protector, *Fragm.*, 12, 2 (Avars; Justin II; Rosamund). Paul the Deacon, *HL*, I, 27 (Avars; Gepids defeat). John of Biclaro, *Chr.VT*, 19 (war dated by 572).
87 Paul the Deacon, *HL*, II, 26.
88 John of Biclaro, *Chr.VT*, 19.

unusual approach could only be interpreted as a request for protection of their national and personal funds, and a sign of a loss of military power.

Nevertheless, the Byzantine Imperial State could barely defend its own borders and in 582 the city of Sirmium was lost again after a two-year blockade to the recently 'appeared' Avars. To justify this conquest, the Khan's ambassador shamelessly explained to the Emperor that this city 'as a former possession of the Gepids rightly belonged to him since the Gepids had been conquered by the Avars.'[89] Four years later, surviving Gepids were clearly vassals of the Khan of the Avars even if around this time a Gepid was also mentioned as a member of the Imperial Guard.[90] In 599, while the Master of the Soldiers Priscus crossed the Danube northwards, between Viminiacum and Singidunum, he encountered three colonies of Gepids, all surprised and drunk while celebrating some festivities. Without any hesitation Priscus slaughtered 3,000 of them and brought back a large number of captives. This was the final end of this restless Germanic people.

Mesopotamia, Syria's Shield and the Key to Romano-Byzantine Defences in the East

The Sassanid Persian dynasty was the most powerful and best organised enemy with a strength comparable to the Romano-Byzantines. The Persians regularly waged war but had few territory gains, as their real goal was to plunder the Empire. The Persian King frequently led his armies in field campaigns, although he had a supreme commander with the title of *eranspahbadh*. *spahbadhs* and *marzbans* were the Persian equivalents to master of the soldiers and dukes. Sassanid armies were always numerous, well-disciplined, with a mass of lightly-armed foot archers, a smaller number of foot soldiers with spear and shield, and an elite heavy cavalry. These heavy cavalrymen, known in Latin as *clibanarii*, wore mail covering their faces, necks and bodies, iron breastplates and helmets, and were each armed with a sword, a mace, a long two-handed spear, a bow with a quiver of 30 arrows and sometimes with a round shield. Like the Romano-Byzantine the Persians used phalanx tactics.[91]

Most conventional and important wars of the period were fought on the dry plains of Mesopotamia, the border province with Persians. It was the upper part of the area called the 'Fertile Crescent' by the American Egyptologist, James Henry Breasted. Mesopotamia meaning 'between two rivers' was delineated by the Rivers Tigris and Euphrates. It was a string of agricultural zones with prosperous cities, bordered to the north by the rugged mountains of Anatolia and to the south by the desert of Syria and

---

89 Menander Protector, *Fragm*., 25, 2 (Avar embassy). B. Bavant, (1984), pp.250–251.
90 Theophylact Simocatta, *HU*, I, 8, 4 (vassals); VIII, 3, 11 (Imperial Guard).
91 A. Cameron, 'Agathias on Sassanians', *DOP*, 23 (1969–1970), pp.78–176; G. Greatrex, *Rome and Persia at War*, pp.52–59.

THE ARMY WATCHES OVER THE BORDERS

Iraq. As a former Roman province, Mesopotamia's border had been pulled back westwards since the loss to the Persians of Nisibis (current Nusaybin in Turkey) and Singara in 363. The Empire's strategy was to stop the Persian invasions Mesopotamia by a network of a few walled cities and forts. While the Persians were attracted to these cities the Romano-Byzantine field armies were gathering for the counter-attack – the two main assembly places were Amida to the north and Dara to the south. Amida was near Romano-Byzantine Armenia: closely bordered by the Tigris 600 metres to the east and overhanging smooth slopes, the city was located in a fertile plain surrounded by dry, rocky mountains. Roman Amida's circuit-walls were the strongest in the East and are the remains are still impressive today. Constans I had built the circuit in 349 with more than four metre thick walls, and 82 two or four floor towers.[92] In 359, Amida was defended by the *Legio V Parthica* and a *turma* of indigenous cavalry. When Mesopotamia was invaded, the city could be reinforced with six legions and one *schola palatina*. C. 400, a crack unit of the Illyrian *scutarii* was garrisoned there.[93] A century later the situation was quite different: from August 502 to January 503, Amida had no garrison and its inhabitants had to defend themselves before the surrender to King Kavadh I after a 97 days siege.[94] Nonetheless the place was retaken by the Romano-Byzantine forces the following year. A few decades later Justinian rebuilt some peripheral forts formerly made of mud brick and restored the derelict outer and the inner walls of the town.[95] Another century later, the place was taken again by the Persians and held from 602 to 628, but finally fell to the Arabs in 639.

The fortress cities of Upper Mesopotamia have always been difficult to besiege. For example, Khosrow I preferred to lower a ransom from 500 to 5 *kentēnaria* rather than continuing the over costly siege of Edessa in 544. Some 130km south-east from Amida stood Dara, the last outpost of the Empire. Before 560, the dozen forts separating Edessa from Dara were rebuilt by Justinian with 'strength and beauty' although they previously had 'ridiculous' walls.[96] Dara or Daras fortress, also called Anastasiopolis (the town of Anastasius, today the dull town of Dara and until recently Oğuz in the province of Mardin in southern Turkey) was then near the border with Persia. It was the first checkpoint on the road leading 1,000km west to Antioch. This road was the main road in East, a string of pearls with walled cities, water supplies and flourishing agricultural valleys.[97] Dara stretched across three low hills crossed by a stream, all dominated to the north by

---

92   F. M. Halifeoglu, 'Castle architecture in Anatolia: Fortifications of Diyarbakir', *Frontiers of Architectural Research*, vol. 2 (2) (2013), pp.209–221.
93   Ph. Richardot, *La fin de l'Armée Romaine*, p.190; *Notitia Dignitatum*, OR.XXXVI.19 (*equites scutarii Illyriciani*).
94   Procope, *BP*, I, 7, 3 (no soldiers); 7, 12–29 (the town fell).
95   Procope, *Aed.*, II, 2, 27–28 (Justinian); II, 4 19 (forts rebuilt).
96   Procopius, *Aed.*, II, 4, 14.
97   R. Dussaud, *Topographie historique de la Syrie antique and médiévale* (Paris: Open Edition Books, 2015), pp.413–501.

BIRTH OF THE BYZANTINE ARMY 476-641 CE VOLUME 2: WATCH THEM FIGHT!

BYZANTINE EAST IN 565 AD

THE ARMY WATCHES OVER THE BORDERS

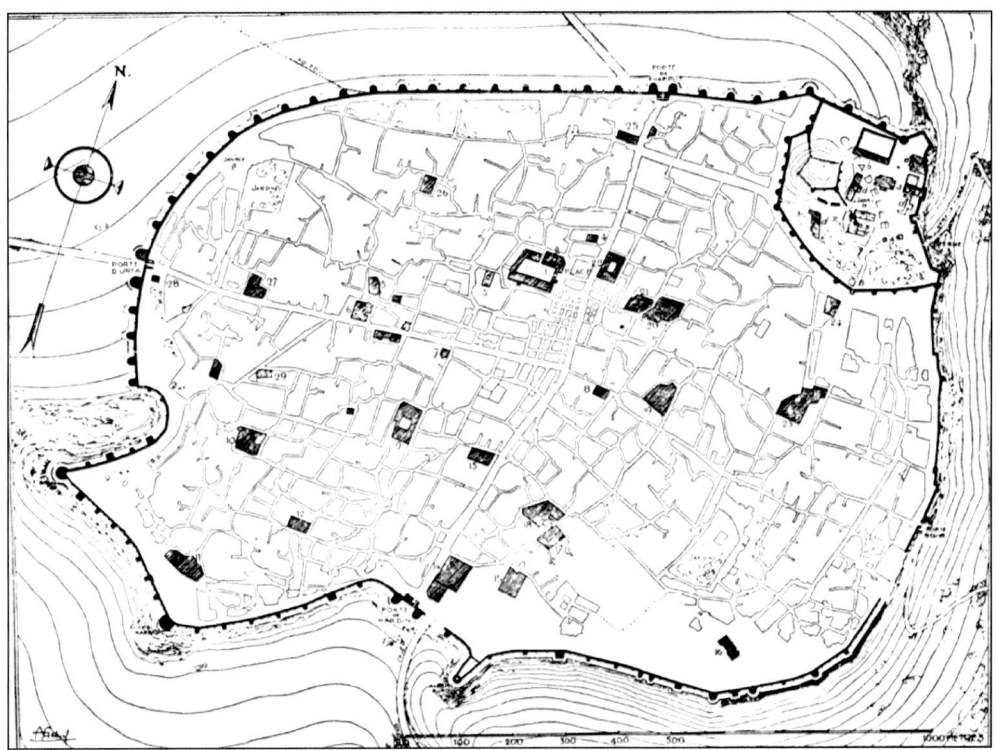

Plan of Amida, main Romano-Byzantine garrison city in Mesopotamia, today Diyarbakır, Turkey. After A. Gabriel, in D. van Berchem, 'Recherches sur la chronologie des enceintes de Mésopotamie et de Syrie', *Syria. Archéologie, Art et Histoire*, 31-3-4, 1954, p. 262.

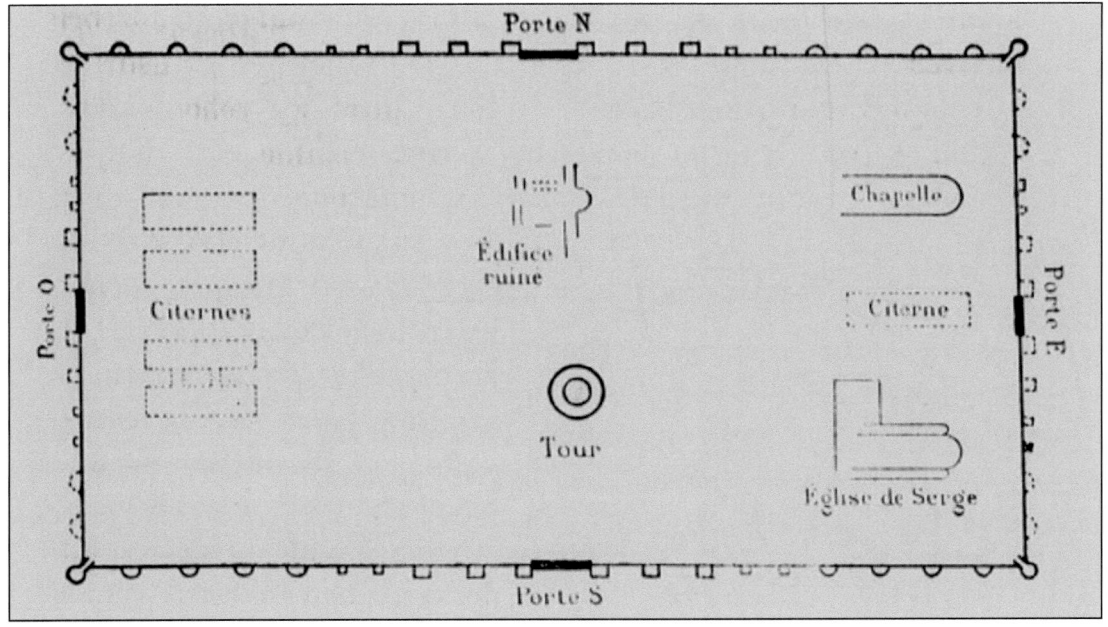

Plan of Resapha-Sergiopolis, a 500 x 300m rectangular fortress with a sanctuary, more a garrisoned caravanserai than a real city. The ditch was still present in 1903 partially filled. After A. Gabriel, in V. Chapot, 'Resapha-Sergiopolis', *Bulletin de Correspondance Hellénique, École française d'Athènes*, 27, 1903, p. 286.

the nearby heights. It overhung the fertile plain of Upper Mesopotamia. According to Procopius, Dara was a village only 28 *stadions* or 30km from the Persian border town of Nisibis.[98] In 505, even before peace was concluded the following year, Anastasius reinforced the walls of Dara. To encourage inhabitants to this insecure region, he built public baths, churches, cisterns, grain silos, and he renamed the city Anastasiopolis – not to be confused with its Thracian namesake. This choice would have been from advice given to him by the Bishop of Amida and by his troops.[99] John the Lydian praised this strategic choice:

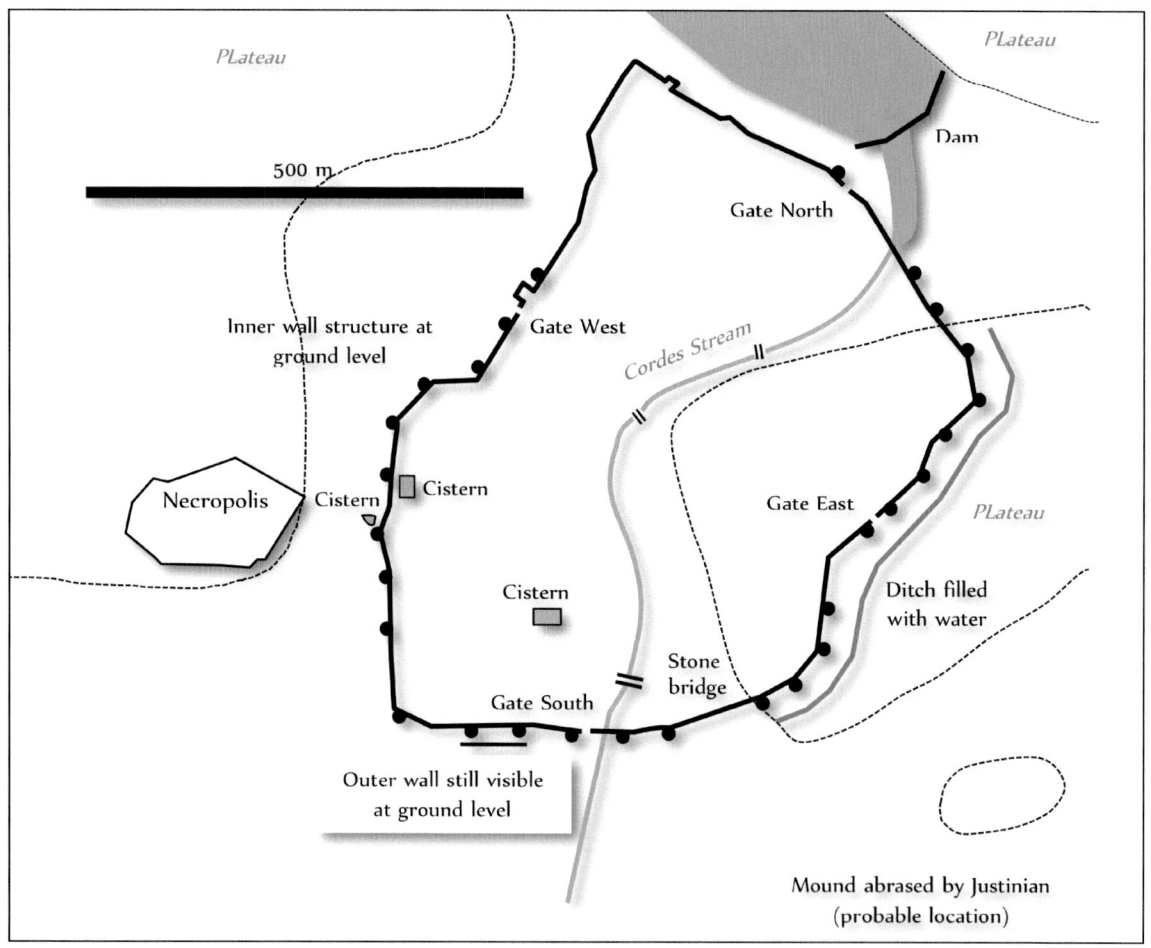

Dara Fortress Reconstructed Under Justinian

After Turkish Museums https://www.turkishmuseums.com/museum/detail/22330-mardin-dara-archaeological-site/22330/4

---

[98] Procopius, *BP*, I, 10, 13. George Kedrenos, *Compendium Historiarum*, vol. 1 (1838), p.130.

[99] John Malalas, *Chrgr.*, XVI, 9. Evagrius Scholasticus, *HE*, III, 37 (public works).

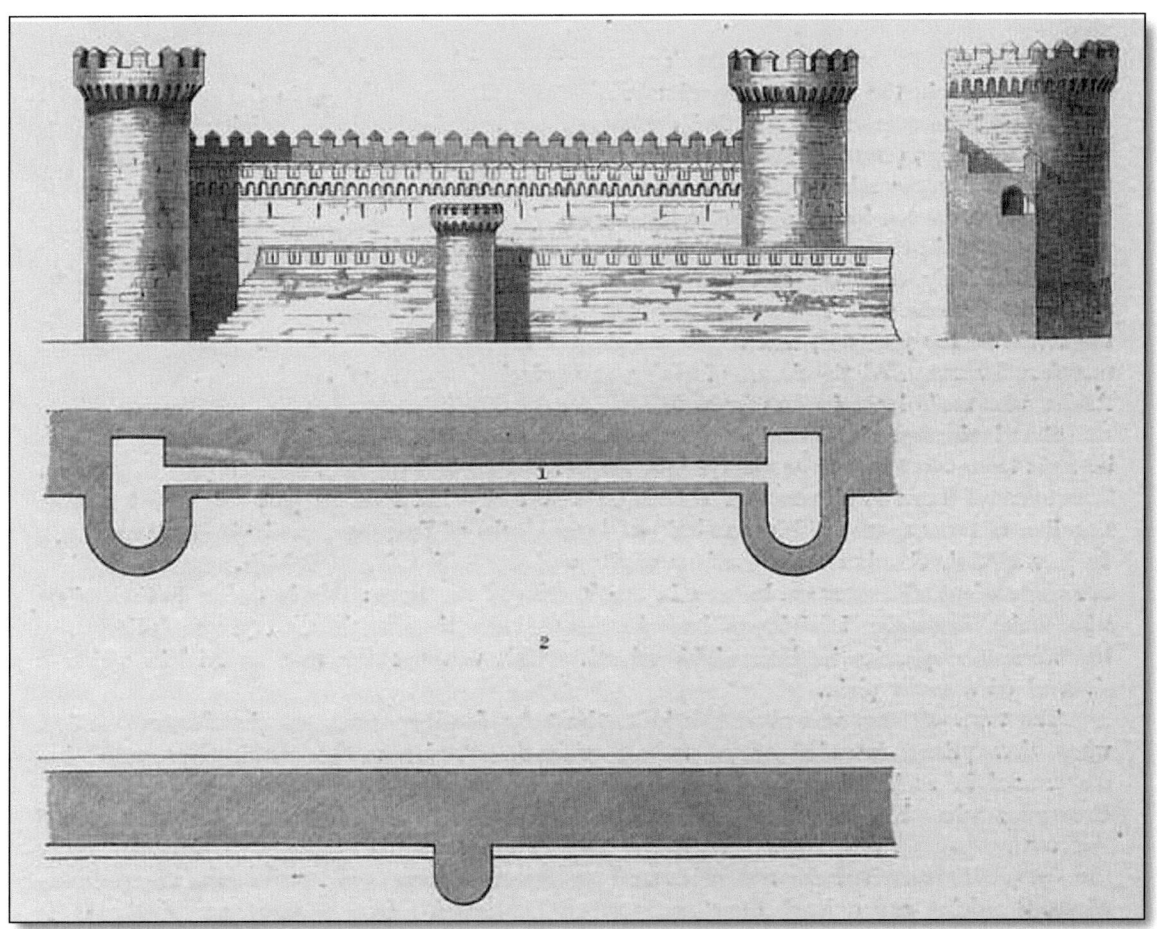

Anastasius did many things for the good of the state; it suffices to name the city he built: Dara say the natives; we call it Anastasiopolis. If God had not removed it from the domination of the Persians, they would soon have seized all the territories bordering the Romans.[100]

After F. M. Ch. Texier, R. Popplewell Pullan, *Byzantine Architecture, illustrated by Examples of Edifices Erected in the East During the Earliest Ages of Christianity* (London: Day & Son, 1864), p.57.

The city most fortified by Justinian was that of Dara, whose walls, built in haste under Anastasius, were ruined because they were built of poor rubble. To correct this poor state of things, Justinian erected an outer wall but took particular care of the main wall. Without rebuilding it, he supported it with powerful cut stone buttresses and raised it so that it supported a vaulted gallery under the parapet walk. This allowed for having a double tier of defenders. The wall rose to two floors and the towers to three:

> The city is surrounded by two walls, the inner one is admirable for its height as each tower reaches 100 feet and the wall to 60, the outer one is smaller but solid and worthy of interest. The space between

---

100 John the Lydian, *De Magistratibus*, III, 47.

the two walls is at least 50 feet and it is here that the inhabitants of Dara bring in their cows and cattle when they are attacked by enemies.[101]

The towers height can be estimated at 29m and up to 15m for the inner walls. The bases of 28 towers and 4 gates have been found. The original apertures of the battlements were reduced to very narrow slits, leaving only the space necessary to pass a man's hand, through and to shoot at the besiegers. A mound looking south and to obstruct an enemy from making mines under the circuit-wall the ground was abrased. Justinian also improved the water supply by huge new underground cisterns. He also reinforced Dara with two external rectangular forts, whose wall were 200m long and defended by 12 towers each, these covering fortifications were called in Latin *praetenturae*. According to Procopius, Justinian also dug a crescent-shaped, water-filled moat defending the south approach where the soil was deep, soft and easy to mine. The south-eastern surviving evidence of ditches 20m east of the east wall, may be the remains of this moat or they may be those from the trenches dug by Belisarius for the Battle of Dara. Important hydraulic works were also made: the course of the River Cordes was changed to make it flow through the city, and a three-arch stone bridge crossed it. The northern entry and southern exit of the river were closed by iron grilles and sluice-gates. To prevent flooding, one of the first arch dams was built following the initiative of an officer. The indirect effect was to create an underground river course thus depriving a besieging enemy of water. The Great Church and the Church of St Bartholomew were also built and the city received the barely used name of Iustiniana Nova (New Justinian [city]). At its peak, Dara had a population 40,000 people. Now only a few ruins from the circuit-wall remain: 2.8km are of the original 4km are still visible and you can visit two well-preserved underground cisterns from Justinian's construction and outside, to the west, a troglodyte rock-cut military necropolis with a church cave dug in the 590s and expanded in the later centuries.[102] For the duration of the defensive war with Khosrow I, Justinian transferred the headquarters of the duke of Mesopotamia to Constantina of Osrhoene. On the other hand, Dara became the operational headquarters of the master of the soldiers to the East in spring 573 when Justin II ordered the besieging the Persian outpost of Nisibis. This offensive turned into a complete rout when a Persian Army moving from the Euphrates to the Khabur and then north attacked the Romano-Byzantines

---

101 Procopius, *BP*, II, 13, 17–18.
102 Procopius, *Aed.*, II, 1, 4–22 (renovation of the walls), 23–25 (moat); 2, 1–21 (water supply). E. Keser-Kayaalp, N. Erdogan, 'Recent research on Dara/Anastasiopolis' in Rizos E. (ed.), *New Cities in Late Antiquity: Documents and Archaeology* (Turnhout: Brepols, 2017), pp.153–175. https://www.turkishmuseums.com/museum/detail/22330-mardin-dara-archaeological-site/22330/4

besiegers from the rear.[103] Using mangonels that the Romano-Byzantines had abandoned at Nisibis the Persian General Bahram Gushnasp, in Greek Bargousnas, took Dara in 573 after a six-month siege but the Persians returned in 591.[104] Like Amida, Dara was subsequently Persian-occupied from 602 to 628 before being taken by Muslim Arabs.

The small fort of Mindouos was not recorded in these events. According to Procopius, Justinian had ordered it to be built in 528, west of the Persian town of Nisibis. Archaeological evidence has identified this small fort near the modern hamlet of Kasriahmethayro, 5km south-east of Dara and 6km east of Nisibis. Mindouos and Thannuris were perhaps two different forts but Procopius seems to merge these in one when he referred to the construction of a fort in 528.[105] This worried the Persians who saw it as a violation of the treaties and consequently they counter-attacked, defeating Belisarius in 528. This episode is sometimes also located in Thannuris, which is sometimes identified as the fort of Tannuri which, *c.* 400, was south-east of the duchy of Mesopotamia and that housed a regular horse archer unit raised from among the Bedouins.[106] Mindouos like Tannuri was not intended to resist a formal siege but simply to raise an alarm. Both indigenous garrisons failed to do this in 573. In the triangle of Amida, Constantina of Osrhoene and Dara stood several forts, of which only two names were given by Procopius: Apadna and Byrthum, two wretched outposts with dry mud walls. Located in the duchy of Mesopotamia, Apadna has existed since Roman times and was home to a unit of indigenous horsemen.[107]

Forty kilometres east of Dara, two days' march for an army, the road came up to Nisibis, a Persian border citadel since 363. When Mesopotamia ceased to be the shield of the Empire, to become the base of attack against the Sassanid Persians, Nisibis was the main objective of the Romano-Byzantine Army. On the initiative of Justin II, Nisibis was attacked unsuccessfully in 573. Some 40km to the east of Nisibis, Sisauranon (also known as Sisauronon, Sisarauna) was located on what was known as a 'tell', a hill possibly of the Bronze Age. Some ruins can be seen today on the Syrian border near the village of Yazryurdu. Then the town controlled the road to

---

103 F. R. Trombley, 'The Operational Methods of the Late Roman Army in the Persian War of 572–591' in in A. S. Lewin, P. Pellegrini, Z. T. Fiema, S. Janniard (eds), *The Late Roman Army in Near East*, pp.321–356.
104 Theophylact Simocatta, *HU*, III, 11, 2–3 (Dara siege in 573).
105 Chr. Lillington-Martin, 'Forts on frontiers facing 'βάρβαροι' et alii', paper was presented at the Late Antique and Byzantine Archaeology and Art Seminar, St. John's College, University of Oxford on 28 May 2015, https://www.academia.edu/1175514/Roman_Persian_frontier_fortlet_Mindouos_?auto=download
106 *Notitia Dignitatum*, OR.XXXVI.17 (*castellum*) and 28 (*equites sagittarii indigenae*). Procopius, *BP*, I, 13, 2 (Mindouos); 16, 7 (in violation of a treaty). (Pseudo-)Zachariah Rhetor, *HE*, IX, 2 (Thannuris or Tannuris in the desert)
107 *Notitia Dignitatum*, OR.XXXVI.8 and 23 (*equites promoti indigenae*). Procopius, *Aed.*, II, 4, 20; L. Dillemann, *Haute Mésopotamie et pays adjacents: contribution à la géographie historique de la région du Ve s. avant l'ère chrétienne au VIe s. de cette ère* (Paris: Geuthner, Bibliothèque archéologique et historique, 72, 1962), p.237.

Assyria and the Tigris Valley, it was formerly a Roman fortress but passed into the control of the Sassanids in 363, was partially razed by Belisarius in 541, probably taken over by Comentiolus the Thracian during his victory in 589, but the Empire was never able to settle there permanently.[108] The region is desperately dry and unfavourable for a summer invasion, as proved by the health crisis that struck the Romano-Byzantine Army after the capture of Sisauranon:

> Many of the Roman soldiers fell ill with a painful fever, as the Persian-held part of Mesopotamia is very arid. The Romans were not used to this, especially those from Thrace: camped in an extraordinarily dry region and living in stifling tents in the middle of summer, they fell so ill that a third of the army was half-dead.[109]

Until Heraclius the Romano-Byzantines were always more comfortable with a defensive role.

Osrhoene a Flaw in the Defensive System

The region of Osrhoene was a region to the south-west of Mesopotamia and bordered the Euphratensis and Syria. It was bounded to the west by the Euphrates and to the east by the River Chaboras (current Khabur). Osrhoene was difficult for a Persian invader coming from Mesopotamia to attack as they encountered powerful fortified cities such as Constantina to the northeast, Edessa to the north, and Carrhae to the south (respectively today Viranşehir, Şanlıurfa and Harran in Turkey). Constantia, called Constantina of Osrhoene or known as Tella, guarded the road to Amida. A century later the place was linked to Mesopotamia and garrisoned by two cavalry units and the *Legio Prima Parthica Nisibena*. By 503 the outer wall was constructed of only a poor mixture of stone with mud and the inner wall was lower with towers too far apart, nevertheless the Persians failed to take the city. Justinian did some important rebuilding: the circuit-wall height and the number of towers were doubled. The towers were upgraded to three floors, and all were square-shaped except the ones flanking the gates, which were semi-circular. A mile-long aqueduct was built to supply the city.[110] Constantina attracted the Persians and a major battle was won

---

108 Procopius, *BP*, II, 19, 24; L. Dillemann, *Haute Mésopotamie et pays adjacents*, pp.83 & 134. A. M. Comfort, *Roads on the frontier between Rome and Persia: Euphratesia, Osrhoene and Mesopotamia from AD 363 to 602* (Doctoral thesis, University of Exeter, 2009), https://ore.exeter.ac.uk/repository/handle/10036/68213, 2009, pp.112 & 326; M. Marciak, *Sophene, Gordyene, and Adiabene: Three Regna Minora of Northern Mesopotamia between East and West* (Leiden: Brill, 2017), p.184.
109 Procopius, *BP*, II, 19, 31–32.
110 *Notitia Dignitatum*, OR.XXXVI.22 (*equites felices Honoriani Illyriciani*); 24 (*equites*

there by Maurice in 582. The whole region had around 20 bridges with arches, many of which remain today. Two days' walk east of Constantina, a bridge crossed the River Arzamon, now Gümüş Çay or Zergan a tributary of the Khabour, on the road linking Persia to the Mediterranean Sea.[111]

This road was controlled both by Constantina and Edessa, located 85km directly east, the capital of Osrhoene which was on a plain crossed by the prone to flood the River Scirtos (today Bar-Daisan). In *c.* 520 a deadly flood killed up to one-third population of Edessa and the city had to be rebuilt. It was temporarily named Justinopolis after the earthquake of 525 when Justin I rebuilt the public buildings and the double wall even extending the circuit to include a hill in the defensive perimeter.[112] Edessa was a such a difficult place to take that in 544 Khosrow I preferred to substantially lower the ransom (from 500 to 5 *kentēnaria*) rather than continuing a too costly siege.[113] About 80km west of Edessa, the Euphrates delineated the border with the province of Euphratensis. The Euphrates River separated the town of Zeugma (literally meaning 'link') in Eufratensis and the city of Apamea which was located on the opposite bank, with the two connected by ferry. Today both these ancient cities are drowned under the muddy waters of the Birecik dam. Zeugma was originally enclosed by walls of loose stones with no suitable barracks for a garrison, but Justinian gave it proper walls and military equipment in order for it to be able resist the Persians. Apamaea then had a 3km wall facing a rich cultivated plain.[114] Located some 40km south from Edessa on the road to Damas, Carrhae had its outer and inner walls rebuilt by Justinian. The main circuit was roughly 4km long with 187 towers, numerous but not impressive. The population of Carrhae was still pagan, and for that reason Khosrow I refused any tribute from them when he invaded the area.[115]

The weak point of Osrhoene was the Euphrates forming an invasion corridor in flat country and flowing south-east towards the impregnable and ever hostile Persian Kingdom. On the left bank lay Circesium, or

---

promoti indigenae); 29 (*Praefectus legionis primae Parthicae Nisibenae*). Procopius, *Aed.*, II, 5, 2–11.

111 Procopius, *BP*, I, 8, 10 (two days from Constantina). A. M. Comfort, 'Roman Bridges of South-East Anatolia' in H. Bru, G. Labarre, *L'Anatolie des peuples, des cités et des cultures (IIe millénaire av. J.-C. – Ve siècle ap. J.-C.). Colloque international de Besançon – 26–27 novembre 2010*, vol. 2, (Collection de l'Institut des Sciences et Techniques de l'Antiquité, 1277-2, 2013), p.335 (localisation).

112 Procopius, *Aed.*, II, 7, 3–5 (flood in Edessa killing a third of the population; reconstruction). John Malalas, *Chrgr.*, XVII, 15 (flood in Edessa); 11–16 (walls restored by Justin I). Evagrius Scholasticus, *HE*, IV, 8.

113 Procopius, *BP*, I, 7, 12–29 (Amida); II, 26, 39 and 27, 46 (ransom for Edessa). Theophylact Simocatta, *HU*, III, 11, 2–3 (Dara).

114 Procopius, *Aed.*, II, 8, 18–20 (Zeugma); C. Abadie-Reynal, 'Séleucie-Zeugma et Apamée sur l'Euphrate: étude d'un cas de villes jumelles dans l'Antiquité', *Histoire urbaine*, 1/3 (2001), pp. 7–24.

115 Procopius, *Aed.*, II, 7, 17 (renovation of Carrhae). Id., *BP*, II, 13, 7 (Khosrow I at Carrhae).

Circesio, the last Imperial outpost in the east (present-day Al-Busayrah in Syria). Built under Emperor Diocletian, *c.* 400 the city was considered as a *castellum* and garrisoned by the *Legio IV Parthica*. Its main weakness was the lack of a wall on the Euphrates' side. At the beginning of his reign Justinian worried about the utter decrepitude of distant Circesium's citadel, so he completed the wall and renovated the entire city, including the baths, and gave it troops led by a duke.[116] By 540, Khosrow I preferred to bypass the city rather than to besiege so strong a place: 'It is the last Roman fortress, named Circesium, very strongly protected by a large river the Abhorra [now the Khabur] which ends its course there and flows into the Euphrates, the fortress is located precisely at the junction of the two. Moreover, outside the fortress a large wall cuts the ground between the two streams and forms a triangle around Circesium.'[117] Circesium was reputedly an impregnable city, but it was of little strategic use as it could be bypassed and did not have a garrison strong enough to stop invading Persians.

Following the right bank of Euphrates to the north-east, three days' journey of over 100km, the Persian invaders fell on the fortified city of Zenobia (today Halabiyah, an archaeological site in Syria). This city, built by Queen Zenobia, was by 540 so 'uninhabited and miserable' that Khosrow I refused to waste time with it, even after the failure of negotiations. Later, Justinian restored the circuit-wall, which now included a hill with a steep base, enlarged the city and protected it from floods, built churches, porticoes, public baths and barracks for soldiers. To do this, Justinian employed two talented young architects, John of Constantinople and Isidore of Miletus.[118]

More than 80km along the Euphrates towards the north stood Callinicum (current Racca or Ar-Raqqah in Syria). In 531, the vicinity of Callinicum had witnessed the defeat of Belisarius' army but the Persians had been unable to go deeper into the Romano-Byzantine hinterland. The Persians were then on the right or southern bank of the Euphrates and after being defeated the Romano-Byzantine troops could retreat on numerous boats to Callinicum on the opposite bank.[119] During the invasion of 540, no record of any military event around Callinicum was noted. Khosrow probably bypassed the city to the south and Romano-Byzantines made no attempt to stop him. In spring 542, contemptuous of any peace agreements, Khosrow I took the same invasion route as in 531 and 540 with the Euphrates on his right. Callinicum had no garrison and its wall was successively demolished in sections to renovate it. Khosrow I found a section of the fallen wall and rushed his troops into it after crossing the Euphrates. He razed the city

---

116 *Notitia Dignitatum*, OR.XXXV.24 (Praefectus legionis quarta Parthicae). Procopius, *Aed.*, II, 6, 2–10. J. Wiesehöfer, 'CIRCESIUM' in *Encyclopaedia Iranica*, vol. V, fasc. 6, (1991), pp.595–596.
117 Procopius, *BP*, II, 5, 2–3.
118 Procopius, *BP*, II, 5, 4 (a three-day walk to Circesium, foundation by Zenobia); 7 (poverty); Procopius, *Aed.*, II, 8, 8–25.
119 Procopius, *BP*, I, 18, 50;

THE ARMY WATCHES OVER THE BORDERS

and deported the population. Justinian rebuilt the city with walls which no longer had anything to fear from the enemy according to Procopius.[120]

Located 25km west of Callinicum, stood the small town of Sura surrounded by an oval circuit-wall 1.7km long, it was at the head of Strata Diocletiana, the military road bordering the desert to the south and a bishopric since the fourth century, today only a ghostly archaeological site. C. 400, Sura was under command of the duke of Syria and garrisoned by the *Legio XVI Flavia Firma*. In 540, under the full weight of the invading Persian Army, it held out just for half an hour as Procopius recorded in his *Buildings*. Nevertheless, in his *Persian War*, he wrote more honestly that Arsace, an Armenian commanding the garrison, fought valiantly before succumbing to an arrow. As a consequence, the small town fell the day after by treacherous surprise during negotiations with the Bishop. Sura was burnt, its population enslaved – Justinian rebuilt it with a circuit-wall equivalent to that of Callinicum.[121]

Around 250km to the south-west where the Strata Diocletiana ran, Sura was covered by Sergiopolis, also called Resafa or Rusafa, which had been strongly fortified by Justinian and is today a well-preserved site. Khosrow I tried but proved unable to take it.[122] Following the road from Sura to about 30km west of the Euphrates the Persian invaders attacked Hierapolis of Syria (formerly Bambyce, and today Manbij), which was known the most beautiful city of the Euphratensis. A wall that is too long on a flat ground made the city indefensible, and after the grim experience of 540, Justinian strengthened the city.[123] After Hierapolis, the road to Syria was open to the Persians. During the 540 invasion Beroea of Syria (today Aleppo) went up in flames but its acropolis resisted for some time until the garrison came to terms with Khosrow I.[124] Antioch, the capital of Syria (today Antakya in Turkey) was the largest city in the East and one might think that it was defended by a strong garrison of troops but it was not. To help Antioch Justinian urgently sent his cousin the Patrician Germanus with only 300 men but promising a greater relief army. Germanus quickly realised that only the side along the River Orontes was really protected. On the opposite side, the wall on the steep rocks known as the Orocasias was not high enough; he therefore ordered the rocks to be scarped. However, the task

---

120 Procopius, *BP*, II, 20, 1 (Persian invasion of 542); 21, 30 (renovation); 31 (wall partly torn down); 32 (city razed; deportation); *Aed.*, II, 7, 17 and 9, 2 (new wall).
121 *Notitia Dignitatum*, OR.XXXIII.6 (*castellum*) and 24 (*Praefectus legionis sextaedecimae Flaviae firmae*). Procopius, Procopius, *BP*, II, 5, 8–33 (Khosrow I); *Aed.*, II, 9, 1–2 (half an hour resistance; fortified by Justinian). M. Konrad, *Der spätrömische Limes in Syrien. Archäologische Untersuchungen an den Grenzkastellen von Sura, Tetrapyrgium, Cholle und in Resafa*, (Mainz: Verlag Philipp von Zabern, Deutsches Archäologisches Institut, Resafa 5, 2001).
122 Procopius, *Aed.*, II, 9, 3–9.
123 Procopius, *BP*, II, 6, 24 (walls too extended); *Aed.*, II, 9, 12–17 (flat terrain; restoration; springs).
124 Procopius, *BP*, II, 7, 12.

very soon appeared impossible and the builders abandoned it because there was not enough time and the work would show the Persians this weak point. The inhabitants preferred to pay ransom to the Persians, but gave up when a body of 6,000 border troops arrived from Lebanon. These reinforcements, fit to hold off desert cattle thieves but unfit to face a regular army chose to desert during the siege, the Persian soldiers even facilitating their passage with cheers, shouts and hand signals.[125] After this disastrous episode which smelled of negligence and cowardliness, Justinian made some adjustments in Antioch. He reduced the length of the circuit-walls, levelled the Orocasias, diverted the course of the Orontes to avoid flooding while taking advantage of the river, had cisterns dug, rebuilt private houses and embellished the city with paved streets, porticoes, theatres, aqueducts and of course baths.[126]

Imperial evergesis was replacing military efficiency. The most successful campaign of Khosrow I was therefore that of 540, where he avoided the fortresses of Upper Mesopotamia and of Osrhoene, skirted the right bank of the Euphrates to avoid the stronghold of Circesium, unsuccessfully attacked Zenobia, passed around Callinicum, and shaved the unfortunate little city of Sura. Arriving in Syria he spared Hierapolis of Syria after it paid a ransom, but burnt and pillaged Beroea of Syria and then Antioch. The account of these events gives the impression of an inglorious disaster and suggest almost total inefficiency: it is sort of 'a version for the media'. But a more strategic insight leads one to think differently.

Probably in 530, Khosrow I invaded Osrhoene a first time. In 540, 542 and 544, he tried again, reaching Commagene in 542 and besieging Edessa in 544, but without achieving anything more than temporary successes and to extort ransom from or plunder several cities..[127] He tried once more in 573 but with a new and wider strategy, ordering his General Adarman to cross the Euphrates in the vicinity of Circesium and to proceed north. Adarman reached Antioch but was unable to take it, then he moved back to Apamea where he enslaved the population as he probably did with Zeugma. Since he only fielded a 6,000-strong army this means Romano-Byzantines had no mobile forces to oppose him.[128] By 581, in order to invade Persia, Maurice, then Master of the Soldiers to the East, reversed the route used by Khosrow I. He first mustered a field army at Circesium and led it to Babylon accompanied by his Ghassanid ally al-Mundir III ibn-al-Harith. From there Maurice intended to reach Ctesiphon, capital of the Persian

---

125 Procopius, *BP*, II, 6, 10–11 (location and weak point); 7, 9 (Germanus); 10–15 (walled unprepared); 16 (ransom); 8, 1 (reinforcements and morale increase); 17 and 24–25 (fleeing of border troops); 8, 8–15 (Persian assault on the weak point).
126 Procopius, *Aed.*, II, 10, 2–25.
127 J. B. Bury, *A History of the Later Roman Empire*, pp.79–89 (first Persian War), 89–113 (second Persian War).
128 John of Epiphania, *Fragm.*, I, 4. Theophylact Simocatta, *HU*, III, 10, 6 (numbers); 8 (crossing near Circesium); 9 (Apamea).

Kingdom. Unfortunately, he had to pull back west to Callinicum where Adarman conducted a strategically successful diversion even if he tactically lost the battle.[129] Subsequently, Mesopotamian and Osrhoenean fortresses were no longer renovated and afterwards proved to have no effectiveness. Amida, once again seized by the Persians in 602, was only recaptured by Heraclius in 628, only to fall into the hands of the Muslims 11 years later. *Sic transit Gloria mundi.*

Armenia Maior, the March of Anatolia

As Mesopotamia and Oshoene were the guard of Syria, so Armenia was the guard of Anatolia and gaining control on it was not an easy task. North of Mesopotamia and south of the vassal Kingdom of the Tzani, Armenia had been a bone of contention between the Persians and the Romans for five centuries. Facing east to west, its mountains did not offer any barrier to invasion. Furthermore, the Armenians showed themselves as an ungovernable people who frequently rebelled, but they were nonetheless too weak to be independent and needed a protector. So, by the treaty of 387, Theodosius I and Sapor III divided Armenia into two buffer states, Persarmenia, the biggest part, to the Persian King; Armenia Maior under Roman domination.[130] In 488, Emperor Zeno removed any form of self-government by dismissing the hereditary satraps of Armenia. From then a duke of Armenia was in charge of the border troops. Byzantine strategy there was more to control the local population than to contain Persian inroads. The warlike Armenians could provide fierce opponents but also good soldiers and generals, as Narses the Eunuch and Heraclius the Elder proved to be.

The key cities of Armenia were Theodosiopolis and Martyropolis (respectively present-day Erzurum and Silvan in Turkey), 200km apart. According to Procopius Martyropolis was located 'on the very bank of the Nymphius (today the River Batman), which divided the Roman from the Persian territory'. The Persian invasion during the Anastasian War in 502 began with the occupation of Armenia in order to outflank Mesopotamia to the north. Only one day's walk separated Martyropolis from Amida in Mesopotamia. According to Procopius Martyropolis' fortifications

---

129 Theophylact Simocatta, *HU*, III, 17, 5–9 (gather at Circesium to attack Babylonia); 10–11 (Battle of Callinicum, which is not mentioned in other sources). John of Ephesus, *HE*, III, 40 (Maurice and al-Mundir march together and find the bridge over the Euphrates destroyed, quarrel because Maurice accuses his ally of having betrayed him. The Romano-Byzantines have accomplished nothing, denunciation to Tiberius II); 42 (2nd Battle of *Callinicum* at the following year, probably an erroneous dating). Evagrius Scholasticus, *HE*, V, 20 (unlocated victory of Maurice over Adarman, betrayal of al-Mundir who refuses to cross the Euphrates).

130 A. Stratos, 'Byzance et la Perse', *La Nouvelle Revue des Deux Mondes,* April (1981), p.35.

were so neglected that Anastasius I, judging the city indefensible, forgave Duke Theodore for having surrendered. In August 502 the betrayal of Constantine, Count of Armenia in charge of civil administration, lost Theodosiopolis but in November the city was retaken when the Persians went south to Mesopotamia. In 505, when negotiations were opened with Persians, Anastasius restored Theodosiopolis' walls.[131] To watch this city, the Persians had erected a fort at Bolum (present-day Bolberd, Turkey). C. 530, the Persarmenian Governor sold the city to the Romano-Byzantines. To fill the gap between Theodosiopolis and Martyropolis Justinian built the fortress of Kitharizon, on the River Keghi, a small town and 'an impregnable fortress on a mountainous site' abundantly supplied with water.[132] Under Justinian, it was the seat of a bishopric and of one of the two dukes of Armenia with Martyropolis according to Procopius.[133] Nevertheless, only one duke of Armenia was previously reported in the *Notitia Dignitatum*. Procopius probably meant a civil governor and a military one.

In 528, as war resumed with Persians Justinian created the rank of *magister militum per Armeniam* (master of the soldiers to Armenia), appointing his brother-in-law Sittas to the post. Previously there had only been dukes, satraps and counts in Armenia, the latter two functions being civil. Justinian gave Sittas forces taken from the two masters of the soldiers present. Sittas rebuilt the walls of Martyropolis, 'destroyed by time' according to Malalas, and installed a troop there, a *numeros* in Hellenised Latin.[134] The 'Eternal Peace' with the Persians of 532 guaranteed to Byzantium the shores of the Black Sea. Armenians held an intermediate status between subjects and allies. These rebellious mountain people revolted alternately against the Persians or the Romano-Byzantines, achieving some successes and a few years of independence before falling back into being a subject people. In 481, when Vahan I Mamikonian raised Persarmenia against the Persian King Peroz, he assembled 30,000 men who crushed the Hun mercenaries sent against them at the Battle of Geran. In 485, Peroz's successor, Kavadh I, covered up the loss of Persarmenia by an agreement with Vahan, who received the title of *marzipan* (governor). With the passing of time, the legal fiction became reality, the Persian domination proved effective and unbearable, especially the anti-Christian persecutions. In 572, the Persian Governor erected a Temple of Fire at Dovin (modern Dvin) capital city of Persarmenia. It was understood as a tentative attempt to impose

---

131 Procopius, *Aed.*, III, 2, 2 (Nymphius River); 3 (neglected walls of Martyropolis); (one day's walk from Amida); 9 (Anastasius); *BP*, I, 10, 18–19 (Theodosiopolis).
132 Procopius, *BP*, I, 13, 2 (Mindouos); *Aed.*, III, 3, 7 (Kitharizon).
133 Procopius, *BP*, I, 15, 32 (Bolum); 24, 13 (Kitharizon was four days distant from Theodosiopolis); *Aed*, III, 2, 1 (duke of Armenia); III, 3, 7–8 (impregnable fortress; water). R. Janin, 'Citharizum' in A. Baudrillart, A. De Meyer, É. Van Cauwenbergh (eds), *Dictionnaire d'Histoire et de Géographie ecclésiastiques*, vol. XII, fasc. 67–72 (Paris: Letouzey et Ané, 1953), col. 997.
134 John Malalas, *Chrgr.*, XVIII, 5 (Martyropolis); 10 (master of the soldiers to Armenia, dukes).

THE ARMY WATCHES OVER THE BORDERS

Zoroastrian religion on the Christianised Iberians and Armenians, the latter then placed themselves under the protection of 'Rome', that is to say Byzantium, according to John of Biclaro. Accordingly, Justin II refused to pay the Persians the tribute they demanded for the religious freedom of Armenian Christians. The peace, like all those concluded with Persians, collapsed again.[135] The cause was a member of the prestigious Mamikonian family, Vardan III, who rebelled against Persians and the following year Justin II helped him by sending an army. These joined forces and devastated the city of Dovin where the pagan Temple of Fire had been erected. In 574, they defeated a 20,000 Persians force supported by elephants at the Battle of Khalamakhik. By 575 King Khosrow I concluded a truce but he broke the following year, suffering a heavy defeat by Justinian, Master of the Soldiers to the East, near Melitene. With some exaggeration and a great deal of chauvinism, Sebeos presented it as a purely Armenian victory.[136]

The Romano-Byzantines also suffered several setbacks with their Armenians tributaries. When Sittas took on the new role of master of the soldiers to Armenia, he had made sure to recruit Armenians in his administration, but 10 years later, in 538, the Armenians, led by Artabanes from the Arsacid dynasty, rebelled against the collection of a new tax. They were also dissatisfied with the fact that two Caucasian peoples subject to Byzantium – the autonomous Tzani and the Lazians who had their own king instead of a Roman magistrate – were better treated. Sittas was killed at the battle, or rather the skirmish, of Oinochalakon with the rebels.[137] Although the rebel Armenians had received help from Khosrow I during this war, that lasted until 545, Byzantium finally reaffirmed its supremacy over them. Neither of the two Empires managed to completely control the whole of Armenia but the Armenians could not escape from this double guardianship.

On the Edge of the Caucasus, Lazica, Outpost of the Empire

The Caucasus was, and is, a patchwork of peoples. On its southern slope along the River Cyrus, (now Kura), up to the Caspian Sea lived the Iberians ancestors of today's Georgians. While Eastern Iberia was under Persian control, west of the Kura was a region called Lazica, Egrissi to the Iberians and formerly known as Colchis. The coastal part was under the rule of Byzantium which kept troops and a fleet based there. Maybe a duke of Lazica was in charge. The loss of Lazica would have allowed the Persians to reach Byzantium through the Black Sea. On the other hand, Lazica

---

135 John of Biclaro, *Chr. VT*, 3 (Armenians and Iberians rebelled); 15 (Justin II final victory). Stratos A. (1981, p.37).
136 Sebeos, *Hist.*, 8.
137 Procopius, *BP*, II, 3, 15–27 (Oinochalakon); 39 (causes of Armenian dissatisfaction).

could have allowed Romano-Byzantine to invade Persarmenia through the Araxes valley.

Lazica itself was a green country with wooded mountains cut by rivers and deep valleys finishing at a swampy coastal plain. The eastern cross valleys were narrow passes generally called by Romans *clausurae*, *kleisurai* in Greek, (closings) and they were walled or palisaded.[138] The River Phasis (now the River Rioni in Georgia) cut Lazica in two from east to west across the middle before plunging into the Black Sea, and served as the geographical boundary between Europe and Asia. It also gave its name to the main Byzantine harbour and stronghold located at its mouth – the present-day Poti.[139] Lazica was rather poorly connected south-westward to Pontus and Anatolia by a strip of land inhabited by the Tzani. The inhabitants were a Christian people called the Lazians or Lazs by the sixth century. According to a Georgian source, King Vakhstan I Gorgasali (Wolf's Head) was at first a vassal to the Persians and inflicted *c*. 485 a huge defeat on Polycarpos, a Byzantine general. But soon afterward, Zeno came to terms with him by giving him his daughter as a wife and granting him the lands between the Rivers Inguri and Kelasuri (Abkhazia).[140] Additionally, to the north the s controlled some vassal peoples from Caucasus; the Misimians, the Apsilians and Abasgians, today's Abkhazs.[141] Even further north of Lazica lived, 'the Alans and the Abasgians, Christians and long-time friends of the Romans, as well as the Zechi and the Huns called Sabeires [Sabirs].'[142] These Sabir Huns could also serve as mercenaries to the Persians

By the mid-sixth century, the Persians carried their main effort into Lazica. This was a real change in strategy, and as a consequence the region suffered a continual state of war, even in ostensive peacetime. The dating of the Lazic War is uncertain and purely speculative, but it is necessary for some understanding. The Persians launched large-scale attacks there in 541, 551, 552 and 554. Procopius declared that, 'and ever since they attacked Colchis, there have been massacres between them, the Lazians and the Romans to this day.'[143] Agathias confirming this pessimistic statement declared that the truce of 551 did not apply to Lazica.[144] The Emperor Justinian clearly understood the Persian strategic goal was to get a foothold on the Black Sea:

> His thoughts led him to fear that the Persians, if they won the war, would take over the entire region. There would then be nothing to

---

138 Procopius, *BP*, II, 29, 25 (*kleisurai*). Agathias, *Hist*. II, 19, 4 (palisades and walls).
139 Procopius, *BG*, VIII, 2, 27–28.
140 Juansher Juansheriani, *The Life of Vakhtang Gorgasali*, p.93.
141 Procopius, *BP*, II, 28, 26 (Christians). Agathias, *Hist.*, II, 18, 4 (s/Colchians); III, 15, 8–9 (Misimians).
142 Procopius, *BP*, II, 29, 15.
143 Procopius, *Anecdota*, XVIII, 24.
144 Agathias, *Hist.*, II, 18, 2–3.

prevent them from fearlessly navigating the Euxine Bridge to voyage all the way into the heart of the Roman Empire.[145]

The eastern entry point into Lazica was the Rikoti Pass in present-day central Georgia. On the other side was the Persian-controlled Iberia, with Mteshketa, near modern Tblissili, being their operations centre. From Rikoti Pass the River Phasis was the more practicable road to the port of Phasis. It was defended by a loose barrier of some high ground, walled towns, and fortresses. At Tekhuri, a northern tributary of the Rioni, was Archeopolis (present-day Nokalakevi), then the capital of the Lazic Kingdom. To the south on the same tributary stood Nesos, present-day Isula (from the Latin *insula*, 'island' and *nēsos* in Greek). Telephis (today Tolebi) was south of the Rioni. These three places were some 30km to 50km east from Poti harbour.[146] Although the area was wooded and mountainous, distances between towns were very short, one to two days of walking:

> The area is well defended and difficult to access because it is surrounded by two rivers. The Rivers Phasis and the Dokonos [Rioni and Tekhuri] descend separately from the Caucasus, at first at a great distance, gradually approaching each other because of the land and are no longer very far apart. So the Romans dug a canal and diverted the course of the Phasis into the Dokonos, and in this way the two rivers met east of Nesos and surrounded the place.[147]

Around 70km south to the harbour and River both named Phasis, the entry point from Persian-controlled Persarmenia was defended next to the Black Sea by the Fortress of Petra of Lazica (today Tsikhisdziri in Georgia). This key position was built by John Tzibos in 535 but was lost in 541 when King Gubazes II of the s invited the Persian invasion of his country. Supposedly in 548, the fickle Gubazes II, hearing that the Persians wanted to assassinate him and to deport his people, called on the Empire for help, hiring Alans and Sabir Huns to attack Persian-controlled Iberia with the promise that they would be paid by the Emperor. As money was money, he also demanded of Justinian 10 years of arrears of pay due to him as a *silentiarius*, a court honorific title whose theoretical task was to silence the chatterers in the Imperial presence. Justinian paid the arrears but omitted to pay the Alans and Huns, instead committing to Gubazes II a 7,000-man field army plus

---

145 Agathias, *Hist.*, II, 18, 7–8.
146 K. Maksymiuk, *Geography of Roman-Iranian Wars Military operations of Rome and Sasanian Iran* (Siedlce: Uniwersytet Przyrodniczo-Humanistyczny w Siedlcach, 2015), pp.72–74 (geographical places during military operations in Lazica c. 541–556). C. Zuckerman, 'The early Byzantine strongholds in eastern Pontus', Collège de France, Centre de recherche d'histoire et de civilisation de Byzance, *Travaux et Mémoires*, 11 (1991), pp.473–486.
147 Agathias, *Hist.*, II, 21, 10.

BIRTH OF THE BYZANTINE ARMY 476-641 CE VOLUME 2: WATCH THEM FIGHT!

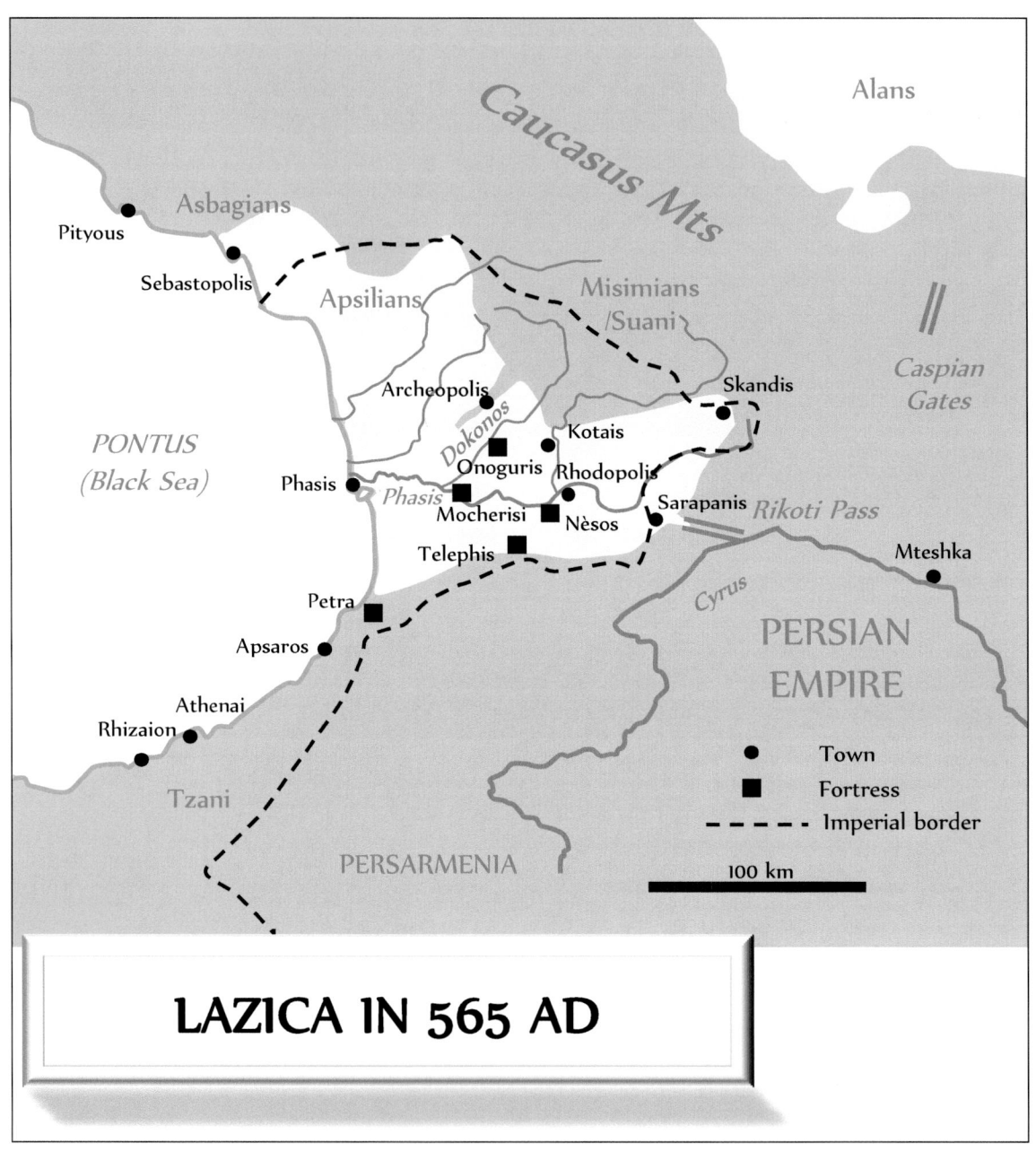

LAZICA IN 565 AD

THE ARMY WATCHES OVER THE BORDERS

1,000 Tzani led by Dagisthaeus, then Master of the Soldiers to Armenia and Lazica. The Romano-Byzantine primary strategic goal was to retake Petra as this fortress was cutting the continuity between Lazica and Tzanica and stood close to the Persarmenian border. Mihr-Mirhoe, a Persian general known in Greek sources as Mermeroes, as general-in-chief led personally a relief force forcing Dagisthaeus to hurriedly abandon the siege of Petra. Then military operations were waged northwards along the River Phasis in central Lazica. Dagisthaeus and Gubazes II's army won two battles, the first in 549 located south of the Phasis and the second in 550 near River Hippis at Mucheirisis or Mocheresis, driving the Persian invasion army back to Iberia. The Battle of the River Hippis was probably the largest during Lazic War, as the Byzantine- army was 12,000 to 14,000 strong against a superior Persian force reinforced by Alan mercenaries.[148] It his worthwhile noting that Mermeroes was not present at these setbacks, but had left in charge two successive Generals Phabrizus, then Chorianes who was killed in action near the Hippis. But these successes were not enough and probably an internal conflict arose. Gubazes II denounced Dagisthaeus as performing poorly since he was too young, and he was replaced with the ageing Goth, named Bessas.[149]

In 550 Bessas put down a sudden Abasgian uprising in northern Lazica – probably a proxy war ignited by Persians. After that Bessas went south to besiege Petra. In the spring of 551, Bessas retook Petra but demolished it, while omitting to fortify the southern path to Persarmenia. It was not a good idea as Persians still had easy access into Lazica and Justinian was angered by all of these actions.[150] While Bessas was operating southwards against Petra, Mermeroes invaded Lazica north-eastwards and besieged Archeopolis. Nevertheless, the city held out and Persian food stocks were short, forcing Mermeroes to withdraw back to Mucheirisis or Mocheresis/Mechlessus/Mochora near the Rivers Tekhuri and Rioni, where he could find out some local resources or get supplied through the Rikoti Pass.[151] In 552, Mermeroes again tried his luck against Archeopolis but in vain. The war went on because Gubazes II stubbornly refused peace proposals.

---

148 N. Khoperia, 'The Byzantine Lazic Phalanx at the Battle of the Hippis River (550 CE)' in *The Journal of Politics and Democratisation-Online Publication*, 4/2, January (2020), pp.18 (estimated forces), 24 (largest battle).

149 A. H. M. Jones, J. R. Martindale, J. Morris, *PLRE*, 3a (1992), pp. 380–382 (Dagistaheus 2).

150 Procopius, *BP*, II, 15, 10–12 and 29, 20–21 (Petra built by John Tzibos under Justinian command); 29, 10 (Dagisthaeus with 7,000 men); 29–32 (Alans and Sabir Huns; Justinian did not pay them in appropriate time); 33 (Dagisthaeus young age); *BG*, VIII, 2, 32–33 (Petra location); 2, 29 (built by 'Romans'); 4, 5–6 (taken by Persians); 12, 28 (Petra retaken and destroyed by Bessas); 13, 11–12 (Bessas negligence). Agathias, *Hist.*, III, 2, 6 (Petra retaken by Bessas; negligence); IV, 21, 1 (rank of master of the soldiers to Colchis and Armenia).

151 Maybe linked to Mochara, *Notitia Dignitatum*, OR.XXXVIII.38 (a cohort under the *Dux Armeniae*)

Possibly in 553, Mermeroes was able to take Telephis Fort and the following year he took Nesos. After several years of positional and inconclusive fighting in Lazica, an exhausted and ill Mermeroes withdrew to his base, Mteshketa in Iberia, where he died in 555.[152]

Mermeroes's appointed successor, Nachoragan, was a less intelligent general, providing a real chance for the Romano-Byzantines military whose cowardliness and probable corruption greatly irritated their Lazian allies. Justinian was warned by Gubazes II of Bessas' idleness and also the idleness of Martin the second in command and of Rusticus the *Sakellarios* or financial intendant. So Justinian confiscated Bessas own property, dismissed and exiled him to the Abasgians. It is worthwhile remembering that Petra of Lazica was a city erected by Justinian's command and with his funds, the latter was also resentful upon being reminded that Bessas had dismantled the place four years earlier. Things did not stop there… Bessas' lieutenants, Martin and Rusticus, denounced Gubazes II to Justinian as a traitor in the service of the Persians. Before Bessas' departure to Byzantium where he was ordered to justify himself, his denouncer Gubazes II was fatally stabbed by John, the brother of Rusticus, in a bloody act of revenge.[153]

The Lazians, torn between the desire to also take revenge and to keep their alliance with Byzantium, informed Justinian of this murder. Rusticus and John were quickly arrested but Martin, the main instigator, was not, so the Lazians were infuriated and would no longer help the Romano-Byzantine troops. Afterwards Martin was ordered to do something against the Persian footholds in Eastern Lazica, to be more precise the fortresses of Onoguris, Mucheirisis and Nesos. Previously, near Archeopolis, east of the River Tekhuri, the Persian General Mermeroes had built a fort at Onoguris (called St Stephen by Christian sources), in order 'to contain the Romans'. It was a Persian thorn thrust into the heart of Lazica. By late autumn 555, Martin and Bouzes went from Archeopolis to besiege Onoguris with no less than 50,000 men and a large number of siege machines. After ambushing a 600-strong Persian vanguard, they did not pay sufficient attention to the approaching 3,000 Persian horsemen led by Nachoragan, a relief force sent from Mucheirisis, and they were pushed into the Tekhuri River drowning many of them, a shameful defeat.[154] The friendship with the Lazians was fully restored in spring 556 when Justinian conferred royal regalia on Tzath II, Gubazes II's legitimate successor, while the General Soterichos especially sent from Byzantium gave large amounts of money to all the Caucasian allies. Gold often was and is the great appeaser of all resentments.[155]

---

152 Procopius, *BG*, VIII, 13, 21 (Nesos). Agathias, *Hist.*, II, 19 à 22.
153 Agathias, *Hist.*, II, 22, 5 (Mermeroes death); III, 2, 1 (Nachoragan); 3, 3 (Bessas, Martin and Rusticus denounced by Gubazes); Agathias, *Hist.*, III, 2, 6 (Petra retaken by Bessas; negligence); (Bessas' disgrace); 3, 1–6 (Gubazes denounced as traitor); 4, 5–6 (Gubazes assassination).
154 Agathias, *Hist.*, II, 22, 3 (Onoguris built by Mermeroes); III, 5, 6–8, 2 (Onoguris, siege and battle).
155 Agathias, *Hist.*, III, 15, 2–5 (Tzath); 6 (Soterichos).

During the summer, Nachoragan mustered troops at Mucheirisis, the second main Persian foothold in eastern Lazica, and headed to Phasis Harbour in a last chance offensive. He was misguided as the walls of Phasis held firm and, worst of all, a Romano-Byzantine Army gathered at Nesos in his rear had followed him. Nachoragan found himself caught between a rock and a hard place. It was time for him to retreat before he was annihilated. For this victorious campaign, Martin was not charged with the murder of Gubazes II but the Army of Armenia and Lazica passed to Justin, the son of Germanus. This was the moment chosen by Justinian to have Rusticus and his accomplice John publicly indicted and subsequently beheaded to satisfy the s. On the Persian side, Nachoragan was also executed for having been defeated, but Khosrow I, after the short-lived satisfaction of his anger and vengeance, found nobody capable of leading his troops in Lazica. So the Hunnic *taxiarch*, Elminsur, with 2,000 cavalry was able to retake Nesos while the Persian garrison patrolled outside or possibly even ran away. In 557, Khosrow I understood it was time to send an ambassador to negotiate a lasting peace in the region on the principle that everyone retained their territorial gains.[156] While the Hephthalites or White Huns threatened the Persian northern border, the truce was confirmed in 562 by the Fifty-Year Peace, or Treaty of Dara, establishing the firm domination of Byzantium over Lazica in return of an annual tribute of 30,000 *nomismata* or *solidi* to Persians, who had made an advantageous Peace since they disliked the cold and snowy weather of the mountainous region of Lazica.

Pacifying the Rebellious Caucasian Tribes

Justinian's reign saw three main pacification campaigns in the Caucasus during the long-lasting Lazic War, one against the Abasgians in 550, the second against Misimians in 556–557, and the third against the Tzani in 558. Although Christianised under Justinian, the Abasgians or Abasgoi, the present-day Abkhaz, rebelled against Romano-Byzantine military occupation and called upon the Persians for help. Justinian ordered Bessas to suppress the revolt. He sent to him Uligang and John the son of Thomas with a large army carried by a fleet probably from Constantinople. As the road into Abasgia was reputed to be impassable for men marching by twos according to Procopius: "The Roman fleet put in between the boundaries of the Abasgi and Apsilii, and John and Uligagus disembarked their troops and proceeded on foot". Then they set fire to Trachea, the main Abasgian city located on a rocky cliff overlooking the Black Sea. The Abasgian wives and children were captured and Opsites. their King. was compelled to flee

---

156 Agathias, *Hist.*, III, 20 à 28 (operations in Lazica); 20, 1–28, 10 (Battle at Phasis); IV, 1, 1–11, 3 (trial and execution of Rusticus); 15, 1–2 (Elminsur); 21, 1 (command in Lazica); 30, 7–10 (peace). Theophanes Confessor, *Chrgr.*, AM 6055, 237 (truce).

to the Sabir Huns, while his country was systematically depopulated,[157] and through this method the expeditionary force restored order. The Misimians are ancestors of the present-day Svans who call themselves Mushüan. They were, and are, settled north of Lazica in the Kodori Valley, a river valley in upper Abkhazia, a mountainous area with snowy winters and large coniferous forests. In 556, General Soterichos, in charge of paying the Caucasian allies and collecting tribute, planned to hand over to the Alans one of their fortresses called Bouchloos. His personal goal was to avoid a painful campaign of this savage march. A poor diplomat besides being lazy, he even beat up the Misimian envoys who protested. In retaliation, the Misimians killed him and his escort, looting the subsidies intended for the other allies. Adding treason to their crimes, and rightly fearful of just reprisals, at the beginning of winter they sent a delegation to Iberia and the Persian General Nachoragan to ask him for protection.

In the spring of 557, a 4,000-strong men punitive expedition set out from Lazica under the command of the *taxiarchs* Maxentios and Theodore the Tzan, soon subordinated to Pharantes the Armenian and Barazes the Lazian. Having reached Apsilian vassal territory, this expeditionary force halted when news came of the arrival of a Persian force to support the Misimians. As a consequence, the summer was spent in inaction. Nevertheless, Maxentios and Theodore with 300 horsemen massacred in a surprise attack a force of 500 Sabir Hun mercenaries who had defected to the Persian, but they had to retreat before the arrival of 2,000 Persian cavalry. The Romano-Byzantines had now to face a limited invasion of Lazica. The loyal Hun officer, Elminsour, with 2,000 horsemen recaptured the city of Rhodopolis abandoned by the Persians, perhaps those mentioned above.

With the winter coming, a new leader, Martin, was put in charge of the indecisive expedition against the treacherous Misimians. Falling ill or unwilling to fight, he sent Apsilian ambassadors to them who were immediately and treacherously put to death. So Pharantes and Barazes were ordered to wage a merciless campaign on the Misimians who, overconfident, failed to keep the narrow path leading into their country. The Misimians panicked, burnt their fortresses and hastily took refuge in the most impregnable of all, Siderus (Steel). After an initial skirmish, the Imperial troops led a loose siege. Martin sent a new, and competent, commander in the person of the Cappadocian General John Daknas. The latter had the city surveyed, and a part of which was located outside the enclosure on a rocky and inaccessible height. An Isaurian scout named Illous spotted a passage guarded by only eight Misimians and used at night to fetch water. John Daknas then formed a night raiding-force of 100 men who cut the throats of the guards, set fire to the wooden huts of the upper city, and slaughtered the population without sparing anyone. A Misimian counter-attack drove out the raiding-force. Eventually, as the blockade dragged on, the Misimians, starving, surrendered. Agathias estimated their losses in

---

157 Procopius, *BG*, VIII, 3, 12–21 (on Abasgians); 9, 11–31 (Abasgian rebellion).

young men at 5,000, and those of women and children at an indeterminate, but larger, number.[158] According to him, the Misimians were on the verge of annihilation. The Misimian population seems to have been low, maybe from 15,000 to 30,000 people? The Romano-Byzantines suffered only 30 fatalities. They did not seek to control this poor mountainous country but to exterminate the troublesome Misimians who did not have enough space to wage any sort of guerrilla warfare. Any flight of the Misimians to a neighbouring people was also impossible since they would have been treated as invaders.

A revolt of the Tzani took place in 558. According to Procopius the Tzani (now the Zans or Chans, a Mingrelian people) settled south of the Caucasus and were 'living as they did a life of solitude among themselves in the manner of wild beasts' in an ever cloudy, often snowy, hilly and forested country, unfavourable to any crops, shut in on all sides by cliffs and inaccessible to horses. After he successfully sent Sittas to defeat and Christianise them, Justinian I built a number of forts with strong garrisons in their territory. He appointed a duke of Tzanica in the very strong, new fortress of Horonôn the entry point for Imperial forces and the meeting-point of three roads between Persarmenia, Lazica and Tzanica. Each year Justinian I gave the Tzani a fixed amount of gold to not plunder Romano-Byzantine territory and some Tzani enlisted in the *Romaiôn Stratos* (Roman Army). Nonetheless, they made frequent raids against Romano-Byzantine and Armenian settlements. Unable to withstand the Imperial Army they retreated to strong fortresses when attacked.[159] Agathias located the Tzani in north-eastern Anatolia:

> They live south of the Euxin Bridge, near the city of Trebizond [modern Trabzon, Turkey]; these Tzani were thus for a long time the allies and subjects of the Romans. While some of them stuck to the previous treaties and did not indulge in any disorder, the population, rejecting the established order, engaged in brigandage: by making raids in the countryside near the Bridge, they looted them and ransomed the travellers. They even attacked Armenia, where it was

---

158 Agathias, *Hist.*, III, 15, 8–9 (Soterichos' project); 16, 1 *sq.* (Misimian revolt); IV, 13, 2 (expeditionary force); 13, 5–6 (operations); 14, 1–4 (action against Sabirs); 15, 1–4 (fall of Rhodopolis); 15, 5–7 (emissaries sent by Martin); 16, 1 *sq.* (siege of Siderous); 17, 2 (John Daknas); 17, 4–7 (Illus the Isaurian); 18 and 19, 1 *sq.* (commando on the upper town); 20, 1–6 (siege of the fortress); 20, 7 (Misimian losses); 20, 10 (Roman losses).

159 Procopius, *Aed.*, VI, 6, 3–5 (woods, hills; unfavourable to crops); 6 (defeated by Sittas); 7 (Christianised); 9 (impossible for horses); 10 (wild beasts); 13 (forts and garrisons); 16 (Horonôn); 17 (duke); 18 (many tribes). *BP*, I, 15, 20–21 (Tzani living south of Caucasus; cloudy and snowy land); 22 (Justinian's annual payment of gold); 23 (raids against Armenians and Romans); 24 (strong fortresses); 25 (enlisted and Christianised).

possible for them, and engaged in looting, behaving no other than declared enemies.[160]

To deal with the 558 revolt Justinian ordered a retaliatory campaign expressly led by a Tzan officer, Theodore, a trusted *taxiarch* who was previously involved against the Misimians. It was a bold choice as Theodore both knew the terrain and his own people that he had to fight. So, he led a quick and efficient campaign. Leaving with a large field army from Lazica, probably from Phasis, Theodore moved to the vicinity of Theodoreias at a place called Rhizaion. There loyal Tzani tribes came to show their allegiance, but the rebels soon launched an attack from a wooded hill against the camp at Rhizaion. Theodore, to quote Patton, 'held onto the attackers by the nose, and kicked them in the ass', as he discreetly committed a detachment to bypass this hill and attack the Tzani from behind. The Tzani were utterly routed, leaving 2,000 dead. Shortly after, the survivors reappeared to accept Imperial rule and pay tax.[161]

A generation later, the so-called Misimians or Suani had to be firmly reminded of the tribute that the Emperor was due. In 576, John of Biclaro wrote: 'Romanus, the son of Anagast the Patrician and Master of the Soldiers captured the King of the Suani. He took him back to Constantinople with his treasure, wife and children, bringing back the province to Roman authority.'[162] All these military operations were very similar to later nineteenth century colonial wars. It contrasts with today's inefficiency and the clearly defined goal was to exploit the natives and to defend a border march.

Pre-Islamic Arabs and Bedouins, Between Raids and Accommodations

Ibn Khaldun, a medieval scholar from the Maghreb, described the Arabs from the 'first era' in this way:

> The Arabs are a nation of nomadic pastoralists; they have tents for shelter, horses for mounts; camels and sheep are their wealth: they breed them, feed on their milk, use their skins and hair to protect themselves against the cold and make their household goods, and use them to carry their burdens. They camp in scattered groups of tents, usually get their daily sustenance from hunting, engage in highway robbery, and are constantly on the move across wide open spaces, sometimes fleeing the heat of summer, sometimes the bitter

---

160 Agathias, *Hist.*, V, 1, 2.
161 Agathias, *Hist.*, V, 1, 3 (Theodore); 1, 4 (Rhizaion camp; loyalists); 1, 5–8 (camp under attack); 2, 1–2 (victory); 2, 3 (Tzani submission).
162 John of Biclaro, *Chr. VT*, 39.

cold of winter, in search of fodder for their sheep and favourable conditions for their camels.[163]

Ibn Khaldun added that Arabs meant 'the men who express themselves clearly.' Although he was a late medieval author his description was well suited to the way early Byzantines considered the Arabs, as nomad pastoralists and sometimes looters.[164] Theophylact Simocatta echoed this rather negative opinion on Bedouins: 'The Saracen tribe is reputed as untrustworthy and inconsistent, their mind is always agitated and their own judgement is not firmly based on prudence.'[165] What pre-Islamic Arabs and Bedouins wanted from war was gold, cattle and slaves or the taking of revenge for an offence. They enjoyed their nomadic way of life and were not interested in conquering the sedentary lands that they could plunder or ransom at will and if needed.

The territory corresponding today to southern Iraq and Jordan formed a kind of strategic buffer zone between Romano-Byzantine and Persian Empires, and no army could pass through, except for the Bedouins. The Romans under Trajan reign had bordered it with a military road that stretched over 1,500km from the Euphrates to the Gulf of Aqaba. A fort stood every 100km with watchtowers in between. This *Limes Arabicus* was renovated and strengthened during the Severan dynasty (193–235).[166] Some fortifications in today's Palestine and Jordan were abandoned during the 530s, or maybe earlier, to the benefit of the Ghassanids, the 'sons of Ghassan', a federation of Christian Bedouin tribes that ruled Arabia Petrea. Greek sources called their leader a *phylarch* (tribal chief or Sheik), and their king was sometimes referred as *archiphylarch*. The other important tribe there was the Lakhmids, who were settled near the Euphrates, loyally pro-Persians and as a consequence a constant threat to the Roman provinces of Mesopotamia, Phoenicia, Arabia and Palestine.[167] In 498, led by their *phylarch* Naaman or al-Nu'man II ibn al-Aswad, the Lakhmids raided Euphratensis and Syria. They were beaten at Bithrapsa in the first region of Syria by Eugenius, Duke of Osrhoene. The same year, led by Jabalah IV ibn al-Harith (Gabalas in Greek), the Ghassanids invaded Palestine and the

---

163   Ibn Khaldun, *Ibar*, t. 1 (1995), pp.137–139.
164   Procopius, *BV*, II, 19, 12.
165   Theophylact Simocatta, *HU*, III, 17, 7. Menander Protector, *Fragm.*, 9.1.
166   D. F. Graf, 'The *Via Militaris* and the *Limes Arabicus*' in W. Groenman-van Waateringe, B. L. van Beek, W. J. H. Willems, S. L. Wynia (eds), *Roman Frontier Studies 1995, Proceedings of the XVI International Congress of Roman Frontier Studies*, (Oxford: Oxbow, 1997), pp.123–133.
167   I. Kawar, 'Procopius on the Ghassanids', *Journal of the American Oriental Society*, 77, 2 (1957), pp.79–87. I. Shahid, *Byzantium and the Arabs in the Sixth Century*, vol.1, part 1, *Political and Military History*, (Washington: Dumbarton Oaks Research Library and Collection, 1995), pp.32–39 and 613–617 (Ghassanids); 42–46 (Lakhmids).

Duke Romanus had to drive them back after a series of fierce actions.[168] In 502, King Jabalah IV submitted the Ghassanids to the Empire and thereafter he was paid annually to watch the desert border.[169] It was undoubtedly better to pay the Ghassanids than to fight them and for the Ghassanids this was a better option as well.

On the other hand, probably because of ancestral rivalry with Ghassanids, the Lakhmids remained loyal allies to the Persians and thus a sporadic threat to the Empire. By the time of Justin I and then Justinian I, their King was al-Mundir III ibn al-Nu'man (Alamoundaros in Greek) who reigned *c.* 503–554.[170] In 503, he raided Arabia Petraea and Palestina Salutaris up to Eastern Egypt, and he led a raid against Syria in 526. Agapius of Hierapolis wrote of his actions: 'Mondhar [al-Mundir III ibn al-Nu'man] raided the Greeks, destroying their homes and taking the population captive.'[171] During the summer of 527, co-rulers Justin I and Justinian I appointed Hypatius as Master of the Soldiers to the East in order to fight the Lakhmids. By October Justinian, now sole Emperor, decided to rebuild and garrison the border city of Palmyra to protect Jerusalem and Phoenicia.[172] Probably in 528, the restless al-Mundir III ibn al-Nu'man killed his Ghassanid rival:

> In the same period, the duke of Palestine quarrelled with the *phylarch* [Jabalah IV ibn al-Harith, Gabalas] of the Saracens subject to the Romans. The *phylarch* went in fear to the inner *limes*. When Alamoundaros heard about this, he went in pursuit, captured him and killed him, took his women and children, and returned. At this the dukes of Phoenicia, Arabia, and Mesopotamia plus the *phylarch* went chasing after him. When he heard this, Alamoundaros fled to Indian territory where none of the Romans had ever been. The Romans captured the Saracen tents and took many of them prisoner, men, women, and children, and [freed] as many Roman prisoners as they found, plus camels, sheep, oxen, and much silk and clothing. In addition, they burnt four Persian forts, and then returned after a great victory.[173]

John Malalas dated this bloody event to April 528, specifying that in retaliation Justinian ordered the dukes of Phoenicia, Arabia and

---

168 Theophanes Confessor, *Chrgr.*, AM 5990, 141.
169 Procopius, *BP*, II, 10, 23.
170 A. H. M. Jones, J. R. Martindale, J. Morris, *PLRE*, 2 (1980), pp.40–42 (Alamoundaros or al-Mundir III ibn al-Numan, son of Zekikē).
171 Procopius, *BP*, I, 17, 41 (raid, 503). Agapius of Hierapolis, *Kitāb al-ʿunwān* (1912), p.425 (raid, 526).
172 John Malalas, *Chrgr.*, XVII, 20 (Hypatius); XVIII, 2 (Palmyra).
173 Theophanes Confessor, *Chrgr.*, AM 6021, 179 (erroneously dated c. 529 after the raid on Antioch).

Mesopotamia as well as the *phylarchs* to attack Lakhmid territory. These expeditionary forces were led by Dionysius Duke of Phoenicia, John Duke of Euphratensis, three *phylarchs* (Arethas, Grouphas and Naaman), plus the *chiliarch* Sebastian, probably the commander of a local border militia. Against them, al-Mundir III ibn al-Nu'man retained a considerable force of 30,000 warriors.[174] In July 529, as the Samarian Jews were rebelling, crowning a certain Julian as Emperor, and Persians were on the edge of declaring war, Lakhmid Saracens launched a deep razzia as far as the suburbs of Antioch. To hold off this raid pushed to the heart of Roman Syria, the Emperor sent the *Lykokranitai* infantry from Phrygia, probably a local militia skilled in counter-guerrilla actions.[175]

After the so-called 'Eternal Peace' concluded with Persians, even with an annual subsidy of 7,200 *solidi* paid by Romano-Byzantines, al-Mundir III ibn al-Nu'man resumed his plundering activities on the Empire's borders. Against him was al-Harith V ibn Jabalah (reign 529–569), called Arethas in Greek sources), who had succeeded his father Jabalah IV ibn al-Harith or Gabalas, who was killed the previous year at the Byzantine defeat of Thannuris/Mindouos, as King of all Ghassanid tribes or *archiphylarch* (commander of commanders of tribes). He gave assistance in Byzantium's wars, raiding the Lakhmid capital al-Hira in 528. Three years later, he led 5,000 men at the Battle of Callinicum.[176] Procopius accused Arethas's men of having broken the line and being responsible for Belisarius's defeat, but Malalas claimed the Phrygians fled first when their commander fell and his standard was captured, then while some Saracens fled Arethas with others continued fighting.[177] Around 537/538 Arethas had to settle a territorial conflict south of Palmyra with Lakhmid Sheik al-Mundir III ibn al-Nu'man.[178]

Tribes other than the Ghassanids and the Lakhmids were playing their own game. To the south, Homerites Saracens or Himyarite Arabs were Yemenite tribes who formed a distant but ever-present threat. To protect Egypt and Palestine from their raids, Justinian built a powerful fortress with a strong garrison at the foot of Mount Sinai where a monastic community was already sited.[179] In 536, following a severe drought, unidentified Saracen tribes from Arabian Peninsula, led by Chabo and Hezido, sought new pastures. Denied access to Lakhmid lands, they invaded the Imperial province of Euphratensis in Northern Syria. Batzas, Duke of Mesopotamia, negotiated the departure of these 15,000 unwanted Saracens migrants. They were probably Kindites and Byzantines allies from the Arabian Peninsula.

---

174 John Malalas, *Chrgr.*, XVIII, 16.
175 Theophanes Confessor, *Chrgr.*, AM 6021, 178 (Λυκοκρανιταί).
176 John Malalas, *Chrgr.*, XVIII, 60 (Arethas 5,000 Saracens).
177 Procopius, *BP*, I, 18, 35–36. John Malalas, *Chrgr.*, XVIII, 60.
178 A. H. M. Jones, J. R. Martindale, J. Morris, *PLRE*, 3a (1992), pp.111–112 (al-Mundir III ibn al-Harith).
179 Procopius, *Aed.*, V, 8, 9.

Some eastern chroniclers mentioned Saracen razzias. The Pseudo-Zachariah Rhetor described these 'Moors' (Saracens) as a people of the desert, 'living from robbery and destruction like the Tayyayē'.[180] (Tayyayē being the Syrian name for the Bedouin). According to Procopius, the desert frontier was ill-defended against these predatory tribes:

> At that time the Saracens invaded the Roman East, from Egypt to the borders of Persia, and wreaked such continual destruction there that all these regions became very poor in men. No man who investigates this matter will be able to discover, I think, the number of those who were killed in this way. The Persians and Khosrowes [Khosrow I] threw themselves three times [540, 542, 544] upon the rest of the Roman Empire and destroyed its cities, killing some of the men taken captive in the cities and in each region and taking the others with them, they depopulated from its inhabitants the territory on which they had fallen.[181]

In 540 Khosrow I asked his Lakhmid ally al-Mundir III ibn al-Nu'man to find a pretext for breaching the 'Eternal Peace' and thus the Ghassanids were accused of border raids.[182] Procopius who obviously disliked Arethas said that the Saracens where unfit for siege warfare but efficient in plundering. So, in 540 Belisarius sent Arethas to raid the Persian province of Assyria.[183] Nevertheless, the rivalry between Ghassanid and Lakhmids was blatant during the Romano-Persians wars and they fought each other from 546 to 562 always with strategically inconclusive results but sowing the seeds of a few 'vendettas'. At the Battle of Yawm Halima near Chalcis (today Qinnasrin), in 554, the Lakhmid al-Mundhir III ibn al-Nu'man was killed by the Ghassanid King al-Harith V ibn Jabalah.[184] Finally, the truce negotiated by Justinian prohibited further clashes between Ghassanids and Lakhmids.[185]

From 569 there was a new Ghassanid king, al-Mundir III ibn-al-Harith (Flavios Alamoundaros in Greek sources). This man should not to be confounded with the previous Lakhmid king, also known as Alamoundaros. Around 572, his persistence in the Monophysite heresy was so abhorrent to Justin II who, angered by a further request for subsidies, sought to have him assassinated. This was followed by three years of a cold relationship detrimental to the Empire, which was once again at war with

---

180 Marcellinus Comes, *Chr.*, a. 536 (Saracen raid). (Pseudo-)Zachariah Rhetor, *HE*, III, 5a (compared the Moors with the Saracens), I. Shahid, *Byzantium and the Arabs*, pp.194–196.
181 Procopius, *Anecdota*, XVIII, 22–23.
182 Procopius, *BP*, II, 1, 2–3.
183 Procopius, *BP*, II, 19, 11 (Assyria); 12 (statement).
184 I. Shahid, *Byzantium and the Arabs*, pp.263–264. G. Greatrex & S. N. C. Lieu (eds), *The Roman Eastern Frontier*, pp.129–130.
185 I. Shahid, *Byzantium and the Arabs*, pp.236–265.

the Persians. After obtaining a pardon, thanks to the mediation of General Justinian, and travelling to Byzantium in 575, al-Mundir III ibn-al-Harith led an expedition against Hira, the Lakhmid capital. Al-Mundir III was invited to Byzantium in 580 where he received a royal crown from the new Emperor Tiberius II. Al-Mundir III unwisely demanded tolerance towards the monophysites, however, although Tiberius II was as ill-disposed to the monophysites as Justin II had been, this did not cause any breakdown in the relationship between the two men. After his return home al-Mundir III ibn-al-Harith led a punitive expedition against Lakhmids who had raided his land while he was at Byzantium.

In 576 al-Mundir III ibn-al-Harith took part to the war against Persians, but he was unfairly charged with treason by Maurice, then Master of the Soldiers to the East, for being responsible of the failure at Ctesiphon. Al-Mundir III ibn-al-Harith had to plead his case before Tiberius II. Under house arrest in Byzantium and losing any hope when his accuser Maurice became Emperor, he fomented a hopeless rebellion, and was exiled to Sicily. His son was captured in 583 and also sent into exile to Sicily. Both were to regain their homeland when Maurice lost power, and his life, in 602.[186] Imperial ingratitude and disloyalty temporarily cooled the Ghassanids' good will, but Maurice's miserable end opened a renewal of trust with Phocas then Heraclius. In 613, the Ghassanids fought alongside the Romano-Byzantine Army but one part of them was pushed back into Anatolia, the other into the Arabian Peninsula by the Persians and the Lakhmids. In addition, the *Limes Arabicus* had vanished since Justinian era. For the early 600s, the watchtowers, the forts of Qasr Bashir, el-Lejjun, Khirbet el-Fityan, Rujm Beni Yasser and Da'janiya show no archaeological sign of occupation. Five years later, lacking a strong defensive network, the Byzantines and the Ghassanids were unable to oppose the Muslim invasion and after the defeat at Yarmuk many of the Ghassanids withdrew to Anatolia again.[187] Those that remained submitted to the law of Islam.

In Egypt, a '*Gendarmerie*' was Sufficient until the Arab Conquest

Egypt was what it is today; a green delta of orchards extended by a narrow ribbon of reeds and irrigated fields bordering the Nile in the shade of palm trees. On either side laid veritable seas of sand, in particular the Libyan Desert, from which the periodic raids of the nomads Blemmyes, Mazices, Goniotai, Nobatai and Mastitai rose as if from nowhere. To face them,

---

186   A. H. M. Jones, J. R. Martindale, J. Morris, *PLRE*, 3a (1992), p.34–37; I. Shahid, *Byzantium and the Arabs*, pp.373–388 (pardon and first visit to Constantinople); 389 (Hira); 389–405 (second visit to Constantinople, crown); 406–463 (campaign against Persians).
187   I. Shahid, *Byzantium and the Arabs*, pp.645–646.

there were few intervention troops, only border guards and civic militias. The border guards, *riparii* or *riparioi*, were scattered across a network of fortresses and forts, since from Alexandria to Syene (current Aswan) was over 1,000km, a great geographic length but with no strategic depth.

Since Justinian, the strategy had been based on a decentralised defence split into five duchies: Egypt, Augustamnica, Arcadia, Thebaid and the Cyrenaica. In Upper Egypt, the Nile Delta was held by three large citadels. To the east, on the coastal road leading to Palestine and Syria stood the capital of Augustamnica Prima, a fortified city named Pelusium (present-day Tell al-Farama). Around 400, Pelusium was garrisoned by a squadron of *Equites Stablesiani*.[188] This area of control extended into the desert of Sinai with the forts of Magdolum and Silē. In about 400, the second fort was guarded by the *Ala Prima Aegyptorum*.[189] To the west, Alexandria was defended by the large fortress of Nikopolis, linked to the Nile by a canal.

At the base of the delta, there was the most massive fortress in the country, dating from the Augustan period and remodelled under Diocletian, its name was Babilona – Babylon of Egypt. In *c.* 400 Babilona's garrison was the *Legio Tertiadecima Gemina*.[190] Rectangular in shape, Babilona was crossed by Trajan's canal, *Amnis Trajanus*, which linked the Nile to the Red Sea. By the beginning of the Byzantine era, this canal had long silted up.[191] Two enormous bastioned round towers stood at the outlet of the Canal into the Nile. One of the two towers is today an archaeological attraction and the other an Orthodox church dedicated to St George, Mari Girgis. Along the surrounding wall, around 20 U-shaped towers protruded every 22m while there were large round towers at the corners. Garrison buildings stood on either side of the canal, probably once connected by a bridge. Today the ruins of this fortress remain in the Coptic district of old Cairo, to the north of the Fostat district, which takes the name of Qasr or Kasr el-Sham (Castle of Syria). In the twelfth century, Michael the Syrian wrote clearly wrote: 'Babylon which today is called Fostat.'[192]

Middle Egypt had a defensive area on the Faiyum west bank of the Nile with from north to south the fortresses of Dionysias, Narmouthis and further south Oxyrinchus (respectively today's Qasr Qaroun, Medinet Madi and al-Bahnasa), 200km from Cairo. Around 400, the *Ala Quinta Praelectorum* garrisoned the fort of Dionysias while Narmounthis was occupied by the *Quarta Cohors Numidarum*.[193]

---

188 *Notitia Dignitatum*, OR.XXVIII.16.
189 *Notitia Dignitatum*, OR.XXVIII.27 (Silē).
190 *Notitia Dignitatum*, OR.XXVIII.15. D. A. Karelin, 'The Reconstruction of the Diocletianic Fortress in Babylon of Egypt: Architectural Decorations and Details' in A. V. Zakharova., S. V. Maltseva, E. I. Staniukovich-Denisova I. (eds), *Actual Problems of Theory and History of Art: Collection of articles*, 9, Lomonosov Moscow State University (St. Petersburg: NP-Print, 2019) pp.180–188.
191 John of Nikiu, *Chr.*, 120, 31 (1883), p.457.
192 Michel le Syrie, *HU*, XI, 7, t. 2 (1963), p.425.
193 *Notitia Dignitatum*, OR.XXVIII.34 (Dionisiada); 46 (Narmunthis).

THE ARMY WATCHES OVER THE BORDERS

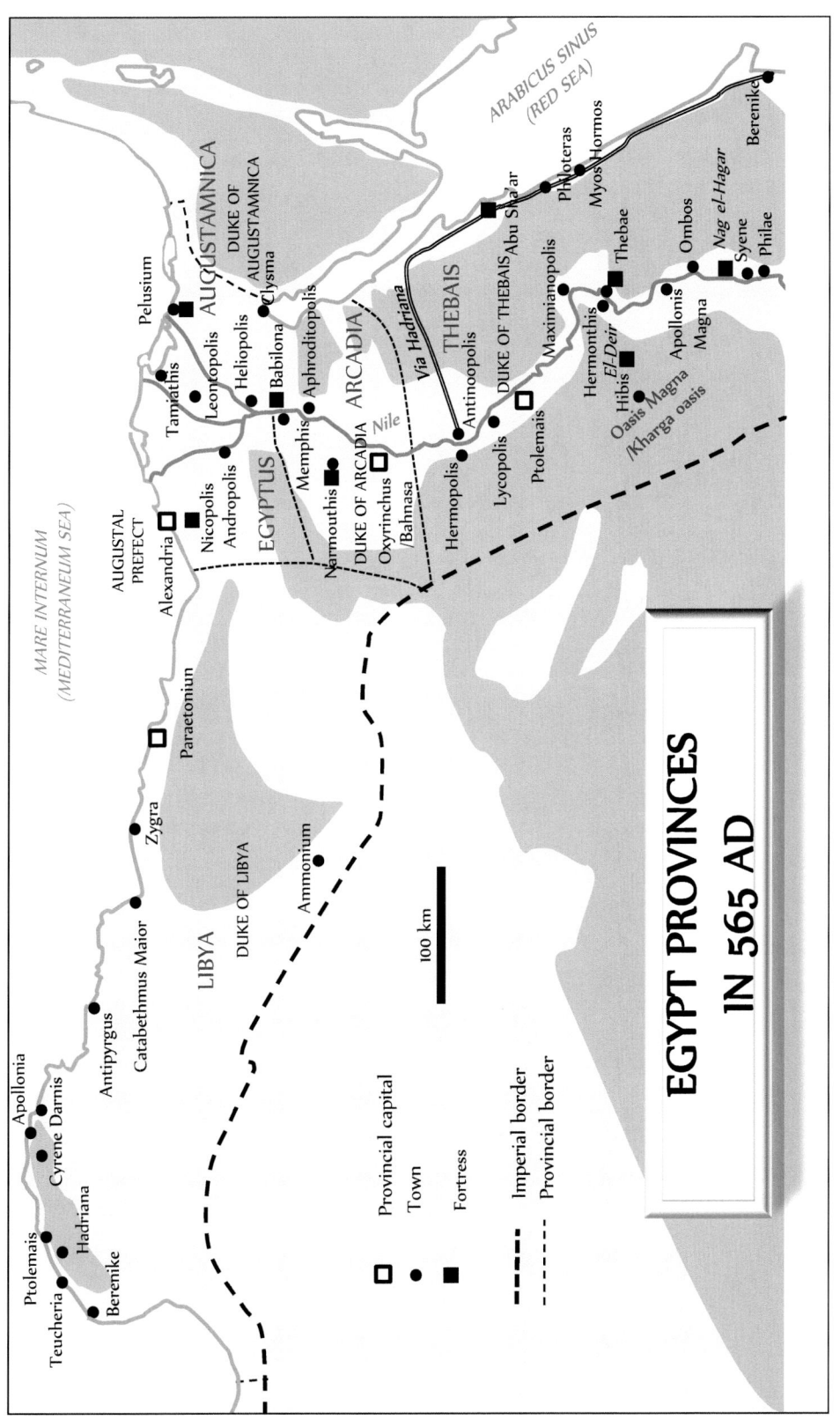

Upper Egypt was defended by two citadels on the right bank of the Nile, Thebes (present-day Luxor) and the Nag el-Hagar fort near Ombos (Kom Ombo). Thebes was held by the *Legio Tertia Diocletiana*.[194] Nag el-Hagar fort was a massive rectangular fortress with square towers at the corners and U-shaped towers along the rampart, grouped in pairs at the three gates. Garrison buildings filled the central space with even a palace, a church and baths.[195] Between the Nile and the Red Sea, a string of forts guarded the six trade routes connected with the Arabian Peninsula and India. To the west, at the confines of the Libyan Desert, the Oasis of Dakhla and Kharga forming the Great Oasis flanked Upper Egypt. This Great Oasis was guarded by two fortresses of Saharan type, that is built with earthen walls with four towers.[196]

Each city had a troop, *numerus* or *arithmos*, commanded by a tribune or a *stratēlátēs*, but subordinate to the *defensor civitatis* (city defender) or *syndikos/ekdikos* (syndic) for judicial missions. The troops were responsible for escorting tax officials, investigating crimes, arresting defendants, suppressing public violence and fighting brigands.[197] These regular soldiers called *stratiôtai* had lost their military efficiency by the time of Justinian. In the rural areas, the *riparii* (border guards) were placed under the orders of a civilian magistrate called a *irenarch*, literally 'Chief of the Peace.'[198] The *koina*, communes, and the *oikoi*, estates, had fiscal obligations of defence, called *munera*. They were used to pay *bucellarii*, their weapons and probably their housing. Townsmen, grouped into *demes*, districts, formed a militia for self-defence. In the remote countryside, part of the surveillance of the territory, largely privatised, was left to groups of *vigilantes* and *bucellarii* paid by the large landowners. The countryside watchmen were called *agrophylachs*, guardians of the fields. The territory of the commune of Aphrodito was divided into *decuries* of two to three shepherds who also served as watchmen. Similarly, the *Philae* sailors were carrying out a surveillance mission. There were mounted forces such as the *caballarii* (horsemen) from Hermontis and the *krommydiôtai* (onion eaters) from the Oxyrhynchus *nome*.[199] On the territory of Pharon there were 800 family groups on horseback, a sort of mounted militia.

In the countryside, landowners frequently paid *bucellarii* and *riparii*. A sixth-century tax document stated that the property of the Teon family had to pay for 65 years for the services of *riparii*. The *bucellarii*, first

---

194 *Notitia Dignitatum*, OR.XXXI.39.
195 D. A. Karelin, 'Imaging of the Late Roman Castrum. Hypothetical Computer Reconstruction of Nag el-Hagar Fortress in Egypt', *AMIT*, 2, 15, (2011), pp.1–20.
196 A. L. Boozer, 'Frontiers and Borderlands in Imperial Perspectives: Exploring Rome's Egyptian Frontier', *AJA*, 117/2, (2013), pp.275–292.
197 J. Maspéro, *Organisation militaire de l'Égypte Byzantine* (Paris: Champion, 1912), pp.88–98 (tribunes and *stratēlátēs* στρατηλάτης).
198 S. Torallas-Tovar, 'Los *Riparii* en los papiros del Egipto tardoantiquo', *Aquila Legionis*, 1 (2001), pp.123–149 (σύνδικος /ἔκδικος).
199 νομός, nomos was a territorial district in ancient Egypt.

mentioned in Egypt around 475, were not a private militia in the service of large landowners. They carried out public order duties at parties or races at the Oxyrhynchus Hippodrome. In wartime, they came under the authority of the duke of Thebaid and fought the Blemmyes, as in 563/568. After the reconquest of Italy, the *bucellarii* of Egypt were also recruited from among the Ostrogoths, to the point where in the following decade the terms barbarians and soldiers were confused and almost interchangeable. In Sinai, the Bedouins of the Pharanithēs *nome* formed the *mehari* militia known as the *Pharanitai*, organised into 800 family groups. They protected the monasteries of the Sinai but were eventually called to Egypt to fight the Blemmyes.[200] This kind of organisation, similar to eighteenth century colonial militias in North America, only made sense when threat was low. The major military weakness of Romano-Byzantine Egypt was the absence of a single commander, as the existence of five duchies led to a decentralised defence that cooperated poorly.

The Arab conquest revealed the military weakness of Egypt. Al-Baladhuri, a ninth-century Iraqi historian, wrote a different account of the conquest. He dated the Muslim invasion of Egypt to the year AH 19 (639) at the initiative of Amr ibn al-As initiative to the great anger of Caliph Omar. Amr's initial strength was only 3,500. Quite logically, Amr began with the fortress of al-Farama, Pelusium, which guarded the road to Palestine. Then he moved south to Alyunah (Babilona), the key to Egypt, which the Muslims renamed Fustat. He made the wise choice to cut Egypt in two, separating the delta from the rest. He received 10,000 to 12,000 reinforcement men from al-Zubayr and Babilona was taken by an assault using ladders. The land was divided between Amr and al-Zubayr. Amr paid tribute to al-Mukaukis, the equivalent of Moqauqas, the leader of the Copts. Some resisted the Muslims but most of Ain Shams submitted and paid tribute.[201]

The ninth-century historian Ibn Abd al-Hakam was an Egyptian and his account is particularly relevant to the conquest of Maghreb and of Spain; he provided some interesting information on Egypt. According to him the siege of al-Farama (Pelusium) was far from easy and lasted a month. Al-Hakam confirmed al-Baladhuri's account when he said Amr had 4,000 men at the start of the campaign before receiving a reinforcement of 12,000 and that the siege of Babilona was intense.[202] Misr was the Arabic word for Egypt

---

200 J. Maspéro, Organisation militaire de l'Égypte Byzantine, pp.67–68, 140 (watchmen and bucellarii); 88–100 (gendarmerie). J. Gascou, 'Militaires étrangers en Égypte Byzantine', BIFAO, 75, 1975, pp.203–206 (Goths). J. Gascou, 'L'Institution des Bucellaires', BIFAO, 76 (1976), p.153 (Aphrodito; Philae; Hermonthis; Pharon; κρόμμυδιοται); 150 (bucellarii for law enforcement or against Blemmyes),154 (Φαρβαιθίτοι), p.156 (Goths).
201 Al-Baladhuri, *Kitab*, V, 1 (1916), p.335 (decision, numbers, year, al-Farama), 336 (Fustat, reinforcements, fall), 337–338 (numbers estimated after various sources: 3,500 men reinforced by 12,000), 339 (al-Mukaukis), 340 (resistance), 341–342 (surrendering of Ain Shams, Fayoum and other places).
202 Al-Hakam, *Futuh Misr* (1998), pp.37 (Farama), 40 (siege de Babylon), 41

and also for a 'fortified city', because in the imagination the country was the 'fine city', but it was also the name for Memphis. The tenth-century Persian chronicler Tabari summed up the campaign as a sort of military expedition ordered by the Caliph Omar to Amr in the twentieth year of the *Hegira* (640). Amr went into the south-east of the delta and ransacked the city of Bilbeis, whose population he enslaved, then he laid siege to Alexandria, which agreed to become a tributary. Heading south to Memphis, Amr fought 'the Prince of the Copts' Moqauqas (literally 'the Caucasian'), in fact the Patriarch of Alexandria, Cyrus Moukaoukis. Amr imposed a tribute on Memphis after a short battle. He settled his camp in what became the district of Fostat or Fustat, in Arabic 'tent' or 'encampment', currently the heart of old Cairo. This city born from the Muslim conquest before being named Cairo (the Victorious) in the eleventh century and absorbing some smaller cities nearby, was first called Fustat-Misr or Misr al-Fustat. From there, Amr left to, victoriously, confront the Coptic Army gathered by Moqauqas at Ain es-Schems (current Ain Schams).[203] Tabari's simplistic account combined a number of facts in a questionable sequence. According to a fourteenth-century Arabic epic *Futuh al-Bahnasâ* (Conquest of Bahnasâ) Amr seized Misr (Memphis), Giza, Alexandria and Lower Egypt on his own initiative. Omar ordered him to plunder the wealthy cities of Ahnas and Bahnasâ/ Behnesa (Héns in Coptic), near present-day Beni-Suef.[204] Ahnas fell after three months, while Bahnasâ resisted in a bloody siege for up to nine months. Around the city there were ambushes and a battle to repel a Greek relief army. Bahnasâ was taken through a tunnel, submitted, but then rebelled and a new siege was needed.[205] Bar Hebraeus was a thirteenth-century Syrian Jacobite Bishop also called Abu'l-Faradg Gamal al-Din, Abu al-Faraj ibn al-Ibri or Abul Faradj in the Arab world and Abulfaragius in Europe. He used Arab sources and, according to him, Kura, Patriarch Cyrus, offered to pay Caliph Omar an annual tribute to prevent him from invading Egypt. Omar agreed but Emperor Heraclius intervened and refused to let Kura go. Manuel an Armenian general was sent with an army to Babilona of Egypt identified by Bar Hebraeus as Fostat. After an insolent reply to the Arab emissary, Manuel fled and Omar invaded the whole country.[206] Muslim sources and Bar Hebraeus struggle to give a cogent account but the seventh-century elaborate narrative of the Coptic Bishop John of Nikiu offers a very different but more precise chronology of events.

For troops moving down from Syria and Palestine along the coastal route, the first fortress to be taken was Pelusium. It was not very advantageous for

---

     (numbers), 42 (reinforcements).
203 Tabari, *Tarikh*, IV, 60, t. 3 (1958), pp.461 (date), 462 (Bilbeis, Alexandria), 463–464 (Memphis) 466 (Battle of Ain Schams/Ain es-Schems).
204 Al-Mo'izz Mohammad ibn Mohammad, *Foutouh al-Bahnasâ* (1909), p.34 and 38 (fall of Misr), 42 (Omar), 43 (Ahnas and Bahnasâ).
205 J. Jarry, 'La conquête du Fayoum par les Musulmans d'après le Futūḥ Al-Bahnasa', *Annales Islamologiques*, 9 (1970), pp.9–20.
206 Bar Hebraeus, *Chr.*, 102–103 (1932), pp.73–74.

them to venture into the canals and marshes of the Nile Delta, especially as the road from Syria ran south along the eastern arm of the Delta, the Bar el-Baqar.[207] This road led directly to the fortress of Babilona (a corruption of Bal al-Yun(ah) - 'Yun(ah) Gate', the former Heliopolis and today Ain Shams a district of Cairo). Amr seems to have bypassed this fortified area and moved into Upper Egypt towards the rich region of Fayoum and against the Duchy of Arcadia. Two Romano-Byzantine officers, John of Barca and John of Maros, were beaten and killed in battle. The latter had only a troop of 50 horsemen and archers in the area of el-Lahoun (today a village about 90km south of Cairo). The city of Bahnasâ finally fell.

The Dukes of Arcadia and Thebaid, Theodosius and Anastasius, then took refuge further north in the citadel of Babilona. In order to guard Aboit, a place located in the *nome* of Lycopolis (today Asiyut), they sent the Prefect Leontius, 'an obese man, without energy and without experience of war.' Theodore, Duke of Egypt, got as far as the city of Faiyum to strengthen Leontius, but the latter panicked and retreated to Babilona. Amr pursued him, crossing the Nile probably at the island of Gezira 6km north of Babilona, near Tendounias, which later became the Coptic quarter. Amr then headed to Umm Dunayn (today in the Azbakeya district of Cairo), and took up a position on the heights of Aoun. From there, he could fall back on Pelusium or receive reinforcements. Some of his forces were still on the west bank, perhaps garrisoned at Bahnasâ, but he obtained from Omar a reinforcement of 4,000 men from Syria or Palestine commanded by Walwaya. Camped at Aoun, Amr waited for the Romano-Byzantine forces with a visible first battle line and set a trap, hiding a second corps north of the Babilona Fortress and a third near the Tendounias Fortress. On the Romano-Byzantine side, without waiting for their colleague the duke of Egypt, the dukes of Arcadia and Thebaid marched on Aoun with a large body of infantry. Their army was surrounded and annihilated by the three corps of Amr.[208] Despite the imprecision of the sources, historiography has etched in stone the date of 6 July 640, for the so-called Battle of Heliopolis, or Ain Schams.[209] The 300 survivors of the Tendounias garrison who had taken part in the battle fled on boats. Amr then took Tendounias, which had been left defenceless. The Governor of Faiyum abandoned his town, which, like Aboit, was left to be looted. The other towns, without any aid,

---

207 L. Chagnon, *La conquête musulmane de l'Égypte* (Paris: Economica, 2008), p.71.
208 John of Nikiu, *Chr.*, 111, 1–3 (1883), pp.433–434 (Theodore informed by Theodosius about the death of the aforesaid John, 50 horsemen); 9, p.435 (fall of Bahnasâ); 13 (Theodosius and Anastase à Babylon, Leontius); 14 (Leontius, Theodore at Fayoum); 112, 1, p.436 (disagreement between Theodore, Theodosius and Anastasius ; march on Aoun with numerous footmen); 3, p.437 (Amr crossing the Nile at Tendounias); 4 (Amr worried about the dispersion of his troops, march on Aoun); 5–6 (Muslim reinforcements); 7–8 (Amr's strategy); 438 (Romans left Babylon and slaughtered); 10 (fall of Tendounias).
209 A. Butler, *The Arab Conquest of Egypt and the Last Thirty Years of the Roman Dominion* (Oxford: Clarendon Press, 1902), pp.221–237.

fell one after the other, and Amr easily established himself as the new local authority. He ordered the city of Delas's boats to bring some of his troops who had remained on the west bank of the Nile. He used Egyptian labour to build a bridge over the Qalyūb canal north of present-day Cairo and a bridge of boats near Babilona, thus blocking navigation and controlling the Nile. He put Roman magistrates in chains, ransomed the rich, doubled taxes, requisitioned fodder and horses and committed many acts of violence. The Romano-Byzantine elite of the region fled in terror to Alexandria, creating a panic and a pitiful exodus of the population, who even abandoned their livestock. But Amr temporarily failed to capture the cities of the delta and returned to Middle Egypt to take those he had left behind. After a long siege, Babilona fell on 24 March 641 on a promise to spare the lives of the garrison. Then Nikiu was abandoned without a fight by its governor and its weak garrison.[210] From a military standpoint, the campaign was over.

One of the reasons for the fall of Egypt, according to Bishop John of Nikiu, was the religious division of the inhabitants:

> Seeing the weakness of the Romans and the hostility of the inhabitants towards Emperor Heraclius because of the persecution he had carried out throughout Egypt against the Orthodox religion, at the instigation of Cyrus, the Chalcedonian Patriarch, the Muslims became bolder and stronger in the struggle.[211]

The Green and Blue factions opposed each other politically, as they did in Byzantium. The dukes of Egypt and Augustamnica Theodore and Menas, belonged to the populist and Monophysite Green Faction, while the dukes of Arcadia and Thebaid, Theodosius and Anastasius, joined the oligarchic and Orthodox Blues. The allegiance of Aboulyânos Duke of Libya remains unknown.[212] Theodore was a loyal follower of Heraclius but was personally disliked by his colleagues.[213] John of Nikiu gave many examples of betrayal, with very varied motives. At the start of the campaign, Jeremiah, leader of a band (brigands, monophysites?) betrayed to the Muslims the hiding place of John and his troops who had hidden in the enclosures and plantations after the capture of Bahnasâ.

With the submission of Faiyum, some Egyptians apostatised the Christian religion and plundered their erstwhile coreligionists along with the Muslims. The militias raised by Theodore in the region of Semnoud refused to fight the Arabs. In the Faiyum region, the inhabitants had

---

210   John of Nikiu, *Chr.*, 113, 1 (1883), p.439 (boats gathered at Delas); 2 (bridge at Kalyub); 3 (boat bridge near Babylon); 4, p.440 (requisitions, violence); 5 (Nikiu resists; exodus); 115, 1 p.441 (Amr's problems in northern Egypt); 117, 1–3, p.447 (fall of Babylon); 118, 8, p.448 (fall of Nikiu).
211   John of Nikiu, *Chr.*, 115, 9 (1883), p.442.
212   L. Chagnon, *La conquête musulmane*, pp.55–56.
213   John of Nikiu, *Chr.*, 112, 1 (1883), p.436.

become tributary to the Muslims and massacred all the 'Roman soldiers' they encountered. Later, in the Misr-Memphis region, Menas and Cosmas, respectively leaders of the Green and Blue Factions, harassed the Roman forces.[214] The *Futuh al-Bahnasâ* reported that the people of Tanbadâ delivered to the Muslims 1,500 'Greek soldiers' hidden in the countryside and that during the capture of Bahnasâ the Copts pointed out the soldiers hidden in the silos and wells.[215] A civil war in Lower Egypt pitted Theodore, head of the Imperial camp, against the partisans of the Muslims. Amr took the opportunity to seize the suburb of Kerioun whose garrison had fled, but Alexandria held out thanks to its inhabitants who threw stones from the top of the rampart onto the Muslim troops.[216]

The Patriarch of Alexandria Cyrus had received from Heraclius the powers of a viceroy, an unwise choice because he would have persecuted the monophysites and thus favoured internal division in the face of the Muslim invaders.[217] Cyrus was recalled to Constantinople, but the death of Heraclius on 11 February 641 allowed him to return to Alexandria around mid-September. It was finally he who capitulated, supported by the regent Martina, the dukes in Egypt and part of the inhabitants of Alexandria. The agreement, dating to late September or October 641, provided for the payment of a tribute to the Muslims, an 11-month armistice, the embarkation of Roman soldiers with their goods and the promise that no other army would return, the delivery of 150 soldiers and 50 civilians as hostages to Amr, the non-interference of Muslims in Christian affairs and the authorisation that Jews could remain in Alexandria.[218] Capitulating and paying tribute were not considered treason since the Bishop of Damascus and the Patriarch of Jerusalem had done the same.[219]

However, not all cities agreed to capitulate, particularly in Augustamnica in the east of the Delta. During the summer following the fifteenth indiction, in June 642 Amr besieged Sakhâ, Tûkh Mazid, Damsis and Tamiathis (current Damietta).[220] The last factor that facilitated the conquest of Egypt was the dynastic crisis opened by the death of Heraclius and then that of his son and immediate successor Constantine III on 25 May 641. This crisis

---

214 John of Nikiu, *Chr.*, 111, 10 (fall of Bahnasâ), 12 (Jeremiah) (1883), p.435; 114, 1 (apostates), 3 (militias), p. 440; 115, 11, p.443 (soldiers slaughtered in Faiyum); 118, 3, p.448 (Menas and Cosmas).
215 Al-Mo'izz Mohammad ibn Mohammad, *Foutouh al-Bahnasâ* (1909), p.129 (Tanbadâ); 208 (Bahnasâ).
216 John of Nikiu, *Chr.*, 119, 1–3 (1883), pp.449–450.
217 L. Chagnon, *La conquête musulmane*, pp.40–41.
218 John of Nikiu, *Chr.*, 120, 1 (1883), p.453 (decision of peace); 17, p.455 (capitulation of Babylon). A. Butler (1902), pp.310–327 (capitulation dated 8 November 641).
219 D. J. Sahas, 'Face to Face Encounter Between Patriarch Sophronius of Jerusalem and the Caliph 'Umar Ibn al-Khattab: Friends or Foes?' in E. Grypeou, M. N. Swanson, D. R. Thomas (eds), *The encounter of Eastern Christianity with early Islam* (Leiden: Brill, 2006), p.36.
220 John of Nikiu, *Chr.*, 115, 1–5 (1883), p.441.

opposed Martina the second wife and niece of Heraclius, who wanted to put their son Heraclonas on the throne, with Valentinian Master of the Soldiers to the East, who supported the 11-year-old Constantine II. This resulted in a coup and the deposing of Martina and Heraclonas in September.[221]

The Empire no longer had the will or the strength to reconquer Egypt, but it was a great loss. The sale of requisitioned wheat in Egypt alone brought in 600,000 to 800,000 *solidi* a year to the state, almost half the tax revenue of the province.[222] However the idea of an easy Arab conquest is contradicted by the military cemetery of Bahnasâ in Upper Egypt where the bodies of 400 emirs killed in action are interred: 'Historians affirm that after the territory of Misr [Memphis] and that of Bohairah [Lower Egypt], there is no country where more martyrs have been found than in Bahnasâ.'[223] With these were buried 70 prophet brothers-in-arms, veterans from the Battle of Badr and 5,000 others Muslim soldiers.[224] Islam brought a tremendous change in war goals as, unlike their precursors and other Saracens, Muslim Arabs were eager to conquer sedentary lands and the souls of their inhabitants.

The Organisation of Border Defences in North Africa

Byzantine strategic goals in North Africa were to protect economically useful areas, the agricultural plains of Tunisia, the fertile valleys of Eastern Algeria, the coastal towns between Morocco and present-day Libya. Byzantium originally possessed the province of Cyrenaica including the north-eastern part of today's Libya, but depended on Egypt. It was a thin coastal strip bounded by an uncontrolled desert. Its very core was 'the Five Cities' – Pentapolis, Berenike, Arsinoe, Apollonia and Ptolemais. According to Procopius, this region was 20 days' march west of Alexandria. Justinian strongly fortified three cities there: Teucheira and Berenike and to the west Boreium (respectively today's Tocra, Benghazi and Bu Grada). South of the Pentapolis Justinian transformed two monasteries into fortresses, Agriolôdē and Dinarthisum.[225] These construction works and Procopius' references to the barbarian raids demonstrate that the Saharan nomads remained unsubdued.[226]

What the Byzantines called 'Libya' corresponded to Tripolitania, Roman Africa, Numidia, Mauritania and, present-day western Libya, Tunisia and

---

221 R. G. Hoyland, *In God's Path: The Arab Conquests and the Creation of an Islamic Empire* (Oxford: Oxford University Press, 2015), pp.66–67.
222 J. Durliat, *De la ville antique à la ville Byzantine: le problème des subsistances* (Rome: CEFR, 136, 1990), p.265.
223 Al-Mo'izz Mohammad ibn Mohammad, *Foutouh al-Bahnasâ* (1909), p.1 (400 emirs), p.3 (the bloodiest conquest Tunisia).
224 Al-Mo'izz Mohammad ibn Mohammad, *Foutouh al-Bahnasâ* (1909), p.214.
225 Procopius, *Aed.*, VI, 2, 3–4 (Teuchira, Berenike); 7 (monasteries); 11 (Boreium).
226 F. Colin, *Les peuples libyens de la Cyrénaïque à l'Égypte d'après les sources de l'Antiquité* (Brussels: Académie Royale de Belgique, 2000).

THE ARMY WATCHES OVER THE BORDERS

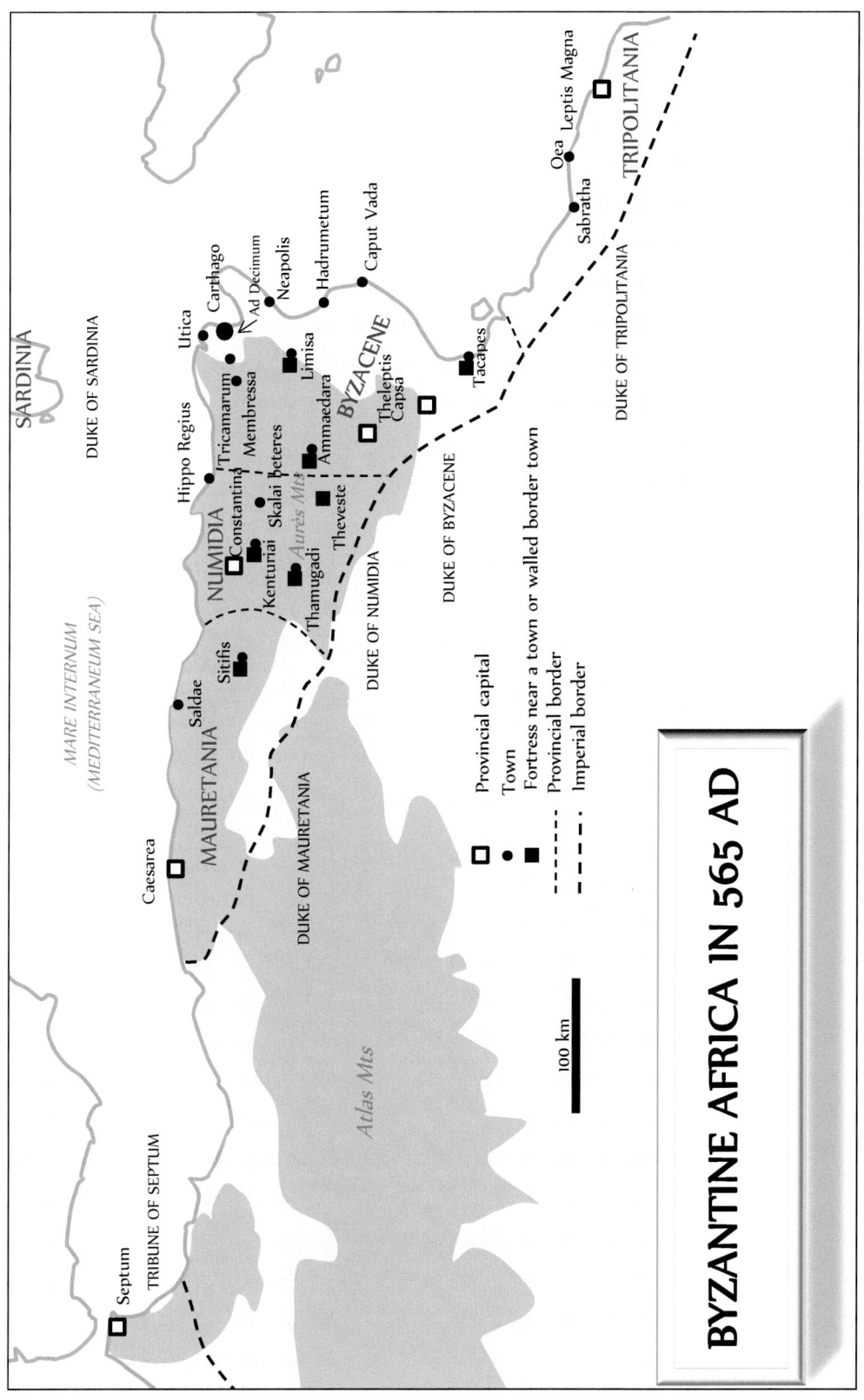

the Algerian coast. Conquering North Africa from the Vandals in 533 was easy, but pacifying the neighbouring Moors took around 10 years.[227] The reason was that the Vandal Kingdom had fluid frontiers defending coastal plains as the Moors were restless neighbours.[228] The Romano-Byzantines found this messy situation and had to fight tribes from the Aures Mountains and the Atlas Range, whom the Romans called Moors – the 'Darks', *Maurus* was the Latinization of the Greek *Mauros*. However, Procopius also specified that some Moorish tribes had very white skin and blond hair, probably those tribes called *Kabyles* by the Arabs.[229] The Moors were the ancestors of the current Berbers, so called by homonym with 'barbarian', a name which shows that prejudices are tenacious.[230] The tribes could unite against the Vandals, and then against the Romans, but remained divided by tribal quarrels. The Aures Mountains, which form the eastern part of the Atlas, was a poorly pacified area as it would later be during French colonisation.[231] A 500-year-long coexistence between Moors and Romans was only a long face to face confrontation with limited and sporadic exchanges and wars but the deep Romanisation failed. The late Roman presence, then the Vandal, had to reach an accommodation with the Moors in an ever precarious but long-lasting equilibrium.[232] The Romans had not been able to build the defences of North Africa on rivers as they had in Europe or the Middle East. Moreover, the Maghreb was too large and too mountainous to build a continuous wall as Hadrian had done in northern Britannia. The Roman strategy taken up by Byzantines was to defend the coastal plains and cities, to contain the Aures Mountains by a chain of forts and to erect few low stone walls south of the Algerian-Tunisian borders. The Vandals proved unable to recover this system and the Moors had increased their domain particularly south of the Aures Mountains and in Numidia. Vandal Mauretania was no more than a chain of urban enclaves on the Mediterranean coast.[233]

---

227 Ph., Richardot, 'La pacification de l'Afrique Byzantine, 534–546' in Coutau-Bégarie (ed.), *Stratégies irrégulières* (*Stratégique*, 93–96, 2009/1), pp.129–158. A. Merrills, *War, Rebellion, Epic in Byzantine Africa. A Historical Study of Corippus' Iohannis* (Cambridge: Cambridge University Press, 2023).

228 Y. Modéran, 'Les frontières mouvantes du royaume vandale' in Cl. Lepelley, X. Dupuis (eds), *Frontières et limites géographiques de l'Afrique du Nord antique, Hommage à Pierre Salama* (Paris: 1999), pp.241–264.

229 Procopius, *BV*, IV (13, 29.

230 V. Zarini, *Berbères ou barbares? Recherches sur le livre second de la Johannide de Corippe* (Nancy: Paris, de Boccard, 1997).

231 P. Morizot, 'Aurès' in *Encyclopédie berbère*, 7 (Aix-en-Provence: 1990), pp.1103–1113.

232 P. Morizot, *Romains et Berbères face à face* (Arles: Errances, Les Hesperides, 2015). A. Merrills, 'Understanding Late Antique North Africa' in A. Merrills (ed.), *Vandals, Romans and Berbers. New Perspectives on Late Antique North Africa* (London, New York: Routledge, 2006), pp.1–28.

233 Ph. Richardot, 'Le plus vieux *limes*: la défense de l'Afrique romaine', *Revue Internationale d'Histoire Militaire*, 76 (1997), pp.15–37.

THE ARMY WATCHES OVER THE BORDERS

Justinian's edict from 13 April 534 set out the defence of Africa, which was entrusted to five dukes and a tribune. The duke of Tripolitania, in the east of current Libya, had his headquarters at Leptis Magna harbour (today a magnificent archaeological site). The duke of Byzacene settled alternately at Capsa and 75km to the north at Theleptis (now Gafsa in central Tunisia and Theleptis, a town 20km from the Kasserine Pass). Theleptis was located on the road between Ammaedara and Tacapes (current Haidra on Algerian border and Gabes harbour). The duke of Numidia was settled at Constantina (today Constantine in Eastern Algeria). In Mauretania the duke was based at Caesarea (current Cherchell on the Algerian coast). A fifth duke was assigned to Sardinia near the Barbaricini (today the mountainous region of Barbagia). A simple tribune was based at Septum (now Ceuta) opposite Spain. Justinian's edict left it to 'His Greatness' Belisarius to assign the strength of infantry and cavalry he deemed appropriate but after reference to the Emperor for approval or amendment.[234] These dukes led both the intervention and border troops, as well as the Moorish *foederati*.[235] In 536, Marcellus, the Governor of Numidia, had five troops under his command, three of them cavalry. These included two troops of *foederati*, the identity of which is unknown, one of these he commanded directly and the other was commanded by Cyril. One cavalry unit and two infantry units were commanded by Barbatos, Terentios and Serapis.[236] The situation in Africa remained unstable until 539, six years after the conquest by Belisarius, and it was difficult to build fortifications. According to the dedications discovered by archaeologists, Solomon assumed the functions of Governor from 539 to 544, and he built the most defences, as some 24 forts referred to him. Subsequently, archaeological excavations reflect either a lack of documentation or fewer activities. Between the reigns of Justin II and Maurice, from 565 to 582, only 8 military sites are dated, and almost as many are of uncertain dating. In all, around 40 military works were erected or restored by Romano-Byzantines.[237]

Solomon resumed the Roman strategy of encircling the Aures Mountains. So, he established a double line of forts 300km long at the foot of Mount Aures, both northern and southern. 15 forts were 60km apart on a 40km to 80km depth. However, the bulk of Africa's defensive system consisted in fortifying cities, a novelty and an admission of military impotence. The work was financed from the treasury of Moorish King Iaudas, captured by Solomon in 540.[238] Solomon surrounded every city with a wall. Even inside Carthage's city wall, he built a fortified monastery 'of solidity to all

---

234   *CJ*, I, 27, 2, 1–3 (dukes and tribunes); 5 (troops).
235   L. Bréhier, *Les institutions de l'Empire byzantin* (Paris: Albin Michel, L'Évolution de l'humanité, 1970), pp.275.
236   Procopius, *BV*, IV, 15, 50–51.
237   J. Durliat, *Les dédicaces d'ouvrages de défense dans l'Afrique Byzantine* (Rome: PEFR, 49, 1981).
238   Procopius, *BV*, IV, 20, 29.

test'. Some border fortresses and fortified villages signalled to the peasants a Moorish incursion by beacon to give them time to take refuge in walled cities. There were more fortified towns in the Aures Mountains than on the Tunisian coastal plain.[239]

Lands formerly occupied by the Romans and lost by the Vandals were reoccupied. This was the case for Tamugadis or Thamugadi (in Greek and Latin respectively, present-day Timgad) and its region. 250m south of Timgad, in c. 539/540 Solomon built a fort identified from a dedication. The building was built on a pagan sanctuary. The fort measures some 111m by 67m internally, divided into two parts by an axial roadway entering the fort at the north gate. The western part contains buildings such as the commander's residence, the headquarters, a small bath-house, a chapel, kitchens, latrines and some non-identified buildings perhaps an arsenal or for food storage. Near the centre, the water tower is located on the former sanctuary's sacred pool. The eastern part of the fort contains the barrack blocks of the rank and file, probably infantry: eight rows with 11 rooms each and three rows are built against the walls of the fort. There is a veranda for each block as during previous period. Sleeping-quarters would have been on the first floor, above a store-room. Each room can hold five men, maybe the *pentarchy*, the sub-unit in the *Strategikon*. The fort thus probably had a 600-strong garrison. The rectangular wall had eight square towers, with one at each corner. The northern gate passed under a tower. The bastioned walls were built by destroying older Roman monuments and using the largest blocks of stone.[240] Following the wars against the Moors between 534 and 547, which were interrupted by just three years of truces, many cities were destroyed. Evagrius Scholasticus claimed that Justinian rebuilt or created 150 of them.[241]

The regular troops which guarded Romano-Byzantine Libya were few in number. In 608, when Heraclius the Elder *exarch* of Africa mutinied, he sent Bonakis, probably the best of his five dukes, to conquer Pentapolis in Cyrenaica. Bonakis took with him 3,000 soldiers and a large number of barbarians recruited at great expense in Tripolitania and Pentapolis.

---

239 Procopius, *BV*, IV, 19, 3 (city walls); 26, 17 (fortified monastery); J. B. Bury, *A History of the Later Roman Empire*, pp.148–149 (double line and warning system). D. Pringle, *The Defence of Byzantine Africa from Justinian to The Arab conquest. An account of the military history and archaeology of the African provinces in the sixth and seventh centuries*, BAR International Series, 99 (Oxford: BAR, 2001), pp.523–526 (precise description with map). P. Trousset, 'Les limites Sud de la réoccupation Byzantine', Ant *tard*, 10 (2003), pp.143–150 (urban fortifications as far as Hodna region).

240 J. Lassus., *La forteresse Byzantine de Thamugadi, fouilles à Timgad 1938–1956* (Paris: Éditions du CNRS, Études d'Antiquités africaines, 1981). D. Pringle, (2001), pp.85–88. P. Morizot, 'Timgad et son territoire' in *L'Afrique, la Gaule et son territoire à l'époque romaine, Mélanges à la mémoire de Marcel Le Glay* (Brussels: Latomus, 226, 1994), pp.220–243. Maurice, *Strategikon*, I, 3, 20 (pentarchēs, πεντάρχης).

241 Evagrius Scholasticus, *HE*, IV, 18.

Heraclius the Younger, the future Emperor, had only boats and many barbarians when he departed Africa for Byzantium.[242] These barbarians that John of Nikiu speaks of were Moors.

The Moors, Auxiliaries and Enemies of the Romans

This improbable duality persisted on into the Byzantine era. The Romans had long been aware of the fighting skills of the North Africans. During the Republic, subduing Jugurtha was a long-term exercise. Julius Caesar hired Numidian cavalrymen in the Gallic War and later the Roman Army recruited Moorish cavalry and infantry. But the Romans had also to deal with sporadic wars on the fringes of their African provinces. The short Vandal domination of the region proved no exception to the Roman experience. King Huneric had to fight a campaign against the Moors from the Aures Mountains in 484, much like his successor Gunthamund did.[243] Nevertheless, the Vandals maintained the Roman tradition of giving the Moorish Kings insignias of their authority, a gilded silver wand, a silver cap resembling a crown, a small white cloak fastened at the right shoulder with a gold clasp, a white tunic with embroidery and gold-covered boots.[244] These gifts maintained good relations temporarily.

In North Africa the Romano-Byzantines experienced some setbacks due to the operational swiftness and political fickleness of the Moors. In 533, Belisarius could rely on the alliance with the Frexes who controlled western Byzacene for 20 years; their King, Antalasm had even inflicted a severe defeat on the Vandal King Ilderic.[245] Although the Moorish Kings had sent many promises of alliance and their children as hostages, they did not provide any concrete help to Belisarius. On the contrary, the Moors of Numidia sheltered the Vandal King Gelimer after his defeat at Trikamaron, and in spring 534, the Moors of Tripolitania launched a surprise attack on Generals Tattimuth and Pudentius.[246] Worse still, following the departure of Belisarius, the entire Moorish tribes of Byzacene and Numidia took up arms against the Romano-Byzantines. Procopius acidly commented these events:

> It is true that this attitude was not foreign to their customs, for the Moors do not fear God any more than they respect men. They pay no heed to oaths or hostages, even if these are the sons or brothers of

---

242 John of Nikiu, *Chr.*, 107, 3, p.421 (Bonakis); 109, 25, p.431 (Heraclius the Younger).
243 Procopius, *BV*, III, 8, 5 and 14.
244 Procopius, *BV*, III, 25, 7.
245 Procopius, *BV*, III, 9, 3.
246 Procopius, *BV*, IV, 5, 10.

their chiefs, and the only reason for peace between them is the fear of an enemy attack.[247]

Belisarius had delegated the command to Solomon. He had also left Solomon a large part of his personal guard and Justinian sent reinforcements jointly commanded by Theodore of Cappadocia and by Ildiger.[248] Nevertheless, the Romano-Byzantine border troops were unprepared and probably not numerous enough. Byzacene and Numidia, now the central Tunisian plains and the eastern Algerian mountains, were devastated by the Kings Cusina, Esdilasas, Iourphoutes and Mesdinissas, while Antalas as well as some other leaders remained loyal to Byzantium.[249] After losing two valuable officers and 500 men to an ambush while on patrol, Solomon inflicted two crushing defeats on the Moors, the first in the plain of Mammes, perhaps Henchir-Ed-Douame, 30km from Kairouan, the second at Mount Bourgaon, Jebel ech Chambi in the Kasserine Pass of Western Tunisia.[250] These Moors took refuge in the Aures Mountains and there joined their forces to King Iaudas who rebelled in late 534 or early 535. Together they ravaged undefended Numidia while the Romano-Byzantine Army was still expecting to be attacked in Byzacene. Some loyal Moorish chiefs urged Solomon to hunt Iaudas in the Aures Mountains. Massonas accused the latter of having killed his father and Ortaias of trying to drive him off his land. Solomon had a seven-day march through deep gorges and cedar forests, and along narrow paths and stony creeks, excellent ambush country. He finally reached the place where Iaudas was supposed to be, the deserted fortress of the so-called Aureus Clipeus, or Mons Aurasius (today the Aures Djebel Chélia in north-Eastern Algeria). Solomon waited for three days, then, running out of food and suspecting a trap set by his allies, he wisely withdrew. Two years later, his supposed ally Ortaias revealed himself a friend of Iaudas.[251] Byzantine generals in Africa were on an insecure ground.

From a tactical point of view the Moors were horsemen and light foot soldiers armed with javelin and skin shields.[252] Maurice's military treatise deemed their javelins good enough to suggest equipping light infantry with them.[253] Such weaponry called for fluid ambush tactics or the assembly of large numbers in a pitched battle to overwhelm the enemy.

---

247 Procopius, *BV*, IV, 8, 9–10.
248 Procopius, *BV*, IV, 8, 23–24.
249 Procopius, *BV*, IV, 8, 21 and 10, 2 (border troops); 10, 6 (rebel Kings); 12, 30 (temporary loyalty of Antalas).
250 Procopius, *BV*, IV, 10, 1–11 (patrol); 11, 15–56 (Mammes); 12, 1–29 (Mount Bourgaon).
251 Procopius, *BV*, IV, 13, 19 (Massonas and Ortaias urge Solomon to act); 13, 33–34 (indecisive campaign); 13, 35–38 (intuition of a trap and retreat); 17, 7 (Iaudas and Ortaias at Skalai Beteres).
252 C. Chadburn, 'Les guerriers berbères dans l'Antiquité', *Prétorien*, 15 (2010), pp.21–28.
253 Maurice, *Strategikon*, XII, B, 20, 10.

Against Moorish bands of looters, the border troops' doctrine was an ambush during the enemy's return, when they were withdrawing home laden with loot and captives, and thus becoming slow and predictable. The tactics employed were more like lion hunting than regular fighting. The first case took place in 534 in Byzacene where two men of great reputation Aigan, *doryphoros* of the House of Belisarius, and Rufinus the Thracian, army *bandophoros*, were in command of two cavalry units. In a narrow pass, they ambushed with their 500 men a party of Moors and freed the prisoners. But shortly after, they themselves were surrounded by tens of thousands of Moors gathered by the rebel Kings. The Romano-Byzantines were surrounded, and fought to the death. The following year, when Iaudas himself raided from the Aures Mountains to plunder the Romans, Althias the duke of Numidia was garrisoned at Kentouriai, a fort about 60km southeast of Constantina. Althias moved out with just 70 Hun cavalry to free the prisoners by ambushing the returning Moors weighed down with their loot, but the terrain, a plain, did not offer him the defile he was looking for. Unable to trap the Moors or fight a pitched battle with his small troop, Althias waited for them at the only watering point in the region, Tigisis, (present-day Ain el Bordj) some 40km south-east of Constantina. There, the Moors, thirsty and unwilling to fight, tried to negotiate keeping third of the spoils for access to the water. As Althias proposed a duel instead, Iaudas took the challenge but ran when his horse was killed, preferring to lose face rather than his head. The Moors fled after him, abandoning their prisoners.[254]

Gold, the Empire's Best Barrier?

War was the justification for the Empire and the army accounted for half to three-quarters of state revenues.[255] In return, war fed war. As they accused barbarians of being looters, Byzantine historians were reluctant to confess that their army did the same and gave few examples of this. An unlocated victory, *c.* 575, between Nisibis and Dara won by Justinian the Master of the Soldiers to the East was presented as a godsend: 'The spoils taken by the Romans were sold with a multitude of Persians, bringing a not insignificant profit to the public finances.'[256] Rather than financing costly fortifications or military campaigns with uncertain results, wasn't it more profitable to bribe the enemy at lower cost? The Roman Empire had practised this double-edged strategy by the fifth century and Attila even held the rank and pay of master of the soldiers present. In 504 the Persians gave back the stronghold

---

254 Procopius, *BV*, IV, 10, 2–11 (Aigan and Rufinus); 11, 23 (500 casualties); 13, 2–16 (Althias).
255 A. D, Lee, 'The Empire at War' in M. Maas (ed.), *The Cambridge Companion to the Age of Justinian* (Cambridge: Cambridge University Press, 2005), p.119.
256 John of Biclaro, *Chr.VT*, 35.

of Amida after receiving a large ransom. Moreover, this inglorious but fruitful bargaining opened peace negotiations. More generally Justinian rewarded the restless border barbarians, to the great irritation of Procopius:

> [Justinian] did not lose an opportunity to make important donations to all the barbarians, to those of the East as well as the West, of the North as of the South, and even to those who inhabited Brittany and to the peoples of the whole earth, of which until then we had not even heard, but of which we learned the name of the race when we saw them for the first time. They, who had come to know the character of this man, flocked to him from all the earth to Byzantium. And he, without delay, all joyous about such a situation and in the idea that it was advantageous to exhaust the wealth of the Romans and throw it to the barbarians or to the waves of the sea, ever sent back each one of them with rich gifts.[257]

Justinian financed Antes and Gepids on the Danube, Kutrigurs and Utigurs north of the Black Sea, Sabir Huns in the Caucasus. Not one of them was a reliable ally. In Asia and Africa, the Lazians, Saracens then Moors were temporary allies on the borders on condition that he paid them. The great game was to play one against another.

In 528, Justinian showered Boa, Queen of the Sabirs, with gifts, silver dishes and a great many gold coins. In exchange, she massacred other Huns who were allied with the Persians and sent to Justinian one of their Kings, Glom, whom she had taken prisoner.[258]

Procopius was not convinced by this generous strategy: '[The leaders of the Huns] after receiving the money, sent several of their lieutenants and their troops with orders to attack the Emperor's country by surprise, so that they too could sell peace to him who wanted to buy it in such a crazy way.'[259] In 551, according to the same author, Justinian cleverly used the Utigurs against the Kutrigurs who were pillaging Moesia and Thrace. He wrote them a letter reproaching them for their inactivity and asking them to attack the Kutrigurs who had remained in the country. In addition, a large sum of money stimulated the martial ardour of Sandil and his Utigurs who, aided by the Tetrix Goths, massacred a Kutrigur horde on the River Tanais, (the present-day Don Delta) taking women and children into slavery. Agathias told a similar story.

After the invasion of 559, Justinian created a deadly quarrel between Kutrigurs and Utigurs Huns by paying the former the latter's annual subsidy. The Utigurs launched a war that led to their mutual extermination

---

257 Procopius, *Anecdota*, XIX, 13–15.
258 John Malalas, *Chrgr.*, XVIII, 13.
259 Procopius, *Anecdota*, VIII, 5 (large sums); XI, 5–6 (border insecurity).

a few years later.[260] Financing a proxy war against a western enemy was also a strategy, and Maurice gave 50,000 gold coins to the Franks to fight the Lombards. John of Biclaro dated this transaction to 584. Gregory of Tours specified that Childebert II invaded Italy at that time, but dated the Imperial gift to the previous year. However, Childebert returned without fighting after the Lombards made him a better proposal and swore allegiance but they were dissuaded from attacking Rome. When Maurice asked for his money back Childebert did not even reply. Subsequently he honoured his commitments in 588 and 590, but his the armies he sent were destroyed by the Lombards or by disease.[261] Taking advantage of the Frankish attack of 588, the Romano-Byzantines were able to regain some lands from the Lombards.[262]

Peace with Persia was always gained by giving gold. So, a good tax minister was the best strategist for the Empire. By the 630s a general paymaster such as Theodore Trithyrios the Sakellarios was also a field army general. It is worthwhile remembering that previously Narses the Eunuch had held this position and had proved worthy of it. However, the subsidy strategy could not be maintained because of the loss of the rich provinces of Egypt and Syria which fell into the hands of the Arabs between 636 and 646, which was the strongest blow to the Empire since the fall of the West. This led to a huge drop in the state's income; a drop which modern historians estimate at 65 percent. This territorial withdrawal gave the Arabs the geographical, financial and human means to expand into the Mediterranean, which ceased to be an Imperial lake.

---

260   Agathias, *Hist.*, V, 24, 1–7; 25, 1–5.
261   Gregory of Tours, *HF*, IX, 25 (588); X, 3 (590).
262   John of Biclaro, *Chr. VT*, 83 (dated this episode to 587, unlike Gregory of Tours).

9

Preparing for a Campaign

> The general who fails to supply his army with the necessary food and with all other necessities prepares his own defeat, even in the absence of the enemy.
> Maurice, *Strategikon*, VIII, 2, 19

Byzantium's Army like its Roman predecessor was the most logistically capable of its time. It mastered great distances and huge quantities of supply. Nevertheless, logistics were under severe strain, as the Empire had simultaneously to feed distant fronts from Libya to Mesopotamia and Italy, while maintaining a guard on the Danube. How could Byzantium do that?

Troop Mobilisation

A horseman gallops towards the ramparts of the city. His garment indicates a letter from the Emperor. The soldiers on guard see it coming with suspicious eyes. Usually, the troops wintered in cities where they remained relatively idle until they were mobilised for a campaign. As the roads were sodden in the spring, the beginning of summer marked the return to military activity. The *Strategikon* recommended going to war when the wheat was ripe, to ensure the feeding of the troops.[1] This was also the period where enemy was expected to attack. Narses the Eunuch wintered in Rome from in 553/554, but in the spring he had to face the Franks allied to the Ostrogoths. He took some measures:

> At the beginning of the summer, the troops were reformed, and all the units were assembled in Rome, according to the orders they had received. Narses commanded them to train more for war: he strengthened their ardour with daily exercises, forcing them to run,

---

1 Maurice, *Strategikon*, VIII, 1, 30.

to make cavalry charges in ranks, to twirl like in a warrior dance, to be often deafened by the trumpet that accompanies the cry of war, so that a winter in inactivity did not make them completely forget the war and that they then show softness in the fight itself.[2]

More or less same scenario occurred on the Danube border in mid-spring 593. When Masters of the Soldiers Priscus and Gentzon met at Heracleia (in the eastern part of present-day Bulgaria). After seven days, they reviewed the allies, counted the army, distributed the annual pay and broke camp ready to fight.[3] When a major siege was expected to be opened, siege machines were built beforehand, as was the case in 555, during the Lazic War. Generals Martin and Bouzes prepared mantlets and mangonels in the plain of Archeopolis before laying siege to Onoguris.[4]

Operations moving armies by sea required more logistics because it was necessary to gather a large number of ships, provide sails and spare ropes, and food for both the soldiers and the sailors. During the reign of Justinian, two expeditionary forces were sent to Africa by sea: the first led by Belisarius in 533 and the second by John Troglita in 546. The immediate problem posed by the first expedition was money. The Praetorian Prefect John of Cappadocia acting as minister of finance frankly opposed the project on the grounds that it would lead to excessive taxation.[5] There remained the question of supplying weapons. Corippus pointed out the matter when describing the expeditionary force of John Troglita: 'On the orders of the Emperor, the ships are filled with soldiers, and after purchasing weapons at the same time, young, inexperienced soldiers are sent to learn fighting under the auspices of a great commander.'[6] Inherited from the later Roman Empire, there still was a network of *fabricae* (workshops) – no less than 15 are listed in the *Notitia Dignitatum* in the East.[7] John Malalas cited the role of the Edessa workshop, mainly in arming the units responsible for fighting the Persians. The Arab conquest in 630s caused the loss of a number of these weapons factories – those of *Nicomedia*, Edessa, Damascus and Antioch. Left were those located at Sardis, Nicomedia, Adrianople, Marcianopolis, Naissus and Thessaloniki and maybe at Caesarea of Cappadocia.[8]

---

2   Agathias, *Hist.*, II, 1, 1–2.
3   Theophylact Simocatta, *HU*, VI, 6, 3–4.
4   Agathias, *Hist.*, III, 5, 9.
5   Procopius, *BV*, III, 10, 3.
6   Corippus, *Joh*, I, v. 125–127.
7   S. James, 'The *Fabricae*: State Arms Factories of the Later Roman Empire' in J. C. Coulston, *Military Equipment and the Identity of Roman Soldiers. Proceedings of the Fourth Roman Military Equipment Conference*, BAR International Series, 394, (Oxford: BAR, 1988), p.265, n. 99.
8   *Notitia Dignitatum*, OR.XI.20 (Damascus); 21 (Antiochia); 23 (Edessa); 27 (Nicomedia). John Malalas, *Chrgr.*, XII, 38 (Diocletian built three unlocated arms factories for the army, arms factories in Edessa for local use, and arms factories at Damascus); J. F. Haldon, 'The Army and Military Logistics' in I. P. Stephenson

Table 13 - *Fabricae* in Eastern Empire according to the *Notitia Dignitatum* (*c.* 400)

Province	Production	City
Orient	*Scutaria et armorum* – shields and weapons	Damascus
	Scutaria et armorum	Antioch
	Clibanaria – armour	Antioch
	Scutaria et armamentaria – shields and other military equipment	Edessa
	Hastaria – spears	Irenopolitana of Cilicia
Pontica	*Clibanaria*	Caesarea of Cappadocia
	Scutaria et armorum	Nicomedia
	Clibanaria	Nicomedia
Asia	*Scutaria et armorum*	Sardis of Lydia
Thrace	*Scutaria et armorum*	Hadrianopolis
	Scutaria et armorum	Marcianopolis
Illyricum	-	Thessaloniki
	-	Naissus
	-	Ratiara
	Scutaria	Horreum Margi

Huge Armies or Small Expeditionary Forces?

The defence of the city of Byzantium relied on a constantly changing force according to the strategic circumstances. In 479, in order to prevent Theodoric the Amal from invading Byzantium, the *tēs Thrakēs stratēgos* (general of Thrace) mustered 2,000 cavalry and 10,000 infantry to which were added 6,000 cavalry and 20,000 infantry, undoubtedly coming from the master of the soldiers present. The total amounting to a very substantial force of 38,000 men.[9] Eighty years later, in March 559, 7,000 Huns Kutrigurs crossed the Danube and reached the gates of Byzantium. The only forces available to fight them were *scholae* from Imperial Guard, armed senators, 300 elite infantry, peasants mustered by Belisarius and an unarmed mob.[10] Should we see in this motley mobilisation the consequence of a regular army and population decimated by the so-called Justinianic plague 20 years before? It appears fairly unlikely. Byzantium's Army was

---

(ed.), *The Byzantine World* (London: Routledge, 2010), p.53.

9   Malchus, *Fragm.*, 18, 2.

10 Agathias, *Hist.*, V, 12, 6 (7,000 Hun horsemen in Chersonese); 15, 2–6 (*Scholae Palatinae*); 16, 2 (300 elite infantrymen and a mob); 3 (numerous peasants). John Malalas, *Chrgr.*, XVIII, 129 (*scholae, protectores, arithmoi*, whole Senate). Theophanes Confessor, *Chrgr.*, AM 6051, 233 (only source with Malalas quoting *arithmoi* and senators).

then overstretched and laid bare the Balkans by maintaining garrisons in Africa, Italy and Lazica. Whatever the efforts of historians to understand and enumerate these pandemic losses, they only produce guesses from opposing maximalist and minimalist approaches. The maximalist approach originates from Procopius who asserted the plague had cataclysmically killed half of population which had survived the earthquakes and wars. For Byzantium itself, he wrote that the plague lasted four months killing 5,000, then 10,000 and more per day. This estimate would reach more 600,000 dead a notoriously exaggerated figure although Procopius was a generally reliable source on military numbers.[11] Plague certainly played some role – as it did later during the Hundred Years' War between the English and the French – without stopping the conflict. A lack of troops occurred again in 626 when the Avars and Sklavenes besieged Byzantium while the field army was fighting the Persians. Overstretching of manpower and resources was the main strategic problem of Romano-Byzantine Empire.

The Balkan area was regularly under attack but never raised huge armies. The number of soldiers in Illyricum in 499 and 548 was strikingly similar, amounting to 15,000.[12] The same remark could be said for the master of the soldiers to the Thraces. In order to push back the Avars in 586 from an area corresponding roughly to current eastern Bulgaria, Comentiolus the Thracian led a 10,000-man force including 4,000 considered unfit for campaigning because of a lack of fighting spirit, probably border guards, and these the latter were left garrisoning Anchialos. The rest was divided into three 2,000 man mobile forces under the command of Castus, Martin and Comentiolus himself. Meanwhile the bulk of Imperial field forces were fighting the Persians.[13]

In the Near East, where the recruitment pool was more important, field armies were substantial. It was a constant of the Roman-Persian wars to put large armies in the field. The largest force raised in the sixth century would be that which the generals of Anastasius I led against the Persians in 503 – 52,000 men according to Joshua the Stylite. This field army was divided into 12,000 men for by Areobindus Master of the Soldiers to the East and 40,000 for Patricius and Hypatius the two Masters of the Soldiers Present. Count Marcellinus gave a lower strength, estimating the forces of Patricius, Hypatius and Areobindus at 15,000 men, reinforced at the end of the year by 2,000 men under Celer.[14] It was nevertheless the

---

11 Procopius, *BP*, II, 23, 2 (death toll in Byzantium); *Anecdota*, XVIII, 43 (half of survivors). C. Whately, *Procopius on Soldiers and Military Institutions in the Sixth-Century Roman Empire* (Leiden: Brill, 2021), p.208 (exhaustive study on various estimations by modern scholars).
12 Marcellinus Comes, *Chr.*, a. 499. Procopius, *BG*, VII, 29, 3 (548).
13 Theophylact Simocatta, *HU*, II, 10, 8 (10,000 including 4,000 unfit due to lack of fighting). Theophanes Confessor, *Chrgr.*, AM 6079, 257 (erroneously 40,000 men garrison at Anchialos and 6,000 field army).
14 Joshua the Stylite, *Chr.*, 54. Marcellinus Comes, *Chr.*, a. 503. G. Greatrex, *Rome and Persia at War*, p.96.

largest mobilisation against the Persians, according to Procopius, who wrote in the 540s-550s, an opinion of course qualified by subsequent events.[15] In 531, the army Belisarius led into battle in Callinicum was only 20,000-strong but fortunately it was only a part of Imperial forces involved in this Persian conflict. Its almost complete destruction was not a strong enough blow to lose the war.[16] Twelve years later, Martin was in charge of a nearly 30,000-strong expeditionary force in Persarmenia and which was slaughtered at Anglon. This serious setback did not effect the defence of eastern provinces.[17] During the Lazic War, in 555, Martin, Bouzes, and Rusticus led some 50,000 men to take the stronghold of Onoguris but were beaten, with no consequence on the broadly favourable strategic outcome of the war.[18] All indicating that Byzantium could withstand considerable military losses.

Later it is more difficult to assess strengths. In 580, when Maurice passed from the rank of Count of *Excubitores* to that of Master of the Soldiers to the East, he was followed by *Excubitores* as well as soldiers from the city of Byzantium, where he recruited many Iberians (Georgians) and Syrians. The raising of his army seemed to have more to do with individual units than with the mobilisation of regular units.[19] It was probably a mixture of volunteers drawn from the elite troops, adventurers hired for the campaign and requisitioned local units. Interfering in a Persian civil war, in 600 Maurice raised a 40,000 strong army, 'with all the war materials and a lot of money' in order to help Khosrow II. The Persian war of 602–628 undoubtedly involved significant numbers. The victory of Niketas the son of Gregory over the Persians in an unlocated battle (Caesarea of Palestine?) in 612 caused losses across both sides of around 20,000.[20] The last large Romano-Byzantine Army in the East was in *c.* 636, when Baanes and Theodore Trithyrios the Sakellarios mustered a field army of 40,000 men, a figure including Bedouin allies. Sebeos and Michael the Syrian gave a 70,000 men strength. According to Tabari, this field army sent from Byzantium reached 50,000 men, divided into marching detachments of 10,000 to 20,000 men. According to him, they were joined by 200,000 men, commanded by the 'King of Rum' Heraclius. According to al-Baladhuri, the Arabs of Syria under the command of Jabalah ibn al-Ayham were only the army's vanguard. He counted 200,000 Greeks, Syrians, Armenians and Mesopotamians. The estimate of the *Chronicle of 1234* went up to 300,000, typical of the epic inflation characterising medieval sources![21] These

---

15 Procopius, *BP*, I, 8, 4.
16 Procopius, *BP*, I, 18, 5.
17 Procopius, *BP*, II, 24, 16.
18 Agathias, *Hist.*, III, 7, 8.
19 John of Ephesus, *HE*, VI, 14 (*excubitores*, soldiers from Constantinople, Iberians and Syrians); 26 (*excubitores*).
20 Agapius of Hierapolis, *Kitāb al-ʿunwān* (1912), p.444 (Maurice army to help Khosrow), 450 (20,000 killed).
21 Nikephoros of Constantinople, *Brev.*, 20 (Theodore Trithyrios as '*stratēgos of*

exaggerated military estimates were far from those of Procopius, a more rigorous historian and a realistic staff officer.

On the African and Italian fronts, the strengths of expeditionary forces were much smaller. Nonetheless Gregorios, cousin of the Armenian Prince Artabanes the Arsacid, was impressed by the field army sent to Africa by 533:

> When Belisarius came there, he had a considerable army and great wealth which the Emperor had provided him; he had in his entourage a large number of military leaders and advisers, he had with him a fleet larger than any we had ever heard of, a strong cavalry, weapons, in short, the whole war apparatus worthy of the Roman Empire.[22]

The strength was as follows: 15,000 men – including 5,000 cavalry – 400 Heruls, 600 Huns, 2,000 naval oarsmen-marines from Byzantium, 30,000 Egyptian, Ionian and Cilician sailors, plus numerous of Belisarius' bodyguards.[23] All this made an approximate total of perhaps 53,000 men, including the *bucellarii*, servants at arms and family members. Elsewhere in his account, Procopius wrote that marauding army servants and even slaves were killed by Libyan peasants.[24] Naval strength excluded, the land forces were only 16,000 plus Belisarius' *bucellarii*. In 540, in Italy, this personal guard was estimated at 7,000 cavalry.[25] Troops committed to Ostrogothic Italy came from Belisarius' Army in Africa and from Illyricum. In 535, the Master of the Soldiers to Illyricum Mundo attacked Dalmatia with an unknown strength corps while Belisarius landed in Sicily with 4,000 'enlisted' soldiers *ek katalogôn* (regular troops) and *foederati*, 3,000 Isaurians, 200 Huns and 300 Moors, plus his *bucellarii*, described as 'numerous and renowned'.[26] Belisarius's invading force probably amounted to as many as 14,500 soldiers.

Anatolia'). Theophanes Confessor, *Chrgr.*, AM 6125, 337 and 6126, 338 (Baanes and Theodore the Sakellarios; 40,000 men in the army for the year of this battle and the previous year), Eutychius of Alexandria, *Annales*, 278–279 (Jabalah; 70,000-strong army), Sebeos, *Hist.*, 42 (unnamed and trusted eunuchs). Tabari, *Tarikh*, IV, 29, t. 3 (1958), p.349 (an initial 50,000-strong force upgraded to 200,000. Al-Baladhuri, *Kitab*, II, 10 (1916), p.207 (leader chosen by the Emperor; 200,000 men). Michael the Syrian, *HU*, XI, 6, t. 2 (1963), pp.420–421 (2nd battle; Baanes, the Sakellarios and the son of Shahrbaraz; 70,000 strong army). *Chr. 1234*, t. 1 (1937), pp.195–196 (three leaders with 300,000 men). W. E. Kaegi, *Byzantium and Early Islamic Conquests* (Cambridge: Cambridge University Press, 1992), p.35 (realistic estimate at 40,000).

22 Procopius, *BV*, IV, 27, 12.
23 Procopius, *BV*, III, 11, 2–19.
24 Procopius, *BV*, III, 23, 3.
25 Procopius, *BG*, VII, 1, 20.
26 Procopius, *BG*, V, 5, 2 (Mundo, regular soldiers mentioned as ἐκ καταλόγων, foederati); 3 (officers); 4 (Huns and Moors, bodyguards).

Table 14 - Structure of the Expeditionary corps in Italy in 535 (ranks in italics are probable)

Officers	Units	Strengths
Commander in chief Belisarius	11	14,500 men
	Including	
'Brigadier generals' *moirarchs*, *chiliarchs* or dukes Constantine (Thracian) Bessas (Thracian) Peranios (Iberian from Caucasus)	regular soldiers and *foederati*	4,000
Ennes (Isaurian?)	Isaurians	3,000
Cavalry unit commanders *tagmatarchs*, counts or tribunes Valentin (Illyrician?) Magnus (Illyrician?) Innocent (Illyrician?)	3 regular plus *foederati* units	500-600 per unit?
Infantry unit commanders *Tagmatarchs*, counts or tribunes Herodian (Greek?) Paul (Illyrician?) Demetrios (Greek?) Ursicinus (Illyrician?)	4 regular plus *foederati* units	500-600 per unit?
Mercenaries' commanders Uldach (Hun)? (Moor)?	2 units Huns Moors	200 300
Private Military Company. Bodyguards of Belisarius		
Commander?	*Bucellarii*	7,000?

By the beginning of 537, the expeditionary force in Italy can be only be estimated, including 5,000 men in Rome, 300 in Naples plus appreciable but unknown strengths in Cumae, Narni, Spoleto and Perugia. Losses are unknown but reinforcements were needed; but these arrived in dribs and drabs. In May 537 around 1,600 Hun, Sklavene and Ante horsemen commanded by Martin and Vitalian arrived. In summer of the same year a large force came from Byzantium to Naples: 3,000 Isaurians under Paul and Conon, 800 Thracian cavalrymen with John the nephew of Vitalian, 1,000 horsemen commanded by Alexander, Marcentius and others. The following year, Narses the Eunuch and Justin Master of the Soldiers to Illyricum came along with 5,000 soldiers and 2,000 Heruls. Later Procopius estimated all of these reinforcements at 10,000 men by adding Narses' *bucellarii* that

PREPARING FOR A CAMPAIGN

he had mentioned.[27] They probably exceeded the troops Belisarius had dispersed in garrisons.[28] This imbalance led to a command crisis between the weakened Belisarius and the too-strong Narses the Eunuch unwilling to follow orders, and Belisarius had to leave. Despite the fact that the so-called Justinianic plague had been decimating the Empire's population since 541, two years later Martin the Master of the Soldiers to the East was put in charge of a 30,000-strong force to attack the fringes of Persarmenia. He therefore had more troops than for the secondary front that Italy was.[29] It must be considered that in 543 nearly 60,000 soldiers and mercenaries were campaigning, stretched over a distance of 3,000 kilometres from Persia to Italy. But the situation of military personnel in wartime is always a volatile notion.

In 545, when he returned to Italy Belisarius had a weaker personal retinue. Therefore, he recruited new volunteers from Thrace by spending his own money. With the help of Vitalius, Master of the Soldiers to Illyricum, partly in charge in Italy, he could muster 4,000 soldiers at Salona in Dalmatia before moving to Ravenna.[30] Although an unspecified number of soldiers from Illyricum were already in Italy, Belisarius semi-failure during his second Italian campaign was due to the lack of troops hampered by having to garrison the main cities. In addition, he found in Italy a deteriorating army strength, as large numbers of the soldiers, long unpaid, had gone over to the enemy.

In 546–547, John Troglita had to fight a new Moorish uprising in Africa. Antalas' messengers tried to impress on John Troglita that his troops were few in number.[31] Needless to say, that troops fighting with Troglita were not available to wage war against the Goths Italy. Despite his urgent requests, Belisarius received reinforcements belatedly and piece by piece. By late 547, senior officers such as Pacurios, Peranios and Sergios came to Italy with only few men, Verus with only 300 Heruls, Varazes with 800 Armenians and Valerian the *stratēgos* of Armenia with more than 1,000 men but including his own personal guard. Valerian did not arrive with the others, because he was unwilling to travel during the winter solstice period of around 21 December, not because of the poor sea conditions but for a lack of supply. Probably in May or June 548, Justinian assigned 2,000 infantrymen to Otranto.

Belisarius found these reinforcements insufficient and he sent his wife Antonina to Byzantium begging more troops from her close friend the

---

27 Procopius, *BG*, V, 14, 1 (300 elite soldiers in Naples under Herodian); 2 (garrison in Cumae); 17, 3 (important garrisons at Perugia, Spoleto); 8 (Narni); 22, 17 (5,000-strong Rome garrison); 27, 1 (Martin and Vitalian); VI, 5, 1 (Paul, Conon, John, Alexander, Marcentius and unnamed others); 13, 17 (Narses); 18, 6, 10,000 including Narses' *bucellarii*).
28 Procopius, *BG*, VI, 9 (Belisarius' troops dispersed).
29 Procopius, *BP*, II, 24, 16.
30 Procopius, *BG*, VII, 12, 10.
31 Corippus, *Joh*, I, v. 483.

Empress Theodora. Unfortunately, the latter died of illness in late June 548. Belisarius himself then had an escort of 900 men, a strength very far from the previous 7,000 *bucellarii* he mustered during his previous Italian campaign.[32] He was therefore now leading a poor man's war in Italy because the Emperor sent few reinforcements, fearing a renewed offensive from the Persians and probably eager to humiliate Belisarius. Troglita's victory perhaps unblocked the manpower crisis in Italy although there were other fronts to deal with. In 548, Justinian appointed Constantian, Bouzes and Aratius to command some 10,000 horsemen reinforced by 1,500, probably mounted, Heruls under Philemuth's command. This 11,500-strong force was raised to fight the Gepids in Dacia and the Heruls disloyal to the Empire.[33] In 550, Justinian I sent Dagisthaeus with 7,000 soldiers and 1,000 Tzani to help Gubazes II against the Persians.[34] Narses the Eunuch was now the commander-in-chief to Italy and Dalmatia Two years later, the Emperor gave him what he had refused to Belisarius, a large sum of money to raise a large army and to solve the arrears of military pay.[35] His army is partially known through the Battle of Taginae and must have had more than 15,000 men.[36] By 554, to fight the Battle of the Volturnus, or Casilinum, Narses had 18,000;[37] his losses had not been replaced because the Lazic War was consuming large numbers of men, e.g. the 50,000 soldiers led by Martin in 555 to besiege the Persian fort of Onoguris.[38]

Sixth-century field armies numbered from 10,000 to 52,000 men, with an average of around 15,000–20,000. By the late ninth century, an average-sized Byzantine Army ranged from 5,000 to 12,000 and the Empire was then half its previous size.[39] These numbers seem very small compared to the geographical area they had to control. But Procopius's or Agathias's strength estimations included only fighting troops, never servants and army followers. These non-combatant personnel at least doubled the overall number. A 20,000 strong expeditionary force was therefore a roughly 40,000 body. If these numbers seem weak, they must be multiplied by 40 to put them in relation to present-day demography and, thus, they appear to be a lot less low.

---

32 Procopius, *BG*, VII, 10, 1–2 (no personal guard; young Thracians; Vitalius and Illyrian soldiers in Italy); 3 (4,000 men at Salona); 27, 2–3 (reinforcements late 547); 27, 13–14 (Valerian); 27, 16 (Belisarius' escort: 700 horsemen, 200 infantrymen); 30, 1 (2,000 infantrymen into Sicily); 3–4 (Antonina). A. H. M. Jones, J. R. Martindale, J. Morris, *PLRE*, 3b (1992), pp.1380–1381 (Vitalius 1).
33 Procopius, *BG*, VII, 34, 40–41.
34 Procopius, *BP*, II, 29, 10 (Dagisthaeus with 8,000 men).
35 Procopius, *BG*, VIII, 26, 5–6.
36 Procopius, *BG*, VIII, 26, 12 (Auduin with 2,000 picked Lombards); 13 (3,000 Herul horsemen; numerous Huns; Asbad with 400 Gepids; Aruth with numerous Gepids); 31, 1–7 (order of battle with 8,000 archers and 1,500 horsemen, plus elite troops, *bucellarii* and barbarians).
37 Agathias, *Hist.*, II, 4, 10.
38 Agathias, *Hist.*, III, 8, 2.
39 Leo VI the Wise, *Taktika*, XII, 24.

Sources give lower strengths data for the mid-seventh century. In 643, when at the Battle of Scultenna Rothari, King of Lombards, was against Isacius the *exarch* of Ravenna this resulted in a 'number of 8,000 men [lost] on the side of the Romans' – this exaggerated figure originates from an anonymous Lombard source used by Paul the Deacon. Historiography attributes to Isacius a more probable force of 2,000 to 4,000 men, but this is only a realistic-looking but unsourced statement.[40] Later in 663, at the Battle of Forino, Constans II had 20,000 men assembled in Naples according to Paul the Deacon.[41]

The Problem of Supply

To make war, wheat was needed first. Bread for the army was some sort of biscuit, *buccellatum*, very different from what is it understood by this term today. Procopius gave a clear definition of it:

> Bread intended to feed campaigning soldiers must be baked twice and baked with enough care to last a very long time and not spoil quickly. Cooked in this way, it necessarily loses its weight. This is why soldiers, when such distributions of bread take place, receive as their portion one-fourth more than the normal weight.[42]

The baking of this military bread was supervised by one of the higher-ranking civil servants, the praetorian prefect of the East. Preparing the campaign of 503 to free Mesopotamia from the Persians, Apion baked 630,000 wheat *modii*.[43] These nearly 4,300 tons of wheat could feed more than 165,000 men for three months or more than 80,000 people for six months, even after a 15 percent loss due to the grinding into flour.[44] Apion saw that an army of 50,000 soldiers was a 100,000 people 'mob' when servants and families are included. A sanitary crisis occurred in 533 when Belisarius's fleet was sailing to Africa. To save baking on wood, the Praetorian Prefect John had the bread heated in the Baths of Achilles in Byzantium. A fortnight after the fleet set sail, the biscuits turned to rotten flour. Five hundred soldiers died

---

40 *Origo Gentis Langobardorum*, 6 (*a parte Romanorum octo milia numerus*). Paul the Deacon, *HL*, IV, 45 (8,000 'Romans' killed) M. Caprioli, '… *a parte Romanonum octo milia numerus*. Considerazioni sulla batalla dello Scultenna (643) e sull'esercito esarcale (VI-VIII secolo)', *Nueva Antologia Militare*, 3, fasc. 9, *Storia Militare Medievale* (2022), pp.7–19.
41 Paul the Deacon, *HL*, V, 10.
42 Procopius, *BV*, III, 13, 15.
43 Joshua the Stylite, *Chron.*, 54.
44 A different view, which estimates the daily ration at 1.3kg of wheat for an infantryman, in J. F. Haldon, *Warfare, State and Society in the Byzantine world, 565–1204* (London: UCL Press, Warfare and History, 2003, pp.288–292.

and many more fell ill.⁴⁵ Probably after this unfortunate accident, the Code of Justinian commanded: 'For baking biscuits, it is appropriate that they be prepared by very zealous soldiers.'⁴⁶ The Imperial state thus provided for the soldiers just as it did for the towns and the needy.

The Roman or proto-Byzantine state was a welfare one. The free distribution *annona* continued in Constantinople and in Rome, where it was continued by the Ostrogoths. Three of Justinian's *Novellae Constitutiones* show the existence of public granaries under control of provincial *praetors* responsible for supplying the chief towns, and indeed all the cities. From the late third century to the age of Justinian, who sought to reduce this advantage, a major city like Alexandria received 2,000,000 *modii* of wheat. In the early seventh century, during a food shortage, the town of Thessaloniki was granted 60,000 *modii* as a first help. In a near contemporary case Ravenna received 50,000 *modii* from the Sicilian lands alone as collected taxes. These examples show that Roman logistics tradition persisted throughout seventh century and that army could still rely on a solid civilian administrative network. However, after the loss of Egypt, the Empire's main bread basket which supplied the state with 24,000,000 *modii* of wheat a year this had become impossible. After a new famine in *c.* 680 Thessaloniki received only little aid and sought for supplies from its own region.⁴⁷ The still existing *cursus publicus*, public post, had its own horses, mules, oxen and carriages to supply the army.⁴⁸ It also had camels until Justinian abolished their use, according to the ever-catty Procopius:

> From ancient times, the state also used to maintain a great number of camels, which the Roman Army as it moved against an enemy in order to carry all the provisions. And, in those days neither the farmers were compelled to provide transportation nor did the soldiers lack of everything; but Justinian as well nearly suppressed all of the camels. Nowadays, when a Roman Army fights the enemy, no necessary measures can be taken.⁴⁹

Sixth-century Egyptian *papyri* reveal both army and church were requisitioning camels from villages, e.g. Nessana, which had to deliver 30 camels and 30 dromedaries. Pack animals were similarly requisitioned as it is revealed by an incomplete inventory from the 560s–580s.⁵⁰ Horsemen were recommended by *Strategikon* and *De velitatione* to carry three or four

---

45 Procopius, *BV*, III, 13, 20.
46 *CJ*, XII, 38, 2.
47 J. Durliat, *De la ville antique*, p.265 (Egypt), 426 (granaries), 481 (Ravenna, Thessaloniki), 483 (supply difficulties, *c.* 680).
48 J. F. Haldon, 'The Army and Military Logistics', p.51.
49 Procopius, *Anecdota*, XXX, 15–16.
50 C. J. Kraemer, *Excavations at Nessana, III, Non-literary papyri* (Princeton NJ: Princeton University Press, 1958), PP.34 (REQUISITION); 35 (INVENTORY).

days' supply of food in a bag.⁵¹ Huge amounts of wheat or biscuits were to follow a field army on pack animals and in waggons. When Maurice, then Master of the Soldiers to the East, was preparing the invasion of Babylonia in summer 581, he gathered a supply fleet filled with wheat at Circesium on the Euphrates. A Persian diversionary attack in Upper Mesopotamia forced him to abandon his project and he had to burn his fleet.⁵² As the soldiers were not exclusively corn and biscuit-eaters the army was probably followed by cattle to provide some fresh meat. Neither should we expect that the army was strict teetotal, and wine carts must have supplied them. However, once these supplies and reserves were exhausted, the army had to live of the country. When the Byzantine fleet landed in Africa in 533, although supplied by the Ostrogoths in Sicily Belisarius had little food left. He thus defined his main campaign goals: firstly, building a fortified camp at the landing point and secondly, defeating the enemy to ensure subsistence, since as he said: 'If we act ourselves bravely, we shall not lack for food, for those who prevail over their enemy also seize all the enemy's goods.'⁵³

Logistics in enemy land simply consisted of winning to eat. But, to reconcile the Romanised populations of Africa, Belisarius prohibited looting and requisitioned Vandal state property. To feed themselves in Carthage the soldiers bought what they needed in the city market without clashes with the natives.⁵⁴

Defending Imperial territory posed comparable problems. The military had to control the terrain and therefore the harvests by the summer time while winter was a period of rest in forts and cities. During the reign of Justinian, Belisarius' *bucellarii* spent the winter 540/541 in Cilicia, a rearward region spared by the Persians but close enough to the threatened eastern border provinces.⁵⁵ During the winter of 588/589, General Priscus took up residence in Byzantium, while his Balkan Army was dispersed across the villages of Thrace.⁵⁶ This shows the absence of a chain of well-supplied fortresses and poses the thorny problem of the cohabitation of the military with its civilian hosts. According to the laws from later Roman Empire it could be an opportunity for abuse. It could hardly be different in the late sixth century; marauding still existed and in 533 troops operating across Emilia plundered methodically:

> At first, they acted in a thoughtful and orderly manner: when they were going to plunder an enemy village or city, they went there in regular formation, and made their attacks in moderation. Their retreats were not in disorder, but in good order, with the rearguard

---

51 J. F. Haldon, *Warfare, State and Society*, p.283.
52 Theophylact Simocatta, *HU*, III, 17, 10.
53 Procopius, *BV*, III, 15, 30.
54 Procopius, *BV*, III, 21, 9 (Carthage).
55 Procopius, *Anecdota*, III, 5.
56 Theophylact Simocatta, *HU*, VI, 6, 1.

remaining in the required place, the troop corps was well organised in a rectangle, the booty kept in the middle, so that it was well protected.[57]

Even before wheat, water is crucial to the survival of both humans and animals. Usually, water courses and wells were provided on the route of march, without having to seek it out oneself, except for individual gourds. Drinking water was a problem for both a long-distance fleet and an army operating in desert terrain. The issue of fodder was another vital issue for the army's animals. Maurice noted that during the months of July, August and September the grass was dry and that nomadic 'cavalry peoples' could not stay in the same place for long.[58] A logistical disaster occurred when water and/or food supplies were lacking. The North African campaign of 546 combined all these problems: water scarcity and therefore grassland, and the cyclical problem of agricultural depletion of the provinces after permanent wars since 533. The army did not know how to operate in the desert of Libya, because John Troglita had not prepared an adequate supply chain.

Logistics is ever superior to strategy. Hunger, lack of water, drought, all caused losses among the army's horses and pack animals, pushing soldiers to maraud and causing many desertions.[59] The desert's victory over classical armies was not only through Byzantine incompetence: Alexander the Great through Gedrosia in 324 BCE, and Emperor Julian in Persia in 363, also experienced such disastrous retreats across the burning sand, as did Bonaparte far later during his ill-fated expedition to Acre.

The Army on the March

Mules, donkeys, hinnies bending under their packs, carts and waggons follow jolting along the stony paths. The clattering army extends as far as the eye can see, signalling its march with a continual cloud of dust. The baggage train was a frequent term used in the *Strategikon* and according to Simocatta 'what the Romans call *touldos* in their native language.'[60] Literary sources deal only exceptionally with the issue of the baggage train. The only known example is the army of the master of the soldiers to Illyricum Aristus who set out to fight the Bulgars in 499 with 15,000 men followed by, '520 chariots loaded with weapons needed to fight': one waggon for every 29 men.[61] The *Strategikon* ideally recommended one light cart per infantry decarchy, loaded with tools and weapons: a hand mill, axe, adze,

---

57 Agathias, *Hist.*, I, 14, 2.
58 Maurice, *Strategikon*, X, 4, 36–39.
59 Corippus, *Joh*, VI, v. 350–360; v. 375–380.
60 Theophylact Simocatta, *HU*, II, 3, 9.
61 Marcellinus Comes, *Chr.*, a. 499.

saw, hatchets, two picks, a hammer, two shovels, a basket, blanket, scythe, leaded darts, caltrops linked by a cord. Like Vegetius he also recommended waggons with ballistae, a packhorse per *logarchy* (line of 16-18 men), 10 to 20 waggons per *arithmos* to carry flour, arrows and spare bows.[62] These recommendations gave some 1,200 to 1,500 waggons for a 10,000-strong army, 1,700 to 2,000 packs animals to the least.

The Roman Imperial Army knew the ratio of one servant to one fighter.[63] According to Procopius, each soldier had an *oiketēs* (servant) or a *therapaina* (governess), *omoskēnoi* (tent companions) and *omotrapezoi* (table companions) whom the soldiers preferred to keep safe with their prisoners and their wealth.[64] This proportion at least doubled the number of those drawing rations. The *Strategikon* gave for every group of three or four common soldiers one paid servant or paid slave plus a pack animal to carry coats of mail and a tent. As he considered the baggage train to be a tactical burden, before a battle, servants, remount horses and soldier' families had to be left behind in the camp. Unnecessary baggage and extra horses were preferably relegated to a fortress 30 to 50 miles (the Roman mile was 1.48km) to the rear and protected by one or two *banda*, with a line of messengers connecting to the fighting force. On the march, the baggage train was placed in the centre and the soldiers were to be march lightly encumbered.[65] One servant for three for four men plus families for mature soldiers could represent 5,000 more people in a 10,000 army. The pack animals, spare horses could be also number thousands.

The marching speed depended on the terrain, climate, composition and security of the troops. The army left its camp at first light.[66] Procopius measured distances in miles only in his work *On Buildings*, but in his *History of the Wars* he only used *stadions* and days of walking, sometimes specifying 'for a good walker'. According to him, seven *stadions* were equal to one Roman mile unlike Pliny the Elder or Strabo who gave the equivalence of eight to one. Procopius estimated a day's march as 210 *stadions* (30 Roman miles, 40km) the distance between Athens and Megara. In fact, the length

---

62 Maurice, *Strategikon*, XII B, 6, 3 (one chariot per *decarchy*); 5–8 (stuff); 8–10 (*ballistae*); 10–11 (*logarchy*); 16–18 (10 to 20 carts).
63 Ph. Richardot, *La fin de l'Armée Romaine*, p.241.
64 Procopius, *BV*, IV, 4, 8 (comrade, ὁμόσκηνος; commensal, ὁμοτράπεζος); *BG*, V, 25, 3 (servant, οἰκέτης, housekeeper θεράπαινα).
65 Maurice, *Strategikon*, I, 2, 59 (axes and scythes); 60–61 (Avar tent); 62–72 (servants); 72–74 (pack animals) 83–85 (spare weapons); V, 1, 1–20 (servants and baggage train away from the battle); 2, 1–11 (spare horses); 3, 1–15 (removal of non-essential baggage train and guard by two *banda*); 5, 1–5 (central position in march); XII B, 6, 1 (one cart per *decarchy*).
66 Theophylact Simocatta, *HU*, VI, 4, 12 (τοῦλδος). Maurice, *Strategikon*, P, 61, 80, 82, 86, 210; I, 2, 69; 3, 39; 5, 22; 8, 7; III, P, 15; 7, 9, 8, 23; IV, 3, 95; 5, 5; V, P, 2, 5. 7; 1, 2, 3, 5; 3, 1, 6, 13, 14; 4, 2; 5, 1, 3, 5; VI, L, A, 14, 2; B, 7, 11; 9, 8, 11; 11, 50; 17, 43, 44; IX, 2, 63; 3, 54; 4, 19, 24, 26, 32; 5, 38; XI, 1, 19, 28; 2, 46, 85; 4, 184, 197; XII, P, 35; B, P, 25; 7, 9; 17, 6; 18, 1, 13; 20, 6, 18, 108; 21. 23, 51; 22, 99, 125.

of the *stadion* was approximate and variable.⁶⁷ Procopius estimated as 90 days of walking along the coast the distance between Gadeira (today Cadiz) in Spain and the extreme limit of Tripolitania. A 75-day trip separated the Pillars of Hercules (modern Gibraltar) to the Ionian Gulf and 120 days the time to walk from Cyrenaica to Epidamnos (Durrës in Albania).⁶⁸

The average speed of march of an army during the Vandal War was 80 *stadions* per day – 14.5km. This was less than Vegetius expected to be covered by an army in a day, 20,000 Roman paces or 29km during summer time and up to 35km when using a 'quick march'.⁶⁹ The explanation is that the army stopped in the middle of the day as Belisarius careful to fortify his camps, and was not keen on forced marches. Stages were even shorter when Solomon led the army in the Aures Mountains, only 50 *stadions*, or 9km, per day.⁷⁰

Simocatta sometimes evaluated the distances by the number of staging camps. In spring 593, Priscus's army had 4 camps from Heracleia to Drizipera (today Marmaraereğlisi on the Sea of Marmara and Büyükkarıştıran in Turkey respectively), then 20 camps to Dorostolon (current Silistra, Bulgaria) on the Lower Danube. As 466 kilometres lay between the latter cities this was a speed of 23km per day. In 595, 15 camps were necessary for Priscus moving from Astikē to Novae on the Danube (today Svishtov in Bulgaria), a distance by road of nearly 255km, with the Balkan Mountains to be crossed en route. It gives a speed of roughly 17km a day.⁷¹ Operational speed was not an advantage of the Romano-Byzantine armies but of the semi-nomadic peoples.

In rough terrain, pioneers endeavoured to prepare the path for baggage train. During his Libyan War between 546 and 547 John Troglita ordered the pioneers to 'flatten the paths in the usual way', according to Corippus who gave no further detail about this.⁷² Crossing the Danube was another logistical problem, the *Strategikon*'s advice to solve this and similar was:

> It is necessary to carry materials to build bridges, if possible, pontoon bridges. In this way you can easily cross the many rivers of their country. Build it in the Scythian way, some erecting the structure, others laying down the planks. You will also need to have bags made of ox or goat skins to make rafts and to help soldiers swim across rivers during surprise attacks against the enemy during the summer.⁷³

---

67   Procopius, *BV*, I, 1, 17 (a day's journey is worth 210 *stadions*). D. Feissel, 'Les itinéraires de Procope et la métrologie de l'antiquité tardive', *AnTard*, 10 (2002), pp.383–400.
68   Procopius, *BV*, I, 1, 14–16.
69   Procopius, *BV*, III, 17, 7. Vegetius, *DRM*, I, 9, 3.
70   Procopius, *BV*, IV, 13, 32–33.
71   Theophylact Simocatta, *HU*, VI, 6, 5 (*Drizipera* to *Heracleia*); VII, 7, 3 (Thracian Plain to Novae).
72   Corippus, *Joh*, II, v. 192.
73   Maurice, *Strategikon*, XI, 4, 75–81.

Some tactical precautions had to be taken as a marching army was in situation of weakness, too stretched tout to be easily commanded and with its flanks vulnerable to an ambush. Moreover, when on the march, soldiers put their coats of mail on the pack mule and bow strings were, for the most part, removed. Neglecting reconnaissance exposed the army to some unpleasant surprises leading the incautious to be crow food. According to the *Strategikon*, the baggage train had to be put behind the infantry, a full bowshot distant. Each waggon had its rear part covered by heavy cloth as a rampart in order to allow drivers to use javelins, slings, metal darts or arrows. *ballistophoroi* that Vegetius called *carroballistae* (catapult-carrying waggons), were to be distributed along the flanks.[74] There are no indications to prove that these sound measures were actually put into use.

Romano-Byzantine generals were mostly aware of the danger when their army was on the march. When Belisarius marched on Carthage, he kept his right flank protected by the sea and his left by Hun horsemen scouting 20 *stadions*, or 3.6km, away. At the same distance before him was a vanguard of 300 elite cavalry. So, he was protected from both a flank and a frontal attack from the Vandals.[75] During the 557 Misimian campaign, an elite reconnaissance force was formed with 40 officers. When ambushed by around 600 barbarians, these officers, experienced officers that they were, took position on a hill, launching counterattacks and earning the necessary time for the army to come in their rescue. Only 40 Misimians escaped alive.[76]

The war against the Moors was essentially a war of ambushes. John Troglita ordered his troops before leaving camp to: 'keep your post, be vigilant: in this way you will defeat the enemy. Let each tribune leave the camp according to his order, meanwhile scouts should search for suspicious valleys and provide easy paths. The whole army will be safe and sound thanks to these precautions: the enemy never surprises the careful ones.'[77] Notwithstanding this order, Troglita's cavalry could not protect themselves from surprise attacks: 'The men have no time to throw their arrows and their javelins. Only the sword can be used in combat to repel the enemy, men can barely avoid injury with their shields.'[78]

The Slavic peoples were the other ambush experts. As a consequence, it was dangerous to cross the Danube and to set up camps in wooded areas, and a campaign had preferably to be waged in winter when no foliage could hide this insidious enemy. A 2,000 cavalrymen *moira* reconnaissance was a strong enough vanguard to be sent ahead the marching army. Even a return movement through an already travelled pass could be perilous

---

74 Vegetius, *DRM*, II, 25. Maurice, *Strategikon*, XII, 18, 9–11 (βαλλιατροφόρος, plural βαλλιατροφόροι).
75 Procopius, *BV*, III, 17, 1–2.
76 Agathias, *Hist.*, IV, 16, 5–7.
77 Corippus, *Joh*, I, v. 569–573.
78 Corippus, *Joh*, II, v. 227–229.

and reconnaissance was always required. Unnecessary cumbersome pack animals were to be avoided. Leaving behind some troops to watch the return path along the Danube was offering an easy prey to the Slavs. Only *dromones* were recommended for such a mission.[79]

The Staging Camp

The Roman tradition was to strengthen the camp and the art of castrametation was one of the three causes of Roman military success according to Vegetius. Camps were set up for just a night during the march or for a longer period during a siege. The *Peri Strategikes* of the mid-sixth century was undoubtedly written by a retired engineer officer. The book is fond of the classic entrenched camp of square or rectangular shape, dug as soon as the troops had pitched their tents and eaten. It also advised surrounding the camp by a wall in the Roman fashion, with the infantry placed on the sides of the camp and the cavalry in the centre.[80] The *Strategikon* proposed a square camp surrounded by an earth embankment, surrounded by traps and a ditch. With one gate on each side, the cross-shaped intersection of two roads divided the interior of the camp. All four entrances were protected by a gamma bend, giving the camp a swastika-like appearance.[81] These two camp models seem highly theoretical and have never been confirmed by archaeology for the Byzantine period. The *Strategikon* insisted that the staging camp when close to the enemy had to be fortified and stocked with provisions.[82] Camps were probably fortified but according to local conditions.

When Belisarius landed in Africa at Caput Vada on 30 August 533, he had protective ditches dug while the general staff and the standards were positioned on a sand dune near a river. Digging ditches is customary in the presence of the enemy. When the John the nephew of Vitalian landed at Ostia in 537, the Isaurian auxiliaries before nightfall dug a ditch, regularly guarded, to protect the port and the waggons. In 547, after disembarking on the beaches of Libya, John Troglita surrounded his camp with cut reeds.[83] When geography permitted, the field army camped around large farms or in cities. During a campaign of pacification in Anatolia against the Tzani in 558, the expeditionary force did not encamp in the nearby town of Theodoreias, but around the place called Rhizaion, probably a large farm

---

79   Maurice, *Strategikon*, XI, 2, 112–118.
80   *Peri Strategikes*, 29, 1–7.
81   Maurice, *Strategikon*, XII, C.
82   Maurice, *Strategikon*, V, 4, 1–16 (staging camp).
83   Vegetius, *DRM*, I, 1. Procopius, *BV*, III, 14, 32. Corippus, II, v. 270 and v. 383–385 (ditch). Procopius, *BG*, VI, 7, 2 (John nephew of Vitalian). Corippus, *Joh*, VII, v. 66; VIII, v. 44 and v. 120 (John Troglita).

PREPARING FOR A CAMPAIGN

with a rampart. This place was dominated by a woody hill from where the Tzani launched a massive attack resulting in a confused battle.[84]

When operating in Slavic countries, it was better to avoid woods or their proximity in building a camp, making the infantry sleep inside the camp and the cavalry outside, with a vigilant circuit of sentries.[85] At Yarmuk in 636, according to Tabari, the Imperial Army crossed the ditch of its own camp to confront the Muslims; nevertheless, once beaten they could not find refuge there. True or false, this version of the battle shows that in the Arab imagination the Byzantines entrenched their camps. In 708 Justinian II's army was massacred by the Bulgars for having ignored any precautions by camping near the walls of Anchialos and going out foraging without protection.[86]

To save the effort of digging, the Romano-Byzantine Army used the waggon circle defence that had allowed the Goths to win the Battle of Adrianople in 378. Its barbarian name was the *carrago* that Ammianus claimed came from the Goths while Vegetius, Claudian, St Jerome of Stridon and the *Historia Augusta* referred it to as barbarian without any specific ethnic group.[87] Unknown in Germania before later Roman Empire, the circle of waggons certainly originated from Steppe nomads. In 537, John the nephew of Vitalian marching to Rome from Calabria with a train of waggons could line up in *karakômatos schema* (circle of waggons formation) when attacked. The *Strategikon* viewed the *karagos* as a standard procedure. Two centuries later, Leo VI the Wise using this term declared that a camp surrounded by ditch and caltrops with an inner palisade was as safe as a waggon circle.[88] The army slept in tents. For Belisarius' personal use a rectangular linen tent was erected, called a *papyleôn*, the Greek form of the Latin *papilio*. Avar-inspired round tents like yurts appear to have been in use in the late sixth century.[89] According to the *Peri Strategikes* men from the same file should be sheltered in one or two tents, so that they might get to know each other and forge bonds of comradeship. Food had to be placed in the centre of the tent and the weapons next to the soldiers. By night a sentry was to guard each tent to face unexpected enemy attack

---

84 Agathias, *Hist.*, V, 1, 4.
85 Maurice, *Strategikon*, XI, 4.
86 Theophanes Confessor, *Chrgr.*, AM 6200, 376. Nikephoros of Constantinople, *Brev.*, 43, 1–10.
87 Ammianus Marcellinus, *RG*, XXXI, 7, 7 (*carrago*). Vegetius, *DRM*, III, 10. A. Chauvot, 'Figure du cercle et représentation des Goths chez Ammien Marcellin', *Ktèma*, 35 (2010), pp.231–241.
88 Procopius, *BG*, VI, 5, 3 (χαρακώματος σχῆμα). Maurice, *Strategikon*, XII, B, 7, 10; 18, 2; 22, 99 and 122; 23, 4; C, 2 and Leo VI the Wise, *Taktika*, XI, 35 and 39 (moated camp as sure as aligned waggons); XIV, 73 and 77 (καραγός).
89 Procopius, *BV*, II, 21, 3 (παπυλιών). Corippus, *Joh*, II, v. 272–273 (linen tents). Maurice, *Strategikon*, I, 2, 60–61 (Avar-style tents).

and also prevent theft.⁹⁰ Corippus gave a vivid description of camp life as he experienced it:

> The brave Roman Army, once the camp was established, then went about various occupations. Some people put the long weapons back in their place, check the quivers and tighten the bows, some put up sails raised by high posts. They thrust spears in lines into soft meadows, tilted shields against javelins across the plains as usual, placed heavy breastplates and helmets on hides beneath them, laid down slingshots and other projectiles. One party eagerly brings together the fast horses who have fought well, to bring them quality food. This one, a fine cook, flies to prepare the meal, placing the cauldrons in the flames he takes care of the food. He draws ice water from a well, prepares table beds in a circle among the herbs then arranges all the trays in their place after cleaning them with water and covering them with dishes.⁹¹

When the enemy was close, soldiers slept with their weapons, their heads on a quiver, while sentries kept watch. Raising the camp followed a specific ritual: as the general gave the order, a trumpet sounded to wake up the men, the tents were dismantled by the servants who also collected horses and lances, the units got into formation then marched out.⁹² In Africa, where the coastal population was favourable to the Byzantines, Belisarius' troops lived in the cities. In Grassē, a place not otherwise identified, the park of a royal palace sheltered the army and satisfied it with various succulent fruits. Once in Carthage, the army quartermasters housed the soldiers in private homes, a method close to the accommodation tickets of Napoleonic armies. The soldiers bought what they wanted at the town market without clashing with the inhabitants.⁹³ The other method was marauding as demonstrated in Emilia by 553:

> When they went to plunder an enemy village or town, they went in regular formation and attacked with moderation. Their retreats were not made in dispersed order, but in good order, the rearguard remaining in the required place, the main body of troops arranged in a rectangle, with the booty set aside in the middle, so that it was well protected.⁹⁴

---

90   *Peri Strategikes*, 27, 2–9 (comradeship); 23–24 (security).
91   Corippus, *Joh*, II, v. 274–287.
92   Corippus, *Joh*, I, v. 509–519 and II, v. 440–450.
93   Procopius, *BV*, III, 17, 8 (Grassē); 21, 9 (Carthage).
94   Agathias, *Hist.*, I, 14, 2.

Byzantium's armies continued to set up staging camps. Even in the late ninth century, Leo VI the Wise devoted the whole of Book IX to camps in even greater detail than Vegetius in his *De Re Militari*, insisting on the need for a camp with a ditch and four gates.

10

The Fleet Sets Sail for a Distant Shore

> In the event of a naval attack by the enemy, they would flee, because they said they were incapable of fighting both the enemy and the sea.
>
> Procopius on Belisarius' soldiers,
> *Bellum Vandalum*, III, 14, 2.

The idea of Byzantium as a thalassocracy is well established in historiography. Before the Arabs invaded the Mediterranean, sea command was still the privilege of the self-calling 'Romans'. In the sixth century Byzantium was still the only power with the capability to send armies across the Mediterranean or the Black Sea, probably the reason why Justinian sought to restore the *Mare Nostrum*. During his reign, this naval transportation power was stretched to the limit, as the Emperor tasked his army with reconquering in one generation what Rome had achieved in three centuries. However, these general observations should not mask the real difficulties faced by the Romano-Byzantine navy.

Military Geography of the Mediterranean in the Fifth to Seventh Centuries

Byzantium controlled a network of insular and coastal bases which were economically profitable and geographically widespread. One strategic constant in the Mediterranean to consider is the maxim: the sea gives wealth and the land gives power.[1] A Romano-Byzantine strategist thought

---

1   Ph. Richardot, 'Du Ve au XVIe siècle: un millénaire stratégique' in *Méditerranée, Les constantes géostratégiques*, Actes du Colloque du Groupe des Écoles du Commissariat de la Marine et Fondation Méditerranéenne pour les Études

THE FLEET SETS SAIL FOR A DISTANT SHORE

of the Mediterranean in terms of distances and seasons. In terms of distance, the Romano-Byzantine Empire no longer had the resources to control the land around the whole Mediterranean, which was occupied to the west by barbarian kingdoms. Additionally, it took a long time to move overland. According to the historian Procopius, it took 347 days to walk around the Mediterranean, 140 to travel from Byzantium to Carthage along the coast, 120 to go from Cyrene in Libya to Dyrrachium, 90 to go from Gades to Tripolitania, 75 from the Pillars of Hercules to the Adriatic, 40 along the coast of Asia Minor on the Black Sea from Chalcedon in Bithynia to Phasis in Lazica, 22 from Byzantium to the Danube Delta.[2] These approximate distances were estimated for a single man on foot – an army on the march could not achieve that pace. Translated into kilometres, the overland distances are impressive: 2,700km from Byzantium to Alexandria via Ancyra in central Anatolia. It is worthwhile to add that it is very rare to find the remains of an ancient roadway, except in very few instances.[3]

The sea thus remained the quickest way to unite two points in the Mediterranean basin. While today's engines have turned the Mediterranean Sea into a lake, in Justinian's time it was an ocean. Ancient and medieval sailors preferred coastal navigation to a straight route with no landmarks. Sailing required many halts to resupply and rest the crews. In addition, good or bad winds could speed up, or slow down, navigation, or even break up convoys. Modern calculations of crossing times based on the supposed ships' performances are too mechanical to be realistic. Ancient and medieval sources gave little indication of the crossing time. Procopius estimated a year was enough to carry a message between Carthage and Byzantium, which seems unreasonably long. It is true that John of Cappadocia wanted to dissuade Justinian from launching an expedition to Africa and had his messenger delayed.[4] In fact, in 533, Belisarius' fleet took nearly three months to sail from Byzantium to the Tunisian coast.[5] This route was the maximum range of action for the Romano-Byzantine fleet. The other major maritime route was the 1,600km between Byzantium and Alexandria in Egypt. In 602, news of Maurice's assassination by the usurper Phocas took just nine days to reach Alexandria. As the event took place on 23 November, it was during supposedly inclement weather that this news was delivered by a 'messenger.'[6] This figure suggests Imperial 'shuttles' were transmitting important news or orders. The last major sea route connected

---

    Stratégiques, Toulon, 25–26 avril 1996, (Paris: Publisud, 1997), pp.87–143.
2   Procopius, *BV*, III, 1, 9–17 (distances in walking days), III, 10, 14 (Byzantium-Carthage).
3   P. Herrmann, *Itinéraires des voies romaines de l'Antiquité au Moyen Âge* (Paris: Errances 2007), p.9.
4   Procopius, *BV*, III, 10, 14.
5   Procopius, *BV*, III, 15, 31.
6   Theophanes Confessor, *Chrgr.*, AM 6095, 291. J. H. Pryor & H. Jeffrey, *The Age of the Dromōn: The Byzantine Navy Ca 500–1204*, The Medieval Mediterranean, Peoples, Economies and Cultures 400–1500, 62, (Leiden: Brill, 2006), pp.333–334.

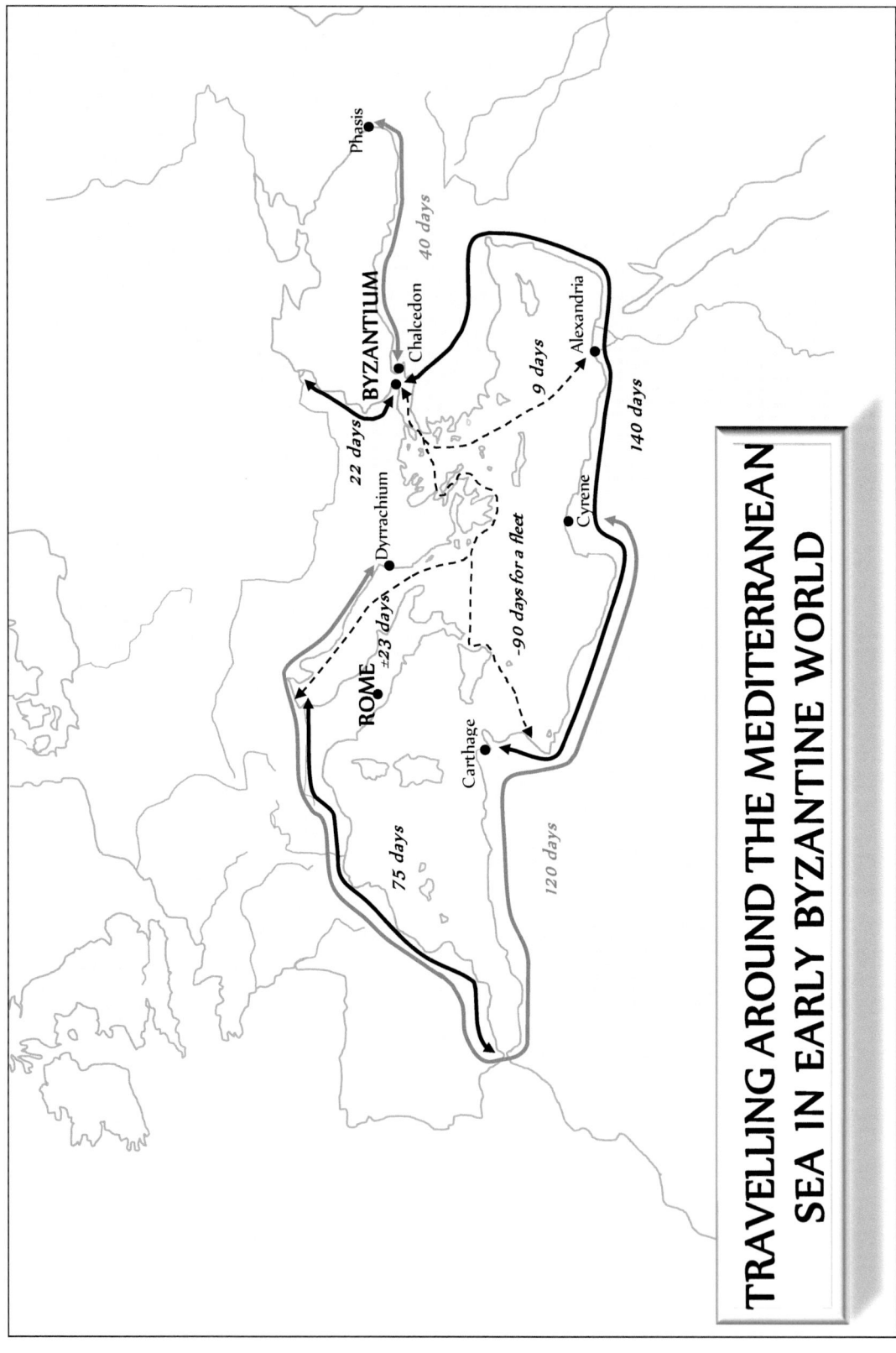

THE FLEET SETS SAIL FOR A DISTANT SHORE

Byzantium to Ravenna. As no historical examples give the duration of this journey, the best approximation was the Venice-Byzantium Sea route for later medieval and Renaissance period. Thus, in 949, the Bishop and Ambassador Liudprand of Cremona took only 23 days to sail from Venice to Constantinople reached on 17 September, which was quite fast and equivalent to what galleys did in fourteenth and fifteenth centuries.[7] Sailing has never been an exact science, especially in pre-industrial era. In 1595, Leonardo Donà another ambassador took 38 days, between 25 August and 1 October, by galley from Venice to Constantinople, or more exactly the outer port of Porto-Lagos in southern Thrace. Only 34 percent of his travel time was spent on navigation, compared to 66 percent in halts.[8] The Crusades give many examples about of sea journeys. From Barcelona or Marseille to Acre the crossing lasted between 15 and 25 days. Paradoxically, some geographically shorter journeys could also be longer: in 1126, for example, Bohemond II took a month to sail from Otranto to Antioch.[9]

The Mediterranean Sea had never been a peaceful sea; storms are relatively frequent and until the middle ages, winter was considered a period of *mare clausum* (closed sea). Until the Renaissance, winter was off-limits to ocean navigation. In 1569, Venice prohibited its ships from sailing between 15 November and 20 January. However, Procopius gives examples of sailing that took place between November and December 533. In November, Solomon was sent from Carthage to Byzantium to report on the situation in Africa. At the beginning of December, 120 ships belonging to the Vandal General Tzatzon sailed from Sardinia to what is now Eastern Algeria in two days. However, probably in late December, Boniface, secretary to the last Vandal King, was unable to leave the port of Hippo for Spain because of the winds that blew him back to the coast.[10]

In the absence of precision instruments, but guided by thousands of years of experience, sailors relied on the customary sea lanes, from port to port along the coast. According to Corippus, John Troglita's expeditionary fleet left Constantinople and, despite a storm, arrived at the same landing beach that Belisarius had 12 years earlier, Caput Vada (today Ras Kaboudia).[11] According to Procopius the beach, called 'cape of the shallows' was 'five days' march from Carthage for a good walker.'[12] This shows a good knowledge of geography and sailing.

---

7   Liutprand of Cremona, *Relatio de legatione constantinopolitana*, 1877, p. 161; D. Stockly, *Le système de l'Incanto des galées du marché de Venise (fin XIIIe-milieu XVe siècle)*, Leyden, 1995, p. 116 (galley's speed).
8   F. Fasano Guarini, 'Au XVIe siècle: comment naviguent les galères', *Annales*, 16-2 (1961), pp.279–296.
9   M. Mollat, 'Problèmes maritimes de l'histoire des croisades', *Cahiers de Civilisation Médiévale*, 10–39–40 (1967), p.351.
10 Procopius, *BV*, III, 24, 19 (Solomon); 25, 16 (Tzatzon); IV, 4, 33–37 (Boniface).
11 Corippus, *Joh*, I, v. 271–281 (storm); v. 366–374 (Caput Vada).
12 Procopius, *BV*, III, 14, 17.

Once Africa was conquered, the Byzantine navy was able to reach Visigothic Spain. Coastal Baetica in south-eastern Spain was conquered in 550–555, at a time when North Africa and Italy served as bases of departure. This radius of action was the privilege of naval power.

The Ships

The Bosphorus is spotted with large and small hulls and white sails coming back or going on from all part of the Empire. Ancient ships reached speeds of between two and eight knots, a speed comparable to that of modern sailing ships, but under oars the average for more than one day is around four knots.[13] In the late fourth century, Vegetius equated the warship term *liburna* to coming from *Liburnia*, a piratic province on Illyrian coast. The *liburna* was a half-decked bireme or trireme with a ram under its prow.[14] Over the sixth century, the word *liburna* almost disappeared being replaced with a new Greek term in official texts and among early Byzantine historians, *dromon* (literally meaning runner). Procopius is dry in his description:

> And they had also warships prepared as for fighting at sea, to the number of 92, and they were single-banked ships covered by decks, in order that the men rowing them might, if possible, not be exposed to the bolts of the enemy. Such boats are called *dromones* by those of the present time; for they are able to attain a great speed.[15]

So, it was a long, low monoreme vessel with a deck to protect the rowers from arrows.[16] The very first occurrence of the word *dromon* appears in a controversial fragment from a historical work attributed to Eunapius of Sardis (died *c.* 414), speaking about 'thirty-oared *dromades* in the form of *liburnae*'.[17] According to another classicising Greek historian, John Malalas, who wrote his *Chronographia* in the 530s, *liburna* and *dromon* are quite equivalent for 'warship'. He said that in preparing for the war against Mark Antony, and implicitly for the future battle at sea at Actium in 31 BCE,

---

13   G. Chabot, 'La vitesse des navires anciens', *Annales de Géographie*, 288 (1942), p.284 (sailing). J. H. Pryor & H. Jeffrey, *The Age of the Dromōn*, p.343 (oar-powered speed).
14   Vegetius, *DRM*, IV, 33. M. B. Charles, 'Vegetius on Liburnae: Naval Terminology in the Late Roman', *Scripta classica Israelica*, 24 (2005), pp.181–194.
15   Procopius, *BV*, III, 11, 15–16.
16   A. P. Kazhdan, 'Dromon', 1991, vol.1, p.662. J. H. Pryor & H. Jeffrey, *The Age of the Dromōn*, pp.123–127 (first mentions of the term); (technical description), δρόμων. Greek form λιβυρνος remained in Egyptian *papyri*, *P. Oxy.*, XVI, 2032, 52 and 54 (sixth century); 2042, 11 (fifth century).
17   J. H. Pryor & H. Jeffrey, *The Age of the Dromōn*, p.123, n. 2 (comment). Fragment only in J. F. Boissonade's edition of Eunapios, *Eunapii fragmenta ex Suida*, vol. 1 (1822), p.525. Not in R. C. Blockley's edition, (2009).

Octavian assembled a cavalry force and 'he also built many *dromon* ships and war *liburna*.'[18] Perhaps a *dromon* is the evolution of the previous *liburna*, however it can be said that they are two kinds of swift galley.

Two fourth-century manuscripts and one fifth-century Latin of the *Aeneid* depict ram-armed galleys with one row of oars, a latticed square sail, a raised prow and a shell stern below a half-moon roofed shelter or a curved stern above the pilot. Gunwales and rams are painted in red; some gilded flame-curved ornaments are fitted above the prow or the stern of very classic ships depicted in the fourth-century manuscript. In addition, the oarsmen's heads are visible on the half-decked boat. In the later manuscript, the oars emerge directly from the hull and rowers are unseen, suggesting a full-decked vessel. The hulls are unpainted except for a red band on the gunwales and along the row of oars, while prows bear a wolf's head turned backwards.[19] The two manuscripts perhaps show roughly the difference between classic *liburna* and the new *dromon*. According to Procopius, there were two types of sail, large ones used in light winds and small ones in good winds.[20] Corippus spoke about 'tall ships' or 'curved boats' and only mentioned a sail, which is in line with the iconography of Romano-Byzantine high sea-going ships.[21] He also praised their bronze prows and long hulls.[22] Unless there is evidence to the contrary, this classical description, which is close to the Greek trireme, seems to be an antiquarian cliché, as Corippus likes to make.

Early Byzantines fleets could be large. The retaliatory expedition against Taranto in 508, with 100 *dromones* and 8,000 soldiers, was qualified as 'piratical daring' by the Count Marcellinus.[23] Numbers of sailors or the presence of cargo vessels for supply is not specified. The hundred or so *dromones* seem to measure the strength of the Eastern Roman Empire's war fleet. This was a force 10 times smaller than the fleet destroyed by the Vandals in 468.[24] By comparison, in classical antiquity in 415, the Athenian thalassocracy was able to send 7,000 soldiers, 134 triremes with 10,000 rowers and 130 transport ships against Sicily. This comparison does not value

---

18   John Malalas, *Chrgr.*, IX, 2.
19   Vergilius Vaticanus latinus 3225 manuscript of the *Aeneid* (fourth century), *dromon* types depicted in ff. 21r, 31v, 39v. Four very classical galleys of liburnian type, with a shell stern below a half-moon shelter, with or without sails, set up in naval squadron on 42r and 47v. The same type alone at 58r: https://digi.vatlib.it/view/MSS_Vat.lat. 3225. Vergilius Vaticanus latinus 3867 manuscript of the *Aeneid* (fifth century) on folios 77r: https://digi.vatlib.it/view/MSS_Vat.lat. 3867. Virgil, *Vergilius Vaticanus facsimile edition* (Akademische Druck – u. Verlagsanstalt ADEVA, 1980).
20   Procopius, *BV*, III, 17, 5.
21   Corippus, *Joh*, I, v. 142, v. 352 and v. 162, 164.
22   Corippus, *Joh*, I, v. 168, 170.
23   Marcellinus Comes, *Chr.*, a. 508.
24   Theophanes Confessor, *Chrgr.*, AM 5961, 116 (1,100 ships). George Kedrenos, *Compendium Historiarum*, vol. 1 (1838), p.613 (1 113 ships). Theodoreus Lector, *Historia Ecclesiastica*, I, 25 (1,100 ships).

Byzantium's naval power with a very much larger empire but demonstrates a potential very similar to Athens *c.* 485, According to the Georgian chronicler Juansher, the Emperor sent 500 *dromones* to Georgia, each of which had 500 men, in order to fight King Vakhtang I Gorgasali. After a supposed Vakhtang's victory over the 'Greek' commander Polycarpos, Zeno came personally with 300 *dromones* to conclude a favourable truce with the Georgian monarch. The fleet size is possibly an epic overestimation, but it shows Byzantium was still then the unrivalled thalassocracy on the Black Sea.[25]

The 500 various ships gathered in 533 for the African expedition were mainly merchantmen with a capacity from 3,000 to 50,000 *medimnoi*.[26] The first category consisted of twenty-metre-long boats. The largest of the Byzantine ships fell into the category qualified as the smallest second-rate ship of the line by the Royal Navy in the early eighteenth century. The merchant navy was undoubtedly mobilised to afford such a heterogeneous force. Nearly 30,000 Egyptian and Ionian sailors manned these transport ships, a ratio of two sailors to one soldier. An average gives 60 sailors per ship, but it is unrealistic to assign the same crew to all boats. The Yassi Ada shipwreck, off the coast of Bodrum Turkey, gives an excellent example of a standard single mast merchantman *c.* 625. It was loaded with 9,000 *amphorae* filled with wine, olives and lentils maybe for the *annona militaris*.[27] Larger ships could have two or three masts as shown by a drawing made by a German traveller in Byzantium *c.* 1574 probably after the Arcadius column. The foremast was usually inclined forward.[28]

Ninety-two 'very fast' *dromones* were used to protect the fleet for Africa in 533. All these carried a crew of 2,000 men, rowers and soldiers, known as *auteretai*, with no superfluous personnel: these were the Marines of the time, undoubtedly the majority of Imperial Navy.[29] With a crew consisting of between 20 and 22 men, they were similar to the lighter *liburna* of the Roman fleet. In a letter dated 467, Sidonius Apollinaris used the Latin term *cursoria*, literally 'courier', to refer to the boat he took on the River Ticino

---

25 Juansher Juansheriani, *The Life of Vakhtang Gorgasali*, p.91 (500 *dromones*, Juansher used a Georgian version of this Greek term), 93 (300 *dromones*).

26 1 medimnos = 51.84 litres (1,000 litres = 1m³). The 155,520 to 2,592,000 litres capacity of these vessels can be today measured as a gross tonnage from 54.95 to 915.90 tons.

27 G. F. Bass, F. H. van Doorninck Jr., *Yassi Ada I: a Seventh-Century Byzantine Shipwreck* (College Station: Texas A & M University Press, 1982); F. H. van Doorninck Jr., 'The Seventh-Century Byzantine Ship at Yass1ada and Her Final Voyage: Present Thoughts' in D. N. Carlson, J. Leidwanger, S. M. Kampbell (eds), *Maritime Studies in the Wake of the Byzantine Shipwreck at Yassiada* (College Station: Texas A & M University Press, 2015), pp.205–216.

28 E. H. Freshfield, 'Notes on a Vellum Album Containing Some Original Sketches of Public Buildings and Monuments, drawn by a German Artist Who Visited Constantinople in 1574', *Archaeologia*, 72 (1921/1922), pp.87–104.

29 Procopius, *BV*, III, 11, 15–16 (αὐτερέται).

bound for the River Po.[30] It is not wrong to equate this riverine stagecoach with the *dromon*, as the *Strategikon* recommended this type of vessel to secure the Danube waters against the Sklavenes incursions.[31] Designed to be swift, *dromones* could only carry a small expeditionary force, such as the one Claudian, Military Governor of Salona, sent against Indulf to retake the fortress of Laureate on the Dalmatian coast in 549. This expeditionary force, defeated straight after disembarking, fled on foot, abandoning its *dromones* and other ships filled with grain and food supply, which were then sent to the Ostrogothic King Totila.[32] The seventh-century Spanish bishop described the *dromon* thus: 'The long ships that we call *dromones* are so called because they are longer than the others, which is the opposite of the *musculus* [muscle], a short ship: *dromon* comes from 'to run', as the Greeks call *dromon to* run.'[33] This short description confirms Procopius but do not add much. The question of a ram for the *dromon* is moot because no ramming was recorded in historical sources. A bronze ram could only slow down a boat nicknamed a 'racer'.

The other question is about the sail – square or lateen? Ancient ships had square sails. Nevertheless, during the Hellenistic period, it was already possible to transform the square sail into a triangular one, using actions described in a treatise attributed to Aristotle and titled *Mechanica, 851 b*; this would be the origin of lateen sailing. A fifth-century mosaic from Kelenderis (today Aydıncık, Turkey) discovered in 1986 shows a lateen rig on a single mast leaning forward. The hook topping the mast was still in use by the early middle ages and its purpose was to facilitate the mast removal. The mast itself stands on a rectangular structure identified as a combat platform, called *xylokastron* 'wooden castle', visible in other ships in graffiti dated from the sixth and seventh centuries. It was not the exclusive prerogative of warships but could also equip merchant ships for defensive purposes. The port and starboard rudders are protected by a wing.[34] In the time of the classic Roman Empire towers existed on larger *liburnae* as Vegetius still described in the late fourth century.[35] This tactical fashion did not seem to have disappeared, even if its distribution is difficult to determine and perhaps became restricted to only dedicated men-of-war. So, when Heraclius the Younger disembarked in Byzantium in October 610, his ships were said to be 'fortified', no doubt carrying defences and towers in the Roman fashion. But they also carried reliquaries and icons of the Virgin Mary on their masts.[36] This late Christian mark is a novelty. The monastic

---

30 Sidonius Appolinaris, *Ep.*, I, 5, 3.
31 Maurice, *Strategikon*, XI, 2, pp.112–118.
32 Procopius, *BG*, VII, 35, 27–30.
33 Isidore of Seville, *Etymologiae*, XIX, 19, 1, 14.
34 P. Pomey, 'À propos de la voile latine: la mosaïque de Kelenderis et les Stereometrica (II, 48–49) d'Héron d'Alexandrie', *Archeonautica*, 19 (2017), pp.9–25. Lateen sail at Kelenderis: https://www.kulturportali.gov.tr/medya/fotograf/fotodokuman/4811
35 Vegetius, *DRM*, IV.44.
36 Theophanes Confessor, *Chrgr.*, AM 6102, after George of Pisidia, *Heraclias*, II, 15.

Sixth-Century Byzantine Merchantmen

Above, two and three-masted merchantmen, from a 1574 drawing by a German visitor to Constantinople probably inspired by the Column of Arcadius.

Below, a merchantman reconstructed after this drawing, of the fifth-century mosaic from Kelenderis (today Aydıncık, Turkey) and by the Yassi Ada shipwreck.

The hooks topped masts in order was to facilitate their removal. The double stern is well attested in the drawing above and on merchant ships from the early middle ages. It is worthwhile remembering that most of sixth-century sea battles at were fought by merchantmen.

site of Kellia in Northern Egypt offers a well depicted graffito dated 600–630, it shows a lateen-rigged ship with *xylokastron*.[37]

A Paradoxical Lack of Naval Experience?

During the fifth century, after the Vandals had seized Roman Africa they launched pirate raids and even pillaged Rome. No Western Roman Navy was able to stop them and a fleet sent from Constantinople suffered a disaster at Cape Bon in 468. After mastering the Mediterranean for half a millennium, the Romans had unlearned the art of war at sea and no sea battles had happened after Actium in 31 BCE until Gallipoli in 324. Both of these were fought between Romans in a civil war. Hence the complete absence of war at sea for three centuries could have led to naval inexperience.[38]

---

37 Institute for the Study of the Ancient World, fig. 51: https://isaw.nyu.edu/research/io-figures/images/fig-51-ship-graffito-from-kellia

38 P. H. Richardot, 'La bataille antique: représentation et modèle', *Prétorien*, 9, avril-juin (2009), pp.233–236.

THE FLEET SETS SAIL FOR A DISTANT SHORE

There was no clear admiralty in the sixth century. Commands at sea were mostly given to generals or senior civilians. For instance, the large fleet sent against Taranto in 508 was commanded by Romanus Count of the *Domestici* and Rusticus Count of the *Scholarii* – basically not admirals. In 515, at the naval Battle of Bytharia, during the civil war between Anastasius I and Vitalian the Thracian, the victor was not even a professional soldier but the Praetorian Prefect Marinus of Syria. Naval warfare was not commonplace in the first third of the sixth century. As a consequence, in 533, generals and soldiers from the Army of the East, then under Belisarius's command, were greatly dismayed when they learned that Justinian wanted to send them to North Africa:

> As for the generals, as they imagined themselves, each individually, to be in charge of the expedition, they were seized with fear and dreaded the magnitude of the danger: even if they had escaped the perils of the sea, they would have to set up camp in a hostile country and use their ships as a base from which to fight a powerful and imposing Kingdom. For their part, the soldiers who had just emerged from a long and arduous war [against the Persians] and had not yet fully tasted the benefits of domestic life, were at a loss: they were being sent to take part in a battle at sea, a kind of combat they had never heard of before, and being sent from the eastern borders of the Empire to the regions of the sunset to risk their lives against Vandals and Moors![39]

This dismay could only be explained by the lack of admirals. Nevertheless, Belisarius's expedition to Africa included a fleet commander named Kalonymos of Alexandria and ranked as 'chief of the ships', who appears to be responsible only for technical advice rather than effective command.[40] Belisarius was also very worried because:

> …the soldiers, who were in mortal dread of sea-fighting and had no shame in saying beforehand that, if they should be disembarked on the land, they would try to show themselves brave men in the battle, but if hostile ships assailed them, they would turn to flight; for, they said, they were not able to contend against two enemies at once, both men and water.[41]

These quite surprising jeremiads from the generals and soldiers bear witness to the fact that, at the time, the Romano-Byzantine troops were not used to

---

39 Procopius, *BV*, III, 10, 4–5.
40 Procopius, *BV*, III, 11, 14 ('chief to the ships', *archēgos té eïs épi nausín*, ἀρχηγός τε εἷς ἐπὶ ταῖς ναυσίν).
41 Procopius, *BV*, III, 14, 2.

travelling by sea and did not have a true Imperial Navy. The fleet had to be improvised to invade Vandal Africa by all means, and the preparations took three years. Improvisation was not in itself a problem, as the great amphibious operations of history all had to resort to it, as with D-Day in 1944. The merchant navy helped to do the job, because the few naval forces of Constantinople still in existence were insufficient to carry out such a big task. Needless to say, the maritime route between Constantinople and Carthage was well-known long before the landings, and diplomatic mail between Justinian and Gelimer was only exchanged by sea.

Nevertheless, Procopius praised Belisarius' professionalism in organising the fleet, even though he had never commanded at sea:

> Belisarius bethought himself how his whole fleet should always keep together as it sailed and should anchor in the same place. For he knew that in a large fleet, and especially if rough winds should assail them, it was inevitable that many of the ships should be left behind and scattered on the open sea, and that their pilots should not know which of the ships that put to sea ahead of them it was better to follow. So, after considering the matter, he did as follow. On the sails of the three ships in which he and his immediate following were carried he painted red from the upper corner for about one-third of their length, and he erected upright poles on the prow of each, and hung lights from them, so that both by day and by night the general's ships might be distinguishable; then he commanded all the pilots to follow these ships. Thus, with the three ships leading the whole fleet not a single ship was left behind. And whenever they were about to put out from a harbour, the trumpets announced this to them.[42]

When the army was embarked on ships, giving a speech to them was impossible. The solution found by Belisarius was to summon those he called his 'companions in command' to his flagship to speak to them.[43] The fleet's route is well known. It set sail from Byzantium on the day of the summer solstice, 22 June 533. The next halt was at Perinth (called Heraclea in Procopius's time and present-day Eregli) on the European coast of the Sea of Marmara, for five days. The next step was Abydos (now Cape Nagara), which closes the Dardanelles, with four days of waiting due to lack of wind. Thanks to violent winds, the fleet doubled Cape Sigeum, leaving the Dardanelles, near Troy (today the Kumkale region in Turkey). Then, after the winds dropped further, the fleet skirted Cape Malea in the south-east of the Peloponnese; at this location the weak winds were a godsend because the ships could have been driven ashore. However, during the night, the ships became entangled. Captains and sailors managed to separate them

---

42   Procopius, *BV*, III, 13, 1–4.
43   Procopius, *BV*, III, 18, 1.

THE FLEET SETS SAIL FOR A DISTANT SHORE

by pushing them apart using oars, with great 'know-how' according to Procopius although it was that of the merchant navy.[44] The fleet rounded Cape Matapan in the south of the Peloponnese and went 5km further to the town of Kainoupolis. It remained there for an unspecified time, before proceeding to the port of Methoni, 20km from Cape Akritas in the southwest of Greece, where Valerian and Martin's advance ships were waiting. Belisarius landed the army and gave it various tasks.

From Methoni, the fleet sailed to the island of Zacynthos to stock up on sufficient water to cross the Adriatic. It took 15 days to reach Sicily because the wind was weak and consequently the water supplies were exhausted. The fleet anchored near Mount Etna and then reached Kaukana (modern-day Porto Langobardo) 200 *stadions* from Syracuse according to Procopius, a great underestimate since in reality the distance was 80km. This was foreign territory, where the fleet could find supplies according to the agreement between Justinian and Amalasuintha, Regent of the Ostrogothic Kingdom of Italy. At this point in the journey, Belisarius still did not know where he was going to land in Africa, probably more out of ignorance of the position of the Vandals than actual geographic ignorance. Thanks to the servant of a Greek merchant from Syracuse found by Procopius, Belisarius was informed of the military situation in Africa and the landing points made possible by the wind.

When the trumpets sounded, the sails were hoisted and the fleet sailed. Having reached the islands of Gaulos (Gozo) and Melitē (Malta), the fleet was pushed by a strong wind towards the African coast. A day later, it arrived at Caput Vada (now Ras Kaboudia in central Tunisia). It was a sandy beach ideal for a strategic surprise landing, and from here it took a good walker just five days to get north to Carthage.[45] However, the absence of a port on this coast and the risk of a storm or an attack on the fleet at anchor prompted Belisarius to disembark immediately. In the end, it had taken more than two months to make the journey.[46] This rather long period of time is explained by the random pattern of winds and the need to frequently feed and get water for 45,000 men and probably 20,000 horses and mules. The fleet had to put into land six times.

The difficulties identified for Belisarius' expedition are not specific to Byzantium; they are found much more acutely in 1249 in the Egyptian crusade of Louis IX. The ship leaving Marseille, which the chronicler Jean de Joinville took, got lost off the Barbary Coast. For two to three days, it went in circles. Having reached Cyprus, the Frankish fleet set sail for Egypt, but the wind only allowed 700 of the 2,800 knights to disembark, as the other ships were scattered and took a long time to return. The French King waited two or three weeks for his brother, the Count of Poitiers, to return. During this interval, the wind turned into a storm and Joinville counted

---

44 Procopius, BV, III, 13, 7.
45 Procopius, *BV*, III, 14, 1–17.
46 Procopius, *BV*, III, 15, 31.

104 vessels 'big and small' that sank with their crews off the harbour of Damiette.[47] The concern of Belisarius' army was therefore understandable since the Mediterranean always presented the same pitfalls. The Gothic War illustrates several disasters due to bad winter weather. In 543, an attempt to supply Rome by sea failed off Naples because of a storm that drove the Imperial ships onto the coast where the Ostrogoths captured them. Five years later, another storm dispersed the relief fleet sent to reinforce Rossano, which was besieged by the Goths. In 550 the fleet led by Artabanes the Arsacid never reached Sicily because winds ran it aground against the Calabrian coast where the Ostrogoths seized the ships while others were sunk or dispersed.[48] Despite a millenary tradition of seafaring, the Mediterranean Sea remained perilous for the transfer of armies and pilotage remained uncertain as the *Odyssey* of Ulysses tells us. It was a permanent factor in ancient and medieval warfare.

Landing in Byzantium in October 610 saw unquestionable logistical mastery but regular sea lanes with Carthage had existed for almost a century. Heraclius the Younger, after some staging in Sicily and in different islands, sailed with the Army of Africa and Mauretania, joined by his cousin Niketas, who came from Alexandria with a large infantry force. The rendezvous was probably at Thessaloniki. Heraclius entered the Sea of Marmara and took Abydos receiving there many allegiances from dignitaries. His next target was Byzantium. He won a short naval encounter with Phocas's fleet near the Kontoskalion, also called the Harbour of Julian/Sophia located in the south-eastern part of the city. Probably the same day and without any further opposition, he landed north at a circular fort near the Hebdomon, a suburb of Byzantium 11km from the city centre. Phocas was killed soon after.[49] This was the first warning of a Byzantine weakness at sea in the face of an organised fleet. Another warning of Byzantium's relative naval fragility came in 624, when the Persians, now masters of Phoenicia, seized Rhodes and several islands in the Aegean Sea without difficulty.[50] However, it has would not be a lasting occupation, as Heraclius reconquered Phoenician ports from the Persians. When the Muslims seized the ports of Syria, Phoenicia Libanensis, Palestine and Egypt, Byzantium's naval control was once again challenged. In 647, Muawiya assembled 1,700

---

47   Jean de Joinville, *Vie de Saint Louis*, 128 (temporarily lost); 147 (Cyprus); 182 (Damietta).
48   Procopius, *BG*, VII, 7, 5–7 (Naples); 30, 10 (Rossano); 40, 14–17 (Artabanes).
49   Theophanes Confessor, *Chrgr.*, AM 6102, 298–299 (4 October, Niketas, Abydos, Long Walls deserted, battle at the Harbour of Sophia). *Chr. Paschale*, a. 610 (3 October, circular fort near the Hebdomon). John of Nikiu, *Chr.*, 109 (1883), p.431 (Heraclius the younger sent to the city of Byzantium with ships and a large force of barbarians; islands and various stations; joined by members of members the Green Faction) 110, 1 (1883), p.432 (no battle at sea but an engagement on the seashore, where the men of the Imperial chariots slew Bonosus, supporter of Phocas). John of Antioch, *Fragm.*, 218.
50   Agapius of Hierapolis, *Kitāb al-ʿunwān* (1912) p.451.

ships to invade Cyprus and the Byzantines were powerless to stop him.[51] Byzantium had now, and for a long time to come, a Muslim rival at sea.

Logistical Coastal Shipping and The Tactic of the Short Hop

The fleet runs along the coast where one can see the army moving in a cloud of dust. Once on the African coast at Caput Vada, Belisarius went along the coast with the bulk of the army and ordered the faster fleet to wait for him south of Carthage at 150 stadions, 27km.

The fleet knew nothing of what happened to the army, and despite the insistence of the Patrician Archelaos, prefect of the army who remained with the fleet, the sailors utterly refused to carry out the orders of Belisarius. The logic of land operations is not that of naval operations. The sailors feared, with some reason, the Kypriana, a storm that regularly occurred in the Carthage region at on 16 September, the feast of St Cyprian. Consequently, they anchored in one of the harbours of Carthage, the Stagnon, at a distance of 40 *stadions*, 7km.[52] Luckily, the rather negligent Vandals did not attack them at anchor. Belisarius did much the same two years later, during the conquest of Sicily, the fleet and his army progressed along the coast more or less together, the masts of the ships even being even used as shooting points from the walls of Palermo. The manoeuvre was repeated the following year, during the move from Reggio to Naples. Belisarius set up his camp near the city held by the enemy but boldly established the fleet in the port of Naples out of range of missiles from the city.[53]

During the initial phases of overseas operations, Belisarius was thus in the habit of not separating the fleet and the army as they progressed together along the shore. Subsequently, the sea played a major role in supplying the field army. In 539 his supplies were transported by sea to Ancona from the cereal regions of Sicily and Calabria. During the rest of the campaign, control of the sea allowed him to blockade Ravenna, the Ostrogothic capital.[54] Coastal shipping had its risks, since in stormy weather ships were driven ashore and, above all, the enemy was always watching. In 543, on its way from Sicily, a large convoy of supplies for Rome was intercepted near Naples by an Ostrogothic squadron of fast ships. Poorly guarded, all the transport ships were captured and many men were killed, although Demetrios, an infantry general, escaped with a few men on a small ship. At the beginning of 546, an episode took place which cannot be described

---

51 Theophanes Confessor, *Chrgr.*, AM 6140, 344. Michael the Syrian, *HU*, XI, 10, t. 2 (1963), p.441.
52 Procopius, *BV*, III, I, 15, 10 (fleet knew nothing); 12–15 (Archealos; Kypriana).
53 Procopius, *BV*, III, 17, 5 (fleet and army); *BG*, V, 5 13–16 (Palermo); 8, 4–6 (Reggio-Naples).
54 Procopius, *BG*, VI, 24, 14 (sea supply); 28, 6 (naval blockade).

as a sea battle. Pope Vigilius sent another supply fleet from Sicily to Rome. Spies informed Totila who hid troops at Portus Romanus where the fleet was captured at the docks without resistance.[55]

Cabotage jump tactic was perfectly suited to a coastline lined with islands, which is the case in Croatia, where there are nearly 1,200 islands and islets lining 1,100km of coastline. In 536, Constantian Master of the Soldiers to Illyricum invaded Dalmatia by sea, unlike his predecessor Mundo the previous year. His army numbered tens of thousands of men, according to the Ostrogoth spies. Its maritime route ran from Epidamnos to Epidaurus, from Durrës in Albania to Ragusa Vecchia or Cavtat, a small port south of Dubrovnik. Then, he approached the island of Lysina (Lesina in Italian or Hvar) in Croatia, from where he launched a reconnaissance towards Salona. He landed near this city and tasked a troop of 500 men with seizing a defile commanding the western access to the city, which was invested shortly after.[56] This amphibious progression is a model of prudence and know-how.

Fighting at Sea

Enemy sails billow across the blue horizon. The alert signal passes from ship to ship. Enemy in sight! The fear of the generals and soldiers before the African campaign of 533 can be explained by the memory of the defeat at Cape Bon in 468. The Vandals had set fire to the Imperial fleet at anchor. The lesson was learned: to protect itself Belisarius' fleet anchored at Caput Vada, the *dromones* formed a circular barrier, while five archers remained on each ship at night.[57] Tactics on the high seas underwent a transformation compared with antiquity. The Greek trier or the Roman liburna were ultimately missiles propelled by oars. Their ram broke the enemy's oars and then pierced the hull. The *dromon* now bluntly rammed their opponents or fought by throwing missiles before boarding. But then the Byzantine navy was characterised by a special weapon.

The biggest sea battle took place in 515 at Sykai in the part of the Bosphorus called Bytharia or Bytharion. It did not oppose two regular navies, as the rebel Vitalian filled all the ships he could with Hun, Goth and Scythian mercenaries. The prefect Marinus of Syria gathered a large force of ships, including military *dromones*. Nevertheless, his victory was due to the use of what historiographical tradition had remembered under the medieval name of 'Greek fire'. John Malalas attributed its invention to the philosopher Proklos of Athens called to help by Anastasius I:

---

55 Procopius, *BG*, V, VII, 6, 24–26 (Naples); 15, 9–14 (Portus).
56 Procopius, *BG*, V, 7, 28–35.
57 Procopius, *BV*, III, 15, 36.

THE FLEET SETS SAIL FOR A DISTANT SHORE

> And the philosopher ordered that a large amount of what is known as elemental sulphur be brought in and that it be ground into fine powder. And he gave it to Marinus saying this: 'Wherever you throw some of this, be at a building or a ship, after sunrise, the building or ship will immediately ignite and be destroyed by dire."

Marinus distributed these incendiary weapons

> ...among all the *dromones* and telling to the soldiers and sailors: 'It is not necessary to use weapons but to throw this on the ships which will come against you and they will burn. And if we reach the houses on the other side where the enemies of the Emperor are, throw it on them."[58]

Part of Vitalian's fleet was set on fire, while the rest was put to flight. Sulphur seems to burn as soon as the containers break. A highly volatile material, finely divided sulphur ignites when ground with silver oxide or oxidising substances, and reacts in the same way with moist sodium chlorite. It even becomes explosive when mixed with lead chloride. These chemical combinations leave plenty of scope for incendiary weapons. But incendiary sulphur was nothing new. Military theorist Vegetius, writing in the late fourth century, mentioned its use during earlier times:

> With ballistas, flaming arrows covered with oakum, *oleum incendiarium* [incendiary oil], sulphur and bitumen, which immediately burn the planks coated with wax, pitch and naturally inflammable resin, are fired at the hulls of enemy ships.[59]

This incendiary oil is reminiscent of what came to be known as 'napalm' in the twentieth century, naphtha and palm oil. Bitumen or naphtha burns on water, making it a formidable threat to ships. Vegetius was republished in Constantinople in 450. He or someone else may have inspired Proklos of Athens in the use of sulphur. On the other hand, Evagrius Scholasticus does not mention the use of this incendiary device at Bytharia:

> When Vitalian had set up camp at Sycae, Marinus the Syrian, mentioned above, was sent by the Emperor with a fleet to fight him. The two fleets met; the first with Sycae at the stern and the other leaning against Constantinople. At first, they stood still, but after a series of insults and exchanges of draft weapons between the two troops, a bitter battle at sea was fought near the place called

---

58 John Malalas, *Chrgr.*, XVI, 16.
59 Vegetius, *DRM*, IV, 44.

Bytharia. After holding out, Vitalian fled in haste, losing most of his forces, just as his partners fled so quickly that by the next day there was not an enemy left in the vicinity of Anaplus or the city.[60]

John of Antioch also failed to mention the so-called Greek fire during the same sea battle.[61] If he did so, Marinus probably equipped his men with jars filled with a sulphur-based mixture. Ships were not yet equipped with the flamethrower tubes. In fact, the great period of bronze siphon-launched Greek fire came later as Theophanes Confessor records it. The very first apparition of flamethrowers, called *siphones* (pumps), is dated from around September 671 to August 672. At this time, the Arab invasion fleet was expected while Constantine IV, 'on being informed of so great an expedition of God's enemies against Constantinople, built large biremes bearing cauldrons of fire and *dromones* equipped with siphons,' and ordered them to be stationed at the Proclianesian harbour of Caesarius.'[62] From April to September 673, the Muslim fleet laid siege to Constantinople, then withdrew for the winter of 673/674 and continued to do so for seven years. Byzantium was then saved by these flamethrowers, invented by a man whose name has been preserved: 'At that time Kallinikos, an architect from Helioupolis in Syria, took refuge with the Romans and manufactured a naval fire with which he kindled the ships of the Arabs and burnt them with their crews. In this way the Romans came back in victory and acquired the wet [Greek] fire.'[63] *Siphones* were also successfully used against Saracens vessels during the siege of Byzantium in 717–718.[64] So, no Greek fire for Justinianic fleet!

If the Vandals no longer had any fleet capable of opposing Belisarius, it was not the case with the Ostrogoths of Italy, who had inherited the remains of the Roman fleet at Ravenna. On the behalf of King Theodoric the Great, his chancellor Cassiodorus drew up precise orders for maintaining a fleet of *dromones* dated to 507–511. In a charter from Ravenna dated to 539, their sailors were called *dromonarii*.[65] The Romano-Byzantines fought three battles at sea against the Ostrogoths. The first was at Salona in 536, opposing warships or merchant ships filled with warriors, while this city was blockaded by sea by the Goths. The Romano-Byzantines put the enemy

---

60   Evagrius Scholasticus, *HE*, III, 43.
61   John of Antioch, *Fragm.*, 214.
62   Theophanes Confessor, *Chrgr.*, AM 6164, 353.
63   Theophanes Confessor, Chrgr., AM 6165, 354 (sea fire, *pyr thalassion*, πῦρ θαλάσσιον; wet fire, *pyr hygron*. πῦρ ὑγρόν).
64   W. L. Rodgers, *Naval Warfare under Oars 4th to 16th Centuries* (Annapolis: Naval Institute Press, 1990), pp.36–37 (siege of 717–719). L. Casson, *Ships and Seafaring in ancient Times* (London: British Museum Press, 1994), pp.96–100. J. H. Pryor & H. Jeffrey, *The Age of the Dromōn*, pp.607–632 (sound appendix on Naval Greek fire).
65   Cassiodorus, *Variae*, II, 31; IV, 15. J. J. Pryor & H. Jeffrey, *The Age of the Dromōn*, p.124.

siege fleet to flight, capturing numerous ships without their crews.[66] The second battle at sea took place near Naples in early 543 and saw the capture of a poorly guarded supply fleet by *dromones* sent by King Totila.[67] At the beginning of 550, the latter still had 400 vessels, probably more civilian than military.[68]

The greatest sea battle of the Gothic War was Sena Gallica (today Senigallia) on the Adriatic in autumn 551. To relieve Ancona, under siege by the Ostrogoths, John the nephew of Vitalian took the initiative of embarking elite troops at Salona on 38 warships. He was joined at Scardone, Dalmatia, by 12 ships from Ravenna under the command of Vitalian the Thracian. Apparently aware of that, the Ostrogoths mobilised 47 ships under the command of Gibal and Gundulf (sometimes named Indulf). Procopius reported an improbable event before the naval encounter: the two fleets stopped, each side drew their ships close together and their admirals harangued the crews.[69] Also according to Procopius, 'The battle was very violent, like an infantry fight, because the two adversaries had drawn up their ships in a line, with their bows facing the enemy, then exchanged arrows.'[70] Although numerically overwhelmed, the Goths chiefly lost because of their very poor naval capabilities. Some of their ships isolated from the rest were attacked separately, others collided with their neighbours and clumped together, pushing each other back with their boat-hooks amid shouts and bickering:[71]

> On the contrary, Romans were skilled in both fighting and handling their ships, orienting their boats head on without never separating far from one another, without never crowding together closer than was necessary, but always keeping their movements towards or from each other in good order; each time they noticed an enemy ship separated from the rest, they easily rammed and sunk it, and whenever they saw an enemy mass disordered and exhausted by the efforts of a chaotic work, they threw a rain of arrows that completely destroyed it.[72]

Gisal was captured and the Ostrogoths escaped with only 11 ships they ran aground and burnt, a disaster.[73] Apparently the so-called *dromonarii* and

---

66 Procopius, *BG*, V, 16, 16–17.
67 Procopius, *BG*, VII, 6, 24–25.
68 Procopius, *BG*, VII, 37, 5.
69 Procopius, *BG*, VIII, 23, 2 (47 Ostrogothic ships); 7 (initiative); 8 (Salona; scardone); 13–28 (exhortation to the soldiers).
70 Procopius, *BG*, VIII, 23, 30.
71 Procopius, *BG*, VIII, 23, 31–33 (inexperienced Goths in sea warfare).
72 Procopius, *BG*, VIII, 23, 34 ('Roman' art of naval warfare).
73 Procopius, *BG*, VIII, 23, 30 (order of battle); 31–33 (Barbarians inexperienced); 34 (Roman art of naval warfare); 38, 11 Ostrogothic ships in flight with Gundulph;

the fleet paid by the Ostrogothic Kings until Ravenna fell into Belisarius hands in 540 and no more existed 11 years later. Unlike the fear previously inspired by the news of the expedition to Africa by sea at Senigallia the Romano-Byzantines mastered sea warfare.

---

39 (burnt).

11

The Enemy is Spotted!

> No effort should be spared to send unceasingly vigilant reconnaissance at regular intervals, by means of spies or patrols, to obtain information on the enemy's movements, strength, organisation, and thus not be surprised by it.
>
> Maurice, *Strategikon*, VII, 3, 4–6.

Waging war requires answering three questions: 'What is the enemy's strength?' 'Where is it?' 'Where to go?' Intelligence is thus a priority for a general disinclined to move and fight like a blinded Cyclops. The early Byzantines were perfectly aware of this.

Strategic Intelligence

Most Byzantine military treatises focused only on tactical matters and were not intelligence manuals. Nevertheless, written at the time of Justinian, the *Peri Strategikes* had a whole chapter on spies who had to hide their activity behind trade and not be of the same race as the enemy or have been mistreated.[1] The *Peri Strategikes* says:

> Spies have a crucial role in providing us with intelligence about the enemy, and can be helpful in letting us know if we can have the advantage or suffer any setbacks. This information may be, for example, the preparation of a campaign against us or neighbouring peoples, or if they plan an enterprise against the enemy.[2]

In *The Secret History*, Procopius criticised the poor intelligence policy of Justinian:

---

1 *Peri Strategikes*, 42.
2 *Peri Strategikes*, 42.

And the matter of the spies is as follows. Since ancient times many men were maintained at the expense of the public treasury, to go into the enemy's country and to get into the Palace of the Persians, either on the pretext of trade or in some other way, and after making a thorough investigation of everything, they returned to the land of the Romans, where they were able to report to the authorities all the secrets of the enemy. These so warned, stood on guard, and nothing unexpected happened to them. Justinian by refusing to pay anything made even the very name of spy disappear in the land of the Romans, and as a consequence of this many mistakes were made and Lazica was captured by the enemy, the Romans having utterly failed to discover in which part of the world stood the Persian King and his army.[3]

It is not a secret to say Procopius disliked Justinian, but he probably had some reasons to accuse him of breaking the Byzantine intelligence service. Even if such a branch was recreated under the following reigns, a thirty-year noncontinuity was disastrous, especially if networks woven and renewed for centuries were torn down. Procopius declared that Kkosrow I was fully informed of what was happening in Justinian I's Court.[4] The Romano-Byzantine Empire probably had poor counterintelligence as well. Subsequently, sources and facts also show that it also had little strategic anticipation and therefore an ineffective network of spies abroad. The disaster of the Battle of Anglon in 543 began with a strategic intelligence failure. The brother of the Christian Bishop of Dubios in Persarmenia informed Valerian, General of Armenia, that King Khosrow I was facing his son's rebellion and that the Persian Army was badly weakened by a plague. On Valerian's unverified report, Justinian I foolishly ordered the Master of the Soldiers to the East Martin to invade Persarmenia.[5]

Procopius gave his own experience of wartime espionage. He makes it fully clear that intelligence on the Vandals, who the Byzantines had not fought for a long time, was weak, and even on northern Africa geography it was poor. This put Belisarius in a state of uncertainty: 'As soon as Belisarius had landed on the island [Sicily], he was irritated, for he was embarrassed. He was tormented by not knowing the kind of men the Vandals, against whom he marched, represented; their warlike abilities, the way he had to fight them and even the place from which he had to launch these attacks.'[6] A general-in-chief who was undertaking a campaign could not be more misinformed. To both questions: 'What is the strength of the enemy?' and 'Where to go?' Belisarius had no answer even a month after leaving

---

3   Procopius, *Anecdota*, XXX, 12 and 14.
4   Procopius, Anecdota, XXX, 13–14.
5   Procopius, *BP*, II, 24, 8–10.
6   Procopius, *BV*, III, 14, 1.

Byzantium. Procopius, then liaison and intelligence officer, *paredros*, was the man of the situation:

> All these reasons, which embarrassed Belisarius, prompted him to send his liaison officer Procopius to Syracuse with the mission of finding out whether the enemy was already waiting in ambush, on the island or on the mainland, for the moment of his sea crossing and where, in Libya, he could find the best anchorage for his fleet and the most advantageous base of operations for waging unceasing war against the Vandals.[7]

Procopius was sent to Syracuse under a cover activity of procuring food for the army. There he met 'a fellow citizen, a childhood friend moreover, whose maritime activities had long brought him to live in Syracuse.' As with any intelligence officer dealing with an honourable correspondent, Procopius does not reveal the name of this precious individual. He was valuable, because one of his servants had timely returned from Carthage two days before with fresh news and answers to all questions. The Vandals did not know that an army from Byzantium was coming to attack them, since their field forces had been sent to Sardinia against the rebel Governor Gôdas and the usurper Gelimer had left Carthage for Hermionē in the interior of Byzacene four days Belisarius could anchor his fleet wherever the wind took it. So a great deal of strategic information was surprisingly coming from a simple servant. Procopius brought this servant to Kaukana (present-day Caucana), where the fleet was waiting, so that he could guide the army to Libya. He justified this requisition to his friend on the pretext that the servant had to meet the general to receive a deserved reward.[8] This episode was exceptional, because ordinarily Byzantine historians did not give the source of the intelligence and preferred the anonymous, e.g.: '[Narses the Eunuch] had already been warned that Leutharis and Butilinus, as well as the armies of the Franks and the Alemanni, had crossed the Po.'[9] Merchants and travellers were common sources of information but dedicated spies could be employed. Procopius confessed that the Romans and the Persians had each other spied upon.[10] When talking about himself, he simply referred to being an 'adviser', never an intelligence officer an ungentlemanly post in every epoch.

---

7   Procopius, *BV*, III, 14, 3 (πάρεδρος).
8   Procopius, *BV*, III, 14, 5 (cover activity); 7–12 (getting information).
9   Agathias, *Hist.*, I, 11, 2.
10 Procopius, *BP*, I, 21, 11.

Tactical Reconnaissance

A group of horsemen cautiously advance on the trail that the entire army must cover one to two hours later. Its mission is to assess the position, direction and nature of the enemy, thwart its traps and obtain intelligence by capturing prisoners. Reconnaissance was called *sculca* in Latin, and according to Simocatta, to post sentinels was 'what the Romans call *sculca* in their mother tongue.'[11] Active reconnaissance demanded to risk a vanguard ahead of the army even for a combat mission. In 533, both the vanguard and left flank guard won the Battle of Dekimon in two separate engagements.[12] In 554, Narses the Eunuch detached a party of 3,000 Romano-Hunnic horsemen under the command of Artabanes the Arsacid and Uldach the Hun. Posted at the observation post offered by Pisaurum (today Pesaro) they were watching like birds of prey the crossing where the Via Flaminia passed along Mount Castigliano on a path narrowing near the Adriatic coast. Practising the best offensive reconnaissance they successfully attacked the Frankish vanguard.[13] Ignoring the principle of conducting thorough reconnaissance was to expose his army to grave perils as illustrated by a setback which occurred in 553 near Parma, where the Franks ambushed the vanguard of a Byzantine force. Fulcaris, the general of the Herul *foederati*, was responsible for this blunder. 'Driven by his foolishness, he made an attack on the city of Parma, which was already occupied by the Franks. He should have sent scouts beforehand who would have given him precise information about the enemy's intentions.'[14] A similar fate was suffered during the disastrous Battle of Anglon in 543 although spies had informed that the terrain was steep and Persians were entrenched, but honour commanded that Martin attack – and to be routed.[15]

Units specialised in reconnaissance were named *skoulkatores* (scouts).[16] This name was already present in Vegetius and the *Notitia Dignitatum*, with the *exculcatores*. The rarer form of *proculcatores* or *proskoulkatores* also existed in Ammianus Marcellinus and John Malalas. During the sixth century, Cassiodorus spoke of *sculcatorias* (naval reconnaissance craft).[17]

---

11 Theophylact Simocatta, *HU*, VI, 9, 14 (*sculca*, σκοῦλκα).
12 Procopius, *BV*, III, 17, 1 (vanguard led by John); 17, 3 (Hunnic flank guard).
13 Agathias, *Hist.*, II, 2, 4–7. F. V. Lombardi, 'Lo scontro franco-bizantino fra Pesaro nel 554 d.C. (Agatia II, 2–3)', *Studia Oliveriana*, 12 (1992), pp.55–62.
14 Agathias, *Hist.*, I, 14, 4.
15 Procopius, *BP*, II, 25, 5–34.
16 Maurice, Strategikon, P, 36; 13, 36; II, P, 15; 11, 1, 4; VII, B, 10, 6; 17, 20; IX 5, 55, 65, 66, 71; XII, D, 24.45.98 (skoulkatôr, σκουλκάτωρ).
17 Ammianus Marcellinus, *RG*, XVII, 10, 1. Vegetius, *DRM*, II, 15 and 17. *Notitia Dignitatum*, OC.V.173 = VII.20; V.75 = VII.122; V.59 = 207 (proculcatore, proskoulkatores). *Chron. Pasch.*, a. 624; a.628. John Malalas, *Chrgr.*, X, 32. John of Ephesus, *HE*, VI, 10. J. Rougé, 'Sur un mot de Cassiodore: Exculcatoriae-Sculcatoriae-Sulcatoriae', *Latomus*, 21 (1962), pp.384–390; Ph. Rance, 'Drungus, Δροῦγγος and Δρουγγιστί', p.309, n. 88; *Id.*, 'Sculca, sculcator, exculcator and

Defending the borders required patrols, observation posts and spies sent into the enemy camp. To defend Lazica in 555 General Martin placed sentries and paid informants, 'those who are paid by enemies to betray their camp and secretly transmit secret information.' Lured by fake news claiming the Persian general was dead, Martin gave up sending spies and his troops no longer monitored the approach routes. Martin paid for his neglect by a devastating Persian surprise attack.[18] When the army operated in foreign territory where roads were poorly developed, local guides had to be used. In an episode reminiscent of the colonial wars, Corippus spoke of a Moor from the Mazax tribe who helped Roman horsemen to discover the enemy camp during the 546–547 campaign in North Africa.[19] Taking prisoners was essential to gain intelligence.

Interrogating Prisoners

Interrogation relied on two modes, spontaneous confessions and torture. Both were confirmed used during the first siege of Rome by the Ostrogoths in 537–538. Two Roman civilians were paid by the Ostrogoths to give drugged wine to the soldiers guarding the rampart near the church of St Peter. One of them told Belisarius everything, the other after being tortured to make him speak was sent back to the enemy with his nose and ears slit and, famously, sitting on a donkey.[20] In most cases intelligence was obtained by capturing prisoners during patrols. During the Libyan War led by John Troglita, a cavalry tribune named Cecilidae Liberatus captured four Nasamons:

> A tribune in person disdains and ordinarily refuses to put down and slaughter men, but he would come and go on his fast horse, trying to take some alive, and, bringing a javelin back, he would continually strike large bodies on the limbs. Seizing four elite Moors from their army, he tied them up, binding their arms in intricate knots, and brought those who might report hidden information to the general, and, with their tongues, deliver secrets to him.[21]

During the same raid, he captured a leader named Varinnus grabbed him by the hair and made him fall from his horse then sat on it and tied his

---

proculcator: The Scouts of the late Roman Army and a Disputed Etymology', *Latomus*, 73 (2014), pp.474–501. Ph. Richardot, *La fin de l'Armée Romaine*, pp.84–85, 89, 93.
18 Agathias, *Hist.*, I, 19, 5 (sentries); 19, 8 (informants); 20, 2 (neglect).
19 Corippus, *Joh*, VI, v. 449–450.
20 Procopius, *BG*, VI, 9, 17–23.
21 Corippus *Joh.*, VII, v. 455–540.

hands behind his back.[22] Cecilidae Liberatus brought all of them back to John Troglita who more lectured the prisoners in a moralising way than interrogated them. Corippus the poet could not really decide whether his hero was a patent torturer and was not. Nevertheless, as a Nasamon answered Troglita insolently, all the prisoners were hanged on patibular forks.[23] The accuracy of Corippus cannot be questioned.

In 555, during the Lazic War, a Persian prisoner gave important information after being whipped by the bodyguards of Justin, the son of the Patrician Germanus.[24] Procopius, Agathias and Corippus did not take offence at this procedure which they viewed as legitimate. Belisarius did not mistreat the prisoners he interrogated and obtained all information he wanted, as with the Vandal messenger sent from Sardinia and the ambassadors returning from Visigothic Spain.[25] Deserters were another source of intelligence. Vandals told Belisarius his Hun mercenaries had been bought by Gelimer.[26] During his second Balkan campaign in 593, Priscus was able to count on a Christian Gepid who acted as his interpreter, spy and lured the Sklavenes into a trap.[27]

Enemy spies always meet with a bad end. On a mere suspicion a Carthaginian merchant was impaled, a torture that filled the army with dread.[28] Mutilation or a gruesome penalty of death was intended to deter espionage. The major difficulty of intelligence is for it to be believed by command. Rome was lost in 547 because Bessas the Military Governor did not believe prisoners who claimed that Isaurian soldiers were going to deliver the city to the Ostrogoths,[29] by the time Bessas, born *c.* 480, was probably not at his best.

---

22   Corippus *Joh.*, VII, v. 463–469.
23   Corippus *Joh.*, VII, v. 475–497 (Cecilides); v. 500–540 (prisoners interrogated then executed).
24   Agathias, *Hist.*, III, 6, 1–3.
25   Procopius, *BV*, III, 24, 1 (messenger from Sardinia); 18 (ambassadors).
26   Procopius, *BV*, IV, 1, 6.
27   Theophylact Simocatta, *HU*, VI, 15-13.
28   Procopius, *BV*, IV, 1, 8.
29   Procopius, *BG*, VII, 20, 12.

12

Catapults Versus Ramparts

> Favourable sites for the construction of a city, particularly if it is close to the border, are elevated with steep slopes that make it difficult to approach. Other favourable sites are those surrounded by a wide river or that can be made so.
>
> *Peri Strategikes*, 11, 2–8.

While the Romans were very formal and even very mechanical in their method of siege warfare, the Byzantines were more pragmatic. Negotiation, trickery and a long blockade were preferred to long, merciless labour supported by an arsenal of machines – economy took precedence over a show of force. This change in attitude can be explained by the fact that Imperial troops had to besiege Roman fortifications which offered a greater challenge than the Celtic *oppida* of Caesar's time. Most of Justinian's wars took place in former Roman provinces and Rome itself was frequently besieged. However, stone walls and high towers were not everything and the *Strategikon* claimed: 'After God, we must place our trust in our weapons and, above all, in our fortifications.'[1]

Military Architecture and Byzantium's Walls

Old Roman fortifications were still in use and new ones were being built. In the West, they were utilised from the mid-third century until *c.* 1300, and even longer for some sections of wall.[2] The same was true in the East. There were no prescriptive standard fortifications but rather a 'family air'. Small semi-circular towers protruded from ramparts; their bases were made of large stones taken from ancient temples dedicated to abandoned

---

1 Maurice, *Strategikon*, VIII, 1, 38.
2 B. S. Bachrach, 'On Roman Ramparts 300–1300' in G. Parker (ed.), *The Cambridge illustrated History of Warfare. The Triumph of the West* (Cambridge, Cambridge University Press, 1995), pp.64–91.

gods. Small stones, almost cobblestones, were piled on top, neatly arranged between thin layers of flat bricks, sometimes forming chevron patterns, all of which was pleasing to the eye and very solid. Under the reigns of Anastasius but, mainly, of Justinian I a new era of construction and renovation began. The big novelty was the alternation between solid towers and hollow towers or bastions. Bastions reveal a development in defensive artillery. All these towers and bastions were of a variety of shapes: square, rectangular and circular, horseshoe or pentagonal and rectangular. A circuit-wall could alternate one up to four different shapes.[3] In Africa, on the Byzacene border, the forts of Theveste, present-day Tebessa, Thelepte and Ammaedera were built by Solomon just after the reconquest. They had a circuit-wall with towers, and a lower outer wall with a moat in front. The space between the two walls could, in haste, accommodate a population seeking refuge. Solomon's African fortifications did not always have ditches or a rectangular shape, as evidenced by the works of Theveste (320m x 275m) and Thamugadi (111m x 68m). The corners were systematically defended by towers, including on small forts.[4] Of the new forts in Africa and the Middle the best preserved are Qsar Lemsa in north Tunisia with arrow slits, probably rebuilt on a third-century Roman fort, and Qasr Bashir in the Jordanian desert on the *Limes Arabicus* built at the beginning of the fourth century. In 556 the fortified port of Phasis was protected by a wall and a water-filled moat.[5]

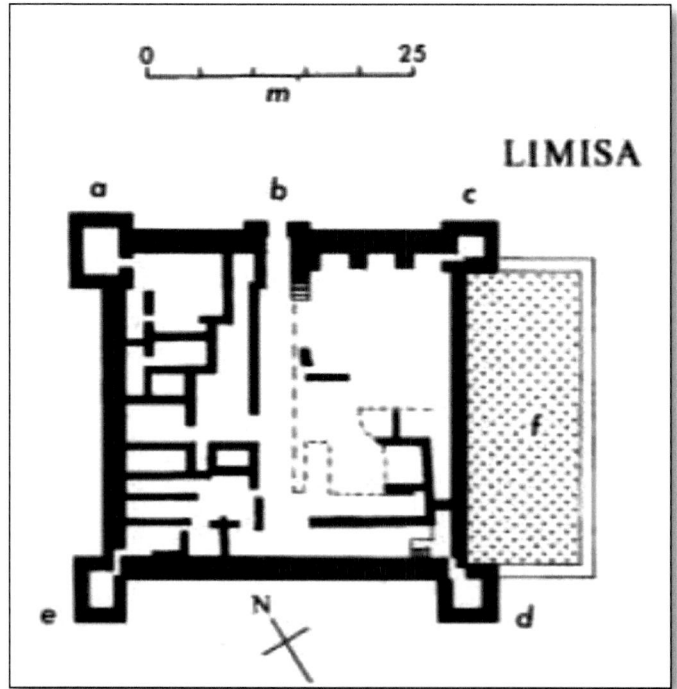

Romano-Byzantine Fort in Tunisia
(*quadriburgium* type fort, built by Solomon in the 530s)
After K. Belkhodja, 'Ksar Lemsa' in *Africa. Fouilles, monuments et collections archéologiques en Tunisie* (Tunis: Institut national d'archéologie et d'Arts, 1968), pp.313–348.

---

3   Sh. Al-Shbib, 'La défense des villes à l'époque Byzantine: alternance entre les tours et les bastions, tradition ou innovation?', *Syria*, 95 (2018), pp.413–430.
4   J. B. Bury, *A History of the Later Roman Empire*, p.149.
5   Agathias, *Hist.*, III, 21, 1–2.

Reconstruction of Ksar Lemsa in Tunisia
This *quadriburgium* type fort, built by Solomon in the 530s may have been erected over a former building. It protected the small hamlet of Limisa and watched the mountain line from where the Moors could break out to plunder the rich and Romanised Tunisian plain. After J.-Cl. Golvin https://jeanclaudegolvin.com/ksar-lemsa/

Maurice's treatise recommended that the towers should not have roofs to install artillery pieces with a curved trajectory called *mangana*, a generic term for machinery and the origin of the medieval term mangonels.[6] Cities in the Near East were rarely protected by a moat, even a dry one. Instead, they had a double enclosure: a low fore wall or *probolos* (outer wall) followed by a higher *peribolos* (circuit-wall) forming the main line of defence.[7] The *Peri Strategikes* is the only known sixth-century treatise on fortification. According to this treatise, the thickness of a rampart should not be less than 3m and the height about 12½m. It advocated hexagonal towers at the corners, with a domed roof and a circular interior. The crenulation was to be reinforced by a parapet mounted on the walkway. It was advisable to have a ditch and a front wall. The ditch had to be 25m wide to discourage mining. The excavated earth formed a terrace between the fore wall and the wall – a peripheral space for sheltering refugees without overwhelming the city.[8] Roofed stone hoardings called *ptera* (wings) were erected on Zenobia's walls:

---

6   Maurice, *Strategikon*, X, 3, 19–22 (*manganon*, μάγγανον, plural μάγγανα).
7   Πρόβολος ; περίβολος.
8   *Peri Strategikes*, 12.

[Justinian] had built some additional structure on the top of the circuit-wall at precisely the place where the cliffs are nearest, designed to serve permanently as a shelter for the men fighting there. This structure was called a 'wing' because it appears like a hanging wall.[9]

The *Peri Strategikes* described a model close to the most powerful defended city of the Empire, Byzantium, which was fronted by a water-filled moat. The city of Byzantium formed a fortified triangle that plunged into the sea with the estuary of the Golden Horn to the north, the Bosporus Detroit to the north-east and the Sea of Marmara, or Propontis, to the south. Byzantium was thus primarily defended by the sea. The western isthmus was barred by a succession of walls and the city was divided in two by the River Lycus.[10]

The Constantinian walls were erected by Constantine I the Great and by his son Constantius II roughly between 324 and 361. They stretched from the Sea of Marmara to the Golden Horn and were 2.8km east of the walls rebuilt by Emperor Severus after razing the city in 196 to punish it for rebellion. The Constantinian walls quickly proved insufficient to contain the rapidly growing 'second Rome', as an extramural area called the Exokionion had been spontaneously formed. So, a second wall, 6.5km long, was built 2km further to the west, which historiography has given the name of the Theodosian Walls, although the wall of Theodosius II was actually begun by his predecessor Arcadius around 404–405. During Theodosius II minority, the Praetorian Prefect of the East Anthemius continued the work until about 414.

On 25 November 437, then again on 26 January 447 or 450 earthquakes demolished a part of the wall. The most catastrophic earthquake was the second, with 57 towers fallen to the ground while Attila was threatening the city.[11]

---

9   Procopius, *Aed.*, II, 8, 14.
10   Van Milligen A., *Byzantine Constantinople. The Walls of the City and adjoining Historical Sites* (London, John Murray, 1899) (numerous nineteenth century photographs and sketches). https://www.gutenberg.org/cache/epub/61475/pg61475-images.html
11   Marcellinus Comes, *Chr.*, a. 447 (57 towers downed; many citizens died from hunger). *Chron Pasch*, a. 447 (collapse of the walls, population fled outside the city, no kill); a.450 (26 January of year 450, maybe the same as 447, population fled outside the city, chanting litanies). John Malalas, *Chrgr.*, XIV, 22 (26 January). *Synaxarium Ecclesiae Constantinopolitanae*, ed. Delehaye H., *Propylaeum ad Acta Sanctorum*, Brussels, 1902, p.425, 6 (a Sunday). Evagrius Scholasticus, *HE*, I, 17 (during Theodosius II's reign, many towers and Long Wall of the Chersonese collapsed – in fact it was erected after this earthquake and after Hun invasion of the same year or in 450-; many villages destroyed; Bithynia, Hellespont and Phrygia suffered from floods). Theophanes Confessor, *Chrgr.*, AM 5930, 93 (severe earthquakes for four months in 437, the Byzantines fled and chanted litanies but walls not mentioned; no more earthquakes for the fifth century in Constantinople) AM 6049, 231 (Monday 16 April 557, earthquake with no damage). B. Croke, 'Two early Byzantine earthquakes and their liturgical commemoration', *Byzantion*, 51

The new circuit-wall now included three additional hills that made Constantinople, a city of seven hills like Rome itself, which was symbolically important. It also included the three largest cisterns of the city; all were built during the fifth century, those of Aspar, Aetius and Mocius. The new wall protected an area of 1,450 hectares and half a million inhabitants, the largest city on the Continent and a beacon of the civilised world. A great novelty was the wide moat in front of the wall perhaps dug during the reconstruction of 447. Five public gates, each defended by two towers and fronted by bridges, allowed for the crossing of the moat. Four to seven military gates served for internal communication with the outer wall. The restoration of the Selymbria Gate gives a good appearance of what the wall must have been like at the beginning of the middle ages. The ramparts were built of small cut stones.

Towers' battlements and enclosure were covered with an inverted V-shaped brick capital, the sharp edge of which did not allow attackers to hold on to it. According to the construction standards defined by Vitruvius, the walls alternated seven to eleven rows of brick and as many of stone, giving greater flexibility and preventing water infiltration from bursting the bottom of the walls. 15m to 20m separated the lower front wall from the main wall and delimited the so-called *peribolos*, a sort of internal ring road accessed by posterns pierced in the main wall. The latter was truly imposing, 12 metres high, 5 to 6 metres wide. It was defended by 96 projecting towers, mostly square, some hexagonal or octagonal, and one pentagonal. They had two floors, the first with six to nine window-arches opening onto the enemy; the second was a crenellated platform. At the north and south ends, close to the sea, the towers were closer together, only separated by about 20m. Access to the rampart walk and towers was facilitated by a staircase that strengthened the wall thickness.[12]

The two focal points were the Marble Tower, to the south, which ensured the junction between the Theodosian enclosure and the wall of the Propontis bordering the Sea of Marmara, and, to the north, the extension which covered the palace of the Blachernes and joined the wall bordering the Golden Horn. This was the weak point of the whole defence because the Golden Horn is only 500m to 750m wide. It was the reason why Theodosius II had chosen to house the fleet in a fortified harbour.

(1981), pp.133–144 (on 447 earthquake).
12   B. Tsangadas, *The Fortifications and Defense of Constantinople* (New York: Columbia University Press, 1980). N. Asufay-Effenberger, *Die Landmauer von Konstantinopel-Istanbul: Historisch-topographische und baugeschichtliche Untersuchungen* (Berlin: De Gruyter, 2007). S. Turnbull, *The Walls of Constantinople AD 324–1453*, Fortress 25 (London: Osprey Publishing, 2004).

BIRTH OF THE BYZANTINE ARMY 476-641 CE VOLUME 2: WATCH THEM FIGHT!

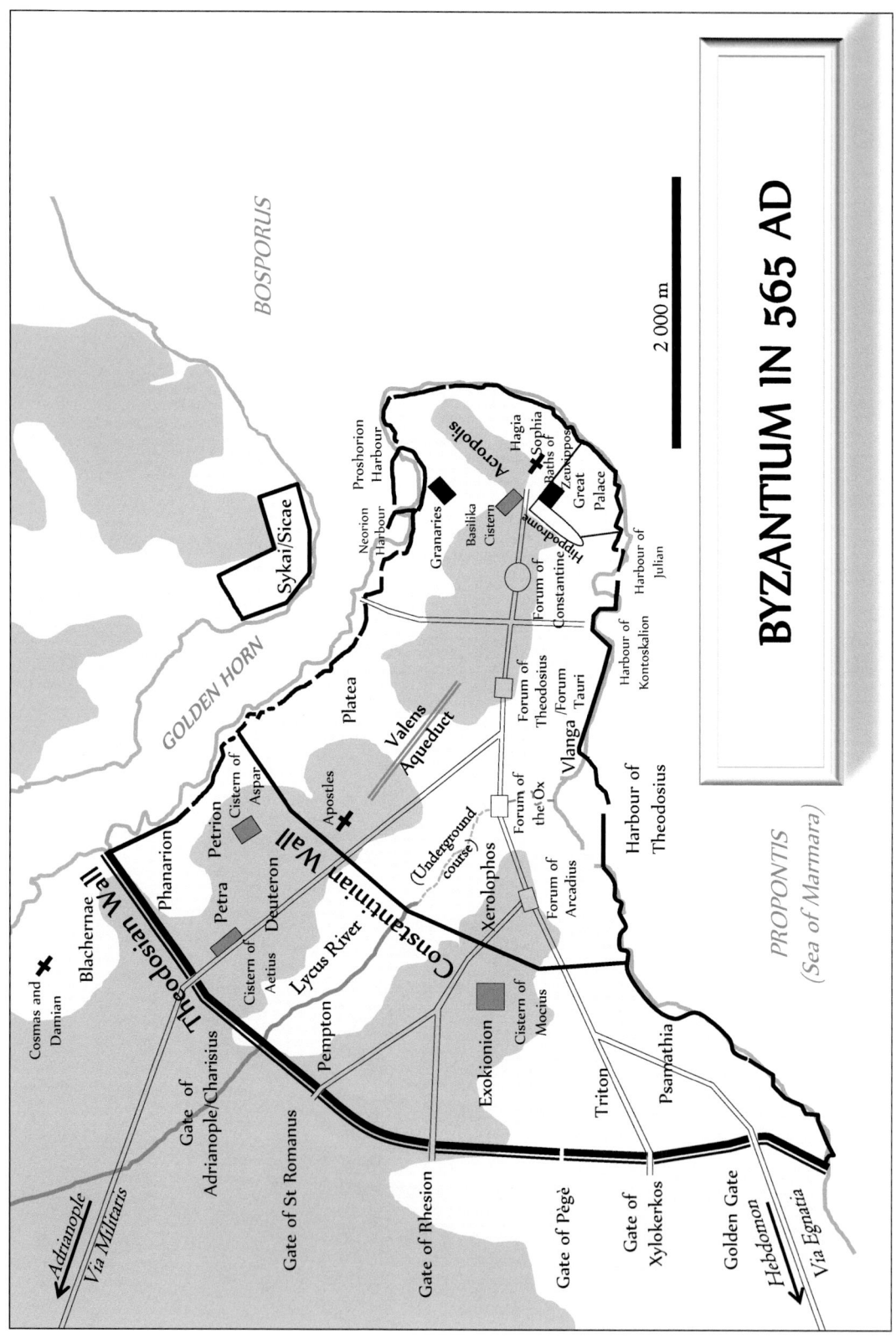

CATAPULTS VERSUS RAMPARTS

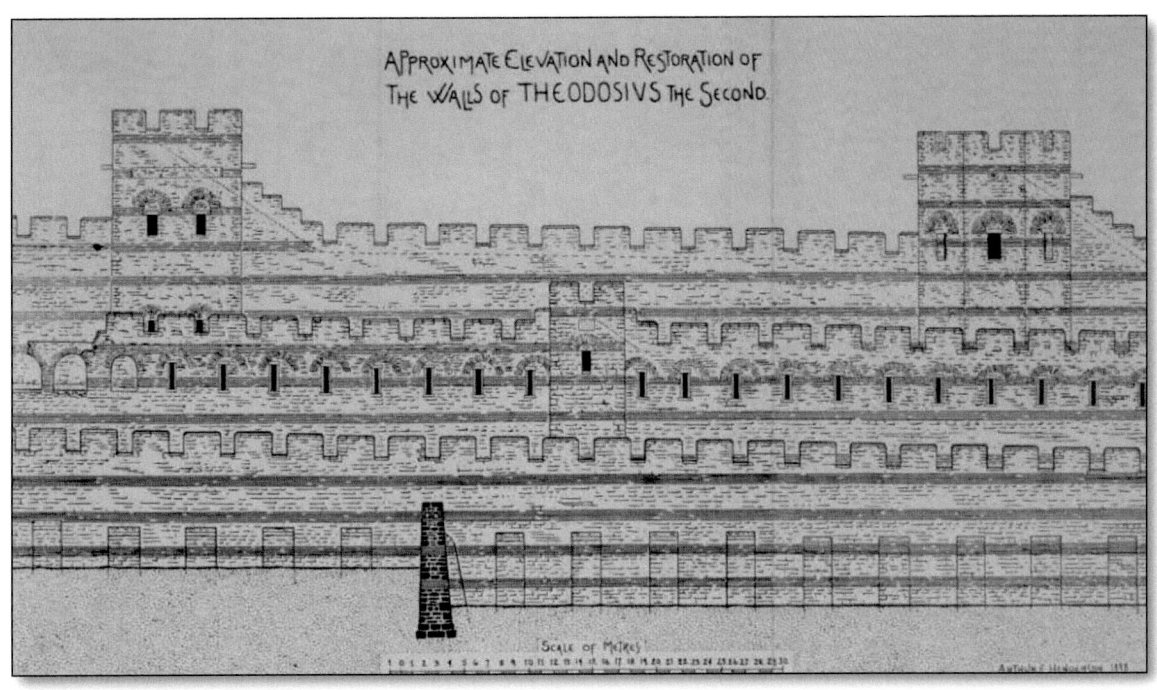

After A. Van Milligen, *Byzantine Constantinople. The Walls of the City and Adjoining Historical Sites* (London: John Murray, 1899), p.107.

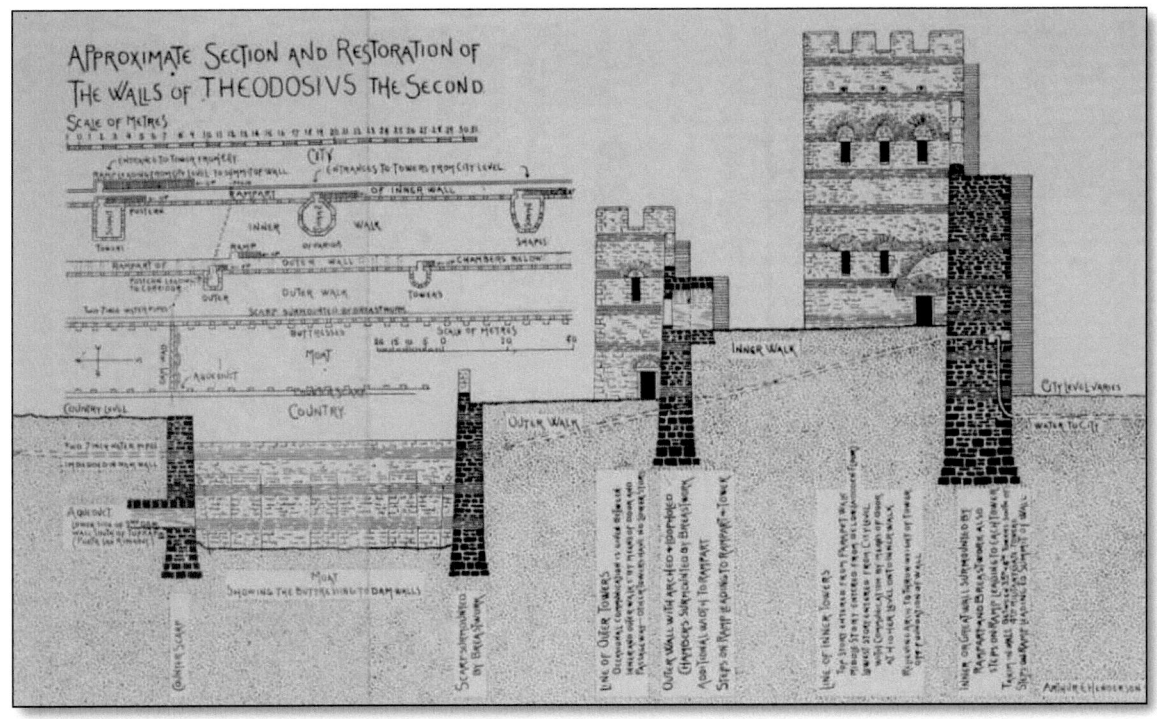

After A. Van Milligen, Byzantine Constantinople. *The Walls of the City and Adjoining Historical Sites* (London: John Murray), 1899, p.106.

BIRTH OF THE BYZANTINE ARMY 476-641 CE VOLUME 2: WATCH THEM FIGHT!

Reconstruction of The Theodosian Walls of Byzantium
(6km long, 70m wide, 82 towers on the outer wall, 96 towers on the inner wall, 15m to 20m wide with a 7m deep moat)
After F. Krischen, *Die Landmauer von Konstantinopel*, t. 1. *Zeichnerische Wiederherstellung mit begleitendem Text* (Berlin: W. De Gruyter, 1938).

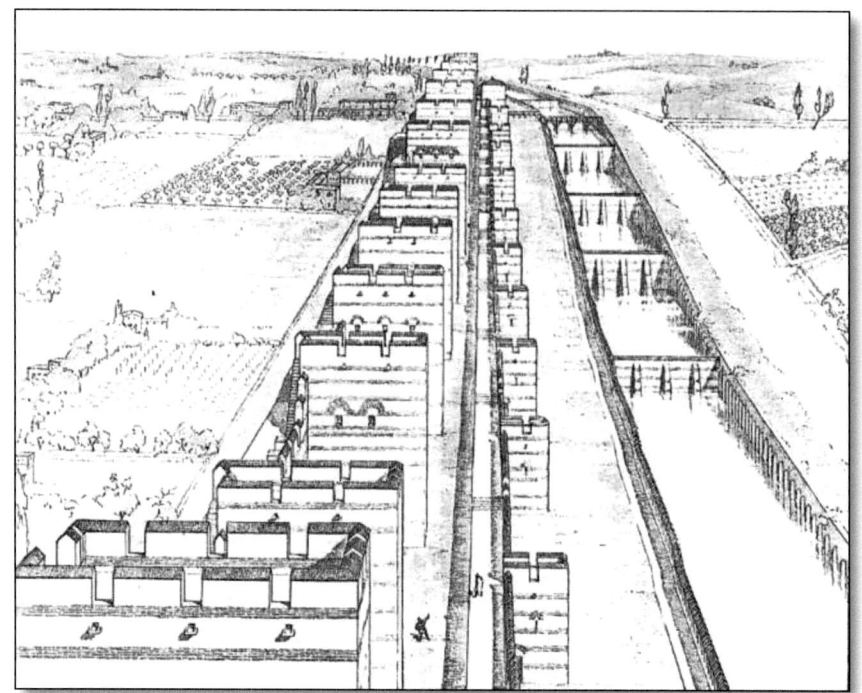

Diagram of The Interior of a Tower on The Theodosian Wall
After A. Van Milligen, *Byzantine Constantinople. The Walls of the City and Adjoining Historical Sites* (London: John Murray, 1899), p.102.

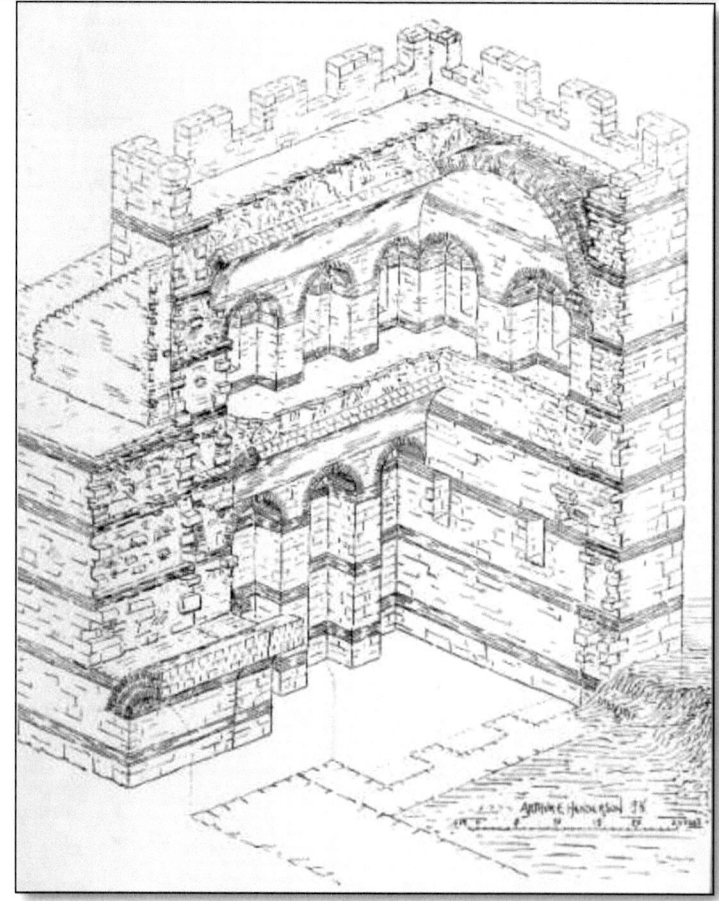

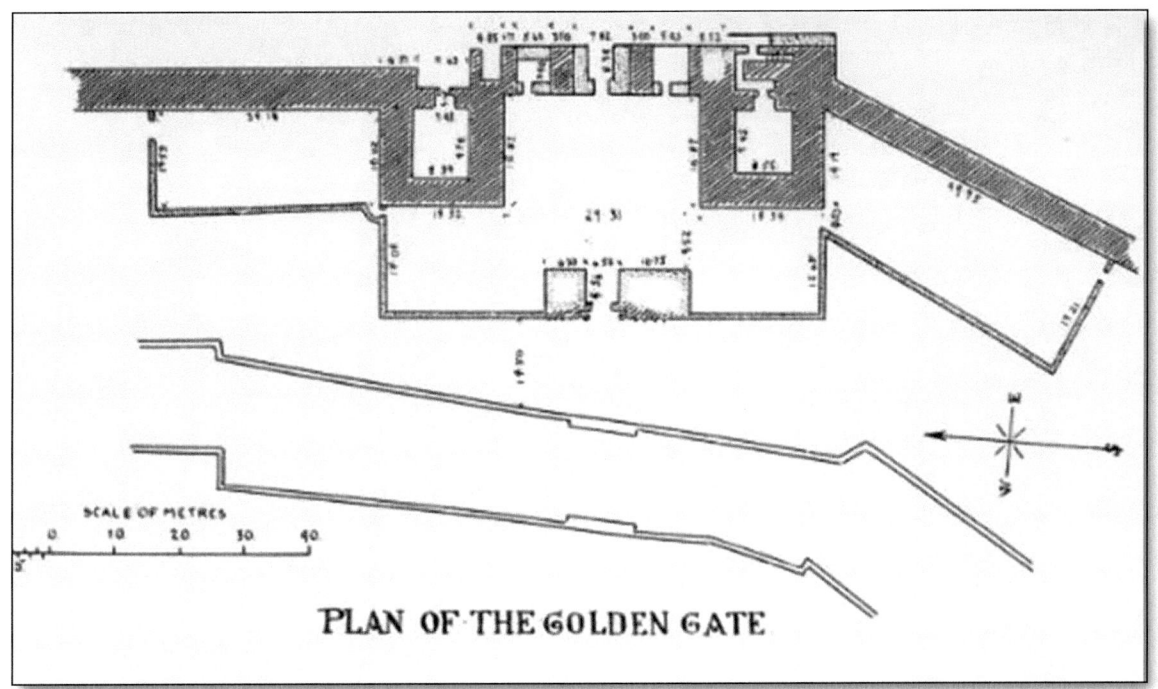

PLAN OF THE GOLDEN GATE

After A. Van Milligen, *Byzantine Constantinople. The Walls of the City and Adjoining Historical Sites* (London: John Murray, 1899), p.60.

But the most impressive defensive work of the Proto-Byzantine period was the line formed by the 'Long Walls'. Its date of construction is uncertain, either before 469 or later under Anastasius I, to whom Evagrius Scholasticus attributed the work:

> One of the greatest and most memorable works was completed by the same Emperor, the Long Wall as it is called, is cleverly positioned in Thrace. It is located about 200 *stadions* from Constantinople and connects the two seas over a distance of 420 *stadions* like a canal. It almost transforms the city into an island rather than a peninsula, and provides very safe passage to those going from Pontus to Propontis and the Sea of Thrace, containing the barbarians arriving from the Euxine Sea, as well as it is called, from Colchis, from Lake Maiotic, from the regions beyond the Caucasus or from those who crossed Europe [administrative district and not the Continent].[13]

The *Chronicon Paschale* also described these walls as 'Anastasian' and dating from 517.[14] Originally 45km long, then extended to 58km by Anastasius, they formed the first line of defence, connecting the Sea of Marmara to the Black Sea, two days of walking, west of Byzantium. Five metres high and two metres wide, the 'Long Walls' irregularly alternated towers and

---

13 Evagrius Scholasticus, *HE*, III, 38.
14 *Chr. Paschale*, a. 517 *pro incerte*.

BIRTH OF THE BYZANTINE ARMY 476-641 CE VOLUME 2: WATCH THEM FIGHT!

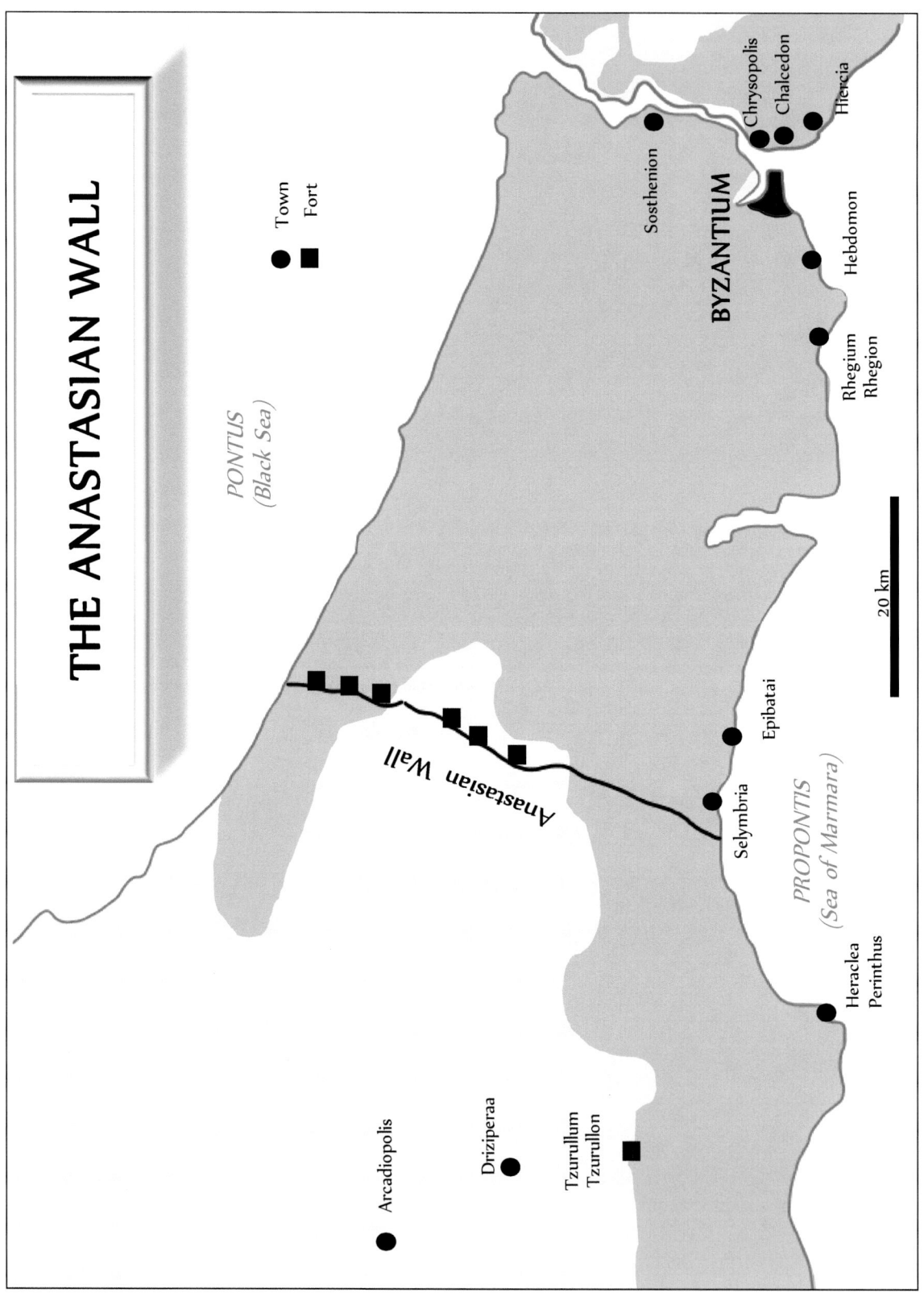

forts prioritising threatened sectors. The towers had a polygonal shape at line breaks and were square elsewhere.[15] Procopius also attributed this construction to Anastasius but was unconvinced of their usefulness:

> The Emperor Anastasius, wishing to put an end to (the barbarian inroads), had a wall built no less than 40 miles from Byzantium, two days' march long, which reached from one sea to the other. He imagined that he had thus secured everything that was included in this enclosure. But in fact, it was the cause of great calamities because the wall was too long to be strong or well-guarded.[16]

Although the Anastasian Long Walls were too lengthy to be defended along their full length, this accumulation of successive obstacles made Byzantium the most formidable fortress in the world. Untaken for six centuries, unless by internal treason in 1204, Byzantium's ramparts only succumbed to the Turkish assault in 1453. No other fortification in history has been so effective.

Attacking Places

The conquest of Italy required mainly siege warfare and few pitched battles. At best, Belisarius had only to occupy unwalled places, as he did in 536 for Reggio and cities of Bruttium.[17] In almost one in three cases the Italian towns were taken without fighting. By contrast, Rome, key of Italy and largest walled city, suffered no less than six sieges or successive occupations: Belisarius entered the city when Goths were fleeing in 536, the Ostrogothic King Vitiges was repelled by Belisarius in 537–538, the Ostrogothic King Totila retook and plundered the city in 545–546, Belisarius reoccupied Rome left by Totila with parts of its walls intentionally destroyed in 547, the Totila again in 549–550, and finally a short siege led by Narses the Eunuch in 552.

According to the *Strategikon* the besieger first had to build a fortified camp with numerous sentries at a distance; forgetting that this could lead to suffering a night attack as happened in 583 during the siege of Aqbas in Arzanene where the Persians captured the Romano-Byzantine

---

15   R. Janin, *Constantinople Byzantine. Développement urbaine et répertoire topographique* (Paris: Institut français d'Études Byzantines, 1964), pp.261–262. B. Croke, 'The Date of the 'Anastasian Long Wall' of Thrace', *GRBS*, 23 (1982), pp.59–78. M. Whitby, 'The Long Walls of Constantinople', *REB*, 55 (1985), pp.560–583. J. Crow, A. Ricci, 'Investigating the Hinterland of Constantinople: Interim Report on the Anastasian Long Wall', *Journal of Roman Archaeology*, 10 (1997), pp.235–262.
16   Procopius, *Aed.*, IV, 9, 6–8 (texte); *BG*, VII, 40, 43.
17   Procopius, *BG*, V, 8, 2–4.

commanders.[18] The construction of such camps is unclear or implied. Procopius detailed it only for the Ostrogoths besieging Rome in 536–537 who had a ditched camp with embankments lined with sharp poles.[19] This episode show the very Romanised way of warfare used by the Ostrogoths explaining partially the difficulties experienced by the Romano-Byzantines in Italy. The second step after setting a safe camp was to negotiate. The *Strategikon* states that terms of surrender should not be too severe and simply demanding horses and weapons can be sufficient, so as not to encourage the besieged to fight bitterly through desperation.[20] Such negotiations were often successful. The capture of Rome by Belisarius on 9 December 536 was resolved by a secret deal with Pope Silverius the son of Pope Hormisdas and the Quaestor Fidelius, both of whom feared the rigours of a siege and judged the Imperial troops as being invincible. The Ostrogothic Governor of Rome, Leuderis, aware of their treason panicked and evacuated his 4,000-strong garrison through the north, while Belisarius was entering from the south. Then Leuderis personally surrendered to Belisarius because he rightly feared the anger of Vitiges his King.[21] Mercy was the most formidable weapon in Byzantine politics. While Julius Caesar massacred and sold off the population that resisted, the Byzantine generals granted safeguards to those who surrendered, as illustrated in 538 by the rapid siege of the barricaded pass of Pertusa Petra (today Passo del Furlo). Martin and Ildiger's 1,000 Byzantine cavalry had no siege engines. After an initial unsuccessful assault with covering hail of arrows against the two entrances, they climbed the cliff overlooking the entrenchments and crushed the barracks with rocks. Unable to fight back, the 400 Ostrogothic warriors agreed to surrender and serve Belisarius on condition that no harm came to them. The Byzantines agreed and, according to Procopius, recruited them 'on a completely equal footing with them'. They even agreed to let their wives and children remain, and some of them remained in Pertusa Petra where they left a garrison.[22] Such mercy was more a matter of skilful psychological action than of humanitarian concern, for the seizure of a city after an assault remained cruel.

During the first five years of the Gothic War, many garrisons surrendered without a fight simply on the promise not to be mistreated as in 538, Tudera and Clusium (today Todi and Chiusi).[23] The same occurred in 552–553 during the last period of this long war, with Tuscan cities opening their gates to Narses the Eunuch under the agreement that they would not to be sacked, which was kept. It is worth adding that these places did not have

---

18   Maurice, *Strategikon*, X, 1, 1–8 (conseil and siege en Arzanene). Theophylact Simocatta, *HU*, I, 12 (Aqbas).
19   Procopius, *BG*, V, 19, 11.
20   Maurice, *Strategikon*, X, 1, 23–29.
21   Procopius, *BG*, V, 14, 4–5 (negotiations); 12 (Goths fled); 14, 13 (Leuderis' surrender); 14, 14 (Belisarius entering Rome).
22   Procopius, *BG*, 11, 10–20.
23   Procopius, *BG*, VI, 13, 2–3.

Ostrogothic Garrisons. By comparison, Lucca suffered a three-month siege due to having a Frankish garrison. To spare the cost of a lengthy blockade or a bloody assault, Narses indulged to psychological warfare. He first came to terms with the most important citizens who pledged that if, after 30 days, the town was not relieved by a Frankish army, it would surrender to Narses. The Franks even gave him hostages and swore oaths. For over a month, the Luccans and Franks temporised and Narses theatrically proceeded to a fake execution of the hostages in the sight of the horrified Luccans. Then he revealed his trick to them, and the hostages who were playing dead got to their feet and went to the city relating how generously Narses had treated them. Procopius concludes: 'These words were soon after had more result than weapons, by calming the quibbling and arguments in the population, and persuading the majority to take the side of the Romans.'[24] Nonetheless Narses had to wait for a further two months, but then he lost patience,

> …believing that it was now intolerable that the Luccans, besieged in such a gentle way, resisted for so long, and had the ramparts aggressively attacked. The siege machines were immediately brought, fiery projectiles were launched towards the towers, and those who showed themselves on the curtain walls were assailed by stones and arrows: a breach was made in the circuit-wall and the prospect of disaster hovered over the city.[25]

The previously freed hostages persuaded their fellow citizens to surrender and the siege was brought to an end.[26]

The Romano-Byzantines were rather more inclined to blockade impregnable places than to spill their blood on the circuit-walls. After erecting a camp, the first thing was to deprive the besieged of food and water.[27] Belisarius proceeded like this with Vetus Auximum (present-day Osimo) of the Marche Region in Italy, a hilly place he surrounded so tightly that prisoners could be taken. The only problem was that besiegers and besieged alike starved. Belisarius resorted to a tactic of poisoning an external cistern using a nauseous cocktail of animal corpses, venomous herbs and quicklime, unnecessarily so because the Ostrogothic defenders could rely on a well inside the city. Nevertheless, they surrendered in summer 539 after losing any hope of being relieved by King Vitiges.[28]

---

24 Agathias, *Hist.*, I, 12, 1 (negotiations); 12, 2 à 13, 7 (fake execution); 12, 8 (efficiency).
25 Agathias, *Hist.*, I, 18, 4.
26 Agathias, *Hist.*, I, 18, 5–8.
27 Maurice, *Strategikon*, X, 1, 8–11.
28 Procopius, *BG*, VI, 23, 1 (Osimo); 23, 5–8 (location of Osimo); 23, 9–39 (siege measures); 24, 1 (starvation of Osimo inhabitants); 24, 2–10 (messengers sent to Vitiges); 27, 11–16 (Vitiges unable to relief Osimo); 27, 17 (Ostrogothic deserters); 26, 2–14 (new messengers to Vitiges); 26, 15 (starvation for Goths); 26, 16

The most efficient blockade during the Gothic War was of Ravenna, forced to capitulate at the beginning of 540. Belisarius had cut off the Ostrogothic capital from land, the River Po and sea access. In addition to this admirable classic manoeuvre, he played dirty by bribing a Ravenna inhabitant to set light to the wheat stores. The Ostrogoths preferred to negotiate rather than endure hunger and finally let the so-called Roman Army enter the city.[29]

Another interesting example of blockade was at Compsa (today Conza della Campania) between winter 554 and spring 555. Narses the Eunuch was blockading this city, defended by Ragnar and 7,000 Ostrogothic warriors. Feeding such a strong garrison was more a burden than a relief for a small city and Ragnar tried to negotiate. Both commanders met, but it was a complete failure as the angered Ragnar shot an arrow at the intransigent Narses; he missed and was killed soon after by Byzantine bodyguards. The surrendering Ostrogothic garrison was sent to Byzantium, where it was probably incorporated into the army.[30]

Frontal assault with ladders was really not the Romano-Byzantine favourite method of taking a city. The *Strategikon* was quite clear on this topic and advocated never committing the entire army in attritional daily attacks. It was really better to target flammable roofs on windy days and shoot incendiary arrows or pots with bows and *petrobola*.[31] Preparatory firing of arrows before an assault was a common practice. While Solomon was campaigning through the Aures Mountains by 540, he came upon Zerboulē, probably more of a ksar with mud walls than a regular fortress. As the rampart was very low Solomon for three days ordered a hail of arrows shot over it, killing the Moorish chiefs. On the fourth day he stormed the place but found nothing as the Moors had silently escaped by a postern the previous night. This incident proves that Solomon had not surrounded Zerboulē, an elementary precaution that he had ignored.

A general assault without proper siege machines was launched when besieging became an unbearable and unsustainable task as Solomon experienced shortly after when blockading Toumar. His soldiers were reduced to drinking only one cup of water per day. While Solomon was planning a cautious assault, a non-commissioned officer spontaneously went to kill the Moorish sentries at the gate. All the army rushed after him, overcoming the battered Moors, while Iaudas, their King, sustained a serious wound.[32]

(starvation for Belisarius); 26, 17–26 (prisoner interrogated); 27, 1–24 (cistern); 27, 28–34 (capitulation).
29   Procopius, *BG*, VI, 28, 3–6. 28, 24; 28, 17–35.
30   Agathias, *Hist.*, II, 13, 4 (7,000 Goths at Compsa); 14, 1–7 (negotiations and rendition).
31   Maurice, *Strategikon*, X, 1, 32–33 (daily assaults); 49–54 (incendiary projectiles).
32   Procopius, *BV*, IV, 19, 23–28 (Zerboulē); 20, 1–21 (Toumar).

Relatively primitive mud or dry-stone fortresses from Atlas or Caucasus did not demand huge breastworks and numerous siege machines. By contrast, attacking a Roman-made rampart in Italy without preparation was a risky, if not bloody, operation. John the nephew of Vitalian had the misfortune to learn it by December 538 when he launched a general assault using ladders against Caesena (now Cesena).[33]

Trickery was another if rare method to take a city. Belisarius ordered Boriades, an officer from his *bucellarii*, with a few troops to take Syllektos in Africa in 533. Early in the morning Boriades entered the city with peasants, probably disguised. Meeting no opposition, he summoned the notables and the parish priest and convinced them to rally to Imperial rule.[34] He was bold – and lucky.

Most of the time, to take a city demanded negotiation, assaults and cunning. When he reached Naples in 536, Belisarius set up a camp in front of the city and his fleet anchored in the port. Soon after this impressive manoeuvre, he received the capitulation of an external fort and welcomed some Neapolitan emissaries. He promised money to the ambassador if the city surrendered, but probably not enough. Belisarius assaulted the circuit-wall in vain, then he cut the aqueduct but Naples' wells also made this measure ineffective. After 20 days, an unexpected example of cunning helped Belisarius: an Isaurian soldier, intrigued by the broken aqueduct, inspected it closely and realised it was possible to enter the city by slightly widening a channel carved into the rock. At night around 400 men infiltrated the aqueduct but suddenly panicked they retreated. Then reduced to 200 men, the force reached a house near the northern rampart. As two towers were occupied, two trumpets of the force gave the signal to attack. The army tried to climb the walls but the ladders were too short, finally two were joined to reach the sentry walk. Nonetheless, caught by surprise the defenders were put flight and the gates opened. On the eastern wall, the troops had no ladders and set fire to the gates; their work was made easier by the desertion of the guards. Only the Jews defending the wall facing the sea fought fiercely.[35]

The last method, the surprise assault, was rarely used but worked, as was the case at Forocornelius (present-day Imola), taken from the Ostrogoths in 539.[36]

---

33 Procopius, *BG*, VI, 19, 20–21.
34 Procopius, *BV*, III, 16, 10–11.
35 Procopius, *BG*, V, 8, 6–18 (negotiations); 41–45 (Belisarius measures); 9, 11–21 (aqueduct); 10, 1–27 (assault); 10, 36 (siege duration).
36 Procopius, *BG*, VI, 19, 22.

The Full Scale Siege

Byzantium inherited all of the machines used by the Roman Army although some developments had occurred since the time of Vitruvius.[37] Nevertheless, Romano-Byzantine field armies did not always have siege machines with them or competent engineers to build siege machines with local resources, as was obviously the case for Belisarius in Africa and Italy. When he besieged Naples, short ladders had to be joined in pairs because the length had been incorrectly calculated for the height of the walls. According to Procopius, Belisarius' soldiers were 'not very acquainted' with the mobile towers and ram's 'tortoise's used by the Ostrogoths.[38] The importance of machines was a constant in siege warfare with the Persians throughout previous centuries, but the Romano-Byzantines had mostly been the besieged and not the besiegers. Nevertheless, they occasionally did use some siege machines as in 555 against the Persian fort at Onoguris in Lazica:

> [Generals Martin and Bouzes] prepared what are known as approach galleries, machines for hurling large stones and all the other machines of war, to assault the rampart if necessary. The gallery is a wicker structure shaped as a roof, impenetrable thanks to its thickness, completely covered on both sides, so that its sides extend downwards and protect what lies beneath. Leather skins and blankets thrown over the top surround this device on all sides and form a protection against hits. Hidden inside, the men carry it unseen and move it as they please. And when they have brought it close to a tower or wall, those inside dig out the earth and remove it, exposing the foundations. Then, striking with picks and mallets, they shake the building.[39]

This description roughly corresponded to what Vegetius called a *vinea* – a vineyard:

> The Ancients called 'vines' what soldiers call today by the barbarian's name *caucia*. This machine is formed of a light frame, seven feet high, eight wide, and sixteen long. It is covered by a double-pitched roof made of planks and racks. Its sides are fitted with a wicker fabric impenetrable to the force of stones and lines; to prevent it from being set on fire, it is covered on the outside with fresh skins

---

37 Ph. Fleury, 'Vitruve et la nomenclature des machines de jet romaines', *REL*, 59 (1981), pp.216–234.
38 Procopius, *BG*, V, 10, 22–23 (Naples); 22, 1 (unacquaintance with siege machines).
39 Agathias, *Hist.*, III, 5, 9–11.

or woollen blankets. Several of these machines are joined in a row, under which the besiegers advance under cover at the foot of the walls whose foundations they undermine.[40]

This type of wooden gallery was called a 'tortoise' or *chelonē* by the *Peri Strategikes* and possibly housed a ram.[41] The *Strategikon* says that the siege artillery consisted of *petroboloi*, a Latin-Greek hybrid word meaning rock throwers. He recommended throwing stones or incendiary bombs, *pyrbola*, against mobile towers.[42] The *Strategikon* also used the generic term *manganon* for both defensive and non-defensive siege artillery. This term is the origin of *manganum* in late Latin and mangonel in English.[43] They were traction mangonels, a kind of artillery invented in China and introduced into the Western world by the Steppe nomads. John, Archbishop of Thessaloniki in the *Miracula of St Demetrios* described the mangonel during the Skavene siege of the city in 597:

> These [*petroboles*] were tetragonal and rested on broader bases, tapering to narrower. Attached to them were thick cylinders well clad in iron at the ends, and there were nailed to them timbers like beams from a large house. These timbers had the slings from the back side and from the front strong ropes, by which, pulling down and releasing the sling, they propel the stones up high and with a loud noise. And on being fired they sent up many great stones so that neither earth nor human constructions could bear their impacts. They also covered those tetragonal petroboles with boards on three sides only, so that those inside firing them might not be wounded with arrows by those on the walls. And since one of these, with its boards, had been burnt to a char by a flaming arrow, they returned, carrying away the machines. On the following day they again brought these petroboles covered with freshly skinned hides and with the boards, and placing them closer to the walls, shooting, they hurled mountains and hills against us. For what else might one term these extremely large stones.[44]

---

40 Vegetius, *DRM*, IV, 15.
41 *Peri Strategikes*, 12, 30, 35; 13, 17, 61, 64, 69, 72, 94, 103, 107, 111, 121, 123; 26, 7 (χελώνη).
42 Maurice, *Strategikon*, X 1, 52.55; 3, 9.17 (πετροβόλος plural πετροβόλοι); 3, 27–18 (πυρβόλος);
43 Maurice, *Strategikon*, X 3, 8, 15, 21, 23, 26 and 40; 4 8 (μάγγανον, plural μάγγανα).
44 P. E. Chevedden, 'The Artillery Revolution of the Middle Ages: The Impact of the Trebuchet on the Development of Fortifications' (unpublished ms., 1991), p.11 after W. T. S. Tarver, 'The Traction Trebuchet: A Reconstruction of an Early Medieval Siege Engine', Technology and Culture, 36, 1 (1995), p.145. S. Vryonis Jr., 'The evolution of Slavic society and the Slavic invasions in Greece: the first major Slavic attack on Thessaloniki, AD 597', Hesperia. Journal of the American School of Classical Studies at Athens, 50 (1981), p.384.

This kind of early mangonel is illustrated by a seventh or eighth century wall painting from the palace of Piandjikent in Transoxania and now in the Hermitage Museum in St Petersburg.

It is difficult to know how many mangonels were used during a siege. When Caesarea of Palestine was besieged from 640 to 641, Muawiya's Muslim Army fielded '72 machines that never stopped throwing stones' according to Michael the Syrian. After a seven-month siege, a breach was made in the circuit-wall, and the general assault was completed by an attack using ladders. Three more days of fighting within the walls were necessary before the surviving garrison fled by ship.[45]

In the West, seventh-century Italy was fought over by the Lombard invaders and Romano-Byzantines had to defend or reconquer walled cities: siege machines were needed. In 663, Constans II employed 'various machines' to besiege Benevento.[46]

The Romano-Byzantines were a long way from the standards of the great Roman siegecraft, as neither the huge works of circumvallation or contravallation, nor assault earthworks are recorded, although some more limited examples are known. In 573 the Patrician and Master of the Soldiers to the East, Marcian, attempted a classic siege at Nisibis, the entry point to Persia. He surrounded the city with a palisade, some sort of contravallation, and he had mobile assault towers and galleries built by engineers. Nonetheless Khosrow I was approaching with an army from the south-West threatening the supply route of his Romano-Byzantines opponents. That move forced Marcian to rapidly abandon the siege leaving behind his intact siege machines. Khosrow I collected all of these to besiege Dara when Marcian took refuge at Marida (current Mardin in Turkey).[47] Unlike Julius Caesar at Alesia, Marcian had not protected his besieging army with a contravallation against Khosrow's relief force. He was dismissed from his command just before he pulled back. The ancient method of undermining, digging a gallery under the wall and building a gallery of pine planks to then set fire to it was recommended by the *Peri Strategikes* treatise, either by use of a mine gallery or under a tortoise. Once the breach has been made, the besiegers had to rush in while screaming to impress and frighten the defenders.[48]

The combination of different approaches was the usual tactic as at the year-long siege of Cumae from 552 to 553. Defended by a numerous Ostrogothic garrison led by Aligern, the place had powerful walls located on 'a steep height and difficult to access.' Cumae is currently an archaeological site about 12km from Naples. Narses the Eunuch first assaulted the circuit-

---

45 Michael the Syrian, HU, XI, 8, t. 2 (1963), p.430 (duration of the siege; machines), p.431 (fall of the town).
46 Paul the Deacon, *HL*, V, 7.
47 John of Ephesus, *HE*, VI, 2 (Nisibis siege); 5 (recuperation of siege machines). Theophylact Simocatta, *HU*, III, 11, 2 (Khosrow I at Dara; Marcian at Mardin).
48 *Peri Strategikes*, 13, 5–21.

walls: he brought together archers and slingers to drive off the defenders on the battlements and deployed various assault machines. Although Agathias did not detail these machines, they were probably mantlets, wooden galleries or even ram tortoises. All assaults failed and after a few days Narses decided to undermine the walls. Noticing a cave under the eastern rampart, he had a gallery dug there supported by beams and covered the noise of the work with simulated attacks where the soldiers shouted more than usual. When the gallery reached under the walls of the city, shrubs and dry wood stored there were set on fire. The gallery collapsed, dragging down a part of the walls and a gate. Archaeology testifies to the effectiveness of this sap. The Romano-Byzantines plunged into the breach, but the debris formed obstacles easily defended by the Ostrogoths and the assault failed again. Narses abandoned the siege but left only a large blockading force after having surrounded Cumae with a palisade. The city surrendered a year later, when Aligern realised that the overall situation of the Ostrogoths was definitely in jeopardy.[49] The besieger was often the winner because he had access to fresh supplies.

The Romano-Byzantines and the Persians no longer had a monopoly on siegecraft as the Germanic and Steppe barbarians learned how to take cities and sometimes had siege machines.

Towns Defended Mainly by Their Inhabitants

The barbarians set up camp within sight of the city. All the inhabitants had gathered on the ramparts to observe this sinister omen. The very medieval image of a population watching on the ramparts and ready to defend their city comes from the later Roman Empire. Since 440 urban 'self-defence militias' had been a legal obligation.[50] An edict from 25 June 539 specified that the category of armourers termed as deputies, in Latin *armificatores* and *deputati*, paid by a tax were obliged not only to manufacture weapons but also to maintain those of soldiers of a local unit. Others, *balistarii* (artillerymen), were stationed in the cities where there were Imperial weapons factories and were supposed to guard the arsenals. Civilian armourers were not to make or sell: 'Bows, arrows, spathas, swords called *semispathas*, armour, spears of any shape, javelins called *monocopias*, shields and helmets.'[51] In the event of a siege, the arsenals probably armed civilians when the number of soldiers was insufficient or there was no garrison.

---

49 Agathias, *Hist.*, I, 9, 1 (assault equipment); 9, 2–5 (first failed assault); 10, 2–9 (mine gallery and another failed assault); 11, 1 (Narses gave up the siege); 11, 5 (blockade and palisade); 20, 5–6 (Aligern surrender). M. Maiuri, 'L'assedio di Narsete a Cuma nel racconto dello storico Agathias', *La Parola del Passato*, 4 (1949), pp.41–46 (archaeological evidence of sap).
50 *CTh, Val.III. N.,*V; IX. Ph. Richardot, (2005), pp.220–223.
51 *Nov J.*, 85, 1 (*deputati*), 2–3 (*balistarii*), 4 (prohibited weapons).

The existence of organised urban militias has not been proven, but there were many cases where the inhabitants defended their town. Each case was different, but the cities of the Balkan area were busy. In 549 in northern Greece, the inhabitants of Topeiros, after their garrison had been wiped out in a reckless sortie, defended themselves by throwing stones, oil and boiling pitch at the Sklavenes. But the latter drove them from the ramparts in a hail of javelins, scaled the walls and slaughtered the entire male population, around 15,000 men. As Procopius estimated the Sklavene horde at less than 2,000 men, these figures show the effectiveness of seasoned warriors over a mass of inexperienced and desperate city-dwellers.[52]

Most of the time, the inhabitants were successful at repelling assaults from barbarians. In the 580s, when the Avar hordes swept across the great plain of northern Thrace, in the centre of present-day Bulgaria, the towns held out fiercely and in 587, not one city fell to the invaders. Simocatta emphasised the courage of the inhabitants and made no mention of soldiers. They could use some positional artillery, a practice which suggests some training of civilian artillerymen. The Avars were pinned down by the mangonels placed on the ramparts of Diocletianopolis (the current Hirsarya fortress in Lovetch, Bulgaria).[53] The following year, the inhabitants of Singidunum even launched raids across the Danube to destroy the invasion boats built by the Sklavenes and the Khan preferred to abandon the siege of the city after seven days.[54]

In Byzantium the only civilian groups with some fighting capacities were the rival factions of the Blues and the Greens, supporters, and sometimes hooligans, of the hippodrome chariot-racing teams. They were probably charged with protecting the Theodosian Walls in 559 although no sources record it.[55] In 602, although the Blues and the Greens numbers were limited to 900 and 1,500 respectively, Emperor Maurice ordered them to defend the ramparts from the approaching mutinous Thracian army.[56] Their military action was nothing since they gave a warm welcome to Phocas and his mutineers. These supporters of chariot hippodrome were more troublemakers, if not gangsters, than patriotic militia. By contrast, sailors accustomed to collective action and solidarity at sea could provide skilful urban defenders. When Thessaloniki was again besieged by the Avars and Slavs in 677–678, the sources make no mention of soldiers, but of locals, in particular sailors, 'experienced in the operation of devices [who] were to be used as stone-throwers and other machines'. Exchanges between mangonels

---

52 Procopius, *BG*, VII, 38, 14–17 (*Topiros*).
53 Theophylact Simocatta, *HU*, II, 16, 1–2 (Beroe, current Stara Zagora, Bulgaria); 17, 1–2 (Diocletianopolis), 3 (Philippopolis, current Plovdiv, Bulgaria), 4 (Adrianople, current Edirne, Turkey).
54 Theophylact Simocatta, *HU*, VI, 4, 1–3.
55 A. Cameron, *Circus Factions. Blues and Greens at Rome and Byzantium* (Oxford: Clarendon Press, Oxford University Press, 1976), pp.105–125. The sources did not mention the Blues and the Greens to defend Byzantium.
56 Theophylact Simocatta, *HU*, VIII, 7, 11 (numbers); 8 2 (orders from Maurice).

on both sides were intense. The Thessalonicians therefore protected the battlements against mangonels with wooden screens and cushions made of a thick cloth stuffed with *papyrus*, which were usually placed under the guests at feasts. They also wielded poles ending in a ploughshare which lifted the wooden tortoises of the Avars then exposing their occupants to fire from projectiles from the top of the walls. No doubt guided by engineers, familiar with siegecraft, they also dug a ditch and placed camouflaged caltrops in front of a sector of the city without a rampart.[57]

The inhabitants of the Romano-Byzantine East also participated in urban defence – because they had no other choice, they had to rely on local human resources. In 530, in Armenia, Martyropolis was saved thanks to an unknown engineer who built inside the city a wooden tower larger than that of the Persians and a machine which crushed attackers by dropping a column, undoubtedly a giant pendulum. Nevertheless, the arrival of the army of the master of the soldiers to the East raised the siege.[58] In 540, the inhabitants of Antioch, especially the young people who were used to competing in the hippodrome, defended themselves bravely, but were cowardly abandoned by the regular troops when the hoardings that increased the surface area of the sentry walk gave way: the soldiers fled on horseback, encouraged by the gestures of the Persians, and the civilian defenders were killed on the spot with a heroism noted by Procopius: 'some of them were covered with weapons but most were naked [without armour] and only threw stones. They repelled the enemies and sang the paean, shouting as if they were victors: Glory to the Emperor Justinian triumphant.'[59] In 544, Edessa faced a major siege, with machines, ladders and by an army outnumbering the garrison. The inhabitants were seized by a black anger that eventually discouraged the Persians:

> The city filled with confusion and agitation and everyone climbed onto the ramparts, men, women and children mixed together. The inhabitants in the prime of life fought vigorously with the soldiers and many peasants distinguished themselves by feats of arms against the barbarians. Children, women and old men collected stones for the fighters and helped them in any way they could. Some of them heated olive oil in cauldrons for the necessary time, all along the rampart then, with containers, they poured this boiling oil which caused great damage to the attackers reaching the circuit-wall. Then the Persians gave up and threw down their weapons, they went to the King to tell him that they could no longer endure this ordeal.[60]

---

57 *Miracula Sancti Demetrii*, I, 14, 152 (screens; cushions); II, 2, 209 (sailors); 210 (poles); 1, 186 (caltrops).
58 John Malalas, *Chrgr.*, XVIII, 66.
59 Procopius, BP, II, 8, 17 (soldiers and youngsters); 24–25 (Persian psychological warfare); 28–29 (heroism).
60 Procopius, *BP*, II, 27, 33–36.

Italian townsmen stood on ramparts defending their city against Romano-Byzantines or, more rarely, against Ostrogoths. Rome was unfortunate in experiencing both cases. This former capital of the Empire was still a huge city when the Gothic War broke out, but with no military power except its ramparts. The so-called Aurelian Wall was erected by the Emperor Aurelian between 271 and 282. It was the largest perimeter wall in Mediterranean world and is still visible today. It had 18 gates and 400 square towers. The rampart was made of a concrete core 3.5m to 3.7m wide composed of mortar mixed with pieces of tuff, covered with curtain brickwork on both sides, it was eight metres high to the crenellated parapet.[61] Many people were needed to defend its 19km perimeter. One man per metre gives a 19,000-man force. Three hours were necessary to walk around according to Vegetius standards.[62] Crossing the city and its maze of streets was probably quite a consuming time process, nearly two hours. However, the Romano-Byzantine garrison was only 3,000 to 5,000-strong, plus an unknown number of civilians. In 537–538 to man the lengthy Aurelian Wall and to avoid a social revolt Belisarius hired hungry proletarians to mix with his soldiers. When in turn Narses the Eunuch besieged Rome in mid-552, the Ostrogoths had a weak garrison and Procopius stated: 'Now the whole circuit-wall was so extraordinary long that neither could the Roman encompass it in their attack nor the Goths guard it.'[63] The Ostrogoths just held a small part of the city around the tomb of Hadrian with an internal wall connected to the Aurelian Wall, but it was still too long to be fully guarded. In 538–539, the inhabitants of Milan helped the Romano-Byzantines to hold their walls but the ratio of a garrison of 300 for a population of over 300,000 is not credible, not because of the garrison's size but because of the exaggerated number of civilians.[64]

The idea that Christianisation morally demilitarised the Roman Empire is refuted by the commitment of monks to the defence of cities. In 502–503, lacking a military garrison, Amida was defended only by its inhabitants who threw beams at the Persian rams which were working ineffectively against the walls. The defenders also undermined an earth ramp too quickly erected by the Persians but at a height greater than the rampart. In the end, it was cunning that won out over art. An old passage roughly blocked with uncemented stones was discovered by a Persian soldier. A small force

---

61 H. Dey, 'Verso una storia edilizia delle Mura Aureliane, da Aureliano a Onorio (271–403 d.C.)' in R. Rita Volpe, R. Santangeli Valenzani, D. Esposito and *alii* (eds), *Le Mura Aureliane nella storia di Roma, 1, Da Aureliano a Onorio, Atti Primo Convegno, 25 Marzo 2015* (Rome: TrE-Press, 2017), pp.13–14. A. Cambeda, A. Ceccherelli, *Le Mura di Aureliano, itinerari d'arte e di cultura* (Rome: Fratelli Palombi Editor, 1990).

62 A. Claridge, *Rome: An Oxford Archaeological Guide* (Oxford: Oxford University Press, 1998), p.59. Vegetius, *DRM*, III, 9 (20 miles per five hours).

63 Procopius, *BG*, VIII, 33, 17.

64 Procopius, *BG*, V, 25, 11–12 (Belisarius hired daily workers as guardians); VI, 12, 40 (Milan 300-strong garrison); 21, 39 (300,000 inhabitants killed after surrender).

rushed through this passage at night and took a tower guarded by sleeping monks. A ladder then allowed them to enter through this tower, then enter the city, which was sacked.[65] This episode in the fall of Amida is sometimes falsely attributed to the betrayal of the monks who let the Persians into the tower they were supposed to guard.[66] The moral support of a man of God could strengthen a city's defences as happened in 610 for the city of Alexandria. In revolt against Emperor Phocas, the inhabitants had to repel loyalist troops. Niketas, the nephew of Heraclius the Elder and leader of the rebels in Alexandria, mustered a motley garrison made up of 'soldiers, citizens of Alexandria, the Green Faction, sailors, archers, with powerful war equipment.' Theophilus the Confessor, a saintly man of Alexandria, advised Niketas not only to fight from the top of the walls, but to open the gate of Aoun and attack. The Alexandrians then lined up with catapults and mangonels. The enemy general got a stone that broke his jaw and knocked him off his horse – dead, his second in command also perished in a similar grim way. When fiercely attacked the besieging forces were soon put into flight.[67]

Urban garrisons from other towns are not recorded. Those of the interior, Byzantium included, had little or none. The Italian campaigns show that Romano-Byzantines and Ostrogoths used garrisons of comparable size in their campaigns. In a letter to Justinian written in 537, Belisarius considered the 5,000 men he initially had to defend Rome against 150,000 Ostrogoths insufficient, a figure undoubtedly exaggerated.[68]

---

65   Procopius, *BP*, I, 7, 12–29.
66   Marcellinus Comes, *Chr.*, a. 502.
67   John of Nikiu, *Chr.*, 107, 46 (1883), pp.426–427 (garrison); 108, 1–7, pp.427–428 (Theophilus the Confessor).
68   Procopius, *BG*, V, 24, 2–3 (strengths).

Table 15, Size of Garrisons during the Gothic War (536–548)

City (year)	Strengths	Source
Naples 536	800 Ostrogoths	Procopius, *BG*, V, 8, 6
Naples 536	300 Romano-Byzantine infantry	Procopius, *BG*, V, 14, 1
Rome 537	5,000 Romano-Byzantines	Procopius, BG, V, 24, 2
Chiusi 538	1,000 Ostrogoths	Procopius, *BG*, VI, 11, 1
Orvieto 538	1,000 Ostrogoths	Procopius, *BG*, VI, 11, 1
Todi 538	400 Ostrogoths	Procopius, *BG*, VI, 11, 1
Pertusa Petra 538	400 Ostrogoths	Procopius, *BG*, VI, 11, 2
Osimo 538	4,000 Ostrogoths	Procopius, *BG*, VI, 11, 2
Urbino 538	2,000 Ostrogoths	Procopius, *BG*, VI, 11, 2
Cesena 538	500 Ostrogoths	Procopius, *BG*, VI, 11, 3
Montefeltro 538	500 Ostrogoths	Procopius, *BG*, VI, 11, 3
Milan 538	1,000 Isaurians, Thracians plus bodyguards 300 Romano-Byzantines	Procopius, *BG*, VI, 12, 26 Procopius, *BG*, VI, 12, 40
Como, Bergamo, Novara 538	700 Romano-Byzantines (out of 1,000 – 300 in Milan)	Procopius, *BG*, VI, 12, 27 Procopius, *BG*, VI, 12, 40
Rossano 548	300 Romano-Byzantine cavalry and 100 infantry	Procopius, *BG*, VII, 28, 6
Rome 549	3,000 Romano-Byzantine	Procopius, *BG*, VII, 36, 1

How to Defend a City

To ensure the defence of a city, it was best to prepare in advance. This is what Belisarius did after he entered Rome on 9 December 536: he built merlons to protect the sentries on guard, he dug a great ditch around the city, transferred the wheat of his fleet to be stored under guard in the public granaries and forced the inhabitants of the neighbouring countryside to bring their supplies in.[69] In an emergency, the first action to be taken was to set fire to the surrounding fields and houses to deprive the enemy of the materials necessary for fascines or for siege machines.[70] Maurice recommended providing the necessary provisions based on what was known of the intentions of the approaching besieger.[71] Organising the defence of a place required no less tactical ability than in a battle. When

---

69 Jordanes, *Getica*, LIX, 311. Procopius, *BG*, V, 14, 12–14 (Rome occupied by Belisarius); 15–17 (circuit-wall restored; food supply).
70 Agathias, *Hist.*, III, 23, 2.
71 Maurice, *Strategikon*, X, 3, 3–5.

the Ostrogoths arrived under the walls of Rome in March 537, Belisarius reinforced the weak points:

> He himself held the small Porta Pinciana and the one on his right called Salarian. At this location the rampart could be assaulted and the Romans could at the same time make sorties against the enemy. The Praenestina Gate [current Porta Maggiore] was entrusted to Bessas. He gave Constantine command of the Flaminian Gate next to the Pincienne, after having had these gates condemned by large stone walls on the inside to the point that they could not be opened. For, since one of their camps was very close, he feared some secret enterprise on the part of the enemies against the city. He ordered the infantry leaders to guard all the other gates. He closed each of the aqueducts as securely as possible by masonry work over a large width to prevent anyone from entering from the outside.[72]

As the population muttered against the fact that the aqueducts had been cut off, that they could no longer wash or grind grain, and that there was also a shortage of food, Belisarius had women, children, old men and servants of the soldiers evacuated to Campania. This mass manoeuvre was only possible because the Ostrogoths could not encircle the immense perimeter of Rome and because they remained close to their entrenched camps. At night, they were afraid of the raids launched by Belisarius' Moorish troops, who massacred, pillaged and then withdrew with impunity.[73] Maurice even recommended getting rid of useless mouths such as women, children and aged people before the arrival of the besieger.[74] During the first siege of Rome by the Ostrogoths led by Vitiges in 537–538, the advantage of siege machines was clearly with the Ostrogoths, but this was not enough. Belisarius's first stratagem was to laugh about it to reassure his troops who treated him as a hypocrite; the second was to demonstrate his talents as an archer to boost the morale of his men before ordering a devastating general fire at the oxen pulling the towers which were thus paralysed.[75] Rome fell on December 546 to a siege led by Totila due to the treachery of Isaurians soldiers and the idleness and greed of Bessas its Military Governor. During the reoccupation of Rome in the summer of 547, Belisarius found a city whose walls had been destroyed during the Visigothic occupation, especially the gates. In anticipation of a fourth siege, he spent 25 days working on fortifications, re-erecting the walls with the rubble, and digging

---

72   Procopius, *BG*, V, 19, 20–24.
73   Procopius, *BG*, V, 20, 5–7 (discontent); 25, 2–5 (evacuation); 6–77 (Ostrogoths stuck to their camps); (afraid by night); 9 (Moorish raids).
74   Maurice, *Strategikon*, X, 3, 6–7.
75   Procopius, *BG*, V, 19, 21, 1 *sq.* (machines); 22, 2–3 (laugh); 4–8 (archery).

a ditch reinforced with stakes. As this was not enough, he had *triboloi* or *tribuli* (caltrops) scattered in front of the gates:

> Four points of the same length are fixed together in such a way that they form a triangle at the base. They are thrown at the fly and three points sink firmly into the ground while the last one stands up and obstructs men and horses. When someone overturns one of these *tribuloi*, the point that was rising up to the sky settles into the ground while another stands up and obstructs those who attack. Such are the *tribuloi*.[76]

Two years later (549–550), Rome was besieged again – and again taken by treachery, and nothing to the reproach of Diogenes, the new Romano-Byzantine Governor, a *doryphoros* from Belisarius own guard. Despite a long blockade, the besieged did not starve because Diogenes had grain sewn inside the circuit-wall. Moreover, by maintaining a strict watch, with only 3 000 soldiers he repelled all the Ostrogoth attempts to storm the walls.[77] One can only say that betrayal prevailed over valour, as it often does.

Agathias described the measures taken to defend the port of Phasis in 556:

> Once behind the gates, the generals organised the guard of the circuit-wall in an orderly fashion, as they considered themselves too weak to engage in a pitched battle. First, Justin the son of Germanus [the Patrician] and his men were positioned in the highest part overlooking the sea. A little further back stood the General Martin with his forces; in the middle, Angilas with Moors armed with shields and spears, Theodore with Tzani infantrymen, Philomathios with Isaurian slingers and spearmen. At a short distance from them, a detachment of Lombards and Heruls stood guard led by Gibros. The rest of the rampart to the east was guarded by troops from the Eastern Army under the command of General Valerian.[78]

In the harbour, the masts of ships that exceeded the height of the rampart were lined with archers.[79] To counter a regular Persian assault, the custom was to unleash a hail of features:

> From the top of the towers and battlements, the Romans resisted with ardour and pushed them back .... Many javelins, thrown from

---

76 Procopius, *BG*, VII, 24, 16–18 (τρίβολοι).
77 Procopius, *BG*, VII, 36, 1–3.
78 Agathias, *Hist.*, III, 20, 9–10.
79 Agathias, *Hist.*, III, 21, 4–5.

the top of the ramparts, injured the enemies, because they fell on an unprotected troop and could not be avoided. Enormous stones were thrown against the galleries, breaking their protective mesh; others, smaller, launched with slings, pierced the helmets and shields of the Medes and prevented them from approaching very close to the rampart by creating a very strong obstacle to them.[80]

The late Roman Army had an effective artillery.[81] 'Scorpion-type' throwing machines were very powerful, confirming what Ammianus Marcellinus had said two centuries earlier: 'The feathered darts prepared for this purpose carried great distances, to the point of piercing and shooting down those who came from afar, with their horses themselves.'[82] These machines played an important role in the defence of Rome:

> Belisarius placed machines called ballistas on the towers. Today, these machines are like a bow, but underneath there is a grooved wooden ramp that projects the lines. This ramp, fixed on an iron structure, is attached to the arch which maintains its freedom of movement. To shoot, we bring back the two limbs of the bow by a short rope fixed at its ends and we place on the ramp an arrow which has half the ordinary length of those of the bows but four times its width. However, this arrow does not have fletching feathers but rather thin pieces of wood which give it the appearance of an arrow despite its thickness, and the men standing on either side release it by a manoeuvre while the grooved ramp throws itself forward then stops discharging the arrow with such force that it goes two bow spans and easily pierces a tree or a rock.[83]

The *ballista* in Latin, *ballistra* in Greek described by Procopius, close to the Hellenistic *katapeltē*, was the same as that of the later Roman Empire, which threw only bolts, and not the stone balls like those of the early Roman Empire.[84]

There still existed 'machines for throwing stones that look like fronds and are called *onagroi*'. This description corresponded to the onager described more than a century earlier by Ammianus Marcellinus, a name derived from the Asian wild donkey.[85] With the *ballista* and the *onager*, the

---

80   Agathias, *Hist.*, III, 25, 3–5.
81   P. E. Chevedden, 'Artillery in Late Antiquity: Prelude to the Middle Ages' in J. F. Haldon (ed.), *Byzantine Warfare* (Aldershot: Ashgate Publishing, 2007), pp.453–496.
82   Agathias, *Hist.*, III, 25, 6.
83   Procopius, *BG*, V, 21, 14–18.
84   Βαλλίστρα.
85   Procopius, *BG*, V, 21, 19 (ὄναγρος, plural ὄναγροι). Ammianus Marcellinus, *RG*, XXIII, 4, 4 and 7; XXXI, 15, 2. Ph. Richardot, (2005), pp.258–259.

lykos (wolf), was also used in the defence of Rome by Belisarius. The *lykos* was a beam with an iron goad and a chain. It was dropped onto the enemy's wooden galleries, crushing them.[86] In addition to the traditional weaponry, there were siege expediencies such as the fortification of Hadrian's mausoleum, a vast rotunda, now known as the Castel Sant'Angelo. On the right bank of the Tiber, this massive complex defended the bridge leading to the Cornelian Gate to the north-west that Procopius called Aurelian Gate. In 537, Belisarius left a weak garrison there because he did not think that the enemy would attack this side. This was an error and the Ostrogoths launched a massive assault here with ladders and under tortoises of shields. As the mausoleum was furnished with magnificent large statues in Parian marble, the Romano-Byzantines broke them and dropped the pieces onto the Ostrogoths.[87] It was an act of vandalism that the Romans had not dared to perpetrate when they defended Rome against the Vandals in 455, nor against the Burgundian *foederati* in 472. The Christian religion also had its share in the siege of 537: between the Flaminian Gate and the Pincian Gate stood the so-called 'cracked wall' which the Romans had not repaired as the Apostle Peter had promised to keep it from any enemy. Belisarius followed the custom and the Saint kept his word as Procopius rightly remarked.[88]

The Best Defence is Sometimes to Attack

Only the defender had the opportunity of transforming the siege into a pitched battle by a sortie en masse. This was the choice that Belisarius made in March 537 on the eighteenth day of the siege. While the Ostrogoths were gathered against the walls of Rome with ladders and machines, he brought out all his cavalry from the Salarian Gate, and probably also through the Labicane Gate, while his infantry remained on the top of the ramparts shooting arrows. Surprised and overwhelmed by the torrent of Romano-Byzantine horsemen, the Goths fled without resisting and were massacred and their siege machines set on fire. Only their entrenched camps saved them from complete annihilation.[89]

During the second siege of Rome in 545–546 by the Ostrogoths, Bessas was forced to hand it over to them. But Totila abandoned the city to campaign against Belisarius, who reoccupied it in April 547. After hastily rebuilding the walls as best he could, he had to defend them over the winter. Fortunately for him the Ostrogoths did not deploy a vast array of machines as they had during the first siege. Belisarius' tactic was, as usual, to launch a counter-attack, even if he was compelled to send reinforcements to stop an enemy offensive. Some time after, he carried out a new tactic: quite simply,

---

86   Procopius, *BG*, V, 21, 19–22 (λύκος).
87   Procopius, *BG*, V, 22, 12–23.
88   Procopius, *BG*, V, 23, 3–6.
89   Procopius, *BG*, V, 22, 1 (Gothic assault); 23, 23–26 (sortie en masse).

he waiting for the enemy in a positional battle in front of the walls. On this occasion Totila's standard-bearer was killed, the Ostrogoths were routed, pursued and massacred. Totila then retreated to Tibur (now Tivoli), after cutting the bridges.[90] Rome was saved but only for two years.

The arrival of a relief force was the best way to end a siege. In 555, the surprise arrival of 3,000 Persian cavalry routed the 50,000 Romano-Byzantines besieging Onoguris in Lazica. The following year, the port of Phasis was besieged by the Persians. As the Romano-Byzantines had no hope of being saved by a relief column, they resorted to a stratagem. Justin the son of the Patrician Germanus went to pray in a chapel outside the city with 5,000 horsemen; that was the pious excuse given by Agathias, who saw the idea as a divine inspiration. Unnoticed as the Persians were attacking the opposite side of the city, the horsemen attacked them from behind causing havoc and winning the day.[91]

Psychological warfare could rebalance the chances of a place besieged by a superior force but required a great sense of improvisation from the general. At Phasis in 556, General Martin gathered his troops and publicly read a letter from a messenger bringing false news of the arrival of a relief army camped nearby. Martin feigned anger and demanded the dismissal of these reinforcements who were entitled neither to the laurels of victory nor to the spoils. He thus restored the morale of his men and worried the Persians who had their spies in the city. The Persian general sent a detachment to block the arrival of these supposed reinforcements and, as recounted above, Justin the son Germanus was able to sally out with the cavalry against the weakened besieging forces.[92]

During the 12 months and 9 days that the first siege of Rome lasted (from March 537 to March 538), Belisarius launched no fewer than 67 cavalry sorties, during both day and night, almost one per week.[93] Nocturnal sorties demoralised the Goths dissuading them from any action outside daylight hours. At night, Belisarius also had musicians playing on the ramparts to confuse the enemy, deployed guard dogs as early warning system and sent small bodies of Moors to near the moat, from where they attacked isolated barbarians.[94] Sorties were also diversionary actions, such as the cavalry fight that Belisarius led in late June 537 north of Rome to mask the arrival of the army's pay to the south. They could also neutralise an imminent danger, as John the nephew of Vitalian did in 538 in defending Rimini from an Ostrogothic wheeled, wooden mobile tower. At night, he went out with the Isaurians to deepen the ditch in the path of this mobile tower. Working

---

90   Procopius, *BG*, VII, 24, 19 (counter-attack); 23–26 (positional battle); 31 (Totila's retreat).
91   Agathias, *Hist.*, III, 7, 1 *sq.* (Onoguris); 24, 7–8 (Justin with 5,000 cavalrymen); 25, 8 (charge); 26, 1 *sq.* (Persian rout).
92   Agathias, *Hist.*, III, 23, 5–12; 24, 1–3.
93   Procopius, *BG*, VI, 2, 37.
94   Procopius, *BG*, V, 25, 9 (Goths stick to their camps); 25, 17 (Belisarius' stratagems).

silently, they were able to return safely to the city. The following day, the Goths' siege tower leaned dangerously when it rolled onto the ditch, which was apparently filled with fagots. They decided to pull it back so as not to have the Romano-Byzantines burn it during a night raid. But Jean went out immediately, caused great losses to the barbarians who, despite everything, saved their precious machine.[95]

Countermines gave the besieged the opportunity to launch an underground counter-attack and take the surprise out of the besieger's hands. In 540, as the Persians dug a mine to take Dara, the Romano-Byzantines, warned by a spy in Persian dress and advised by a certain Theodore expert in mechanical science, made a trench between the outer and the inner walls then unexpectedly fell upon the incoming enemy sappers. Khosrow I, having seen his ruse foiled accepted 1,000 pounds of silver to lift the siege and keep his honour unsullied. The countermine also allowed the besieged to safely set fire to an attack terrace, *agesta*, like the one that Khosrow I had built in front of Edessa in 544 with wood, stones and earth. The Romano-Byzantines dug a gallery to the middle of the terrace where they created a chamber which they filled with dry tree trunks coated with cedar oil, sulphur and bitumen. The fire grew gradually but during the afternoon the smoke could be seen from Carrhae, about 40km to the south. Khosrow again preferred to come to an agreement.[96]

A besieged city communicated with the outside world sending a courageous messenger who crossed enemy lines discreetly at night, carrying an oral or written message and most of the time was successful in doing so. This was a quite easy task from Rome, whose nineteen-kilometre perimeter was too large to be effectively watched by the besiegers. It was more difficult to perform when a smaller city was closely surrounded by the besieger. In August 538, while John the nephew of Vitalian was besieged at Rimini, he sent a messenger who crawled through the enemy sentries and was able to carry a plea for help to Belisarius. John was fortunate enough for his appeal to be heard. During the siege of Milan by the Ostrogoths and Burgundians in February 539, Mundilas sent Paul, leader of the Thracian soldiers, to cross the enemy blockade and swim across the River Po to persuade Martin and Uliaris, who were encamped nearby, to come to relieve the city as Belisarius had previously ordered. The two generals cynically sent the same messenger back bearing a promise which they would not keep. At the same time, Martin wrote to Belisarius that he had inadequate forces to face the multitude of barbarians and requested for reinforcements.[97] Milan fell and his fate was hardly enviable.

---

95 Procopius, *BG*, VI, 2, 1–24 (Belisarius' diversion); 12, 1–25 (Rimini mobile tower).
96 Procopius, *BP*, II, 13, 26–28 (Dara); 27, 1–17 (Edessa).
97 Procopius, *BG*, VI, 16, 14–16 (Rimini); 21, 1–11 (Milan).

Plate A. The Theodosian Walls
(Illustration by Renato Dalmaso © Helion & Company)
See colour plate commentaries for further information.

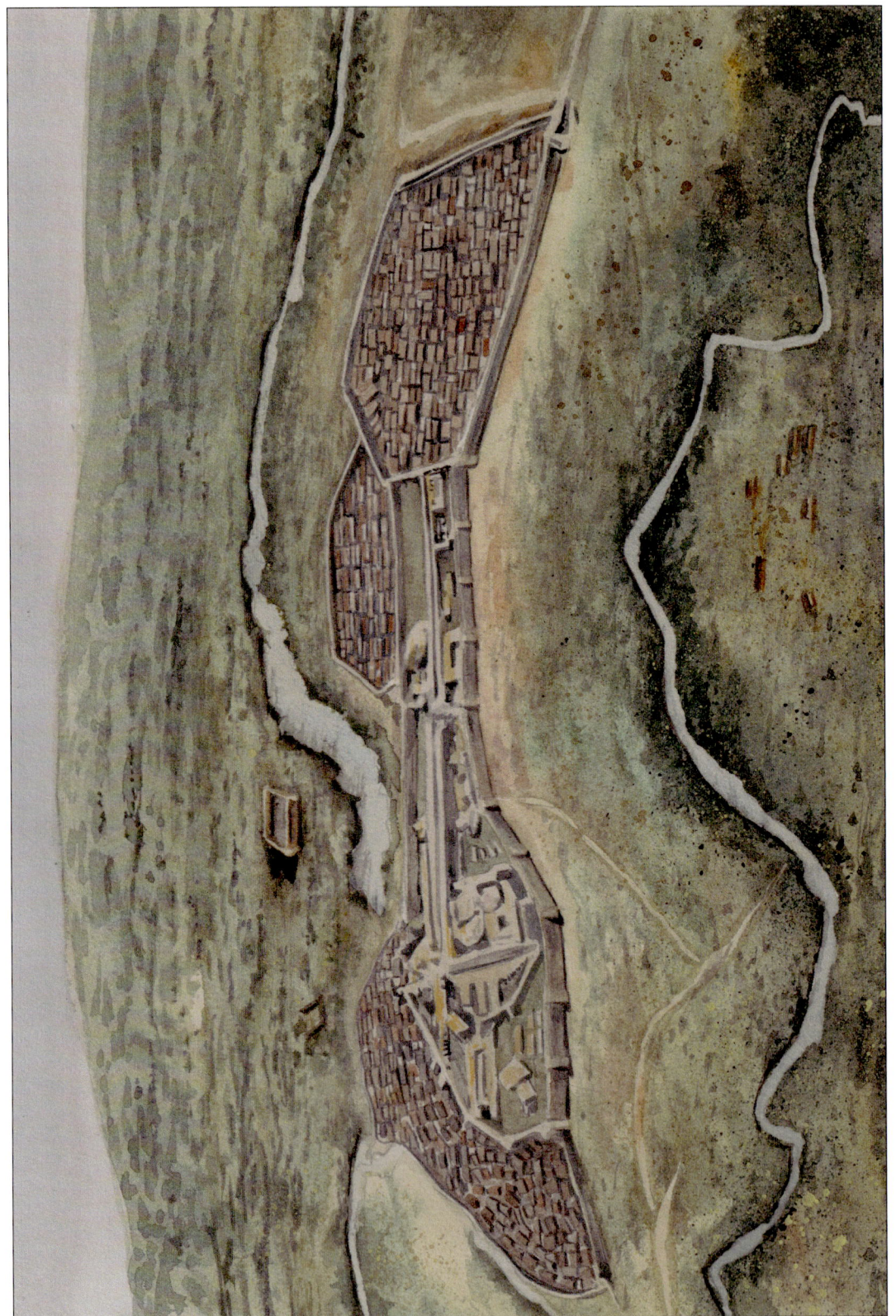

Plate B. Iustiniana Prima
(Illustration by Renato Dalmaso © Helion & Company)
See colour plate commentaries for further information.

Plate C. Mid-6th Century Heavy Cavalry
(Illustration by Renato Dalmaso © Helion & Company)
See colour plate commentaries for further information.

Plate D. Late Sixth Century cataphract
(Illustration by Renato Dalmaso © Helion & Company)
See colour plate commentaries for further information.

Plate E. Seventh Century Syrian infantryman
(Illustration by Renato Dalmaso © Helion & Company)
See colour plate commentaries for further information.

Plate F. Junior Officer
(Illustration by Renato Dalmaso © Helion & Company)
See colour plate commentaries for further information.

Plate G. Byzantine footman in Lazica second half of the Sixth Century
(Illustration by Renato Dalmaso © Helion & Company)
See colour plate commentaries for further information.

Plate H. Sixth-Seventh Century foot archer
(Illustration by Renato Dalmaso © Helion & Company)
See colour plate commentaries for further information.

'Woe Betide the Defeated': the Capture of a City

> I have often witnessed the taking of cities and I know very well what happens in such cases. Men of all ages are killed, and the women, though they beg to be killed, are not given the chance but are dragged off to suffer the most abominable and pitiful outrages. The children, who are deprived of the supports of their education, are doomed to be the slaves of the most odious men of all, those who have on their hands the blood of their parents. That is not all, my dear Stephen, for I have not mentioned the conflagration which destroys all the goods and all the beauty of the city.

Belisarius sincerely added in this letter that he had no control over his men, especially the barbarians, who had lost friends and relatives fighting under the walls of Naples.[98] The city fell and its fate did not differ greatly from Belisarius' warning while the classic trilogy of 'kill, pillage and rape' inevitably applied. The soldiers killed the men, captured the women, children and slaves then pillaged the goods. Like the pagans that they were the Huns even massacred those who had taken refuge in churches. Notwithstanding Belisarius put an end to the atrocities, asking his troops not to make enemies of the Neapolitans by mistreating them. He freed the captives and reconciled the soldiers with the surviving Neapolitans, who were able to recover the money and valuables they had previously buried.[99] The Neapolitans miserably asked Belisarius for forgiveness and, as a sign of goodwill, killed the two public figures who had called them to resist. It is worthwhile to consider that Naples was a Roman city destined to join the Empire and had to be spared as a gesture of good politics. This was not the case of Siderous, the principal fortress of the restless Misimians, which was taken at night in 557:

> The Romans, coming to meet them at the gates themselves, as if to welcome them with the sword, made a great massacre of them. Some were killed as soon as they emerged, others were arriving or were about to arrive, and there was no respite for their suffering, for they were all being hunted down. Many of the women who had risen up flocked to the gates in supplication, but the Romans, carried away by their anger, did not even spare them; they too were cruelly massacred, paying the price for the mad pride of men. One of the most distinguished of them, a torch in her hand, a spear stuck in her belly, was dying miserably. One of the Romans seized the torch and set fire to the houses, which, being made of wood and thatch, burnt

---

98   Procopius, *BG*, V, 9, 24–26 (Belisarius letter); 9, 28 (no control).
99   Procopius, *BG*, V, 10, 29–36

very quickly.... Then a greater number of barbarians died en masse: some, inside the houses, were consumed by fire and buried under the rubble, and for those who rushed outside, death by the sword awaited them. Many children, who wept and called out for their mothers, were seized and the soldiers crushed some by throwing them against rocks, while others were carried like bundles after being thrown into the air and then caught in flight on swords, as if for fun.[100]

However, massacres followed by pillage were the rarest, since usually a city preferred to capitulate before this bitter ending.

When the defence was successful and the siege continued on, there came the dark riders of Famine and Pestilence, the two inseparable companions of War and Death. This happened in late March 538 in Rome after a year and nine days of blockade by the Ostrogoths who were also affected. But as their blockade was incomplete, Belisarius had the resources to bring food into the city from Campania and Bruttium via the Tiber. More affected than the Roman population, the Ostrogoths lifted the siege.[101] This was the exception, because without outside help, a city was doomed to fall. This is what happened to Milan, after a long blockade, probably around the beginning of March 539. Defended by a garrison of 300 Romano-Byzantines soldiers commanded by Mundilas, the city starved and the inhabitants ate dogs, rats of course, and 'animals that had never been eaten by man'. No doubt to soften the lamentable news of surrendering a city to the enemy in exchange for their lives, Procopius gave Mundilas a heroic speech to his 300 worn out men, urging them to sally out with arms in hand. His men refused, the city was surrendered and burnt to the ground, 300,000 civilians were said to be massacred and the women enslaved, while Mundilas and his troops were only taken prisoner – victorious warriors respecting their defeated enemy.[102] It was the greatest defensive siege failure of the Empire and the largest massacre of the sixth century, but the overall number of deaths claimed is highly questionable.

When Totila recaptured Rome the 17 December 547, he proved to be cruel towards the city and its inhabitants probably because the population had helped the Byzantines:

> Totila entered Rome on the kalends, the sixteenth day of January; he demolished the walls, set fire to several houses and took the property of all the Romans as booty. He took these same Romans as prisoners

---

100 Agathias, *Hist.*, IV, 19, 3–5.
101 Procopius, *BG*, VI, 3, 1 (hunger and pestilence); 4, 16–17 (Goths); 10, 13 (siege duration and ending).
102 Procopius, *BG*, VI, 12, 27 (Paul leader of the Thracians); 40 (300-strong garrison); 21, 26 (hunger); 21, 27–28 (negotiations); 21, 29–37 (speech); 39–40 (Milan destruction and Mundilas surrender).

to Campania. After this devastation, Rome was so desolate that for 40 days or more neither man nor beast remained there.[103]

When a garrison was not paid, such as the 3,000 Imperial soldiers who defended Rome in 549–550, betrayal rather than a protest was to be expected although most soldiers remained loyal. Only the Isaurians negotiated with the Ostrogoths after the long siege, and they opened the gates of the city. On 16 January 550, some of their comrades were fooled by a fake attack signalled with trumpets on the side of St Paul's Gate on the Tiber, others were slaughtered by the Goths entering the city, and the rest fled, most of them via the road to Centumcellae (current Civitavecchia), where an ambush awaited them, Diogenes, the commander of the garrison, was wounded there but after that he resolutely defended Centumcellae. But 400 horsemen under Paul's orders still resisted near the Hadrian's mausoleum defending the bridge to the church of St Peter, 300 took refuge in churches. Starving and with no hope except to seek a glorious death, they were offered the options by Totila to either return to Byzantium on foot and disarmed or to join him. In fact, they had inflicted heavy losses to the Ostrogoths and Totila was afraid of suffering more losses. These 700 soldiers passed into Totila's army, only an officer and a loyal Isaurian were allowed to rejoin Byzantine lines under escort.[104] This time, far from martyring Rome as the barbarian he was supposed to be, Totila called a meeting of the Senate, rebuilt the buildings he had destroyed and held a chariot race held.[105] For him Rome was the main city of his Kingdom not an enemy city place to plunder.

The Persians sought more to ransom than to conquer. Nevertheless, like other contemporary peoples they were particularly cruel when they took a city that had resisted. In 503, as a result of their too-long resistance, the inhabitants of Amida were massacred: 80,000 to 85,000 killed according to contemporary sources. This figure is likely because, during the siege of 359, the population had swelled from 20,000 to 120,000 with the influx of refugees.[106] At the beginning of the campaign of 540, Khosrow I decided to make an example of the small town of Sura on the River Euphrates, which had resisted for only one day. The city was burnt to the ground, part of the population was massacred, the other part was held for ransom and died in captivity.[107] When they captured Antioch shortly afterwards, the Persians massacred all those old enough to bear arms and took the rest of

---

103 Marcellinus Comes, *Chr.*, a. 547.
104 Procopius, *BG*, VII, 36, 7 (Isaurians); 8–10 (Totila's diversion plan); 11 (ambush on road to Civitavecchia); 12 (diversionary attack); 13–15 (Romano-Byzantine rout; Diogenes); 16–23 (Paul's horsemen); 24 – 28 (surrender).
105 Procopius, *BG*, VII, 37, 3.
106 (Pseudo-)Zachariah Rhetor, *HE*, VII, 4; Joshua the Stylite, *Chr.*, 53; *Zuqnin Chronicle*, II, 5 (85,000. Ammianus Marcellinus, *RG*, XIX, 2, 14.
107 Procopius, *BP*, II, 5, 26 (destruction and massacre); 32 (death).

the population for ransom.¹⁰⁸ Another example of this cruelty to civilians happened after the capture of Jerusalem in 614 by General Shahrbaraz. The latter offered the city the chance to surrender before applying the rigours of a siege. According to Sebeos, the authorities of Jerusalem offered to pay tribute to Shahrbaraz who accepted but some excited citizens of Jerusalem killed the Persian emissaries. A 19-day siege ensued, which ended on 19 May. Strategius said that the siege lasted 21 days (15 April to 5 May) with artillery bombardments and assaults using galleries and mantlets. During this period, a Romano-Byzantine relief army led by the monk, Abba Modestus, arrived but quickly pulled back when they saw the numbers of the Persians. Finally, on the last day of the siege, treachery won out. When the Persians broke through, they exterminated the Christians, who took refuge in cellars, cisterns and churches. Strategius put civilian losses at 66,509. Sebeos gave a figure of 35,000 captives and 17,000 killed after three days of massacre. The Jewish community took part in the massacre of the Christians and was allowed to remain in the city. The surviving Christians, including Patriarch Zachariah, were taken captive to Babylon. Churches were burnt down and the true cross was taken as loot but then returned in 629 after Heraclius has raided Ctesiphon, retaken Jerusalem and obtained peace with Siroes, the successor to Khosrow II.¹⁰⁹ Ten years later, the Muslim conquest was also punctuated by massacres. When Caesarea in Palestine fell into their hands between 639 and 641, Mouawiya's men killed 7,000 Romans according to Theophanes Confessor, a figure which corresponds to the garrison according to Michael the Syrian and part of which fled by ship while the population was forced to give up its riches. Elias of Nisibis overestimated the massacre at 100,000 people.¹¹⁰ During the conquest of Egypt, the fate of the cities that fell into Muslim hands was tragic. Thus, like Bahnasâ the city of Nikiu was mercilessly treated: 'They massacred everyone they met, in the streets and in the churches, men, women and children, without sparing anyone.'¹¹¹

Case Study: the Avars at the Gates of Byzantium in 626!

From the high crenellated walls of the second enclosure, the people of Byzantium look in fear at the columns of black smoke escaping from the

---

108 Procopius, *BP*, II, 8, 34 (massacre of those old enough to bear arms); 9, 14 (ransom).
109 Strategius, *The Capture of Jerusalem by the Persians in 614*, ed. Conybeare, *English Historical Review*, 25, 1910, pp.502–517. Sebeos, *Hist.*, 34, 115 (negotiations and siege), 116 (losses).
110 Theophanes Confessor, *Chrgr.*, AM 6133, 341. Michael the Syrian, *HU*, XI, 8, t. 2 (1963), p.431. Elias of Nisibis, *Op.Chr.*, 65.
111 John of Nikiu, *Chr.*, 111, 10 (1883), p.435 (Bahnasâ); 118, 8, p.448 (Nikiu).

villages and farms of the suburbs. This is the first of three attempts by the Avars to take the city. The first in 578 was more a raid of devastation on the outskirts than a siege.[112] The second in 623 was what might be called a 'surprise' in the modern military sense. Emperor Heraclius, at war with the Persians, had spent the previous year reorganising his forces in Asia Minor and sought to negotiate with the Avars. On Sunday 5 June, he naively waited for their Khan near Heraclea on the Propontis to conclude a peace agreement with him, accompanied by a civilian escort made up of priests, merchants and supporters of the Blue and Green Factions, as the army was in Asia Minor. He even wanted to hold a chariot race in Heraclea on the occasion. The Khan treacherously sent a troop through the Long Walls, part of which had been ruined.[113] This troop infiltrated Byzantium's walls as far as the Golden Gate and the outer part of the Blachernae district where they plundered the church of St Cosmas and St Damian. On the verge of being captured, the Emperor only escaped by wearing ordinary clothes. According to the *Chronicon Paschale*, the Avars camped in front of the city on the plain called Hebdomon to show that they had nothing to fear. Then they returned home with 270,000 captives, a figure undoubtedly exaggerated but covering the result of their entire military campaign. The dating is also a matter of controversy, since Nikephoros places the event at the beginning of the reign of Heraclius but after the conquest of Egypt by the Persians. Theophanes, a later source, dated this event to the year of the world 6110, i.e. *c.* 618–619, stating that the Emperor had left Byzantium and was lured into a trap by the Khan promise to conclude peace. He mentioned the capture of Heraclius' baggage and escort and the ensuing plunder of Thrace.[114] Whatever the fog of history may be, this nearly catastrophic incident gave the Khan a hope of taking Byzantium. By then he had a formidable military power with his nomadic people of expert horsemen armed with long spears, composite bows and long straight swords. Their highly innovative helmets and lamellar breastplates were both light and strong, even today impenetrable to small calibre pistols. Avars combined mobility, armour, shock and fire power.[115] Within 50 years, they had become a power almost comparable to Attila's Huns.

---

112 Agathias, *Hist.*, V, 12, 7 (Siege of 559). John of Biclaro, *Chr. VT*, 46 (577).
113 Procopius, *Aed.*, IV, 9, 9.
114 *Chr. Paschale*, a. 623. Nikephoros of Constantinople, *Brev.*, 10, 16–29 (Heraclius); 39–38 (270,000 prisoners). Theophanes Confessor, *Chrgr.*, AM 6110, 302 (surprise attack; baggage train; Thrace). Theodore Synkellos, *In depositionem pretiosae vestis*, ed. Combefis F. dans *Historia haeresis Monothelitarum*, Paris, 1648, pp.751–786. Id., translated by A. Cameron, 'The Virgin's Robe: An Episode in the History of Seventh-Century Constantinople', *REB*, 49 (1979), pp.42–56. M. Whitby (tr. into English) *Chronicon Paschale. 284–628 AD* (Liverpool: Liverpool University Press, TTH, 7, 2007), pp.203–205.
115 K. Nagy, 'Notes on the Arms of the Avar Heavy Cavalry' in *Proceedings of the First International Conference on the Medieval History of the Eurasian Steppe*, Szeged, May 11–16, 2004, Part II (Szeged: Akadémiai Kiado, *Acta Orientalia Academiae*

Helped by Sklavenes, the Khan besieged Byzantium during the summer of 626. The Bulgars and Gepids may also have participated in this siege.[116] On 29 June, a vanguard of 30,000 Avars crossed the Long Walls and arrived in front of the Theodosian Wall, preventing the Byzantines from grazing their animals outside the walls. Nevertheless, for 10 days, as the enemy did not appear, soldiers, their servants and civilians went out to harvest crops a few miles from the city. A skirmish took place, which was favourable to the Romano-Byzantines, who would have massacred the Avars had they not had to defend the non-combatants. After that, 1,000 enemy appeared north of the Golden Horn, in the district of Sykai or Sycae, lighting fires to signal themselves to the Persians arriving on the opposite shore of Bosphorus near Chrysopolis.[117] Anastasius who commanded the forces around Adrianople brought 12,000 cavalry as reinforcements.[118] A month later, on 29 July, the Khan and his army appeared in front of the Byzantine walls to intimidate the population. They launched an attack on 31 July. Their front was extended from the Pempton Gate to the Polyandrion Gate, punching against the central part of the Theodosian Wall, nearly 1,200m in length.[119] It was a hilly area crossed by the Lycus. Against other parts of the wall, the Sklavenes formed the first line of an assault force followed by Avar armoured infantrymen: a diversion where they served as expendable small charge. George of Pisidia, probably in an epic exaggeration, estimated this mass of barbarians at 80,000![120] The fight lasted from dawn to the eleventh hour. In the evening, the Khan disposed the mantlets and siege machines against the Brachialion (literally bracelet), probably the front wall of the Theodosian defences. This event took place on 1 August according to the *Chronicon Pascale*: the Avars placed 'a multitude of siege machines' on their axis of effort, forcing the defenders to concentrate also machines in this sector. The assault was contained, but in the course of the day the Khan brought out the big artillery.[121]

Almost a rolling tannery advanced towards the walls of Byzantium. The Avars had their siege machines covered with freshly skinned cowhides to prevent fire. The Khan formed a battery of stone-throwing catapults, and concentrated 12 mobile towers plus wooden galleries of tortoise-type, between the gate Polyandrion and the gate of St Romanus. That was cutting the possible front of attack in half. In the besieged city, everyone understood the issue. Under the leadership of the Patrician Bonus, civilian sailors assisted the population in defending the rampart. One of them distinguished himself by his ingenuity, raising a mast to attach it an aerial

---

Scientiarum Hungaricae, 58, 2, 2005), pp.135–148.
116 Theophanes Confessor, *Chrgr.*, AM 6117, 315 (only source with Bulgars and Gepids).
117 *Chr. paschale*, a.626, (2007), p.171.
118 *Chr. paschale*, a.626, (2007), p.172, (12,000 horsemen).
119 *Chr. paschale*, a.626, (2007), p.173.
120 George of Pisidia, *Bellum Avaricum*, v. 217–219.
121 *Chr. paschale*, a.626, (2007), p.174.

bucket from which he tried to set fire to the enemy's assault towers.[122] In the Golden Horn, the fleet attacked some of the *pirogues* that the Slavs had brought from the Danube against the bridge of St Kallinikos. The *pirogues'* sailors were no match against a Byzantine thalassocracy. On 2 August, the Khan asked to negotiate. His aim was to impress the Byzantine delegation, made up of the Patricians George and Athanasius, the Patrician and *logothete* Theodosius, the *Commerciarius*, or tax agent, Theodore and the Bishop Theodore Synkellos, the future historian of this siege. The Khan counted on the presence of three Persian Ambassadors and the help of 3,000 soldiers from the *Shahrbaraz* or *generalissimo*, Salabaras, or Sabaros, in Greek, who had arrived on the opposite bank of the Bosphorus. The Greeks were not impressed and the meeting ended miserably with mutual insults. The Persian emissaries re-embarked at Chalae (now Bebek) to return to the eastern bank of the Bosphorus, but were intercepted at sea. One was sent to the Khan with his hands cut off and the head of the second as a necklace, while the head of the third was sent to the Persians with a message falsely stating that the Khan had made peace with Byzantium.[123] The profession of the diplomat has always had its risks and Byzantine fair play had its limits.

In the evening, a fleet of Sklavene *pirogues* crossed the Bosphorus from Chalae to ferry the Persians across. Against them the Romano-Byzantines launched 70 ships but their approach was hampered by the wind. These were biremes and triremes armed by the Patrician Bonus, regularly named *Magistros* by the *Chronicon Paschale*, and certainly the master of the soldiers Present.[124] According to Sebeos, the Persians tried to get into the city from ships and lost 4,000 men at sea to the Byzantine fleet. Unlike Theodore Synkellos, he did not mention the role of Sklavenes in ferrying Persians, the Persians had no fleet of their own there.[125] It was undoubtedly a total massacre, for Nikephoros wrote that the sea was stained with blood and that among others were the floating corpses of Sklavene women.[126] Undeterred, on Wednesday 6 August the Khan launched an assault on the Blachernae district at the northern end of the city. The Avars forced open both gates but were driven back.[127] The next day, the Sklavenes and the Bulgars crossed

---

122 *Chr. paschale*, a.626, (2007), p.174, (stone-throwers; Polyandrion and gate St Romanus; 12 mobile towers covered with hides; aerial bucket episode). Theodore Synkellos, *De Obsidione Avarica Constantinopolis*, 306, 13–19 (machines covered with hides). Nikephoros of Constantinople, *Brev.*, 13, 15–17 (mobile towers and tortoises).
123 *Chr. Paschale*, a.626, (2007), pp.175–177.
124 *Chr. Paschale*, a.626, (2007), p.178. Nikephoros of Constantinople, *Brev.*, 26–28 (Bonus the Patrician's biremes and triremes).
125 Sebeos, *Hist.*, 38 (told erroneously King Khosrow being present at this naval encounter). Theodore Synkellos, *De Obsidione Avarica Constantinopolis*, 307, 8-308, 2.
126 Nikephoros of Constantinople, *Brev.*, 32–36.
127 George of Pisidia, *Bellum Avaricum*, v. 403–406. Theodore Synkellos, *De Obsidione Avarica Constantinopolis*, 308, 2–28 (6 August).

the Golden Horn in small canoe-like boats, at the point where the walls were weaker.[128] The Imperial fleet again sank again most of this force, and then Armenian soldiers sallied out from the wall of Blachernae and set fire to the portico near St Nicholas blocking any land attack from that side. The remaining Sklavenes dived from the *pirogues* into the sea, desperately trying to escape but those who returned to the shore were merciless executed on the Khan orders. A second assault made by the Avars who had disembarked was repulsed by the Armenians.[129] The Khan's intention was to use the attack across the Golden Horn as a diversion while his troops attacked Blachernae, but the Sklavenes attacked too soon.[130] Crest-fallen by this bloody day, the Sklavenes decided to abandon the siege.[131]

After this disaster the Avars retreated, lifting the siege with great professionalism: the siege machines were brought back, their 'fireproof skins' were removed and the palisade which protected their camp was dismantled. By night all this was set on fire. The following day up until the 7th hour, present-day 1200 to 1300, a cavalry rearguard covered the retreat setting fire to two churches and many suburbs before it withdrew.[132] Synkellos wrote that Byzantine inhabitants burnt canoes and corpses of the enemy impaling their heads on the wall and that the authorities had to prevent the angered population from sallying out.[133] To save face, the Khan bombastically let the Byzantines know that he was not leaving out of fear but out of lack of provisions and threatened to return.[134] Reinforcements led by Theodore Kouropalates, brother of Heraclius, arrived shortly after the Khan's departure. Although they did not intervene in the defence, the announcement of their arrival may have decided the Avars to abandon the siege.

According to Theophanes, the siege of Byzantium lasted only 10 days, causing heavy losses to the Avars, while the Shahrbaraz and the Persians who were besieging Chalcedon spent the winter there.[135] Synkellos wrote that the Persians continued to besiege Chalcedon for some time but finally retreated.[136] The *Chronicon Paschale* attributed the happy outcome of the siege to the favour of God and the protection of the Blessed Virgin. During

---

128 Theophanes Confessor, *Chrgr.*, AM 6117, 316 (huge canoe fleet across Golden Horn). George of Pisidia, *Bellum Avaricum*, v. 409–12 (Bulgars on canoes).
129 *Chr. paschale*, a.626, 2007, p.178 (Armenians; portico; retreating Sklavenes slain by the Khan). George of Pisidia, *Bellum Avaricum*, v. 441–474. Theodore Synkellos, *De Obsidione Avarica Constantinopolis*, 310, 38–40 (7 August); 311, 7–312 (Golden Horn attack).
130 Theodore Synkellos, *De Obsidione Avarica Constantinopolis*, 311, 10–12.
131 *Chr. paschale*, a.626, (2007), p.179.
132 *Chr. paschale*, a.626, (2007), p.179, (Avar retreat).
133 Theodore Synkellos, *De Obsidione Avarica Constantinopolis*, 312.
134 *Chr. paschale*, a.626, (2007), p.180.
135 Theophanes Confessor, *Chrgr.*, AM 6117, 316 (reinforcement sent by Heraclius; 10-day siege; Chalcedon).
136 Theodore Synkellos, *De Obsidione Avarica Constantinopolis*, 313, 14–27.

the siege, the morale of the population was maintained by the Patriarch Sergius who relied on the Marian relics of the churches of the Blachernae district and who placed icons of the Virgin at the gates of the city, usage that continued in the fortifications of the Balkan region until the Renaissance.[137] This was the origin of an important moment in Greek Orthodox liturgy, the Akathist Hymn to the Blessed Virgin, whose holy icon and the clothes that once belonged to her were carried around the ramparts, along with a piece of the true cross and an Acheiropoitic icon of Christ. The people thanked the Virgin with a night of standing prayer, *akathistos*.[138] The failure of the siege put an end to the tribute paid by the Empire and signalled the decline of the Avars. The following year, the wall was extended around the Church of Theotokos (Mother of God) in the outer part of the Blachernes district.[139]

---

[137] Theodore Synkellos, *De Obsidione Avarica Constantinopolis*, 303 and 304. N. H. Baynes., 'The Supranatural Defenders of Constantinople' in *Byzantine Studies and Other Essays* (London: The University of London, Athlone Press, 1955), pp.248–260.

[138] D. Stiernon, 'Bulletin de théologie mariale Byzantine', *REB*, 17 (1959), pp.201–250. (Ἀκάθιστος ὕμνος).

[139] *Chr. paschale*, a. 627.

13

Elite Cavalry and Second-Class Infantry?

> The general will be well advised to have more cavalry than infantry. The latter is only good for close combat, while the former can easily pursue or retreat, and when its men are dismounted it can serve as infantry.
>
> Maurice, *Strategikon*, VIII, 2, 85.

While the force of the Roman armies had resided in the infantry, nicknamed the *murus*, 'the wall', by the time the *Strategikon* was written it had become a secondary weapon. Indicative of the times, the *Strategikon* discussed cavalry battle formations in Book II but the infantry only in the second part of Book XII. Influenced by nomadic peoples from the Eurasian Steppe, early Byzantine cavalry achieved remarkable tactical flexibility, both in partisan warfare and in pitched battles. Generals did not hesitate to put themselves at its head in combat. This trend, born under the late Roman Empire, reached maturity in the sixth century then dominated military history throughout the middle ages. Was the cause to be found in training, weaponry or recruitment?

Cavalry Defensive Equipment and Armour

For Procopius the most powerful type of cavalryman was the shielded mounted archer:

> Today's archers go into battle covered in a cuirass and knee-length leggings. Their arrows hang from their right side and their shield from their left. Some also carry a spear and a small shield without a handle around their neck to protect their face and neck.[1]

---

1   Procopius, *BP*, I, 1, 12 (mounted archer).

ELITE CAVALRY AND SECOND-CLASS INFANTRY

Iconography suggests armour other than mail was worn as the nearly muscular breastplate shown on the Barberini Ivory with leather pteruges covering the upper arms and the thighs: a model inherited from the Hellenistic and Roman periods with only the spaulders being a genuine Byzantine novelty. On the Barberini Ivory, the Emperor is not wearing spaulders but his officer is. This kind of armour is frequent described on Orthodox military saints but was certainly not for the rank and files. A sixth-century fresco found in room 6 of the Coptic monastery of Baouit shows St Sisinnios as a horseman, very similar to the Barberini Ivory, with the same armour, the same cloak turned to the left, the same spear but without the Imperial diadem, the Saint is bearded, bareheaded and, of course, has a halo.[2] In room 17, St Sisinnios is unarmoured and mounted; the Saint is dressed in a long white embroidered *manicata* tunic and *braccae*, or trousers, and wears a reddish cloak. Nevertheless, he his killing a female demon with a long spear, and is holding a small oval shield bordered in light brown-orange with a green oval centre adorned by a black cross cercelee.[3] The same monastery also has a painted wooden plaque depicting St Theodore bearded and with the same clothing, except for the long tunic descending to above the knees and two decorative armbands on the forearm. The hilt of a sword hanging from a shoulder strap can be supposed on his left side, the side where he has a round shield that is resting on the ground. Theodore's right hand holds a spearshaft topped by and iron cross. The brown colouring of the pteruges suggest leather while the grey colour of the corselet and spaulders indicate iron. Even if he is shown on foot St Theodore wears the equipment of an elite cavalryman.[4]

Isidore of Seville wrote about the *squama*, scale or lamellar armour: 'The *squama* is iron body armour (*lorica*) made of bronze or iron plates linked together in the manner of fish scales and named for their glittering likeness to fish scales. Body armours are both polished and protected by goat-hair cloth.'[5] The first evidence of lamellar body armour is on the gold *nomisma* or *solidus* depicting Anastasius I (r. 491–518) in military dress with a spear and an oval shield.[6] The best-known depiction of lamellar armour is of the horseman engraved on the sixth-century silver Isola Rizza dish, preserved in Verona's Museo Civico di Castelvecchio. This helmeted,

---

2   D. Bénazeth, 'Calques de Baouit archivés à l'Ifao', *BIFAO*, 105 (2005), pp.1–12.
3   J. Clédat, 'Le monastère et la nécropole de Baouît', *MIFAO*, 12, 1 and 2 (1904), colour plate LVI.
4   Raffaele D'Amato, *Roman Heavy Cavalry (2) AD 500–1450*, Elite Series 235 (Oxford, Osprey Publishing, 2019), p.10, (Coptic Museum Cairo, inv. 9083).
5   Isidore of Seville, *Etymologiae*, XVIII, 13, 2 (*Squama est lorica ferrea ex lamminis ferreis aut aereis concatenata in modum squamae piscis, et ex ipso splendore squamarum etsimilitudine nuncupata. De ciliciis autem et poliuntur loricae et teguntur*). R. D'Amato, V. Pflaum, 'Two Suites of Lamellar Armour from Kranj (Carnium), Slovenia, in the light of Archaeological Analogies, Written Sources and Contemporary Iconography', *Acta Militaria Medievalia*, 15 (2019), p.17.
6   R. D'Amato, V. Pflaum, (2019), p.19.

lance-armed cavalryman was maybe a Lombard killing Sklavenes or more likely a Byzantine warrior dressed according to the military fashion of the Steppe nomads.[7] Early seventh-century frescoes from the monastery of Bawit also offer three more individuals dressed in a lamellar cuirass of the same type as depicted on the Isola Rizza dish. Two are infantrymen but St George has his horse nearby. He is clean shaven with a halo, wearing a short iron lamellar breastplate with iron decoration, a triple row of gilded or iron pteruges at the waist and the upper arms. A crimson sash and harness

of the same colour is worn over the cuirass. A thin black baldric suspends a sword on the left side. A large, light orange, oval shield is held at left.[8] Excavations at the Svetinja site in the fortified town of Viminacium have uncovered some 553 scales or strips of a cuirass dating to the late sixth or early seventh century, each measuring 7cm to 8.5cm long and 1.8cm wide. They are drilled with a hole at the top and bottom, two series of two holes on the sides to let through leather straps, some of which are preserved. Most are notched on the right side. It is a very specific model which differs from the Germanic or Avar examples.[9]

Fifth or Sixth-Century Horse Archer in Scale Armour
This horse archer is wearing scale armour on a leather *subarmalis*. His composite bow is easily visible. His crested helmet with visor is unattested from archaeology. It is probably an artistic convention reminiscent of the older, classical Thracian helmet. After a fifth or sixth-century ivory from Egypt depicting an escort, today in the Rheinisches Landesmuseum, Trier.

---

7   I. Lebedynsky, *Les Scythes. La Civilisation des steppes (VIIe-IIIe siècles av. J.-C.)*, (Paris: Éditions Errance, 2001), p.106. G. Esposito, 'The Isola Rizza Dish', *Medieval Warfare*, 4/6 (2014), p.58.
8   D'Amato R, V. Pflaum, (2019), p.22, (fresco reconstruction).
9   I. Bugarski, 'A Contribution to the Study of Lamellar Armours', *Starinar*, 55 (2005), pp.161–162 (size and dating), p.164 (difference with models from Niederstotzingen, Schrandzheim, Kirsheim am Reis, Kunszentmarton, Tiszavasvari, Kertch).

ELITE CAVALRY AND SECOND-CLASS INFANTRY

Sixth or Seventh-Century Byzantine Lamellar Body Armour
David clad in lamellar armour with short sword and round convex shield. He wears a reddish, or pinkish, long-sleeved tunic and gaiters. From a Coptic fresco in the monastery of Bawit, Egypt, Chapel III. After J. Clédat, *Le monastère et la nécropole de Baouît*, MIFAO 12, 1 and 2 (Cairo: Imprimerie de l'Institut français d'archéologie orientale, 1904), pl. XVII.

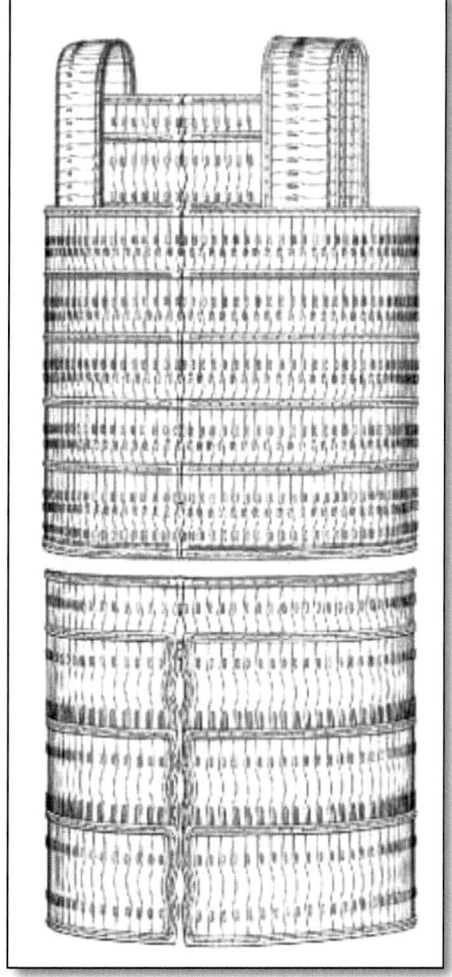

Sixth/Seventh Century Reconstructed Lamellar Armour
A reconstructed Germanic lamellar armour found in Niederstotzingen Germany. Other lamellar armours were discovered in Romano-Byzantine context such as that from Satala, Turkey. This kind of armour was widespread among Germanic peoples, Avars and Byzantines. It could be folded by fitting the strips inside each other like a nesting doll. After P. Paulsen, *Alamannische Adelsgräber von Niederstotzingen (Kreis Heindeinheim)*, (Stuttgart: Müller & Gräff, Kommissions Verlag, 1967), Taft 22.

BIRTH OF THE BYZANTINE ARMY 476-641 CE VOLUME 2: WATCH THEM FIGHT!

Mid-Sixth-Century Heavy Lancer from the Isola Rizza Dish

This heavy cavalryman is identified as Byzantine. He is wearing a Spangenhelm type helmet with a mail neck guard and a horsehair tuft on top and lamellar body armour. He wields his *kontos/kontarion* with two hands as during the late Roman Empire. He is using stirrups. After the Isola Rizza dish, a sixth-century silver dish with a relief medallion in the centre depicting a fight between and two unarmoured Goth infantry, today in the Castelvecchio Museum.

Mid-Sixth-Century Heavy Cavalryman with Lance

Horseman clad in lamellar armour with a segmented Baldenheim type helmet. Like earlier Roman and Persian *cataphractii* he is carrying his kontos with two hands. He is more stable due to the use of stirrups He is also a horse archer and the quiver is visible on his right side. The bow is hanging down on his left side. After the Isola Rizza silver dish and a quiver from a thirteenth-century Serbian icon of Saint George with a pattern close to Steppe nomad quivers.

ELITE CAVALRY AND SECOND-CLASS INFANTRY

Mid-Sixth-Century Heavy Cavalryman with Lance and Bow, in Lamellar Armour

This heavy cavalryman has all of the weaponry Procopius describes at the very beginning of his *Wars* (*BV*, I, 1, 12-13). The posture with the long cavalry lance (*kontos/kontarion*), the segmented helmet with plume, and the lamellar armour are inspired from the Isola Rizza dish. The leather thong is added allowing the use of the bow. The quiver is hanging on his right, the *gorytos* with the composite bow is hanging at his left side. The small shield without handle depicted by Procopius is well shown on the Sassanid cataphract reliefs of Taq-e-Bostan, Iran.

Far from the dazzling gilding of Corippus' descriptions, the ideal horsemen equipment for the years 560–570 was described without any poetry in Maurice's *Strategikon*:

> They must wear complete *zaba/zava* (coats of mail) down to the ankles with a *skaplion* [cape shoulder protection] and held in place by straps and buckles, saddlebags, *kassida* [helmets] topped with *touphia mikra* (plumes, literally tufts), bows suited to the strength of each and not more, and even rather less, cases large enough to hold the bows, spare strings in the saddlebags, quivers with 30 to 40 arrows, files and an awl on their harness, Avar-style *kontaria kaballarika* [cavalry lances] with a strap in the middle of the shaft and a *phlamoula* [pennon] at the end, *spathia* [swords], Avar-style round *peritrachēlia stroggula* [gorgets] made with strips of linen on the outside and wool on the inside.[10]

---

10   Maurice, *Strategikon*, I, 2, 10 (ζάβα, plural ζάβαι; σκαπλίον, plural σκαπλία), 12

The small shield previously mentioned by Procopius for the 530s has disappeared. Unknown to Procopius, the *zaba* was a widespread term which appeared in the sixth century, perhaps coming from the Arabic *jubbah* designating a long tunic. An edict from Justinian dated 539 and the *Law of the Visigoths* equated *zaba* to the Latin word *lorica* (body armour).[11] A century later, the first variant of *lorica* that Isidore of Seville talked about was made of *circulis ferreis* (iron rings). In the tenth century, Leo VI the Wise used *zaba* and *lôrikion* as more or less synonymous. He recommended the lôrikion to be fastened with *lôriôn kai krikelliôn* (thongs and rings) and to be made completely of *panta alusidôta* (mail) but also of materials such as horn, boiled leather or not, felt or dried hide. Describing the *zaba* he said each infantryman and cavalryman should have: 'Complete *zabas* reaching to their ankles, fastened with thongs and rings, along with their carrying cases.'[12] An unclear passage from Simocatta said that in 598, Comentiolus' soldiers were ordered to equip themselves at dawn. They 'put on their breasts with cloaks of iron' thinking that they were going to be reviewed. As soon as the sun had risen, they saw the Avars in battle order then they all armed themselves in proper military fashion.[13] It is likely that the soldiers wore additional personal protection for battle but which was perhaps unsightly for a review.

During the siege of Byzantium in 626, while launching an attack on 31 July the Avar Khan formed his first rank with unarmoured and dispensable Sklavenes, but infantry in the second rank were clad in *zabas*.[14] S*kaplion* came from the Latin *scapula* (shoulder) and may be a mail or scale protection preserved from the late Roman Army. It was a

---

(κασσίς, plural κασσίδα, μικρόν τουφίον, plural μικρά τουφία), 18 (κοντάριον καβαλλαρικόν, plural κοντάρια καβαλλαρικά), 19 (φλάμουλον, plural φλάμουλα), 20 (σπαθίον, plural σπαθία; περιτραχήλιον στρογγύλον, plural περιτραχήλια στρογγύλα).

11 Nov. J., 85, 4 (*et quae vocantur zavae sive loricae*). *Leges Visigothorum*, IX, 2, 9 (*zabas vel loricis*).
12 Leo VI the Wise, *Taktika*, V, 3, 19 (λωρίκιον, plural λωρίκια made with thongs and rings, λωρίων καὶ κρικελλίων), 20, (made completely of mail, πάντα ἀλυσιδωτά), 22 (made of other materials); VI, 2, 9 (long *zabas* made with thongs and rings λωρίων καὶ κρικελλίων); 3, 24 (*phlamoula mikra* on the shoulders); 13, 60, 62, 65 (*zabas* covered a loose, padded mantle with very broad sleeves in order to protect it from humidity and to mask its brightness); 15, 78 (pack animals to haul *zabas* and tents); 18, 90, 94 (*zabas* put in hide cases behind the cantle across the horse's hindquarters to avoid to be left out and ruined in the open and to alleviate the weight for the soldiers); 21, 122–123 (*zabas* or *lorikia*, apparently not synonymous); VII, 54, 372 (*zabas* or *lorikia*); 56, 393 (*zaba* with greaves). Isidore of Seville, *Etymologiae*, XVIII, 13, 1 (*lorica vocata eo quod loris careat; solis enim circulis ferreis contexta est lorica*). Ch. du Fresne du Cange Ch. and *alii*, *Glossarium mediæ et infimæ latinitatis*, ed. Favre L, Niort, 1883–1887, t. 8, col. 425a.
13 Theophylact Simocatta, *HU*, VII, 13, 10 (τοῖς σιδηρείοις χιτῶσι τὰ περιστέρνια φράτουσιν); 14, 1 (they all armed themselves in proper military fashion)
14 John Malalas, *Chrgr.*, XIII, 23 (Greens with *zabas*). *Chron Pasch*, a.626 (Avars in second rank with *zabas*).

protection independent of the coat of mail, as the *Strategikon* suggested that unarmoured soldiers could borrow it from those fully equipped to deceive the enemy from afar during a siege.[15] Nevertheless, there is also some controversy in interpreting it as a mail coif or a flexible neck guard.[16] The *peritrachēlia stroggula*, throat collars, were probably some sort of padded protection, like the gambeson from the late middle ages, but here limited to the protection for the neck, maybe an aventail or a scarf. This *peritrachēlion* throat protection is depicted on a painting of Joshua from the monastery of Hosios Loukas (St Lucas), Greece.[17] There is another controversy, as a *peritrachēlion* could be a padded neck guard in Leo VI's *Taktika*: 'Let those who do not have neck pieces of iron mail be protected by those made of quilted material on the inside and leather (linen in some versions) on the outside.'[18] Take advice that in theory a mail *skaplion* could be put with a *peritrachēlion* for a perfect protection. In summary, the Romano-Byzantine horseman was not merely a copy of his late Roman predecessor.

Some body armour had a pectoral harness with a chest girdle and two shoulder straps. They can be seen throughout most of the Byzantine period in the hagiographic and in ninth to eleventh century military iconography. Its first and only literary mention was related to the Edict Concerning the Sale Price of Goods of Diocletian from 301 under the name of *subalare babylonicum* (Babylonian chest strap) with a cost of 100 *denarii* and listed among the leather goods.[19] This 'Babylonian bra' is depicted on a quilted *suburmalis* on the third-century tombstone of Severus Acceptus, Istanbul. Although frequent in iconography this harness is never mentioned in Byzantine sources and its proper name remains unknown. Perhaps alluding to this item, Simocatta said that the soldiers of the Danube, 'clasp their iron tunics around their chests.'[20] The other interpretation is that it was a rank insignia as it can be worn on woollen tunics. Its origin is debated, and is sometimes erroneously called 'Varangian', other times it is attributed to the Persians since 'Babylonian bra' was its Roman name. It was worn on a tunic as well as on mail, scale, lamellar or muscular breastplates, and appears on the seventh-century silver plates depicting the story of David

---

15   Maurice, *Strategikon*, X, 1, 20 (τὸ σκαπλία τῶν ζαθάτων). T. G. Kolias, *Byzantinische Waffen. Ein Beitrag zur byzantinischen Waffenkunde von den Anfängen bis zur lateinischen Eroberung* (Vienna: Verlag der Österreichischen Akademie der Wissenschaften, *Byzantina Vindobonensia* 17, 1988), pp.43–44.
16   P. L. Grotowski, *Arms and Armour of the Warrior Saints. Tradition and Innovation in Byzantine Iconography (843–1261)*, The Medieval Mediterranean 87 (Leiden: Brill, 2010), p.158, n. 134.
17   Simon Macdowall, *Late Roman Cavalryman, 236–565*, Warrior Series 15 (Oxford: Osprey Publishing, 1995); P. L. Grotowski, *Arms and Armour of the Warrior Saints*, pp.158–159, n. 135.
18   Leo VI the Wise, *Taktika*, V, 3.
19   *Edictum de pretiis rerum venalium*, X, 1, 10.
20   Theophylact Simocatta, *HU*, VII, 13, 10 (τοῖς σιδηρείοις χιτῶσι τὰ περιστέρνια φράττουσιν).

versus Goliath. It can also be found on a seventh-century mosaic depicting David versus Goliath, looted in Syria during the 2010s. The sub-pectoral ribbon designating officers from the Hellenistic period was still found in the representation of many saints throughout the middle ages – is it an artistic convention or a military permanence?

At the time of Justinian, the *Peri Strategikes* affirmed that front-line horses should have iron protections on the muzzle, neck and chest.[21] It was probably a Sassanid influence from that shown on the rock-cut equestrian figure of Taq-e-Bostan, Iran. The *Strategikon* recommended that the horses of officers in the front rank should wear half-armour: 'The horses of officers and elite soldiers in the front rank of the line of battle must have an iron protection on the muzzle and an iron or felt bard on the chest, or a mane and chest bard after the fashion of the Avars.'[22]

Most of the horses were unarmoured unlike in the late Roman Army when *cataphratarii* and *clibanarii* made up around 15 percent of *comitatenses* cavalry.[23] The terms *cataphratarii* and *clibanarii* even disappeared from the vocabulary in the sixth century and did not reappear until the ninth century. They probably corresponded to what Procopius and Agathias called *tethorakismenoi*.[24] Nevertheless, the context shows that Procopius and Agathias spoke of a rider's armour and not armour including that of horses. More significantly, *cataphratarii* and *clibanarii* also disappeared from Byzantine iconography and it has to be admitted that this type of ultra-heavy horseman likely no longer existed, or perhaps only in the limited form suggested by the *Strategikon*. During the Battle of Nineveh in 627, Heraclius rushed into battle, his horse wearing light armour suited to a campaign in mountainous regions: 'The Emperor's tawny horse called Dorkon was wounded in the thigh by an infantryman who struck it with a spear. It also received several blows of the sword on the face, but, wearing as it did a *cataphractus* made of sinew.'[25]

By the mid-sixth century some cavalrymen could carry shields. According to Procopius mounted archers had small bucklers without a grip-handle and attached by a strap around their neck. It was borrowed from the Sassanid Persians as depicted on a fourth-century rock relief from Taq-e Bostan, Iran.[26] In 556, when the Romano-Byzantine cavalry of Justin the son of Germanus fought the Persians at the siege of Phasis, the shields played a paradoxically offensive role:

---

21 *Peri Strategikes*, 17, 13–14.
22 Maurice, *Strategikon*, I, 2, 35–39.
23 J. F. Haldon, 'Some Aspects of Early Byzantine Arms and Armour' in D. Nicolle (ed.), *A Companion to Medieval Arms and Armour* (Woodbridge: The Boydell Press, 2002), p.68.
24 Procopius, *BP*, I, 1, 12; 5, 5; 24, 51; *BV*, III, 26, 1; *BG*, V, 9, 15; 16, 11; 22, 4; 23, 19; VI, 5, 14; VII, 4, 21; VIII, 8, 17. Agathias, *Hist.*, I, 9, 4; IV, 20, 1; V, 22, 4. R. D'Amato, (2019), p.6 (τεθωρακισμένοι).
25 Theophanes Confessor, *Chrgr.*, AM 6118, 318.
26 Procopius, *BP*, I, 1, 13.

ELITE CAVALRY AND SECOND-CLASS INFANTRY

Late Sixth-Century Byzantine *Cataphractus*
This heavy cavalryman rides a lamellar-half-armoured horse in the Sassanid-style, with *touphia mikra* (small plumes) on it. His segmented helmet is also topped by a *touphion mikron*. His main weapon is a long cavalry lance with a leather thong in the Avar-style, allowing it to be carried easily during marches and to use his composite bow during battle. It has a small pennant ornamentation it but it was preferable to remove this before a charge. A long *spatha*-style sword is hanging on his left side. The quiver hangs from his belt at his right side. A long coat of mail or *zaba* protects the body. Mail chausses or metal greaves protect his lower leg down to the ankles, and a mail *skaplion* offers supplementary protection for the shoulders. A linen and woollen scarf is wrapped round the throat in the Avar way. A large Avar cloak in the Steppe fashion covers the body in a more practical way than a *kandys*. From Maurice's *Strategikon* and the Sassanid cataphract relief of Taq-e-Bostan, Iran.

Immediately striking some with their spears, others with their sarissas and their swords, they killed all those in their path, violently charging the ranks of the enemy and pushing them back with their shields, they created disorder in their formation.[27]

The *Strategikon* did not propose a shield for officers, NCOs, *foederati* and *bucellarii*. The shield was only the defensive weapon of second category horsemen like the new recruits for *foederati*: 'Young foreigners inexperienced with the bow must have *kontaria* (spears) and *skoutaria* (shields).'[28] Early Romano-Byzantine cavalry was more mobile than its late Roman forerunner but still remained heavy cavalry.

---

27 Agathias, *Hist.*, III, 25, 9.
28 Maurice, *Strategikon*, I, 2, 21–22 (κοντάριον, plural κοντάρια; σκουτάριον, plural

Sixth-Seventh Century St Sisiniolos Dressed as a Light Cavalryman
Saint Sisiniolos is slaying a charming, but nevertheless evil, female demon with his lance. He is protected by a small flat oval shield and is dressed in an embroidered, long-sleeved tunic and large trousers which was a stylistically barbarian dress. Coptic fresco in the monastery of Bawit, Egypt, Chapel XVII. After J. Clédat, *Le monastère et la nécropole de Baouît*, MIFAO 12, 1 and 2 (Cairo: Imprimerie de l'Institut français d'archéologie orientale, 1904), pl. LVI.

Fighting on Horseback

In pitched battles from all times, cavalry brought a little elegance to what would be a vulgar brawl. Cavalry combat often began with an exchange of arrows, and the bow was the first offensive weapon mentioned by the

---

σκουταρία).

ELITE CAVALRY AND SECOND-CLASS INFANTRY

Strategikon. Then the elite soldiers from the Imperial Army were the mounted archers, *hippotoxotai*. Procopius praised them, uncharitably mocking them by comparison to the archers of the Homeric era who went on foot without armour and fired shots without strength by bringing the string of their bow to chest level:

> (Today's archers) are excellent horsemen and can fire from both sides when their horse is galloping, as well as when the enemy is pursuing them or fleeing. They draw the string of their bow from their forehead to their right ear and the weapon shoots the arrow so hard that whoever is hit is inevitably killed, no shield or armour can stop the blow.[29]

Romano-Byzantine cavalry used the efficient Hunnic method of firing a bow that consisted of grasping the string with only the thumb to draw the bow, known as the 'Mongolian draw' or 'thumb draw'. The Persians were less efficient as they drew the string with the three lower fingers of the right hand, while the index finger pointed towards the target.[30] Iconography shows that the Romano-Byzantines used composite bows, with double curvature and made of layers of wood and bone and whose appearance is characterised by a bulging of the upper and lower branches.[31] All iconography shows the bow hanging on the right in a *gorytos*, a leather bow case, with the quiver hanging on the right. In addition, Corippus was confirming that Romano-Byzantine cavalry knew how to shoot backwards against pursuers, imitating the Parthian style.[32] This was not a new tactic, as in the 360s and 370s the officer and historian Ammianus Marcellinus already saw the archer with a shield as a formidable fighter. In his time cavalry was gaining importance in the Roman Army but infantry remained the decisive melee weapon. Two centuries later, the infantry no longer formed the heart of Romano-Byzantine military power, its mission was to fix the enemy which left the lion's share of the fighting to the cavalry

The *Strategikon* insisted that all Roman soldiers under the age of 40 should have a bow and a quiver whether they were expert or just average archers. A light bow was enough for the less experienced to practice, but all riders had to have two lances, one of which was a spare.[33] The bow, however, was only a preliminary weapon of attrition. In the *Johannis*, combat with the bow and javelin represents only about a fifth of the losses, while the clash with the spear and the sword inflicted the remainder. The spear was

---

29 Procopius, *BP*, I, 1, 9–11 (Homeric archer); 12–15 (mounted archer).
30 N. Khoperia, 'The Byzantine Lazic Phalanx', p 22.
31 Stephenson I., *Romano-Byzantine Infantry Equipment* (Stroud: Tempus, 2006), p.123–127 (bows also used by infantry).
32 Corippus, *Joh*, VI, v. 681–682.
33 Maurice, *Strategikon*, I, 2, 28–30 (bow and quiver); 30–32 (lances); 32–34 (light bow).

the horseman's primary weapon in hand-to-hand combat. Early Byzantines used ash spears that could be used as javelins.[34] According to the *Strategikon*, cavalry lances were decorated with an ornamental *phlamoula* (pennon) on parade, useful during an inspection or a siege, but the rider had to remove it when the enemy was in sight because the pennon hindered the accuracy of arrows. The pennons were to be removed at a distance of one mile, or two kilometres, roughly five minutes from the enemy.[35]

Fighting with a spear was fast and furious, as in the duel between Anzalas and the deserter Coccas before the Battle of Taginae in 552:

> Coccas then made the first run and charged at his enemy to pierce him with his spear, pointing the weapon at his stomach. But Anzalas, by making a volte, rendered his enemy's charge useless. By this manoeuvre he had positioned himself to the side of his enemy and thrust his spear into his left flank and Coccas fell from his horse to the ground as if dead.[36]

Worthy of a samurai film was the mounted duel between Valaris the Ostrogothic giant and Artabazes the small Armenian. In the very first charge Artabazes pierced and killed Valaris, who remained upright on his saddle the lance stopped. Believing his opponent was still alive, Artabazes made a second pass to finish him, but Valaris' spear slipped over his armour and cut an artery in his neck. Artabazes died of a haemorrhage a few days later.[37] In the ensuing battle, John Troglita pierced the chest of one enemy with his spear, which he then hurled into the back of another, but he struggled to remove it from the vertebrae where it had lodged.[38] An experienced officer like Bessas could spear three Ostrogothic horsemen in the same engagement.[39]

Cavalry lance fencing was to strike the enemy's chest: 'You try to reach the breasts of the enemy.'[40] The technique was not yet that of the spear lying under the armpit inaugurated in the eleventh century. The spear was held in both hands like a pike or brandished like a dagger.[41] Held with both hands, the cavalry lance took advantage of the kinetic force of the mounted charge and thus gained great penetrating power. Ricinarius literally pierced Eilimar: 'Piercing the chest of the one who charged him with the iron against

---

34 Corippus, *Joh*, V, v. 612.
35 Maurice, *Strategikon*, II, 10, 1–4 (pennons for inspection and siege); 5–9 (causing some trouble); 11–13 (out when one mile distant); VII, B, 16, 5–6 (out for charge); 7 (out when one mile distant); 17, 14–16 (bulky).
36 Procopius, *BG*, VIII, 31, 11–15.
37 Procopius, *BG*, VII, 4, 21–29.
38 Corippus, *Joh*, VIII, v. 391–396.
39 Procopius, *BG*, VI, 1, 3.
40 Corippus, *Joh*, IV, v. 165.
41 Corippus, *Joh*, VI, v. 650.

him, he broke his vital organs, having broken his ribs, and his spear pierced his back with great force.'[42] Twice, Corippus mentioned a spear piercing an enemy's shield and ribs, and a javelin that did the same.[43] Far from being a poetic exaggeration, it was an outcome made possible by the horse's charge. In the Napoleonic era, light horsemen were advised to *rendre sa lance* (give up his lance) when they had pierced an enemy. When a cavalryman no longer had a lance, the fight went to the sword. The Byzantine long sword or *spathion*, had a formidable efficiency when striking with the cutting edge, which accounts for nine out of 10 strokes in the *Johannis*.

Two-thirds of the blows were delivered to the head and collar to achieve rapid lethal effect. By contrast cutting strikes against the body, protected by the rib cage, were rarely fatal as Vegetius explained.[44] Corippus and later the celebratory songs described the cutting power of spathion. Using his 'solid sword' properly John Troglita split two Moor Manzerasen in half.[45] The fatal blow was struck on the collarbone of an unarmoured opponent. A Moorish leader named Iammada in vain threw several javelins at Peter, a Byzantine officer, who in retaliation sliced his skull with a single slash of his sword.[46] Such a blow is attested by a recovered Germanic skull dated to the third or fourth century. Solomuth, John Troglita's officer, performed a real butchery:

> He slits Meuzzen's throat with his sword, pushed Laltin off his horse, and struck the courageous Sinisgún and Varinnus, whom the destinies had not yet claimed. His sword splits his shield, reaches his left hand and cuts the ends of the nerves with one blow. But, defeated, he fled through the armies, dropping his shield, his wounded left hand hanging with bloody fingers.[47]

The weakness of a Moorish leather shield, similar to that of the later Tuareg shield, made such blows possible. Thrusting blows were rare in Corippus who only cited two, to the belly and the neck.[48] Facing armoured horsemen, it was difficult to strike decisive blows: death in battle was a slow haemorrhage of multiple blows. In the battle near the Milvian Bridge, the Ostrogoth Wisandus Vandalarius was left for dead after receiving 13 wounds from Belisarius' horsemen; laying on the battlefield for three days, he was saved by his comrades who were preparing to bury him with the others.[49] During a melee, cavalrymen could be unhorsed and horses killed with lances or javelins; the fall was often fatal to their rider who was

---

42 Corippus, *Joh*, V, v. 73–79.
43 Corippus, *Joh*, V, v. 139, 239 (lance); 252 (javelin).
44 Vegetius, *DRM*, I, 12.
45 Corippus, *Joh*, V, v. 120–121.
46 Corippus, *Joh*, VII, v. 432–434.
47 Corippus, *Joh*, V, v. 318–324.
48 Corippus, *Joh*, VIII, v. 405–406.
49 Procopius, *BG*, V, 18, 29–33.

crushed.[50] The tribune Marcianus had his horse killed by a javelin to the forehead. After his fall, he fought as an infantryman under the cover of his shield and drove back the Moorish cavalryman that he faced, then boldly pursued him with a drawn sword.[51]

Procopius liked to tell such stories of cavalry battles. During a skirmish that occurred during the siege of Rome on the plain of Nero by December 537 several of Belisarius's *bucellarii* sustained wounds. Kutilas, a Thracian *doryphoros*, received a javelin strike in his head and Arzes, a *hypaspist*, took an arrow between his nose and his right eye, but neither of the two stopped fighting. Bochas, a Hun *doryphoros*, was struck without effect on his armour, *thorakos*, by the spears of 12 Ostrogoths, was wounded in the upper right arm by a blow given from behind, while another blow received from the front pierced him in the right thigh, causing him to be evacuated by Martin while Valerian took his horse by the bridle.[52] This ferocious combat shows that the face and limbs were most exposed. Two other examples of wounds suffered by Belisarius' *doryphoroi* confirm these areas of vulnerability. A blow from a lance severed the tendons in Sinthoues' right hand and disabled him permanently. Trajan received an arrow above his right eye, whose head detached itself from the shaft and remained embedded in his skull and which partially came out five years later without any pain.[53] As far as a poet can be believed, Corippus gave a very wide range of injuries in cavalry combats.

---

50 Corippus, *Joh*, V, v. 310–313.
51 Corippus, *Joh*, V, v. 201–212.
52 Procopius, *BG*, VI, 2, 15–18 (Kutilas and Arzes); 2, 21–24 (Bochas).
53 Procopius, *BG*, VI, 4, 15 (Sinthoues); 5, 21–27 (Trajan).

Table 16, Causes of Injuries in Cavalry Combat According to Corippus

Kind of Injury	Weapons	Arrow	Javelin	Lance	Sword
Body sliced in two	2 (2.9 percent)				2
Split skull	1 (1.5 percent)				1
Beheading	10 (14.5 percent)				10
Temples	5 (7.2 percent)	1			4
Face	1 (1.5 percent)				1
Neck	4 (5.7 percent)				4
Throat	3 (4.3 percent)				3
Belly	3 (4.3 percent)	1		1	1
Heart	2 (2.9 percent)		1	1	
Chest	16 (23.2 percent)	2	4	10	
Back	2 (2.9 percent)			2	
Flank	5 (7.2 percent)		2	2	1
Groin	1 (1.5 percent)			1	
Collarbone	2 (2.9 percent)				2
Severed arm	1 (1.5 percent)				1
Left hand	3 (4.3 percent)			1	2
Leg	2 (2.9 percent)	1			1
Severed leg	1 (1.5 percent)				1
Crushing after fall from horse	5 (7.2 percent)		3	2	
Total (percent)	69 (100 percent)	5 (7.4 percent)	10 (14.4 percent)	20 (29 percent)	34 (49.2 percent)

Little Confidence in the Infantry

A mass of scared men drop their shields and spears, running to the rear, mercilessly trampling upon those who stumble. The cavalry reaps this moving field of panicked heads and bent backs. In 493, 499 and 505, in a very short period, the Army of Illyricum was beaten twice by Bulgars and once by Ostrogoths, two peoples of horsemen. At Bismideon (Tell-Besmai) in 502, the cavalry fled without fighting when it saw the numerical superiority of the Persians, abandoning the infantry which bravely fought and was destroyed on the field.[54]

---

54 Joshua the Stylite, *Chron.* 278.

Justinian's generals, however, did not have confidence in their infantry. In 533, Belisarius in his campaign against the Vandals to assigned the infantry to guard the camp or even prefer it to arrive almost a day later, while the cavalry fought victoriously alone at Dekimon and Trikamaron. In the latter case, the arrival of the infantry persuaded the Vandals to abandon their entrenched camp without fighting, an obstacle which the cavalry faced without effect after its success in the field.[55]

Distrust of the infantry was characteristic not only of Belisarius. His successor in Libya, Germanus cousin of Justinian I, lacked tactical know-how and even was afraid to fight with his cavalry alone, but he assigned the infantry only a passive support role, known in Latin as *defensores*. Thus, at Skalai Beteres in the spring of 537, he confronted the deserters of Stotzas, whom Belisarius had already defeated but not decisively. Germanus had better odds, probably one-on-one, while Belisarius had faced Stotzas with one to five at best. Germanus placed a line of chariots to shield the centre held by his infantry. Positioned in this way, the infantry, unable to advance theoretically formed an impenetrable barrier to a cavalry charge. But they fled without a fight as soon as the cavalry of the right wing had been driven back.[56] The inefficiency of the infantry was demonstrated during the Battle of Onoguris in 555. While 50,000 Romans laid siege to the town, only 3,000 Persian cavalrymen routed them and seized their camp, their logistics and their property.[57]

The most striking example of the lack of confidence in the infantry appears when the infantry wanted to convert into horsemen as at the Battle of the Field of Nero when Belisarius, besieged in Rome in 537, wanted to sally against the Ostrogoths:

> And even most of the infantrymen did not want to remain in their usual condition, but, since they had taken horses from the enemy and were not ignorant of horseback riding, they were now mounted. And since the infantry was no longer numerous enough to form a substantial phalanx, and since it had never engaged in combat with the barbarians, but had fled at the first contact, he considered it unsafe to lead it far from the fortifications, but that it was better to leave it in position where it was, near the ditch to catch a possible rout of the Roman horsemen and repel the enemy.[58]

---

55 Procopius, *BV*, III, 19, 11 (Dekimon); IV, 2, 2 (Belisarius left Carthage with the infantry one day after the cavalry); 3, 19 (late arrival of infantry in Trikamaron).
56 Procopius, *BV*, IV, 17, 2 and 4 (waggons in front of the infantry).
57 Agathias, *Hist.*, III, 7, 1 *sq.*
58 Procopius, *BG*, V, 28, 21–22.

ELITE CAVALRY AND SECOND-CLASS INFANTRY

On this occasion, Belisarius's staff even advised him to use mounted infantry officers with the cavalry, who did not fight in line with their men, but simply rode along the battle line and sometimes fled before the battle.[59]

Was fighting on foot tactically outdated? Of course not. There were supporters of the infantry in Justinian's Army. At the same Battle of the Field of Nero, a Pisidian officer named Principios and an Isaurian named Tarnuntos, both *doryphoroi* of Belisarius, reminded him: 'It is from the Roman infantry that the ancient Romans drew their power.' Both officers added that the cowardice of the infantry was due to their leaders who mounted horses and fled rather than fight. They therefore asked Belisarius for command of the infantry. Belisarius granted it, however Principios died with 42 infantrymen and Tarnuntos later perished from his wounds.[60] *Quod erat demonstrandum*. However, during the defence of Rome by Belisarius, infantry were used for raids 'not arrayed in a phalanx, but mixed with the horsemen.'[61] During a battle against the Persians and Alans in Lazica in *c.* 550, General Philegagos dismounted his Romano-Byzantine and Lazians cavalrymen and arrayed his troops in a thick phalanx. The Persians, seeing their horses repelled by spears and shields, unleashed a rain of arrows. The Imperial forces and Lazians retaliated in kind. Although the enemy's rate of fire was faster, the phalanx's shields stopped most of the arrows. At this point chance decided the battle between the two sides, when the Persian general was killed, causing his men to flee, mercilessly pursued by the Romano-Byzantines and the Lazians.[62] As the cavalry also achieved success by fighting dismounted, one might think that the recruitment of the infantry was poor. Infantry was thus the weakest part of Justinian's armies and probably remained so after his reign.[63]

Arming Infantrymen

'These carry arrows and bows, shining weapons resound on the broad shoulders of these. The spears and shields shine, and the heavy armour and plumes that stand on their helmets.'[64] These were, in the expeditionary force of John Troglita in 546, the light and heavy infantrymen. For the latter, Corippus evoked 'troops clad in iron' and 'maniples covered in bronze.'[65] Of the Romano-Byzantines, he wrote: 'For them iron was their tunic.'[66] In battle, Troglita's infantrymen were armed with javelins, a sword and a

---

59   Procopius, BG, V, 28, 25–26.
60   Procopius, *BG*, V, 28, 23–28 (argumentation); 29, 38–44 (heroic death).
61   Procopius, *BG*, VI, 1, 2.
62   Procopius, *BG*, VIII, 8, 31–36 (Lazica).
63   G. Ravegnani, *Soldati di Bisanzio in Età Giustinianea* (Rome: Jouvence, 1998), p.58–65.
64   Corippus, *Joh*, I, v. 441–443.
65   Corippus, *Joh*, I, v. 427 and v. 440.
66   Corippus, *Joh*, VIII, v. 189–190.

shield.[67] The Justinian period infantryman, like that of the fourth century, had a very different appearance from the classic Imperial legionary.[68] Nevertheless, the shield continued to characterise the combatant in the very early middle ages. Jean Lydus, a fifth-century encyclopaedist, described the shield, in Latin *scutum*, as 'robust and compact …. light because it is thin but solid, and is not easily pierced by blows'. He added: 'It is a peculiarity of the Greeks to use very light shields in war; the barbarians have *thureoi* (long shields), and at the height of the battle, they bring them up above them and use them as a shelter.'[69] The *Strategikon* called the heavy infantryman *skoutatos*, a Hellenism of the Latin word *scutatus* (shield bearer). According to him, the shields of an infantry *arithmos* or *tagma* were to display the same colour.[70]

In the late fourth century, Vegetius complained that infantrymen under Emperor Gratian had abandoned helmets and body armour, which they considered to be oppressive with the result that they were slaughtered by enemy archery.[71] It was no different a century later; according to the *Strategikon* heavy infantrymen had to wear a crested helmet, to carry a spear with a pennon, and a shield. The best soldiers, at least two per file in the first and last ranks must have been equipped with a coat of mail, iron or, surprisingly, wooden greaves.[72] An infantryman wearing a coat of mail was called *abatos*.[73] The *Peri Strategikes* recommended equipping the first two ranks, the last two and flankers with coats of mail and greaves, but that all should wear mail over a padded garment a finger thick. He also suggested felt and leather headwear instead of iron helmets. His idea of a spiked helmet usable as a weapon is not attested for the period, but this type of weapon was manufactured in Persia until the eighth century and called *Kulah Khud*, perhaps a Turco-Mongol innovation.[74]

The *Strategikon* and the *Peri Strategikes* dreamt of an ideal army but did their military dreams correspond to reality? In good part yes, because Agathias confirmed the difference in defensive armament between the first and the last ranks at the battle of in 554: 'The front ranks, covered in breastplates down to their feet and wearing very strong helmets, formed a

---

67   Corippus, *Joh*, II, v. 227–230.
68   Simon Macdowall, *Late Roman Infantryman, 236–565*, Warrior Series 9 (London: Osprey Publishing, 1994).
69   John the Lydian, *De Magistratibus*, I, 10, 4 (scutum); 6 (Greeks and barbarians).
70   Maurice, *Strategikon*, XII, B, 4, 1 (skoutatos, σχουτάτος, plural σχουτάτοι); 2 (specific colours for each unit; σχουτάριον, plural σχουτάρια).
71   Vegetius, *DRM*, I, 20.
72   Maurice, *Strategikon*, XII, B, 4, 3–4 (helmet, κασσίς, plural κασσίδα, petits panaches μικρά τουφία; pennon φλάμουλον, plural φλάμουλα); 5 (coat of mail, ζάβα, plural ζάβαι); 6–7 (greaves, περικνημίς, plural περικνημίδα).
73   Maurice, *Strategikon*, XII, 1, 19–20 (covered with a coat of mail, ζαβάτος, plural ζαβάτοι); XII, B, 23, 16.
74   *Peri Strategikes*, 16, 21–22 (cloak, imation, ἱμάτιον); 27–30 (spiked helmet); 54–56 (ranks and equipment); 59 (headeear).

continuous line of shields. Behind them, the others stood in close ranks, all the way up to the missile men – all those carrying light arms or throwing weapons stood behind, waiting for the moment when they could use their weapons.'[75] The question is what kind of breastplate is this about, because Procopius and Agathias, steeped in classical Greek culture, use the term *thorax* and apply it to both cavalry and infantry.[76]

The *Strategikon* endorsed two offensive weapons for the *skoutatos*: The first was the *spathion Erouliskion* (Herulic sword). Although it is not clear what this type corresponded to, the *spathion* was derived from the Roman *spatha*, a sword 'longer than the usual sword' according to Vegetius. This weapon was very effective in slashing and was used in earlier times by the auxiliaries and cavalry and then by fourth-century infantrymen.[77] It was perhaps inherited from the long blade sword of the Scythian horsemen.[78] In the tenth century Leo VI wrote that cavalrymen or infantrymen, 'should have swords hanging from their shoulders, in the Roman manner, as well as daggers or large knives on their belts.'[79] Nevertheless, there are some occurrences of short swords like those in the Cairo Museum.

The second offensive weapon for any *skoutatos* was the spear, called *kontarion* in a Hellenisation of the Latin *contus*, and carrying a pennon called a *phlamoula*.[80] In the 380s, Vegetius already mentioned the flammula among Roman insignia, and the term is still used today as in the word *oriflamme* in French.[81] Simocatta reported that during the riots in Constantinople on 2 February 602, Emperor Maurice distributed to his bodyguards iron sledgehammers called *distria* in Roman idiom.'[82] These weapons, capable of breaking arms as well as heads, avoided the need to draw a sword and perpetrate a massacre. Nevertheless, they could also be useful against armed soldiers, such as Persian or Avar *cataphratarii*.

More than late Romans, the Romano-Byzantines attached importance to distance weapons. The *Peri Strategikes*, taking up the same advice as an anonymous sixth-century archery treatise, gave three objectives to archery: shooting precisely, powerfully and quickly. He distinguished high

---

75 Agathias, *Hist.*, II, 8, 4 (heavy infantry); 5 (light).
76 Procopius, *BP*, I 1, 15; 13, 36; 18, 33; II, 25, 27; 25, 31; *BV*, IV, 26, 1; *BG*, V, 9, 21; 23, 9; 23, 11; VI, 2, 22, VII, 4, 22; 14, 22; VIII, 11, 35. Agathias, *Hist.*, I, 9, 4 (iron cuirass worn by taxiarch Palladios); III, 25, 7 (infantrymen and cavalrymen); 28, 5 (also worn by Persians). The word used by both authors was θώραξ, plural Θώρακες).
77 Maurice, *Strategikon*, XII, B, 2, 2–3 (Herulic sword σπαθίον Ἐρουλίσκιον, plural σπαθία Ἐρουλίσκια). Vegetius, *DRM*, II, 15 (*spatha longior gladius dicitur*); Ph. Richardot, *La fin de l'Armée Romaine*, p.278.
78 I. Lebedynsky, *De l'épée scythe au sabre mongol: Les armes blanches des Steppes* (Paris: Errances-Actes Sud, 2021).
79 Leo VI the Wise, *Taktika*, VI, 2, 18–20.
80 Maurice, *Strategikon*, XII, B, 2, 3 (lance, κοντάριον, plural κοντάρια; pennon, φλάμουλον, plural φλάμουλα φλάμουλα).
81 Vegetius, *DRM*, III, 5.
82 Theophylact Simocatta, *HU*, VIII, 4, 13.

trajectory shooting from flat trajectory shooting.[83] The *Strategikon* insisted on training in rapid archery, according to the Roman or Persian style, and added the practice of long-range shooting with the javelin and the sling. You had to know how to shoot while carrying a shield and while running. Skirmishers, *psiloi*, were lightly protected by a small shield.[84] During the Battle of Callinicum in 531, the Persians had more experienced archers but their arrows shattered on the helmets, *thorakes* (breastplates) and shields of Romano-Byzantine soldiers. By comparison:

> The shots of the Romans are always slower, because they are launched from very strong and strongly drawn bows, one can also say by more robust men, and they easily wound those they touch, much more than the Persians, no armour protects from their impact.[85]

These were undoubtedly composite bows. The light infantry had large quivers with 30 to 40 arrows and small ones for the bolts of wooden crossbows, called *solēnaria xylina*.[86] The *Strategikon* wanted all *psiloi* who were not experienced archers to carry Sklavene javelins, *lankidion Slkabiniskion*. This javelin must be very specific because Maurice chose to use the word *lankidion* whereas for all other javelins he preferred *akontion*.[87] He also prescribed slings and leaded darts called *martzobarboula* stored in quivers. According to Vegetius, the latter equipped two Illyrian legions under Diocletian and Maximian under the name of *martiobarbuli* (little beards of Mars). Still an efficient weapon the *Strategikon* even wanted the heavy infantry to train with and for it to be stored in equipment waggons. Three centuries later, Leo VI the Wise still spoke about this Roman weapon, which in his day was called *saliba*. Just as Vegetius wanted to train the legionaries to use the sling, the *Strategikon* wanted all *skoutatoi* (shieldmen) to be armed with it.[88] It is worth recording that bows and slings were deadly

---

83 *Peri Strategikes*, 44. O. Schissel von Fleschenberg, 'Spätantike Anleitung zum Bogenschiessen', *Wiener Studien*, 59 (1941), pp.110–24; 60 (1942), pp.43–70 (Anonymous treatise on archery from the sixth century).

84 Maurice, *Strategikon*, XII, B, 3, 1 (skirmisher, *psilos* ψιλός, plural ψιλόι), 2–3 (bow training and javelin); 5, 3–4 (small shield, σχουτάριον μικρὸν, plural σχουτάρια μικρά).

85 Procopius, *BP*, I, 18, 34.

86 *Strategikon*, XII, B, 4, 1–2 (bow and javelin); 5, 2–3 (big quiver, κούκουρον μεγάλον, plural κούκουρα μεγάλα), 4 (arbalète σωληνάριον ξύλινον, plural σωληνάρια ξύλινα). J. F. Haldon, '*Solenarion*-The Byzantine Crossbow', *Historical Journal of the University of Birgminham*, 12, 1970, pp.155–157. G. T. Dennis, 'Flies, Mice, and the Byzantine Crossbow', *Byzantine and Modern Greek Studies*, 7 (1981), pp.1–5.

87 Maurice, *Strategikon*, XII, B, 4, 5 and 6 (light infantry, sklavenic spear λαγκίδιον Σκλαβινίσκιον, plural λαγκίδια Σκλαβινίσκια), VII, A Pr, 43; IX, 2, 22; XI, 4, 44 and 74; XII, A, 7, 58; B, 20, 10, 8 (ἀκόντιον).

88 Vegetius, *DRM*, I, 17 and 20; II, 15 (*martiobarbulus*, plural *martiobarbuli*). Maurice, *Strategikon*, XII, B, 2, 2–3 (training of heavy infantryman with *martzobarboulon*,

ELITE CAVALRY AND SECOND-CLASS INFANTRY

effective, as shown during the heroic defence of the fort at Abgersaton in Osrhoene in summer 531: 'The garrison inside killed 1,000 of the Persians by showering down their arrows; and when they ran out of arrows they used slings and killed many of them.'[89]

The Appearance of the Infantryman

Iconographic or statuary representations of proto-Byzantine Army soldiers are rare but consistent. The most interesting are those in colour that are found in icons, manuscripts, wall paintings and mosaics.

For the fifth-century Roman Army, the most interesting colour miniatures come from the Virgil's *Aeneid* in a Vatican manuscript, known as *Vergilius Romanus*:[90]

On folio 74v Aeneas wears a gold helmet with cheek guards and a gold crest and a frontal band to give an archaic aspect. From the crest protrude very long individual red feathers curving forwards. A pink cloak fastened on the right by a round *fibula* brooch covers the left shoulder. Aeneas carries a spear in his left hand and leans on a round, convex shield with a cone-shaped shield boss, or *umbo*. The *umbo* and the border are gold, the shield is purple. An orange open quiver decorated with red bands is laid aside. The long sleeves of his tunic are a soft green with a gold border at the wrist. Shoulders, thorax and abdomen are protected by an iron scale breastplate as the light grey colour suggests. The edging scales are gilded. *Pteruges* cover the upper arms. The tunic skirt is pale yellowish with a pink border. The trousers are white, tight with horizontal grooves maybe indicating some calf bands. These main features, except perhaps the fanciful colours, still remained in early Byzantine iconography.

Folio 163r of *Vergilius Romanus* shows five soldiers without armour. Three are wearing embroidered long-sleeved *manicatae* in various colours: carrot orange, unbleached white and light green. They are wearing tight, circle-spotted braids in purple or orange. Their shoulders are covered by cloaks fastened with a golden fibula brooch on the left or right, and the range of colours remains showy: light brown, orange, purple and green. They are all wearing light brown, orange or red Phrygian caps. One, representing

---

μαρτζοβάρβουλον, plural μαρτζοβάρβουλα); 4, 2–3 (heavy infantry, herulic sword), 4 (heavy infantry, sling *sphendolon*, σφενδόβολον, plural *sphendola*, σφενδόβολα), 5, 6 (light infantry, sklavenic spear λαγκίδιον Σκλαβινίσκιον, plural λαγκίδια Σκλαβινίσκια), 8 (*martzobarbulon*, sling); 6, 6 (*martzobarbula* stored in carts with essential assets). Leo VI the Wise, *Taktika*, VII, 3 (μαρτζυβάρβουλον also called σαλίβα).

89 John Malalas, *Chrgr.*, XVIII, 61.
90 Inv. MS Vaticanus latinus 3867. https://digi.vatlib.it/view/MSS_Vat.lat. 3867. Virgil, *Vergilius Romanus facsimile edition* (Zurich: Belser Verlag, 1985). J. Ruysschaert, 'Lectures des illustrations du Virgile Vatican et du Virgile romain', *Monuments et mémoires de la Fondation Eugène Piot*, 73 (1991), pp.25–51.

Ascanius, hunts a deer and strings a composite bow with an orange tubular quiver with red stripes placed on the ground. The others are spearmen of which three hold large round convex shields with gold, pointed *umbos* with a border of the same. Two shields are purple, one is green.

More interesting is folio 188v where stylised Greeks and Trojans fight. The latter wear Phrygian caps, a symbol of the East, while the Greeks wear gold helmets that cover the ears and neck with a crest of red feathers. All warriors are wearing a cape fastened on the left or right for reasons of balance of the design. As before, these are short cloaks or capes which fall above the thighs and which the Romans called *sagum* and the Greeks *sagion*. Except for a Trojan archer, all the warriors are armed with spears. Ordinary warriors wear long mauve or light brown tunics. The Greeks wear mustard-brown calf bands. All wear brown sandals that rise above the ankle. The two heroes fighting in the centre wear scale cuirasses that stop at the waist but cover the upper arms; these are made of iron but the edges are gold. Their khaki-green clothing is long, with red edging on the bottom, and gold embroidery on the wrists. All visible shields are of the same round, convex model except but in varying colours of violet, orange and red while their umbos are made of iron or brass, and the shields' rims are rawhide or brass (or perhaps yellow leather?).

On folio 235v Aeneas visiting Neptune is draped in a *chlamydia*, a long ceremonial, orange cloak, he wears a dark green tunic, a crested helmet of the same model as elsewhere in the manuscript and a scale cuirass. Socket, tapered and rounded spearheads at the base are found in most illustrations.

Folio 101r shows three Trojan soldiers carrying large oval shields with leather borders and iron shield bosses.

A fine sixth-century mosaic in the Archaeological Museum of Argos in Greece exhibits a month of March Mars dressed as a soldier and bearing a *bandon* banner. He is wearing an iron bandenhelm-type helmet, with cheek guards and a probably mail neck guard. A yellow pectoral band is around a gilded muscle-breastplate with a row of small semi-circular scales ornamenting the lower edge. Pteruges cover the upper arms and thighs. Between the highly probable *subarmalis* and the gilded breastplate, there appears to be a three-pointed yellow apron, perhaps a rank indicator. The God is wearing a long-sleeved red tunic, long boots and white socks with bare legs.

In Egypt, the Coptic church of Deir Abu Hennis in the old village of Antinoa has frescoes dating from the late sixth to early seventh century. A scene of the Massacre of the Innocents shows two legionaries carrying large, white, oval shields bordered with a light blue band with red edge and armed with a red spear. They are wearing iron helmets with visor, neck guard and cheek guards and with crest of red feathers.[91]

---

91   R. D'Amato, 'A Sixth or Early Seventh Century AD. Iconography of Roman Military Equipment in Egypt: The Deir Abou Hennis Frescoes' in Theotokis G., Yıldız A., *A Military History of the Mediterranean Sea* (Leiden: Brill, *History of Warfare*, 118,

St Catherine's Monastery in Sinai has a pilaster with a sixth-century fresco depicting the sacrifice of Jehpthah's daughter. Jehpthah himself wears an elongated gold helmet, a white tunic, a red cloak decorated with short gold circles covering his left shoulder following the military fashion, leather pteruges suggest a breastplate that is not visible, and boots with on bare legs. He draws a long sword from a black scabbard.[92]

Dated to the late fifth to early seventh century, the Pentateuch of Tours also known as Ashburnham Pentateuch is in the collection of the Bibliothèque Nationale de France:[93]

Folio 50r is decorated with a miniature in which the Pharaoh authorises Jacob to travel to the land of Canaan. Jacob is wearing a gilded Intercisa-type helmet also with a gilded metal crest. Three bodyguards are armed with long swords hanging at the left side, and a dressed in a long red tunic and yellow trousers, a white tunic with green trousers and a green tunic with a white cloak and purple trousers.

On folio 68r, the Pharaoh's army drowns in the Red Sea. The oval shields are painted with an orange, crimson, blue or white background. Emanating from the shield boss are patterns like ringed cross or sun wheel of eight branches. The armour scales are gilded or iron grey with spaulders and pteruges of the same on the upper arm. The helmets are gold or iron grey with cheek and neck guards, Attic headband, and a very large crest of the same metal as the breastplate flared into petals, with a fleur-de-lys frontal motif. Long, tight tunics and pants are worn under the armour.[94]

The Bibliothèque Nationale de France also possesses a Syrian Bible dated to the late sixth or early seventh century:[95]

On folio 8r, a miniature frontispiece depicts Moses and Aaron brought before the Pharaoh, behind them are standing three guards armed with spears. It is these figures that are of interest here. Two are bareheaded and dressed in long red tunics with no embroidery. Behind the monarch stands a soldier wearing a pale blue cloak and an iron helmet with cheek guards and a red crest, very similar to the Intercisa-type helmets of the late Roman period.[96]

2018), pp.105–152.

92 A. Shams, 'The treasures of the Holy Monastery of St Catherine at Mount Sinai: from the treasury of Sixth Century CE to the museum of Twenty First Century CE', Management and Development of Cultural Heritage, PhD Student, IMT Institute for Advanced Studies, Lucca, Italy (2011), p.7.

93 Bibliothèque Nationale de France, Paris, inv. MS NAL 2334. https://gallica.bnf.fr/ark:/12148/btv1b53019392c

94 B. Narkiss, 'Scribes and Artists of the Ashburnham Pentateuch' in *Tributes to Jonathan J. G. Alexander. The Making and Meaning of Illuminated Medieval & Renaissance Manuscripts, Art & Architecture* (London: H. Miller, 2006), pp.141–158.

95 Bibliothèque nationale de France, Paris, Ms. Syriaque 341. https://gallica.bnf.fr/ark:/12148/btv1b10527102b

96 F. Pacha Miran, *Le décor de la Bible syriaque de Paris (BnF syr. 341) et son rôle dans l'histoire du livre chrétien* (Paris: Geuthner, 2020), pp.199–202.

Goliath Wearing Sixth/Seventh-Century Byzantine Body Armour
Goliath in armour with pale yellow *subalare babylonicum* and a short reddish military cloak. The shoulder *pteruges* seems to be in iron. He is wearing an iron helmet (a stylised Spangenhelm?) and carries a convex, round shield. Note the sword with a buckle-shaped pommel. From a Coptic fresco in the monastery of Bawit, Egypt, Chapel III. After J. Clédat, (1904), pl. XVIII.

The Bawit Monastery presents two infantrymen on wall paintings. The first is David, in chapel 3 on the north wall; he is wearing lamellar armour, draws a medium size sword and carries a round, orange, convex shield decorated with two question mark motifs. The second is of course Goliath wearing a very stylised iron helmet, an iron harnessed breastplate and brandishing a spear, his shield is green.[97]

The sculptural representations have no colour but provide other information. The cathedra of Archbishop Maximian of Ravenna, preserved in the Museum of Antiquities in Ravenna and dated between 545 and 553, features ivory panels carved with religious scenes. Three panels depicting the life of Joseph, inspired by Genesis, show groups of two or four infantrymen representing his guard. They are anachronistically dressed in sixth-century military fashion. The most significant panel depicts the reunion of Joseph and his father. Like the barbarians of the Barberini Ivory, two of them are wearing 'bell-bottom' pants with a wide band of embroidery on the front and at the bottom. On all the soldiers a round *fibula* brooch fastens a military cloak which covers the left shoulder. A breastplate is suggested by a double row of fringed pteruges which protects the upper thighs and arms. The only visible breastplate has scales yellow pectoral band and has a row of small semi-circular scales ornamenting the lower edge. The scabbard for one of the swords is studded on each side as on the Barberini Ivory. Two soldiers in the background appear to be carrying a spear. On the panel where Joseph sits

---

97   J. Clédat, 'Le monastère et la nécropole de Baouît', *MIFAO*, 12, 1 and 2 (1904), colour plate XVII (David); XVIII (Goliath).

on a throne and watches over the recording of the harvests, a soldier carries a spear, similar to that on the panel where he Joseph presented to Pharaoh. On this panel, two soldiers have clearly visible studded sword scabbards. All soldiers have long, ruffled sleeves. Their helmets have an obusal shape, simplified cheek guards looking like curved blades and beaked visors with a question mark pattern above the ears, but no crest. They resemble Macedonian and Hellenistic helmets.

The *pyxis* of Sion (Sitten) in the Musée Valere belongs to the same iconographic family. It is a sixth-century ivory box that shows soldiers resting during a visit to the Holy Sepulchre. Its origin is disputed – Egypt, Syria or Constantinople – but Byzantine in any case and of the Eastern Mediterranean school. Two soldiers carry composite 'B' or 'W' shaped bows. All wear short scaled breastplates or mail with *pteruges* on the upper thighs and arms. Two have short cloaks fastened on the right and covering the left shoulder. Two are bareheaded with bowl-shaped hair, as on the Barberini Ivory. The others are wearing stylised helmets with a sort of visor that rises up to form a 'burgonet-like' form. Five hold small, oval shields with a flat *umbo* from which a cross-shaped motif emerges. They have bare legs and wear low shoes.[98]

Another sixth-century ivory *pyxis* from the Hermitage Museum in St Petersburg which depicts the three youths of Babylon in the burning furnace shows a soldier wearing a stylised helmet with crest and cheek guards, a cloak and carrying an oval shield.[99]

The British Museum has a pyxis illustrating the martyrdom of St Menas.[100] Dated to the sixth century and sculpted in ivory, it depicts a soldier brandishing a long sword. The latter is dressed in a long *manicata*-type tunic embroidered at the neckline and along the torso and is wearing trousers. A second soldier has a helmet similar to those on the other *pyxides* or on Maximian's throne. He is protected by an oval shield with a motif of eight petals radiating from the *umbo*, a mail or scale cuirass with pteruges, and is armed with a spear. A short cloak covers his shoulders. This *pyxis* comes from Italy, but experts believe it was made in Alexandria.[101]

The Museum of Macedonia in Skopje has a series of terracotta plaques found at Vinica and showing Romano-Byzantine soldiers from the sixth to seventh centuries depicting Joshua and his companion Caleb, two biblical heroes, in the episode where he stops the sun above Gabaon.[102] The

---

98   P. Elsig, M. Cl. Morand (eds), *Le Musée d'histoire du Valais, Sion. Collectionner au cœur des Alpes* (Sion, Paris: Somogy Ed. d'Art, Musée d'histoire, 2013), pp.102–103.
99   Hermitage Museum, St. Petersburg, inv. W-7.
100 British Museum, London, inv. 1879,1220.1.
101 A. Eastmond, *The Glory of Byzantium and Early Christendom* (London: Phaidon, 2013), p.81.
102 E. Dimitrova, *The Ceramic Relief Plaques from Vinica. The most significant values of the cultural and natural heritage* (Skopje: Directorate for protection of cultural heritage, 2017), pp.20–21.

BIRTH OF THE BYZANTINE ARMY 476-641 CE VOLUME 2: WATCH THEM FIGHT!

Sixth-Century Byzantine Heavy Infantryman

This soldier is wearing a coat of iron mail over a leather *subarmalis* whose *pteruges* are visible at the thighs. Sometimes *pteruges* also cover the upper arms. The wide trousers are of barbarian origin but were in use in the Romano-Byzantine Army as portrayed on the cathedra of Archbishop Maximian of Ravenna (545-553). The design of the shield is inspired from the sixth-century ivory *pyxis* showing the martyrdom of St Menas (British Museum, inventory number 1879, 1220). In both representations, the soldiers wear scale armour with *pteruges* and a stylised visored helmet. Instead a Leiden-type segmented helmet has been preferred to the Hellenistic-like artistic convention. The shield's colours are inspired by the frescoes, dating from late sixth to early seventh century, in the Coptic church of Deir Abu Hennis in the old village of Antinoa. The belt is based on late Roman examples.

representations are quite crude. Joshua wears a scale breastplate of rising scales that covers the shoulders and goes down to the thighs. He has a short cloak tied at the neck. The two warriors wear high boots and long tunics, helmets with cheek guards, nasal and a very stylised crest seen from the front and pointing to the front, probably metallic. They are holding wide iron spears. Caleb seems to be covered in some kind of gambeson, difficult to pinpoint. He is carrying a medium size, round shield with a pattern or reinforcement of 13 rays emanating from the flat *umbo*.

The Metropolitan Museum of Art in New York holds six of the nine silver plates from the so-called 'Cyprus Treasure'.[103] All of these depict the warlike exploits of David and are dated around 613–630 – undoubtedly with the aim of glorifying Emperor Heraclius as a new David. The best-known of the group shows, in the centre, the duel between David and Goliath. Behind the antagonists stand two soldiers symbolically depicting the Hebrews and the Philistines, they are identical and armed in the Romano-Byzantine fashion as is Goliath himself. All soldiers are bare-legged with high boots showing the toes and short tunics. They wear a short mail cuirass with a pectoral band decorated with festoons on the abdomen, a row of pteruges on the thighs and upper arms, spalieres and a short cloak covering the left shoulder. They hold a spear in the right hand and hold a round convex shield with eight large petals in their left. A long sword hangs at the left side. All have a pointed-visored elongated helmet, covered with decorated fabric with a crest. Another plate depicting the armament of David shows that the pectoral harness worn over a breastplate or over a tunic.[104]

A lost mosaic in Syria depicts the same scene between David and Goliath where both warriors are wearing segmented helmets, mail body armour on a leather *subarmalis*, and are carrying round shields and spears.

Ultimately, the appearance of an Imperial soldier could resemble that of a warrior of a Romano-Germanic kingdom. Only the shield emblems, the standards, certain classicizing elements of the armor such as the *pteruges*, the pectoral Babylonian harness gave him a "Roman" air.

---

103 Metropolitan Museum of Art, New York, inv. 17.190.396. K. Weitzmann, 'Prolegomena to a Study of the Cyprus Plates', *Metropolitan Museum Journal*, vol. 3 (1970), pp.97–111.
104 Metropolitan Museum of Art, New York, inv. 17.190.399.

BIRTH OF THE BYZANTINE ARMY 476-641 CE VOLUME 2: WATCH THEM FIGHT!

Heraclius Era Infantryman Probably Stylised in a Classic Style

Foot soldier dressed in full military array with a leather *subarmalis* worn under a classically shaped breastplate but of mail. Another soldier depicted in the same plate wears scale armour. He is wearing the *subalare babylonicum* (Babylonian chest strap). The oval shield remains that of the Late Roman Empire. The most unusual thing is the helmet which is Hellenistic in shape, but which may actually be a leather or felt helmet cover on a Spangenhelm type helmet. This odd headgear is adorned with a horsehair plume. After the battle of David and Goliath from the Cyprus Treasure, aka the David Plates, a set of nine silver plates made in Byzantium between 613 and 630 and today in the Metropolitan Museum of Art, New York.

Seventh-Century Byzantine Infantryman from Syria

This infantryman wears a red tunic, light beige trousers, long white long decorated socks and black boots. He is carrying a pinkish-colour shield bordered with red and white, a conical segmented helmet, a short coat of mail strengthened by a yellowish leather *subalare babylonicum*. Under the body armour he has a brown-white *subarmalis* with *pteruges* and decorated upper sleeves, a sort of 'buff coat'. On the original mosaic the black scabbard is hanging on his right-hand side, an unrealistic position to draw the sword. There is no classicising and aesthetical effects as appear on items in the Cyprus Treasure. After a lost Syrian mosaic showing the fight between David and Goliath, which is a recurrent theme in early Byzantine art.

ELITE CAVALRY AND SECOND-CLASS INFANTRY

Late Sixth-Century Byzantine Infantrymen
The left hand infantrymen is wearing a brass scale armour with red leather *subalare babylonicum* and carries a round shield, interpreted from the silver plates of the Cyprus Treasure. His iron Spangenhelm type helmet has a large mail neck guard on a piece of cloth which could also be of leather. The right-hand soldier wears a more elaborate Baldenheim type helmet and a short coat of mail. Only the standard-bearer has a brass muscle corselet of the classical fashion like the crest of his helmet. The standard is a late Roman style *labarum*. White leather *pteruges* are well attested for thighs protection. Courtesy of the Numerus Invictorum.

The Helmets

Of all these representations, the helmet is the most stylised item but also the item most found in archaeology. The two do not fit well. It seems that the helmet of the Romano-Byzantine infantryman is a simplification of that of the later Roman Empire. From the sixth century, across the whole of Europe, the most-common helmet was of segmented type, also known as Spangenhelm type. It was made of four or more curved iron plates. This was not a new form, as it is found on the Trajan Column among Dacian horsemen, and some historians believe it to be of Sassanid, or even east-Asian, origin.[105] Roman horsemen of the *scutarius* type are wearing them on the Arch of Galerius in Thessaloniki from the beginning of the fourth century. Cavalrymen and infantrymen now appear to have the same helmets. Generally elongated in shape, the skull, of four convex rhomboidal

---

105 A. L. Kubik, 'Introduction to studies on late Sasanian protective armour. The Yarysh-Mardy1 Helmet', *Historia I Świat*, 5 (2016), pp.77–105.

pieces, was held together by riveted bands that met at the top and rested on a circular band where cheek guards were attached by iron hinges. The interior was lined with a leather cap. This model is best illustrated by a helmet dated to around 400–600, found in Egypt preserved in the Rijksmuseum voor Oudheden, Leiden.

Romano-Byzantine Segmented, Spangenhelm Type Helmet from Egypt, 400–600
Roman or Byzantine iron Spangenhelm type helmet with cheek guards, interior leather trim and fasteners, and no neck guard unless it was leather or linen and has thus not survived. After a specimen discovered in Egypt on the head of a mummy, 618-628, today in the Rijksmuseum voor Oudheden Leiden.

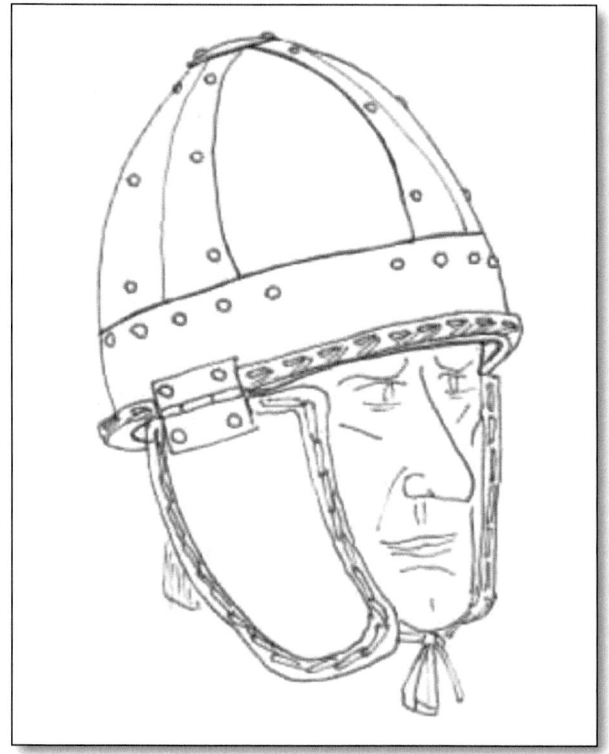

The Regional Museum of Cetinska Krajina in Sinj, Croatia, has in its collection a segmented helmet, dated to 568–628 and very similar to that in Leiden. It is undecorated and elongated with cheek guards probably held to the bowl of the helmet by a leather thongs.[106] A hemispherical bowl helmet dating from the late sixth or early seventh century was found in Jerusalem in the Temple district. It has no wide bands and is very similar to the Baldenheim type discussed below. The cheeks guards were attached by the leather thong around the inside of the helmet.[107] Around 30 iron helmets were found in Novae, on the Danube in present-day Bulgaria, in

---

106 Inventory number MCK-AZ-118, Museum of the Cetinska Krajina Region, Sinj. Z. Vinski, 'Ein völkerwanderungszeitlicher Helm aus Sinj', *Starohrvatska prosvjeta* 3712 (1982), pp.7–34.

107 G. D. Stiebel, 'A Spangenhelm-type helmet' in E. Mazar, *The Temple Mount Excavations in Jerusalem 1968–1978. Directed by Benjamin Mazar. Final Report II. The Byzantine Period*, (Jerusalem: The Hebrew University of Jerusalem, Qedem, Monographs of the Institute of Archaeology, The Institute of Archaeology 2003), pp.43–46.

ELITE CAVALRY AND SECOND-CLASS INFANTRY

a building called *ptochotrophion* a refuge which welcomed pilgrims who came to honour St Luppos. An earthquake in 557 crushed the helmets but also preserved them. They have small, unornamented cheek guards. The helmets' shape is original because it is asymmetrical with, under the head band a piece of metal which gradually widens from the forehead towards the back of the head and covering the latter.[108]

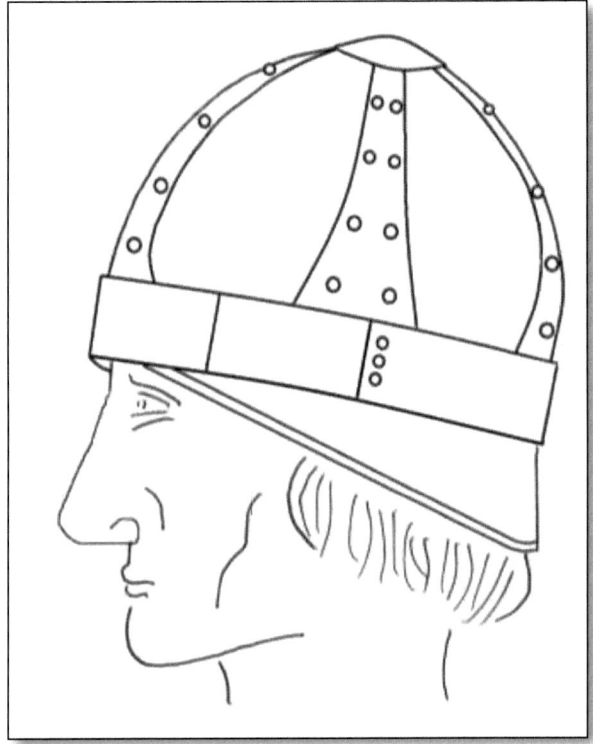

Sixth-Century Byzantine Segmented, Spangenhelm Type Helmet from the Area of Thrace
After specimens of rib or hoop iron helmets excavated from the early Byzantine city of Novae (now Svištov in northern Bulgaria) in the Diocese of Thrace. The first instances of these models appears in the Third and Fourth Centuries in Sassanid's Persia and they were later adopted by the late Roman Army. Some models have iron cheek pieces and a mail neck guard.

The other shape of segmented helmet, called bandenhelm, or broadband, has a hemispherical bowl shape with a two-part skull riveted together by a wide central band and a circular band at the base. Spaced groups of three rivets hold the central strip. It could be a development and simplification of the late Roman Intercisa-type helmet. The two best-known examples, near-enough identical, are from Narona (Sveti Vid in Croatia) and dated to the fifth or sixth century, in the collection of the Kunsthistorischen Museum, Vienna.[109] The Museum hesitates to identify them as local late Roman or Alan-origin.

---

108 B. Bohlendorf-Arslan, A. Ricci (eds), 'Early Byzantine Iron Helmets from Novae (the Diocese of Thrace)', *BYZAS*, 15, *Byzantine Small Finds in Archaeological Contexts*, DAI Istanbul, (2012), pp.91–104.
109 Kunsthistorischen Museum in Vienna, inv. A 1998a and A 1998b.

Romano-Byzantine Bandendelm-type Helmet from Egypt, 400–600
Some of these hemispherical helmets were found in Danube area and are sometimes linked with Alans (either by use or manufacture). As cheap model, they were in common use with the late Roman border troops. There is neither iron cheek nor neck guard. Here the linen neck cover and the scarf protection are inspired by a tenth-century fresco from St Lucas Monastery. In a Mediterranean summer or a desert climate, the use of a linen neck cover is later echoed in their use on the kepis of the *Légion Étrangère* in the Sahara. After a specimen found in Egypt, now in Rijksmuseum voor Oudheden, Leiden.

Tenth-Century Byzantine Helmet with Linen Neck Cover and Scarf
The scarf may be equated to the late sixth-century *peritrachèlion stroggulon*, some sort of padded tissue protection of Avar origin. After a colour fresco from the monastery of St Lucas (Hosios Loukas) in Boeotia, Greece.

An example of the bandenhelm family from Thebes in Egypt is in the Brooklyn Museum and is dated to the seventh century. Two blade-shaped cheek guards like earflaps and a mail neck guard hang from the helmet. It has embossed bronze bands lining the base and the parietal sides with relief of grapevine motif.[110]

---

110   Brooklyn Museum, New York, inv. 37.1600E.

ELITE CAVALRY AND SECOND-CLASS INFANTRY

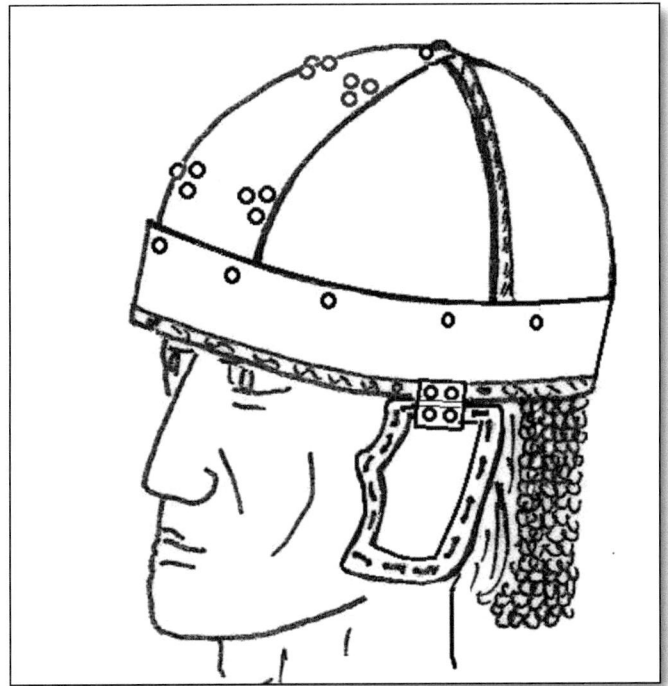

Seventh-Century Bandenhelm with Ear Guards and Mail Neck Guard
This hemispherical helmet found in Thebes, Egypt has iron ear guards and a short mail neck guard. Later base and lateral bronze bands with a grapevine motif were added to the bowl. It is the last variation of the Late Roman Intercisa helmet type. After specimen 37.1600E in the Brooklyn Museum, New York.

The other variant, known as the Kreuzbandhelm, was found in the fort of Voivoda in Bulgaria, which was destroyed in the second half of the fifth century.[111] More elaborate, this variant has a four-part cap riveted together by golden copper strips forming a cross. Decorative gilded ribbons join at the top and form a cross. The circular band is also golden but notched at the level of the eyes and sketches a nasal pattern. This model appears to be derived from late Roman helmets of the Burgh Castle or Concesti type, which have pronounced nasals and wide cheek pieces. Kreuzbanhelm-type helmets without decorative ribbons have been found at Shorwell in the United Kingdom, in a tomb where there is a copy of a Byzantine *solidus* gold coin, at Trivières in Belgium and at Bretzenheim in Germany, a copy of which survives only in iconography and a cast. Dated to the sixth century, they reflect a European military fashion.[112]

A more elaborate helmet than the Baldenheim type was the Spangenhelm, used by officers, elite cavalry and Germanic chieftains. The eponymous model comes from a grave excavated in July 1902 in a field in Baldenheim, and is today in the Archaeological Museum of Strasbourg.[113]

---

111 L. Vagalanski, 'Ein neuer spätantiker Segmenthelm aus Voivoda, Schumen Gebiet (NordostBulgarian)', *Archaelogica Bulgarica*, 2 (1998), pp.96–106.

112 B. Ager, 'West Wight, Isle of Wight: Anglo-Saxon Grave Assemblages (2004 T187)', in *Treasure Annual Report 2004* (London: Department for Culture, Media and Sport, 2006), pp.68–71. https://www.britishmuseum.org/collection/object/H_2006-0305-67 (Shorwell).

113 Musée Archéologique de Strasbourg, Strasbourg, inv. MAS 4 898.

Dating from around the late sixth century or the beginning of the seventh century, the bowl is divided into six elliptical plates of silver-plated iron, riveted together by six bands of gilded copper alloy resting on a gilded crown band. The crown band is decorated with round and lozenge-shaped medallions displaying various motifs of plants, winged figures, animals and riders. A hollow point adorning the top of the bowl suggests it once had a tufted crest. The cheek guards are decorated with a guilloche pattern. At the time of the discovery, pieces of mesh ribs were found, probably from a flexible neck guard. Pieces of leather forming the inside of the cap have been preserved.[114] This type of helmet is often found alongside Imperial coins in Germanic tombs showing the Byzantine influence or perhaps indicates former *foederati*.[115] Forty or so examples of this type of helmet have been found from Libya to Scandinavia and as far as Ukraine and Russia, but mainly in the Danube area and are dated throughout the 550s–650s – all have a Romano-Byzantine origin. Among the barbarians, these helmets are associated with tombs or lakes, while in Byzantine area, they are found in habitats and forts.[116] In a Byzantine context, the most interesting specimen is the sixth-century helmet from Salona. The skull is made from four conical iron pieces. The four riveted fastening pieces, the crown band and the cheeks guards are gilded. Eucharistic symbols of a grapevine motif are raised in relief on the crown band. The cheek guards are engraved with small details. Three remaining rings suggest a mail neck guard. The helmet was topped by a hollow point used to fix a horsehair plume. The conical segmented helmets made the traditional crest impracticable.

A variant of this type of helmet, dated to the late fifth or early sixth century, was found in Macedonia in a basilica on the site of Heraclea (today Heraklea Lyncesti).[117] It is conical and symmetrical, with cheek guards and narrow connecting bands, and a decorated crown band showing the usual raised relief of the grapevine motif. An intermediate type between Baldenheim for the pattern and Voivoda for the indentation above the eyes, probably worn by a Germanic chieftain. It was found at Villeneuve in Lake Geneva, and is in the collection of the Landesmuseum, in Zurich.[118] The

---

114 M. Vogt., *Spangenhelme: Baldenheim und verwandte Typen*, (Mainz: Verlag des Römisch-Germanischen Zentralmuseums, Kataloge vor – und frühgeschichtlicher Altertümer, 39, 2006).

115 D. Glad, 'The Empire's Influence on barbarian Elites from the Pontus to the Rhine (Fifth-Seventh Centuries): A Case Study of Lamellar Weapons and Segmental Helmets' in S. Ivanišević, M. Kazanski, *The Pontic Danubian in the Period of the Great Migration* (Paris-Belgrade: Collège de France/ CNRS, Centre de Recherche d'Histoire et Civilisation de Byzance, Monographies 36-Arheološki Institute Beograd, Posebna Izdanja, Knjiga, 51, 2012), p.357.

116 M. Kazanski, 'Les casques du type Baldenheim en Europe orientale: les origines' in M. Kazanski, P. Perin (eds), *Autour du règne de Clovis, Les grands dans l'Europe du Haut Moyen Âge, Histoire et archéologie* (Leuven: AFAM, 31, 2021), pp.230–229.

117 E. Maneva, 'Le casque à fermoir d'Héraclée', *Archaeologia Iugoslavica*, 24 (1987), pp.101–111

118 Landesmuseum, Zurich, inv. A-38925.

ELITE CAVALRY AND SECOND-CLASS INFANTRY

Sixth-Century Byzantine Officer in Spangenhelm type Helmet from Salona
This helmet has brass bands and cheek guards on an iron skullcap. It has a mail neck guard. A horsehair plume was probably fixed at the top point, as shown on the Isola Rizza silver dish. The vineyard grape motif is typical of this kind of helmet for officers, and is a Christian reference to the Christ's blood and the resurrection. This specimen is attributed to a Romano-Byzantine officer or an Ostrogothic chieftain, and was found in Salona, today in Croatia.

four pieces that form the skull are made of silver-plated iron. The hollow butted tip, the riveted T-shaped axial bands and the circular headband are gold. The latter is decorated with an interlacing with vine vines and birds. The punched holes at the base of the helmet suggest it had a leather interior cover. The cheek pieces and neck guards are missing. The origin of this helmet is Byzantine according to the Landesmuseum's curators.[119] The only clear sixth-century iconographic representation of a segmented helmet with a top horsehair plume is on the Isola Rizza silver dish, contemporaneous to the Gothic War.[120]

---

119 C. Borel, 'Spangenhelm' in Martiniani-Reber M. (ed.), Byzance en Suisse, catalogue d'exposition (Genève: Musées d'art et d'Histoire, 2015), pp.400–405.
120 G. Esposito, 'The Isola Rizza Dish', p.58.

The most accurate iconographic representation of a Byzantine segmented helmet comes from later, in the tenth century, in a fresco from the monastery of St Lucas in Greece, depicting Joshua, the Hebrew general at the Battle of Jericho.[121] It shows a white cloth neck guard which may protect against the sun and may also have been a protection against blows. The fight of David and Goliath on the silver plate from the Cyprus Treasure shows a fabric helmet cover with visor, flexible neck guard, with a tufted plume at the top extended to the rear by a horsehair mane.[122] Specific to Byzantine and Arab this headwear was called a *kamelaukion*, a name now associated with the cylindrical headdress, generally black, worn by Orthodox priests and monks.[123] In the Merovingian Frankish area, the bandhelm-type helmet found in Trivières in Hainaut, Belgium, shows traces of a leather cap on the inside and another on the outside.[124] These caps protected helmets from rust and the head from the heat.

Iconography almost never represents Spangenhelm type helmets widely in use but often depicted helmets with a visor and crest that have never been found by archaeology. Byzantine art was keen on military characters from biblical or hagiographic themes. Hellenistic paintings were the source of inspiration for representing heroic military equipment. The Arkeoloji Müzeleri in Istanbul has a second century BCE painted stele with a *thorakitēss* equipped with a mail shirt, a gilded bronze helmet with a red plume and a triangular visor. A painted grave stele in Dioskourides, Ptolemaic Egypt, represents a *thyreophore* from the side wearing a bronze Macedonian helmet with a visor, question mark pattern on the bowl, cheek guards and red plume.[125] The same type of helmet, but with a metal crest, can be found on a *missorium* depicting the story of Achilles and Briseis, dated to the fourth century and found *c.* 1656 in the Rhône.[126] All this illustrates a backward-looking iconographic tradition which depicted the Thraco-Macedonian helmet, militarily obsolete, but present in the late antiquity visual universe as a demonstration of tradition. This helmet and the Achilles-style armour were part of the process of heroisation and historicisation. The segmented helmet was considered too 'modern' by the artists and undoubtedly unbecoming for biblical heroes or saints.

Another question is the recovery of enemy weapons, including helmets, by the Byzantine Army. According to Procopius after the fall of Petra, a lot of Persian equipment was captured because: '[Chosroes had] deposited there such an abundance of weapons that when the Romans took

---

121 M. Chatzidakis, *Byzantine art in Greece, Mosaics – Wall Paintings. Hosios Loukas* (Athens: Melissa, 1997, p. 9.
122 Metropolitan Museum of Art, New York, inv. 17.190.396.
123 Leo VI the Wise, *Taktika*, XIX, 278 (*kamelaukion* 'black in colour and raised on a spear as a signal'). Stephenson I., (2006) p.33 (καμελαύκιον, headgear).
124 G. Faider-Feytmans, A. France-Lanord, 'Le casque mérovingien de Trivières', *Revue Belge d'archéologie et d'Histoire de l'Art*, tome 20, fasc. 4 (1951), pp.265–272.
125 *Thorakites*, θωρακίτης, plural θωρακίται; θυρεοφόρος, plural θυρεοφόροι.
126 Bibliothèque nationale de France, Paris, inv. 56.344.

possession of them as plunder, five men's equipment fell to each soldier, and this too in spite of the fact that many weapons had been burnt on the acropolis.'[127] A colourful Byzantine mosaic from a tomb in Siverik, Turkey, shows a warrior or a hunter struck down a giant bird. The figure has long fair hair, and is wearing a long-sleeved, white tunic, a red belt with a round purse, rose-red trousers, light brown shoes; the man could be a Slav. His scattered equipment consists of a short spear, a cylindrical red and tan-yellow quiver, and a round shield with a conical iron boss. The shield is decorated with three concentric rings (rose, burgundy and light brown) and he has a black baldric. Near him lies an iron helmet from a model close to the Batumi/Staritsa/Perm type. All these sixth and seventh-century helmets are hemispherical or conical, monopartite, hammered and could have a mail aventail riveted to a ring of dozens of individual loops. The Batumi example is precisely dated to the year 557, the Perm and Staritsa-type helmets date from the late sixth century or early seventh century. Other examples have been found in the Russian Federation and Uzbekistan and one in Afghanistan. The Batumi example seems to be a Romano-Byzantine re-use.

---

127 A. L Kubik., O. A Radyuš., L. A. Vyazov, 'On one series of the VI Century AD Iron One-Piece Asian Helmets', *Bulletin of the Institute of Oriental Studies*, 3(1) (2023), p.70. Procopius, *BG*, VIII, 12, 17.

14

The Pitched Battle: Tactics and Practice

> When you are getting ready to fight, expecting to encounter no difficulties is neither humane nor in keeping with the way of the world.
>
> Archelaos, military prefect, Procopius, *Bellum Vandalum*, III, 15, 11.

The pinnacle of tactics was the pitched battle, rare because of its uncertainty and the high stakes. The *Peri Strategikes* recommended not engaging in a formal battle if the enemy was in better condition or if the chances were equal.[1] The *Strategikon* said to avoid battle if it did not offer some advantage.[2] Most battles were decisive, because the defeated side was no longer able to fight another battle. Throughout the sixth century, Imperial troops won most of their battles, a skill that afterwards diminished. How can this relative decline be explained?

The Exhortation to Fight

A man on horseback travels along the army's front. All eyes are turned towards him and everyone is listening to him. As a reality of psychological warfare or a mere topos from ancient historiography, the general-in-chief harangued his men before fighting. Procopius, Agathias or the poet Corippus almost never recount an important battle without the general-in-chief's harangue, a common practice among Imperial troops, Vandals and Ostrogoths.[3] Two questions arise: how did the general make himself heard

---

1　*Peri Strategikes*, 33, 16–17 (condition); 25–26 (equal chances).
2　Maurice, *Strategikon*, VIII, 2, 86.
3　Procopius, *BV*, IV, 1, 12–25 and 2, 1 (Belisarius at Trikamaron); 2, 8–32 (Gelimer and Tzatzon).

by the whole army, and what was the real content of his speech? Before Taginae in 552, Narses the Eunuch gathered his army in a narrow space to harangue them in the manner perhaps of a union speech. The following year, during the siege of Lucca, Narses came 'into the midst of his army' to speak to them. This central position made it easier to be within earshot, but in front of several thousand men, his voice had to be loud.[4] When the army was drawn up for almost a kilometre, it proved far more difficult. Before the Battle of Mammes, Solomon made a speech to his 'companions-in-arms' in battle before the Moors.[5] Was it heard by everyone? Did he repeat the same ideas several times while strolling along the front line? Procopius does not say.

The content varied according to the morale of the army and the overall situation. It aroused or tempered the aggressiveness of men and also gave tactical instructions. The foundations of psychological warfare are found in some of John Troglita's harangues: the enemy was bad, the cause was legitimate and victory would be certain because Mars (!) supported the Romans, they would have to stand fast in combat then he concluded by giving the order to advance.[6] The evocation of Mars by the poet Corippus may have been more epic than historical, but recourse to divine protection has always been a recipe for psychological warfare.

A defeat was a circumstance where a harangue proved more necessary but not easier. This was the case in 553 during the Italian campaign after a detachment of troops was ambushed by the Franks, when Narses the Eunuch had to restore the morale of the troops gathered in Lucca. They had not been involved in the defeat but, among themselves, exaggerated the disaster of their comrades in arms and the strength of the incoming enemy. Then Narses speech opposed good and bad examples, comparative strengths and weaknesses of 'Romans' and their enemies. He began by criticising angry men, accustomed to success and quickly discouraged. It was a way to indirectly castigate his men without mentioning them. After Narses used flattery to make the men want to place themselves in this category. He then relied on a sentiment that reflected the mentality of the time, demonstrating that the setback suffered was due to a barbarian general in the service of the Empire, Fulcaris; thus it was not the 'Roman soldier' and the military art of Byzantium that was to blame. In so doing, he lessened the impact of his defeat. Then he appealed to honour, claiming that it would be shameful to give up. He then evoked another virile virtue – resolution. After this emotional salvo, Narses switched to military reasoning. He included his soldiers in the general's calculations of an analysis of strengths and weaknesses. The enemy's strength came from their large numbers, while that of the Romans came from their discipline. The enemy's weakness was that they came from Gaul without supply. The Romans, on the contrary, had an abundance of

---

4   Procopius, *BG*, VIII, 30, 1 (Taginae). Agathias, *Hist.*, I, 16, 1 (Lucca).
5   Procopius, *BV*, IV, 11, 22 (Mammes).
6   Corippus, *Joh*, IV, v. 406–456.

food. Their strength was also of being able to take refuge in a network of cities and fortresses. Franks did not benefit from such an advantage. Finally, Narses released the last argument which closed almost all the harangues of Romano-Byzantine generals: 'The Almighty is with us.'[7]

It was rare that the harangue did not work. Belisarius experienced it bitterly in 531 at Callinicum. He wanted to avoid an uncertain battle and rationally presented his arguments to the troops: why risk it when the enemy was retreating? God did not help those who deliberately sought danger; the army was hungry and lacked cavalry. For an answer he only received insults and had follow his troops' wishes, who were eventually beaten.[8] In periods inexperienced troops or a crowd respond more to emotion than reason. Belisarius still had this to learn.

The Preliminary Duel

Two men stand out from the opposing armies which are lined up face to face. They fiercely rush towards each other with the intent of killing their opponent. The practice of preliminary duels before battle did not exist in the later Empire. But across the sixth century, the heroic and even Homeric culture of duelling before battle reappeared in a world where Greek culture was dominant. The practice of duelling was part of the virile *ethos* or *andreia* resonating in Procopius' stories. It was not just a decorative literary motif, but a code of honour, a way of life and death, shared with and understood by all warrior peoples.[9] Byzantine officers owed their promotion to their fighting spirit.[10] They had to inspire their men by proving their valour in arms.

A duel between John the son of Sisiniolos and Stotzas, the commander of an army of deserters was reported by Corippus and Procopius. If Corippus is suspected of poetic embellishment, Procopius was not. The duellists were driven, the historian argued, by an old hatred not heroic emulation: 'They both left their troops and walked towards each other.' Without concern for elegance, John the son of Sisiniolos shot Stotzas with an arrow, fatally wounding him in the femur according to Corippus and in the right groin according to Procopius, probably cutting the artery.[11]

The preliminary duel was not just a sordid settling of scores in an individual killing – it was a ritual. At Faenza in early 542, Valaris, an

---

7   Agathias, *Hist.*, I, 16, 1–9.
8   Procopius, *BP*, I, 18, 16–23 (speech); 24 (insults); 50 (defeat).
9   M. E. Stewart, 'Contest of Andreia in Procopius' Gothic Wars', *Parekbolai*, 4 (2014), pp.21–54 ($\alpha\nu\delta\rho\varepsilon\iota\alpha$).
10 M. P. Speidel, 'Who fought in the Front' in G. Alföldy, B. Dobson, W. Eck (eds), Kaiser Heer und Gesellschaft in der Romischen Kaiserzeit. Gedenkschrift für Eric Birley (Stuttgart: Franz Steiner Verlag, 2000), pp.473–482.
11 Corippus, *Joh*, IV, v. 171–172. Procopius, *BV*, IV, 24, 10–11.

THE PITCHED BATTLE: TACTICS AND PRACTICE

Ostrogoth horseman, came out of the ranks to challenge the Romans. The Armenian officer Artabazes took up the challenge and killed the Ostrogoth with a single blow from his spear, but was wounded in the neck and died three days later. At Taginae in 552 Coccas, a 'Roman' deserter who had joined the Ostrogoths, who had a 'great reputation as an active combatant', approached the army of Narses the Eunuch to propose a single combat. An Armenian cavalryman named Anzalas took up the challenge and killed Coccas with his lance. The 'Roman' army roared in victory.[12] In this case two 'Romans' opposed each other. It is worth noting that most of the time the hierarchy did not oppose this practice or punished champions who acted of their will.

The fact the two armies stood by and watched the duel proves there was a tacit understanding. The duel's heroic culture was understood by the Romano-Byzantines as well as by the barbarians. It would have been dishonourable to capture an enemy who came to bring a challenge. On the barbarian side, after the unfortunate fight where Coccas was killed, Totila took the moral momentum by offering a show of arms and also gained time until the arrival of 2,000 reinforcements. To the admiration of both armies he gave a show of horsemanship and handling of the spear which he skilfully threw and caught; he was magnificently clad in purple and golden armour, certainly composed of metallic scales and dyed leather. After this equestrian show, he went behind the lines and returned with common armour so as not to become a target.[13]

Duelling before battle was seldom practised by the Germanic peoples, whereas Agathias claimed that the Franks preferred to settle the fate of a battle by a judicial duel in their civil wars. Frankish sources were unlikely to mention this.[14] The duel could exceptionally replace the battle. It was offered by the Hun Althias to the Moor Iaudas for possession of a spring. Tall and strong, Iaudas overconfidently accepted since Althias was small in stature, but he was unpleasantly surprised by the Hun's agility. While their horses were galloping, Althias used his right hand to retrieve the javelin thrown at him by Iaudas and his left hand to draw his bow then he shot the Moor's horse. Althias behaved in a 'chivalrous' manner, and he did not finish off Iaudas on the ground. He let someone bring a second horse to Iaudas who ran without fighting more. Despite the disproportion of forces – 70 Huns against thousands of Moors – the ethics of the duel and of keeping one's word prevailed over the military logic of numbers.[15] After all, they were warriors and not later professional soldiers. During a siege, the duel had a very strong Homeric resonance. When Solomon was campaigning from the Aures in *c*. 450, an *optio* named Gezon, gripped by an inexplicable fury, set off alone to attack the Moorish stronghold of Toumar. The three

---

12 Procopius, *BG*, VII, 21–29 (Valatis and Artabanes); VIII, 31, 11–15 (Totila).
13 Procopius, *BG*, VIII, 31, 17–21.
14 Agathias, *Hist.*, I, 2, 7.
15 Procopius, *BV*, IV, 13, 7–16.

Moors guarding the entrance thought he had come to challenge them and went out, also faithful to the ethics of the duel. As the narrow terrain only allowed them to arrive in one at a time, Gezon killed them one after the other. His feat prompted the whole army to storm Toumar stronghold. The heroic emulation was obvious.

The greatest duellist in Justinian's Army was Andreas. Surprisingly, he was not a soldier but simply General Bouzes' personal bath attendant, which says a lot about the oriental luxury of the Byzantine high command. Before handling the towels and aromatic oil, this Byzantine servant was the *pediotribe* of a *palestra*, or trainer in sports centre. By 530, when at the opening of the Battle of Dara a young Persian horseman challenged the Imperial Army, Andreas took up the challenge. He overthrew his challenger with a spear and finished him off with a penknife. Vexed, a Persian Warrior with grey hair and tall stature issued another challenge. Despite General Hermogenes' prohibition on duelling, Andreas again took up the challenge. The two antagonists knocked each other down, but the faster Andreas finished off his opponent with a spear. Procopius points out that Andreas was physically strong and well trained. It was the muscular victory of the sportsman over the warrior. These unfavourable omens led the Persians to retreat and the battle was postponed.[16] However, the most famous preliminary duel of the time was that between Heraclius and the Persian General Rahzadh before the Battle of Nineveh on Saturday 12 December 627. It was a mounted duel in which Heraclius knocked Rahzadh off his horse without injuring him, since the two opponents were most likely armoured as *clibanarii*. Immediately afterwards, Heraclius had to confront and kill two other Persian champions. The first probably stepped forward to protect Rahzadh as he was laying on the ground, the second to restore the Persians' faltering morale and honour. Rahzadh was killed in the ensuing battle.[17] Who won the duel, won the battle!

Cavalry Tactics

'Having immediately assembled the horsemen who accompanied him and having placed them in regular formation, he ordered the standards to be displayed high and all to set to work.'[18] This was how Justin, the son of the Patrician Germanus, acted as a squadron leader. Officers fought in the front rank, setting an example to their soldiers.[19] The *Peri Strategikes*, treatise written in the time of Justinian, said the usual tactic was the 'horse phalanx' a five rank formation, leaders in the first rank, common soldiers to the rear. Horsemen could not be tightly packed as in an infantry phalanx, but had to

---

16 Procopius, *BP*, I, 29–38.
17 Theophanes Confessor, *Chrgr.*, AM 6118, 318.
18 Agathias, *Hist.*, III, 25, 8.
19 M. P. Speidel, 'Who fought in the Front' in G. Alföldy et al, pp.473–482.

THE PITCHED BATTLE: TACTICS AND PRACTICE

have the space to charge at the gallop.[20] By contrast, the *Strategikon* preferred a 10 rank formation and the charge at the trot like medieval knights and French cuirassiers.[21] Open order was used to manoeuvre and close order to charge. The *Strategikon* blamed 'Romans' and Persians for using their cavalry in a single line or *parataxis*, sealing the fate of tens of thousands of men in one unique charge. It preferred Avar and Turkish tactics of having several squadrons deployed two or three lines deep.[22] It preferred to deploy cavalry in two lines: *phoideratoi*, Illyrians, vexillations in the first, *optimatoi* and *tagmata* in the second. Although ancient authors preferred four ranks per *tagma*, the *Strategikon* declared: 'As it is true that the number of elite soldiers capable of fighting at the head of the line in each *tagma* is limited, it is necessary to limit the depth of the ranks proportionally to each unit.'[23] So, each file was a *decarchy* variable in size: seven cavalrymen for *phoideratoi*, vexillations and *optimatoi*, eight for Illyrians or 10 in other *tagmata*.

A cavalry unit was set in motion when the *tagma* leader raised his hand or his shield, a trumpet sounded, a lance pennon movement or an order was shouted: *Move* (read *mowé*) with the same meaning as in English. The halt command was: *Sta!* (Stay in place).[24] Within three or four bowshot's range from the enemy, the *tagma* drawn up in order of battle. All commands were given in Latin. The tribune shouted: *Iunge!* (tighten the ranks). This brief command was followed by a long palaver, again always in Latin, aiming to appease the soldiers so that they held onto their nervous mounts. 'Thou' was used to individualise the collective order:

> Stay silent! Nobody holds back, nobody goes beyond the banner. If thou advance, do so while remaining in line, the banner in sight. Follow thy banner, soldier, that is what a good soldier does. If thou leave thy banner, thou will not be victorious. Soldier, keep thy position and thou ensign bearer keep yours. If thou fight, if thou pursue the enemy or stay in the ranks, do not charge impetuously, otherwise thou will break the formation.[25]

---

20   *Peri Strategikes*, 17, 1–2 (ἱππική φάλαγξ and formation).
21   Maurice, *Strategikon*, III, 2 (10 ranks and open order); 3 (close order); 5, 29–33 (charge).
22   Maurice, *Strategikon*, II, 1, 20–26 (παράταξις, battle line).
23   Maurice, *Strategikon*, II, 6, 20–21 (decarchy with 7 for foederati); 23 (7 for vexillations); 24 (8 for Illyrians); 26 (8–10 for others).
24   Maurice, *Strategikon*, III, 5, 11–13 (μοβε for Latin *move*; στα for sta),
25   Maurice, *Strategikon*, III, 4, 3–4 (range); 5 (ιουγγε for Latin iunge); 5, 2–8, (Latin transcribed into Greek: Σιλεντιον, νεμο δεμιττατ, νεμο αντεκεδατ βανδουμ, σικ βενιας βερο αικουαλις φακιες, βανδουμ καπτα, ιψω σεκουε κουμ βανδο μιλιξ, ταλις εστ κομμοδουμ μιλες βαρβατι, σι βερο βανδουμ δεμιττες εο μοδο νον βερο βικες, σερβα μιλιξ ορδινεμ ποσιτουμ, ιψουμ σερβε ετ τον βανδιφερ, σιβε σεκουες ινιμικουμ σιβε αικουαλις φακιες νον φορβτε μιναρε ουτ νε σπαργες του σουουμ ορδινεμ. - *Silentium, nemo demittat, nemo antecedat bandum, sic venias vero aequalis facies, bandum capta, ipso seque cum bando miles, talis est commodum militis barbati, si*

The tribune shouted again: *Iunge!* Then the cavalrymen advanced at a trot. Once within range the horse archers in the rear ranks delivered an indirect volley into the enemy. The order to charge was given: *Percute!* (Charge). Leading from the front rank *dekarchs* and *pentarchs* raised theirs shields to protect their heads and the neck of their horses. They kept the lances upwards advancing 'not too fast but at the trot' in order to keep the ranks in order.[26]

Reality was quite different from theory. Cavalry fighting was most often a fluid series of repeated actions as Procopius reported of an engagement against the Persians near Satala in 530, a city in Roman Armenia: 'Each of the two sides rushed against each other in charges followed by rapid withdrawals, for all were on horseback.'[27] The Romano-Byzantines won, although half the number of their enemy, because of the heroic actions of a Thracian squadron leader who seized the enemy general's banner before being killed. The Persians, and their Hun allies, no longer seeing this banner, were thrown into disarray and were routed with heavy losses. This was the classic pattern of a defeat: surprise, disorder and rout. Every troop losing cohesion and morale fled, being slaughtered from behind by the enemy. As turning your back was always an invitation for the enemy to pursue, one of the Byzantine cavalry favourite tactics was the feigned retreat then return to counter-attack. It was a borrowing from the Parthians and the Steppe nomads. This stratagem resulted in diverse fortunes. A people of horsemen like the Vandals of Africa were not taken in. At Trikamaron in 533 Belisarius twice sent his mounted *hypaspists* in small numbers to attack the Vandals' centre. Each time, these cavalry details were put forced to run, but the Vandals did not commit the error of pursuing them. Nonetheless a people of foot soldiers like Franks were very vulnerable to this stratagem. Thus, near Rimini in 553, Narses the Eunuch committed 300 horsemen who failed first to defeat a 2,000 man Frank 'phalanx' with cavalry on the wings. He then simulated a retreat pushing the Franks to break their ranks and pursue the fleeing troop, a fatal error as Byzantines horsemen turned back and massacred the now rabble-like crowd.[28] The Ostrogoths, who had a culture of heavy cavalry, and therefore of frontal combat, were also vulnerable to the simulated retreats as proven during the siege of Rome in 537. Three times, Belisarius employed 200 to 300 cavalry to approach the enemy camp, with orders to empty their quivers against those who came out and then to take refuge under the walls where *ballistae* stood ready. The Ostrogothic cavalry lost 4,000 men without coming to close quarters. A few days later, they tried in vain to copy this Romano-Byzantine tactic, sending 500 horsemen near

---

vero bandum demittes eo modo non vero vices, serva miles ordinem positum, ipsum serve et tu bandifer, sive pugnas sive seques inimicum sive aequalis facies non forte minare ut ne sparges tu suum ordinem).

26 Maurice, *Strategikon*, III, 5, 26 (ιουγγε for Latin *iunge*); 29 (περκουτε for *percute*); 29–33 (charge).
27 Procopius, *BP*, I, 15, 15.
28 Procopius, *BV*, IV, 3, 10–12 (*Trikamaron*). Agathias, *Hist.*, I, 21, 4 (Franks strengths); 21, 5 (Narses strengths); 21, 6–7 and 22, 1–8 (Rimini).

THE PITCHED BATTLE: TACTICS AND PRACTICE

the walls, but Belisarius had them surrounded by 1,000 mounted archers shooting arrows from behind, killing most of the Ostrogoths. The second time that the Ostrogoths tried, 500 of their elite horsemen were cut to pieces by a 1,500 strong cavalry force sent out to meet them.[29]

A tactic borrowed from the Avars, or more likely the Huns was the division of the cavalry into groups of *cursores* and *defensores* (runners and defenders), transcribed into Greek as *koursores* and *dephensores*. The former were dedicated to the assault, the latter to covering them. According to Maurice's *Strategikon*, the *cursores* were horse archers placed on the flanks which charged the enemy and then retreated, the *defensores*, constituted two-thirds of the manpower in the centre of a *meros*, and followed the *cursores* in good order and offered them refuge in case of retreat.[30] The other form of combat borrowed from Steppe cavalry was the *droungisti* or swarm charge;[31] This type of combat was illustrated by numerous sorties by the Roman cavalry, particularly the Huns, during the siege of Rome by the Ostrogoths in 537. The Field of Nero, near the Cornelian Gate, was ideal for this type of mobile skirmish. Procopius described 'small numbers of horsemen from both sides' whose combat was degenerating into duels and where 'horsemen in small groups went in all directions.'[32]

The surprise charge with drawn sword on an enemy in marching order obtained good results. In 554, Roman-Hunnic horsemen commanded by Artabanes the Arsacid and Uldach the Hun were guarding a coastal route. As soon as an advance guard of 3,000 Franco-Alamanni appeared, they revealed themselves and charged with swords, knocking some of the enemy down to the bottom of the cliffs, and routing the rest. Artabanes the Arsacid and Uldach pursued this advance guard as far as Fano, about 12km distant, but refused combat when they saw the bulk of the Frankish army arrayed in line of battle.[33] Another sudden action by 600 'Roman' horsemen commanded by Dabragezas and Usigard, two barbarian officers, routed an advance guard of 3,000 Persian horsemen.[34] Around March 537, at the Milvian Bridge near Rome, an encounter pitted a reconnaissance force of

---

29 Procopius, *BG*, V, 27, 4–14.
30 Maurice, *Strategikon*, P, 27; I, 3, 27 (tactical role); 8, 27; II, P, 6; 3, 1–3 (distribution in a *meros*); 5, 23; III, 5, 38–39, 43, 70, 74, 90, 94, 98, 101, 102; 6, 6, 9; 12, 7, 9: 13, 8; 15, 6; VI 1, 3; 2, 3.7; 3, 3, 5, 8, 9, 13; 4, 4; VIIB, 16, 5, 15; XI, 2, 92, 94; XIIA, 1, 11; 3, 24 (δηφένσωρ, plural δηφένσορες). P, 27; I, 3, 26, 29 (tactical); II; P, 6; 3, 1–3 (distribution in a *meros*); 5, 23; 6, 34; III 5 37, 38, 42, 70, 74, 89, 93, 101, 102, 106; 6, 4, 9; 12, 5, 9; VI 1, 3; 2, 3, 5; 3, 4, 6, 13; 4, 4; VIIB, 16, 3, 16; XI, 2, 93, XIIA, 1, 10; 3, 2 (κούρσωρ, plural κούρσορες); S. Janniard, 'Procope, les Huns et les transformations tactiques de la cavalerie romaine au VIe siècle' in G. Greatrex & S. Janniard (eds), *Le monde de Procope/ The World of Procopius,* (Paris: O&M, 28, 2018), p.209.
31 Maurice, *Strategikon*, P, 77; III, 5, 48, 65, 82, 111, 118; 12, 20; 14, 6; IV, P, 6; 3, 80;5, 1, 6, 10, 19; XI, 2, 41 (δρουγγιστί).
32 Procopius, *BG*, VI, 1, 20–21.
33 Agathias, *Hist.*, II, 2, 4–7 (ambush); 3, 1 (retreat).
34 Agathias, *Hist.*, III, 6, 9 ('Roman' strength and command): 7, 1 (Persian strength); 7, 2 (Persian rout).

1,000 cavalry commanded by Belisarius against the Ostrogothic vanguard, who had already crossed the Tiber. Although superior in number, the latter was put to flight after losing 1,000 men, 'of those who fight in the front rank,' added Procopius. On the 'Roman' side, losses were not given but were sustained by the best men, including Maxentius, a bodyguard who sought to defend an endangered Belisarius. Only the firm Gothic infantry was able to repel Belisarius and his impetuous horsemen.[35]

Tactical excellence always required training. However, the sources are quite poor on this point. The *Strategikon* noted two customary exercises with *tagmata*: Scythian and Alan. The first was to circle around a simulated enemy with two squadrons crossing in opposite course without colliding. The second was to simulate retreat and counter-attack.[36] At the beginning of summer 554, Narses the Eunuch assembled his troops in Rome and had them intensively trained for the next campaign, especially the cavalry:

> Narses commanded them to train more for war, he enhanced their ardour with daily exercises, forcing them to run, to make orderly cavalry charges, to twirl as if performing a war dance, to be deafened by the trumpet that accompanies the war cry so that a winter of inactivity has not made them completely forget the war and that they are not softened at the time of combat.[37]

By the mid-sixth century, the Imperial cavalry had a clear superiority over its opponents. This was no longer the case during the 570s when it was regularly outperformed by Lombards. However, cavalry remained highly trained. Ninth-century Muslim author, al-Waqidi had Emir Khalid ibn al-Walid said that at the Battle of Emesa in 635, 'These Roman horsemen are the strongest of the warriors. There are no weak or cowards among them.'[38] The tradition of elite heavy cavalry has endured and its memory perpetuated but some flaws were quoted. Maurice said that the Avars and the Turks did not organise their horsemen in a single line of battle, like the Romans, 'sealing the fate of thousands of men and horses in a single charge.'[39] Tactical flexibility remained with the Steppe horsemen and shock power passed to the Lombards. In a battle near Benevento by 663, the Imperial cavalry fled after one of its members, qualified as a 'little Greek' by Paul the Deacon, was pierced and lifted from his saddle by a Lombard lancer.[40] This story, without exceeding the possible capability of a strong man, may have been invented, although the defeat of the Romano-Byzantine horsemen was a fact.

---

35 Procopius, *BG*, V, 18, 1 *sq*.
36 Maurice, *Strategikon*, VI, 1.
37 Agathias, *Hist.*, II, 1, 1–2.
38 Al-Waqidi, *Futuhl a-Sham*, 2, 57 (2013, p.245.
39 Maurice, *Strategikon*, II, 1.
40 Paul the Deacon, *HL* V, 10.

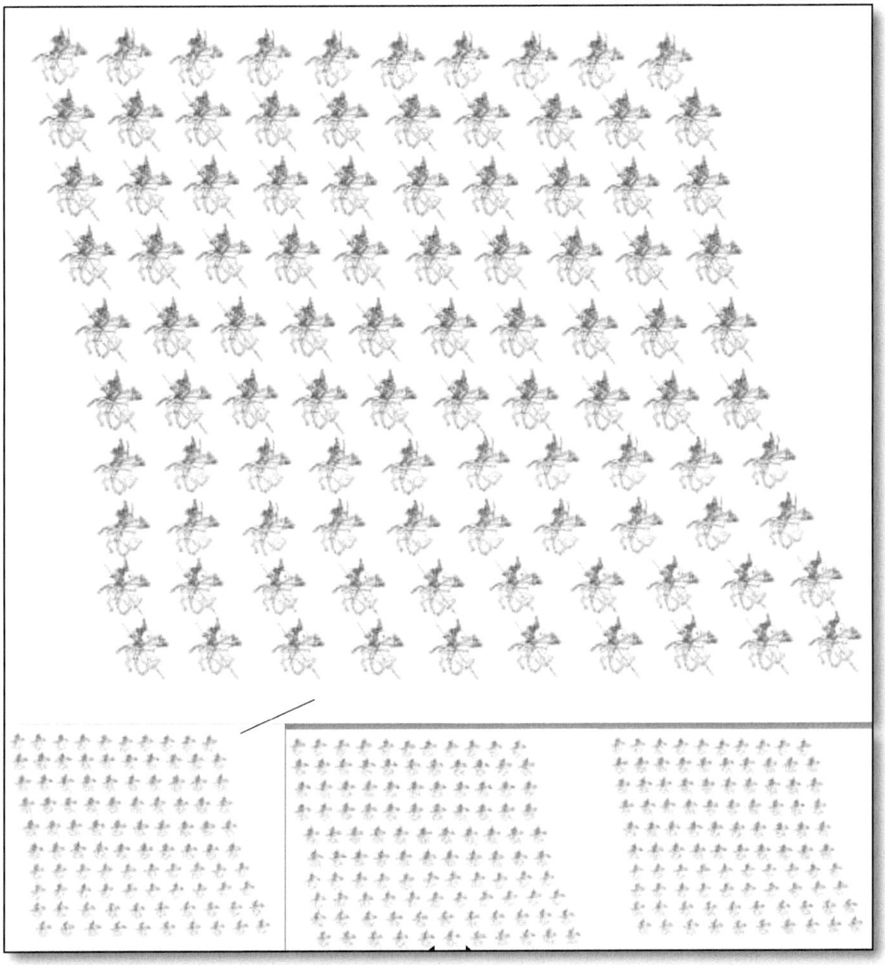

THE PITCHED BATTLE: TACTICS AND PRACTICE

Late Sixth-Century Cavalry *Tagma* in Open Order

A tagma was displayed in three phalanxes in open order when manoeuvring before the charge. Each side of the phalanx was ten files of ten ranks except the central one with eleven. After Maurice's treatise, the *Strategikon*. Commander's phalanx with the *bandon* were in the centre.

Combatant Types in A *Tagma* from The *Strategikon*

There were four types of combatant: NCOs with lance and shield in the two first ranks, cavalrymen with bow, cavalrymen with every kind of weapons, horse archer with shield in the rear ranks.

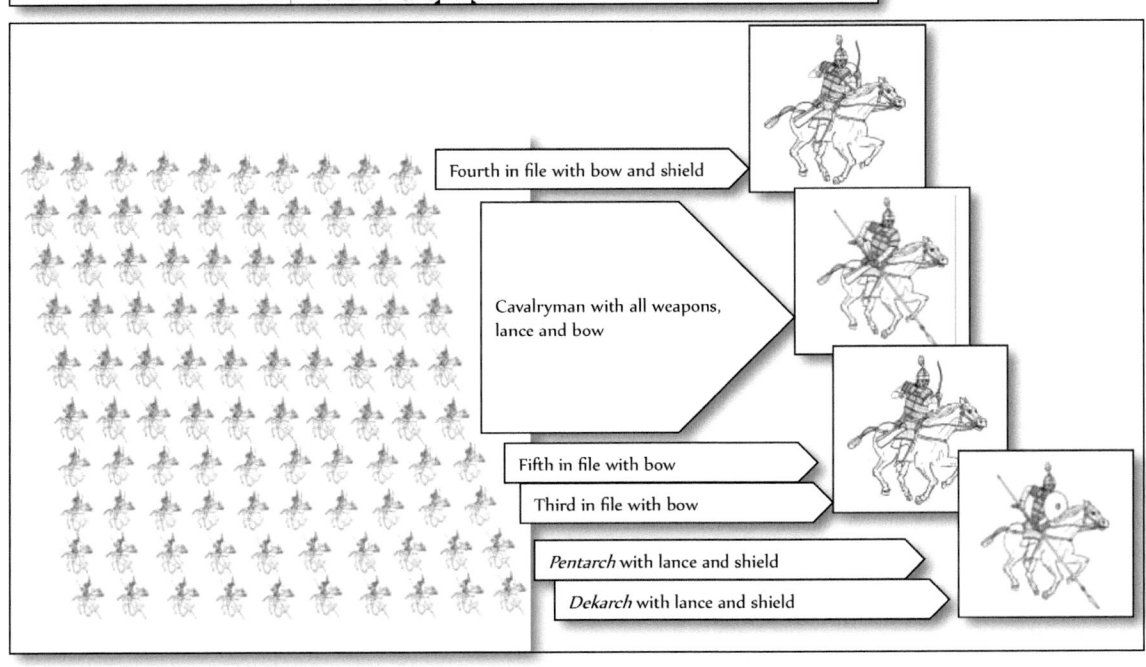

Fourth in file with bow and shield

Cavalryman with all weapons, lance and bow

Fifth in file with bow

Third in file with bow

Pentarch with lance and shield

Dekarch with lance and shield

219

Shock Effect of the First Two Ranks
The *dekarchs* and *pentarchs* were better armoured and the best fighters in a hippic phalanx. Their job was to open a breach in the enemy line then the following ranks exploited the tactical breakthrough.

Infantry Tactics: the Phalanx Again, Maybe the *Phoulkon* as Well

In the years 380–390, Vegetius complained about the use of the 'long square', *fronte longa quadro exercitu*, more directly called the phalanx, which overstretched the fighting line, was disrupted by the unevenness of the terrain and could easily be defeated by the enemy.[41] However, there were some mixed feelings if not sheer contradictions about the phalanx. 'For this reason, did our forefathers call the infantry a wall (*murus*)' stated Vegetius referring to the solidity of the battle line.[42] In Justinian's time, the *Peri Strategikes* described a whole panoply of phalanxes: narrow, wide, oblique, *protaxic*, *entaxic*, *epitaxic*, *hypotaxic*, parabolic, double, with single or double envelopment, square, oblong, two-sided, *amphistomic*, *heterostomous*, a Hellenistic tactician's veritable mumbo-jumbo! The treatise pointed out that, in his day, few people were familiar with tactics and only square or oblong phalanxes were formed. As 'the phalanx designates a formation of armed men whose mission is to contain the enemy' it was in use with cavalry.[43]

Emperor Maurice believed, like Vegetius, that extending the battle line too far was dangerous and placed great emphasis on flank-guards, whose mission was as much to screen the line as to overrun the enemy.[44] Romano-

---

41   Vegetius, *DRM*, III, 20, 1–3.
42   Vegetius, *DRM*, I, 20, 12 (*Unde enim apud antiquos murus dicebatur pedestris exercitus*).
43   *Peri Strategikes*, 15 (phalanx definition; use), 17 (cavalry phalanx), 31 (phalanx types).
44   Maurice, *Strategikon*, VIII, 2, 82 (overstretched phalanx); III, 13 and 14 (flank-guards).

Byzantines were also addicted to phalanx tactics as they were easier to form and maintain in the chaos of battle. During the summer of 538, at the foot of the hill on which the fort of Ancona stood, and which he was defending, Conon was unwise enough to draw up a long, thin phalanx of infantry – as if for hunting. His soldiers fled without fighting when they saw the great numerical superiority of the Goths and most were subsequently killed in the pursuit. Some of Conon's troops were saved by the inhabitants of Ancona, who threw them ropes from the ramparts.[45]

The last great battle of the Gothic War took place at Mons Lactarius probably in late 552. As this steep location proved unsuitable for cavalry, a frontal clash between two phalanxes of dismounted horsemen, mixed with simply infantry, ensued. The Romano-Byzantines soldiers drew themselves up without order, units combined and intermixed and without hierarchical precedence or tactics. It was a two-day brawl, with the night between spent near the battlefield. The Ostrogoths finally gave up and sued for peace negotiations.[46] The depth of such phalanxes remains unknown. Syrianus Magister spoke of a phalanx in three ranks that planted their spears in the ground, but he wrote during the ninth century.[47] Corripus described the phalanx in the way that Vegetius did:

> The very dense battle line, bristling with intertwined shields, extends far away across wide plains. The bodies are hidden by dense armour like walls. Only the two-pinned (axes) and the tops of the helmets, with their crests and dazzling tips, appear behind the shields. But a plain of iron bristles above, once the spears are raised.[48]

Corippus took some poetic licence as he quoted the anachronistic terms of maniples and cohorts.[49] He also mentioned the *cuneus* (wedge) a sturdy assault formation recommended by Vegetius and used from the fourth to the sixth century to define a truncated cone like a pig's snout.[50] As phalanx and wedge were used by the Germans it could be seen as a Germanisation of Romano-Byzantine tactics. This seems to be borne out by a formation that the *Strategikon* called *phoulkon* and that historiography renders as *fulcum*. It consisted of forming what we call a *testudo*: the first rank held their shields in front, while those following put them above their heads.[51] A little etymology is necessary: the term *phoulkon* could derive from the old Saxon *folc* or the old Norwegian *folk* both of which mean 'army', 'troop',

---

45 Procopius, *BG*, VI, 13, 7–13.
46 Procopius, *BG*, VIII, 35, 18 (neither commands nor rank privileges); 19 (phalanxes of dismounted horsemen).
47 Syrianus Magister, *De Strat.*, XXXVI, 3–8, 14–20.
48 Corippus, *Joh*, IV, v. 557–560.
49 Corippus, *Joh*, I, v. 577.
50 Corippus, *Joh*, V, v. 244. Vegetius, *DRM*, I, 26.
51 Maurice, *Strategikon*, XII, A, 7, 53; B 14, 9; 16, 30 (φοῦλκον).

BIRTH OF THE BYZANTINE ARMY 476-641 CE VOLUME 2: WATCH THEM FIGHT!

Fighting Postures of Heavy Infantry
The first four ranks are in postures according to Maurice's *Strategikon*. The first and second ranks are kneeling with the spear butt firmly planted in ground. The third and fourth ranks used their spear for thrusting or even throwing. The space between third and fourth ranks is inspired from Vegetius giving possibilities for manoeuvring and filling gaps. In any case, throwing and stabbing as the *Strategikon* suggested demand some space. The following ranks were archers or javelinmen.

'people' and even 'crowd' in its French derivative *foule*. In old Norwegian, the verb *fylkia* has the meaning of 'arranging warriors in battle'. A Slavic survival of this term was the *pulk* (troop) which characterised the Cossacks.

Phoulkon and phalanx were synonymous in the *Strategikon* which recommended a thin rectangular formation in four ranks. The first two ranks formed a wall of shields where the shields of the second rank passed over the heads of the first rank whose shields they touched. In the rear ranks the men were 'almost glued to each other'. The *ouragoi* (file-closers) prevented desertion and slowed down retreats while the leaders, *lochagoi*, led the fight.[52] Commands – Silence! Follow orders. Do not worry. Keep your position. Follow the banner. Let no one leave the banner and pursue the enemy![53] – were given in Latin by the *mandatôr* or *kampidouktôr* but could be given by trumpet or horn.[54] As units commonly had 16 ranks, they had to be deployed in eight or four when ordered to be in combat formation. The orders were: 'By eight (ranks)!' or 'March out (in four ranks)!' When the battle line became uneven: 'straighten out the front!' When the troop came about two or three bowshots distant from the enemy: 'Close ranks. Form the *phoulkon*!'[55]

---

52 Maurice, *Strategikon*, XII, 16, 13–29.
53 Maurice, *Strategikon*, XII, 14, 2–4 (Latin transcribed into Greek: σιλεντιον, μανδατα καπτατε, νον βος τουρβατις, ορδινεμ σερβατε, βανδο σεχυτε, νεμο δεμιττατ βανδνουμ ετ ινιμικος σεκουε – *silentium, mandata captate, non vos turbatis, ordinem servate, bando sequite, nemo demittat bandum and inimicos seque*).
54 Maurice, *Strategikon*, XII, B, 16, 2–6.
55 Maurice, *Strategikon*, XII, B, 16, 11 (αδ οκτω ἤ εξι – *ad octo, exi*); 14 (εξι -*exi*); 17 (διριγε φροντεμ – *dirige frontem*); 22 (ιουγγε – *iunge*); 33 (αδ φουλκον – *ad fulcum*) - *Ad octo, exi. Exi. Dirige frontem. Iunge. Ad fulcum!* Ph. Rance, 'The *Fulcum*, the Late Roman and Byzantine *Testudo*: The Germanisation of Roman Infantry

THE PITCHED BATTLE: TACTICS AND PRACTICE

Then the unit leader ordered: *Parati!* (Ready). The second in command shouted: *Adiuta!* (Help). Then all soldiers replied in chorus: *Deus!* (God).[56]

The archers shot over the heavy infantrymen who were advancing to within javelin range. At this point the infantry would put their spears in the ground to throw darts or javelins. If they did not have light projectiles, they would move closer to throw their spears like a javelin and then draw their swords. Rear ranks held their shields over their heads to protect themselves from arrows, a useful precaution for unarmoured fighters according to the *Strategikon*. This was undoubtedly the special feature of the *phoulkon*, similar to the Roman *testudo*. Losses were piling up, no doubt troubling the minds of the less seasoned. At this moment the officers shouted: *Non vos turbatis!* (Do not worry). Soon the order was: *Percute!* (Charge). Then the phalanx was going to crash into the opposing ranks. Jostling and screaming, a forest of helmets and low blows, the wounded, groaning, were moving moaning to the rear, we had to stay together: *Ordinem servate!* 'Keep your position!' The fight was on and blood was spurting on shields and greasing swords, the enemy was beginning to waver and some tempers were blaring: *Nemo dimittat bandum and inimicos seque!* (Let no one leave the banner and pursue the enemy). The phalanx was not limited to fighting on the spot, it could also push the enemy back: 'striking some with their javelins, others with their *sarissae* and with their swords, they killed those who were in their path; by making very violent charges against the ranks of the enemies and pushing them back with their shields, they broke their good order.'[57]

The *Strategikon* specified that the first three ranks were compacted together, interlocking their shields, fixing their spears 'in the ground' and angled to impale the enemy. The first two ranks pressed their shoulders against the shield. They were perhaps kneeling because the two following ranks struck the enemy with their spears like daggers or threw them – so the third rank is unlikely to have fixed their spears in the ground.[58] *Phoulkon* as described by the *Strategikon* was very reminiscent of the *Ektaxis kata Alanon* (Battle Line against the Alans) that Arrian, Governor of Cappadocia, theorised *c*. 135: four rows of heavy infantrymen in phalanx preceded another four rows of light infantrymen firing missiles at enemy horsemen.[59] During the Battle at the River Hippis in Lazica, the Romano-Byzantine infantry phalanx joined by dismounted cavalrymen withstood a numerically superior force of Persian and Alan cavalry discharging a rain of arrows on them.[60] In 598, the phalanx was effective against the Avar horsemen who blocked the entrance of the Shipka Pass to the army of

---

Tactics', *Greek, Roman and Byzantine Studies*, 44 (2004), pp.265–326.
56   Maurice, *Strategikon*, XII, B, 16, 41 (παρατι, Latin *parati*); 42 (αδιουτα, Latin *adiuta*); 43 (Δεους, Latin *Deus*).
57   Agathias, *Hist.*, III, 25, 9–10.
58   Maurice, *Strategikon*, XII, A, 7; B, 16 and 24.
59   Arrian, *Ektaxis contra Alanos*, 16–18 (first four ranks with *kontoi*); 15–21, 26 (skirmishers); Ph. Rance, 'Drungus, Δροῦγγος and Δρουγγιστί', pp.297–298.
60   N. Khoperia, 'The Byzantine Lazic Phalanx', p.21.

Comentiolus the Thracian. After suffering casualties, the army was formed into a *phalanx* and cleared the barbarians.[61] This tactic could fail, as at Tell-Besmai in 502 when Persian heavy cavalry defeated a *chelonē* or *testudo* according to Joshua the Stylite who used both Greek and Latin words for the formation.[62]

The infantry phalanx or *phoulkon* was also a rallying point for friendly retreating cavalry, as happened at Callinicum in 531.

> A small part of the infantry fought against the entire Persian cavalry. Nonetheless, the enemy could not defeat them or dominate them in any way. Constantly massed against each other, shoulder to shoulder in a narrow space, and forming with their shields a very solid wall, they shot at the Persians more easily than these could shoot back. The Persians frequently retreated to return again to the charge and destroy their line, but in vain. Because the horses, shocked by the wall of the shields, came back, throwing confusion at themselves and their riders.[63]

During the engagement at the Field of Nero in 537, the retreating cavalry fell back to what Procopius named a 'phalanx' which fled in turn, because it was partly made up of Roman citizens without military training. Nevertheless, Principios and Tarnuntos stood firm, stopping the Goths and allowing the rest of the army to withdraw. This courage came at a cost, Principios was killed on the spot and Tarnuntos, mortally wounded, was barely evacuated by a cavalry detachment commanded by his brother.[64]

---

61 Theophylact Simocatta, VII, *HU*, 14, 9.
62 Joshua the Stylite, *Chron.*, 277.
63 Procopius, *BP*, I, 18, 45–48.
64 Procopius, *BG*, V, 29, 38–44.

THE PITCHED BATTLE: TACTICS AND PRACTICE

Fifth/Sixth-Century Foot Archer
This foot archer has a composite bow, and a cylindrical quiver as depicted in the a fifth-century manuscript of the *Vergilius Romanus* (the *Aeneid*). He is wearing a long tunic and a Phrygian cap often shown in the manuscript. This kind of light infantry followed the heavy infantry and provided some indirect before the melee. From Ms Vat. lat. 3867, *Vergilius Romanus*.

Sixth-Century Armoured Foot Archers
These resting foot archers have a composite bow and wears scale or mail body armour on a leather *subarmalis* with leather or linen pteruges at the shoulders and thighs. One of the two is helmeted and has an oval shield like the common infantry. After the so-called Sitten *Pyxis* Ivory, Museum of Valere, Sitten.

Order of Battle Practice

Classical Greeks and Romans from the Republican era each had a stereotypical order of battle: the phalanx for the former and the *triplex acies* for the latter. The preconceived order of battle found in Maurice's *Strategikon* was largely theoretical. The Romano-Byzantines were much more pragmatic than their predecessors and every battle had its own tactical army deployment. The only great stereotypical aspect of the order of battle was still to divide the line into three: left and right wings and flanking the centre. The alignment of ranks was also a constant. The poet Corippus described 'the dense armies with their shining shields and helmets.'[65] Nonetheless at the Battle of Skalai Beteres in 537, the Roman deserters of Stotzas abandoned the manoeuvres in ranks and files: 'As for the rebels, who took position facing them [troops of the Patrician Germanus], far from showing themselves disciplined they presented themselves as the barbarians tend to do, in scattered mob.'[66] They lost the battle. On the battlefield the Romano-Byzantines could quickly change formation if needed. To free the city of Martyropolis, besieged by 6,000 Persians, Imperial troops fought two battles. The first was a brute frontal assault but the stubborn enemy could not be beaten. The second, however, relied on the old trick of simulated flight. Overconfident the Persians broke ranks to pursue the apparently fleeing Romano-Byzantines. Unexpectedly counter-attacked the Persians lost a third of their men killed or captured, abandoned their standards and their officers, and an unknown number of the Persian Army was drowned in the River Nymphos.[67]

Belisarius did not use classic or even complicated battle tactics. At Dara in 530, his greatest victory, he faced 50 000 Sassanids, commanded by King Peroz in person, with only 25 000 men. The fortress at his back, he protected his front with three trenches, one forward two back, defended by infantry. The main corps of the cavalry were deployed at far left and right flanks. John the Lydian and Bouzes respectively commanded the right and left wings with their cavalry placed at ditch extremities, not behind entrenched positions. Two 600-strong bodies of Hun horsemen were in the centre, the left one led by Sunicas and Aigan, the right by Simmas and Ascan. The infantry stood along the centre. Belisarius himself commanded the centre with Hermogenes, their *bucellarii* standing behind as a reserve. Belisarius's ace was Pharas and 200 Herul cavalry hidden in a fold of land on his left wing. In case of a setback, the city of Dara was close to the army's back. After the general's speech to boost the morale and a preliminary duel, both sides exchanged showers of arrows in the centre, which was crossed by the road between Dara and Ambar running south. The Persian infantry in the centre did not attack, simply forming a covering force for their cavalry

---

65 Corippus, *Joh*, IV, v. 530–531
66 Procopius, *BV*, IV, 17, 7.
67 John Malalas, *Chrgr.*, XVIII, 65.

THE PITCHED BATTLE: TACTICS AND PRACTICE

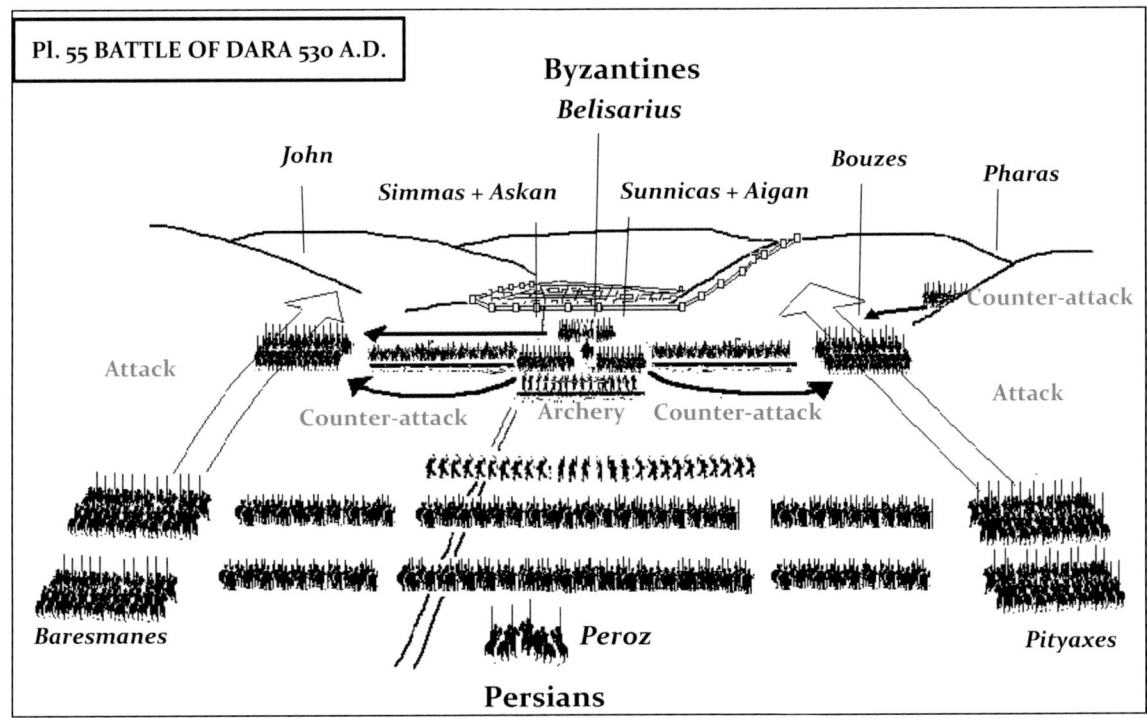

Battle of Dara in 530

which first attacked Bouzes and his men on the Romano-Byzantine left wing. The same action was repeated on the Romano-Byzantine right wing. Belisarius had anticipated a pincer attack from the Persian cavalry against his, probably weak, wings. So as the enemy attacked successfully, Belisarius counter-attacked the pincers from the back and the front with the Huns, the Heruls and his *bucellarii*. The Sassanid Persians lost the day with more than 5,000 killed in action, and Belisarius decided to not pursue the fleeing enemy.[68]

In Africa, Belisarius only attacked the Vandals with his cavalry. His infantry guarded the camp or threatened that of an already defeated enemy. Belisarius relied on three methods: beating the enemy in detail before the latter could gather his whole army (Dekimon), spotting the enemy's weaknesses and suddenly striking at that with all his strength (Membressa), probing and crushing enemy's centre by the progressive commitment of centre and wings (Trikamaron). Belisarius' deployent was quite simple: his personal guard or his best elements stood in the centre and the rest on the wings. In a battle like Dekimon, in its first phase Belisarius detached cavalry troops to the front and flank guard sufficiently strong and autonomous for a distant combat of which he was only informed of the outcome after its conclusion. By the summer solstice of 537 (20 June) when Belisarius defended Rome, the double battle north of Porta Pinciana and the Field of Nero was a diversion to mask the arrival from the south of Euthalios

---

68   Procopius, *BP*, I, 13–39 to 14, 1–52,

with the pay for the army. Belisarius then launched 600 cavalry under the command of three *doryphoroi*, Artasires, Bochas and Kutilas, from the Porta Pinciana to attack an Ostrogothic camp. At the same time, he sent Martin and Valerian with 1,600 horsemen to the Field of Nero, opposite the Cornelia Gate and near Hadrian's mausoleum. Two confused cavalry melees engaged separately. At the Porta Pinciana, the adversaries fought fiercely and received reinforcements, but the Romano-Byzantines were victorious. At the Field of Nero, the Ostrogoths won and Belisarius had to send the Hun Bochas to put the enemy to flight. But Bochas pursued too far and received a serious wound forcing him to retreat.[69] This double battle, which enabled Euthalios to enter Rome, had the constant feature of cavalry combat that the last troop to charge won the fight. From all these examples, it is clear that Belisarius had an intuitive touch and was not playing a game of chess or simply applying tactics according to the manual. He saw battle as a projection of forces; first probing attacks were launched then the decisive one at the right time in order to destroy the enemy.

The Battle of Skalai Beteres could explain the distrust of some great generals for the tactical figures of the manuals. The Patrician Germanus, cousin of Justinian I, who was then less experienced and had only book knowledge of tactics, used the tactic of the oblique order. This ancient manoeuvre consisted in strengthening one wing while refusing the other to unbalance the adversary and break his. It is first recorded as used by Epaminondas with the Theban Army at Leuctra in 371 BCE and was used by Alexander the Great with the *Agema* of the elite mounted Companions at Issus in 333 BCE. At Skalai Beteres, the Patrician Germanus used a variant of the oblique order. He placed his best cavalrymen with him on his left wing. On his right wing, the other cavalry were divided into three squadrons, one commanded by John Troglita, the other two by Ildiger and by Theodore of Cappadocia. The infantry held the centre. This classic plan was foiled because its device was too obvious to deserters from the Imperial Army familiar with such tactics. The mutinous Herul *foederati* asked Stotzas to be deployed against the Romano-Byzantine right wing which they promised to break because it was weak. Stotzas also put himself and his elite troops with them. Seeing their right wing in rout, Germanus' infantry fell back, for fear of being surrounded. For his part, Germanus drove in the enemy with his left wing, racing to envelop the enemy first, since the two adversaries were essentially employing the same tactical idea. The situation was saved by Germanus' speed and by the confusion that ensued in this battle between 'Romans' wearing the same dress and speaking more or less the same language. Germanus was quick enough to order that all those who did not know his word of the day for the battle should be killed. His men struck first when in doubt and narrowly defeated the enemy.[70] The case

---

69   Procopius, *BG*, V, 27, 1 (Martin and Valerian strengths); VI, 2, 8–14 (Porta Pinciana); 2, 19–24 (Field of Nero).

70   Procopius, *BV*, IV, 17, 5 (Germanus); 17, 14–15 (Heruls); 17, 16 (Stotzas with

THE PITCHED BATTLE: TACTICS AND PRACTICE

of Skalai Beteres shows that stereotypical tactics were easily countered by seasoned fighters.

Justinian's two eunuch generals, Solomon and Narses, invented or used tactics adapted to each battle. Solomon was the more imaginative of the two and won the Battles of Mammes in 534 and Mount Bourgaon in 535 against the Moors. He gave up the advantage of his cavalry: a radically different concept from Belisarius. At Mammes, as the Moorish cavalry disorganised his troops, Solomon dismounted his cavalry to fight on foot with shield and sword. However, he did not choose a defensive battle but attacked the Moorish camp, slaughtering the wall of camels that frightened his horses. This simple and pragmatic solution took advantage away from the Moors. At Mount Bourgaon, Solomon had 1,000 infantry occupy the summit and trapped the Moorish camp between two forces when he attacked from below with the rest of the army. In both cases, the enemies were disconcerted and were massacred as they fled.[71] Like Belisarius, Solomon was aggressive and sought to seize the initiative. Narses opportunely used classic tactics but gave up the initiative to the enemy.

His masterpiece was in 552, the so-called Battle of Taginae in Umbria. In fact, Totila was camped there, on the Via Flaminia, although Procopius never actualy said that this was the location of the battle. Coming from the north after retaking Ariminium (Rimini), Narses left the Via Flaminia and encamped at a place Procopius named as Busta Gallorum (Pyre of the Gauls) where he pretended that the Roman dictator Camillus had defeated Gauls. Procopius made some confusion with the Battle of Sentinum (now Sassoferrato) in the Marche Region, where a confederation of Samnites, Umbrians and Gauls were defeated by two Roman consuls in 295 BCE. This place was according to Procopius 200 *stadions* or *stades* north-east of Taginae, or a day's march according to him, some 38km or 24 English miles. The two towns are separated from each other by a mountain which is crossed by a pass.[72]

The Battle of Taginae was fought in a valley surrounded by the wooded Apennine Mountains south of Sentinum, probably at what is now the Berbentina industrial zone. Narses outnumbered his enemy by two to one and the day before the fight offered a proposal of negotiations, but Totila refused and had the intention of launching a surprise attack, although Narses was aware of it. On the actual day of the battle, Totila swiftly reached the valley of Sentinum and attempted to take a small, bare hill on Narses' left flank. As the whole terrain was like a corridor, this position was important. But Narses was not to be foiled again and had preventively occupied this

---

elite soldiers); 17, 17 (Germanus' right wing and centre at trouble); 17, 20–24 (Germanus victory).
71 Procopius, *BV*, IV, 11, 15–54 (Mammes); 12, 3–25 (Mount Bourgaon).
72 Procopius, *BV*, I, 1, 17 ('Now one day's journey extends 210 *stadions*, or as far as from Athens to Megara'). *BG*, VIII, 26, 29, 3 (Totila encamped at Busta Gallorum, 200 *stadions* distant from Taginae), 4–5 (Narses at Busta Gallorum).

hill with 50 elite infantrymen, and the Ostrogothic cavalry attack was repelled. Totila was waiting for a 2,000-man reinforcement led by Teias before engaging in the real fight, and he used some delaying strategems. The first was a preliminary duel between Coccas, a Romano-Byzantine deserter who has joined him, and Anzalas a *bucellary* of Narses. After the ominous open of the defeat and death of Coccas, Totila himself, dressed in golden and purple shining armour, offered a show in arms handling and horse riding along the space between the two opposing armies; Narses army applauded. Totila ended his circus act demonstration with the arrival of Teias and regained his lines to change his dressing into a duller and more anonymous one. He unimaginatively arrayed the army in two phalanxes: the cavalry in front and the infantry behind, then he launched a charge with all his strength: a desperate tactic.

Narses intention was to entice Totila's Ostrogoths into what Procopius called a 'crescent' and which corresponded to the 'scissors' in Vegetius. The Byzantine troops were first lined up in a phalanx and then, on an order from Narses, took up the crescent formation by extending the wings just before the engagement.[73] On the left wing, he placed the 'best of the Roman Army' under his personal command and John with the *bucellarii* and some picked Huns and probably Persians. To the far left were 1,500 horsemen, 500 for reserve behind the infantry, 1,000 ordered to outflank the charging Gothic infantry. In the centre he deployed, in two groups, some 8,000 archers on foot 'from the regular troops', *ek katalogôn*. It is worthwhile reminding that the English had only around 6,000 to 7,000 bowmen at Agincourt in 1415 when they crushed the French chivalry. In the centre Narses stationed the least reliable troops, dismounted so that they could not flee easily, namely the *foederati*, 5,000 Lombards, 3,000 Heruls, Huns and Persian deserters. They are estimated to number 8,000–10,000 men, a target to trap and to catch the Ostrogoths. At the junction of the centre and the right were another 4,000 foot archers. The right wing was commanded by Valerian, John Phagas 'the Glutton' and Daguistheus along with the rest of the 'Romans'.

Engulfed in Narses' trap the Ostrogoths and the Romano-Byzantine deserters allied with them were wiped out, suffering 6,000 killed in action and a great many prisoners. Totila, dressed as a common soldier during the fight, fled with only five followers but was mortally wounded by the lance of Asbad a Gepid officer, and later died in Capras from his wounds.[74]

In late 553, near Rimini, Narses the Eunuch with 300 cavalry crushed a troop of 2,000 Franks using the stratagem of a simulated retreat and an offensive return to an enemy overwhelmed by the pursuit. Much better

---

73   Procopius, *BG*, VIII, 32, 5.
74   Procopius, *BG*, VIII, 26, 12 (Auduin with 2,000 picked Lombards); 13 (3,000 Herulic horsemen; numerous Huns; Asbad 400 Gepids; Aruth with numerous Gepids); 29, 3 (Totila encamped at Busta Gallorum, 200 *stadions* from Taginae), 4–5 (Narses at Busta Gallorum); 31, 1–7 (order of battle); 32, 5 (crescent formation).

THE PITCHED BATTLE: TACTICS AND PRACTICE

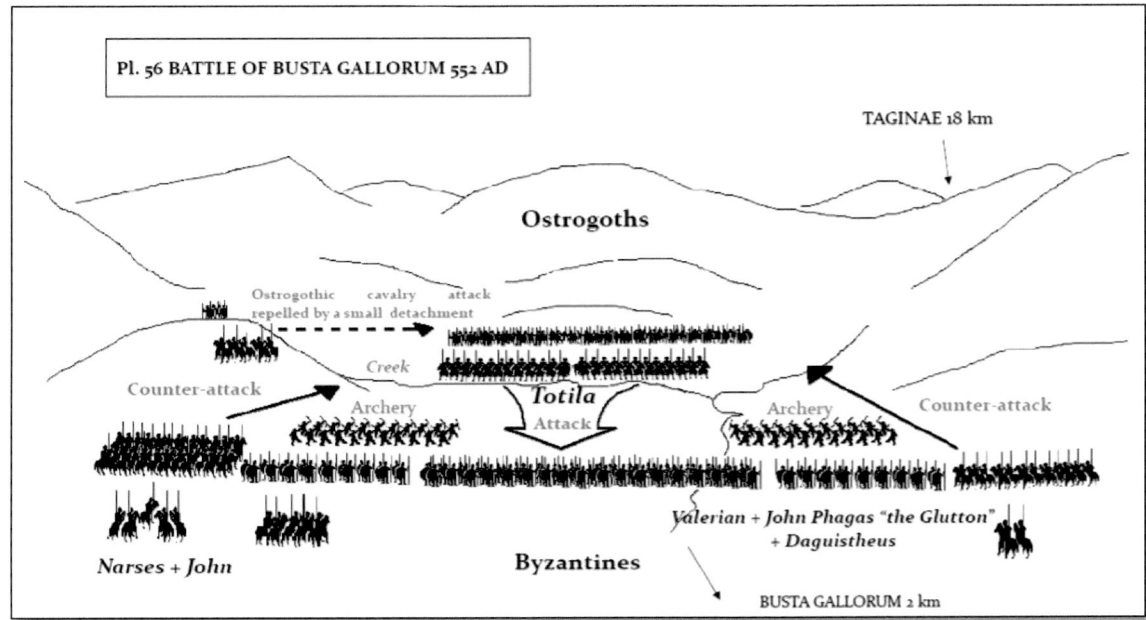

Battle of Busta Gallorum, 552

prepared and larger was the Battle on the Volturnus River in 554. The battle is also called Casilinum from an ancient city that is engulfed now in the modern Capua. There was the crossing of the Volturno on a still visible three-arched stone bridge. A strategic place where the Via Latina from Rome ended and a crossing point for the Via Appia to the port of Brundisium (present-day Brindisi). This is why Narses chose to stop the invader from the north at this location. With an army estimated at 18,000 men, Narses defeated some 20,000 Frankish and Alemannic warriors led by Butilinus or Buccelinus. The numbers were nearly equal after one-third of Butilinus army died from dysentery, and the remaining Franks and Alemanni were probably not at their best. The opponents, had each built fortified camps on either side of the river, and observed each other for several days and Narses sent a party to attack the Frankish raiders. This provocation pushed the Franks into offering battle. As at Taginae, Narses prepared a fairly complex stratagem; he stood on the right wing with the army's servants, no doubt to inflate the appearance of his numbers. On his far left, he hid the cavalry of Valerian and Artabanes the Arsacid in a wood for a surprise flank attack. In the centre, the infantry lined up a phalanx of heavy infantry in the front ranks, followed in the second echelon by medium infantry in close ranks. The light infantry remained to the rear. In the centre stood the Heruls, fighters considered unreliable as at Busta Gallorum. Herul deserters even warned the Franks that their fellows would refuse to fight because they had quarrelled with Narses. This event became a tactical advantage, for it played into Narses' intention by drawing the Franks to the centre. The tip of the gigantic force of the Franks had no difficulty in breaking into the front ranks, but in doing so it locked them in. Narses folded in his wings of horse archers who shot at the back of the Franks. The Heruls then understood the best hope for them was to intervene and closed the gap in the middle of the first line. The Romano-Byzantine troops tightened the net around the Franks who were exterminated, including their leader Butilinus.[75] It is a plan comparable to Cannae in 216 BCE with the successful double encirclement of troops in the enemy the centre. Narses has a taste for enveloping his opponent with both wings. The successes of Taginae and Casilinum were made possible by an impetuous and brutal enemy who, systematically attacking in the centre, was trapped and annihilated. While Belisarius sought to defeat his opponent, Narses sought to annihilate his.

In a battle near Viminacium on the Danube *c.* 599, Priscus divided his line into three corps (*merē*) united into a single phalanx (*ektaxis*) to secure their camp, deciding not to use their bows but to fight hand-to-hand with spears, while the Avars divided themselves into 15 squadrons, *systēmata*. The traditional Greek phalanx again won over loose charges, with a body count of 300 Romans killed to 4,000 of their enemy, although Simocatta did not specify whether these were cavalry or infantry.[76]

Some Advice for The Novice

Vegetius, the last great Roman military theorist, stated: '*amplius juvat virtus quam multitudo*' (valour prevails over numbers).[77] Belisarius said the same to his soldiers before the Battle of Trikamaron: 'War will not to be decided neither by numbers of men nor by bodily stature, but by valour of soul.'[78] It was an idea deeply rooted in the Romano-Byzantine culture of war. Before facing an immense Moorish Army, Solomon in his exhortation to battle opposed quality to quantity:

> And yet, it is easier to see a small group of perfectly well-prepared combatants defeat a crowd of men with no warrior bravery than to see them defeated by them. For the valiant soldier places his confidence in himself, while the soldier without courage finds himself caught up in a mass of people whose sheer numbers usually end up dangerously reducing his capacity for action.[79]

Belisarius had nothing but contempt for the mutineers of Stotzas, deprived of discipline and tactical intelligence, and made it clear to the loyal soldiers: 'Because in war, superiority is not usually measured by the number of

---

75 Agathias, *Hist.*, I, 21, 4–6 (Rimini); II, 4, 10 (strengths in Casulinus); 6, 1–9 (camps; skirmish); 8, 1–9 (orders of battle); 9–10 (battle).
76 Theophylact Simocatta, *HU*, VIII, 2, 10–12 (μέρη, corps; ἔκταξις, battle line; συστήματα, squadrons). Dagron G., (1990), pp.279–281 (noted the two tactical styles but omitted the Roman victory).
77 Vegetius, *DRM*, III, 26.
78 Procopius, *BV*, IV, 1, 16.
79 Procopius, *BV*, IV, 15, 29.

THE PITCHED BATTLE: TACTICS AND PRACTICE

fighting forces, but by how well organised and courageous they are.'[80] In both cases Solomon and Belisarius prevailed over a larger enemy army. However, it was in being surrounded by a larger Moorish Army that Solomon and his bodyguards were killed.[81] Very different on this matter was the first great Byzantine military treatise, the *Strategikon*: 'It is not true, as inexperienced people believe, that wars are decided by courage and numbers, but, with God's help, they are decided by tactics and the art of command.'[82]

The *Strategikon* gave very interesting recommendations for fighting against the enemies of the Empire. Facing the Persians, the general had to choose a flat ground, without gulleys likely to break the ranks. He had to attack quickly once he reached bow range to avoid being slaughtered by a hail of arrows. On uneven ground, it was important not to leave your horsemen in the front line, but to place the infantry there. It was risky to engage in battle against the Persians when the army was not ready and, in this case, prudence dictated avoiding it by setting up ambushes. The sudden counter-attack was a good tactic against them provided you attacked their flanks and enveloped them.[83] Against the nomadic horsemen known as 'Scythians', that is Avars, Turkish and 'others whose way of life resembling that of the Hunnish peoples', the art was to post sentries at all corners and to find a good defensive position, if possible, on open ground backed to a watercourse. As it was dangerous to send men out for supplies, it was essential to have sufficient supplies of food and water for both men and animals. In battle, it was best to reinforce the flanks and keep a cavalry reserve on hand.[84] The 'blond peoples', such as the Lombards, Franks and other Germans, were characterised by a courage that declined over time. Once they had been demoralised by ambushes at the start of the campaign, the battle could be fought. It was best to choose wooded terrain that reduced the advantage of their spears. A classic order of battle was enough.[85] Fighting the Sklavenes, on the other hand, required fluid tactics. The light troops had to attack from several directions, pouring down a rain of arrows of which the army had to have a large reserve. In the event of a major battle, a flank attack or simulated retreat was to be preferred to a frontal attack. The general had to keep in mind that the Slavs always had a staggered and a disguised depth, very difficult to encircle.[86]

---

80   Procopius, *BV*, IV, 15, 29.
81   Procopius, *BV*, IV, 21, 26–28.
82   Maurice, *Strategikon*, VII, Preface and VIII, 2, 73.
83   Maurice, *Strategikon*, XI, 1.
84   Maurice, *Strategikon*, XI, 2.
85   Maurice, *Strategikon*, XI, 3.
86   Maurice, *Strategikon*, XI, 4.

The Fury of Battle

Unlike today's battles, where soldiers have the impression of fighting a landscape from a distance with an enemy impersonated by killing smoke bursts, the ancient and medieval warrior saw the enemy lined up at two or three bow shots distance with colourful standards, shining helmets, a threatening line of shields and a forest of spears. As both a poet and a witness, Corippus is a good source to describe the real fury of the fighting. Putting aside some epic exaggerations, he gives a multitude of small, realistic details. The fight began with a preparation shooting by ranged weapons. The sky was darkened by a hail of arrows at 300m to 100m, then at shorter range by the *plumbatae* darts or javelins at 60m down to 30m. Javelins made a distinctive noise. They even intercepted the enemy's javelins in mid-course 'quite often', but many caused injuries on arrival. Javelins of those killed were recovered for throwing back. The shields were pierced by those missiles and looked like pincushions.[87] Subsequently the two lines clashed in hand-to-hand combat. Was there then a battle of a myriad of duels between individuals or a sort of vast rugby scrum with groups pushing each other? Perhaps something inbetween it can be understood. The aim for infantrymen was to stay in close order shield against shield, stabbing at the enemy's legs and thighs as piercing the femoral artery is a mortal blow.[88] Cavalry fighting was more fluid except for those heavily armoured. During the skirmishes outside the vast circuit-wall of Rome: 'The horsemen in no great numbers armed themselves many times for battle, but the struggles always ended in single combats, and the Romans were victorious over all of the enemy.'[89] First rank officers and elite soldiers were the natural fighters punching holes in the enemy bodies leading the common soldiers who acted as followers and pushers. All were 'blinded by the tumult and fury.'[90] Procopius said that the men were infuriated by the clamour of battle.[91] An animal ferocity seized the combatants, who growled and bared their teeth, to the point where Corippus weirdly compared John Troglita to a tigress

---

87 Corippus, *Joh*, V, v. 52–53 (sky darkened); v. 55–64 (projectiles intercepting each other); v. 65 (javelin's noise); VI, v. 715 (recovering projectiles from those killed); v. 736 (shields pierced by javelins). Re-enactment trials from Tod's Workshop: *plumbata* darts and pilum with mail coats, https://www.youtube.com/watch?v=xK96h2dyJfI; https://www.youtube.com/watch?v=SLd2JPL7UAg

88 Plutarch, *Vita* Caesaris, XLV, 2–3: 2… the cohorts ran out from where Caesar was posted, not hurling their javelins, as usual, nor yet stabbing the thighs and legs of their enemies with them, but aiming them at their eyes and wounding their faces. 3 They had been instructed to do this by Caesar, who expected that men little conversant with wars or wounds, but young, and pluming themselves on their youthful beauty, would dread such wounds especially.

89 Procopius, *BG*, VI, 1, 20.

90 Corippus, *Joh*, V, v. 68–69.

91 Procopius, *BG*, VI, 2, 13.

THE PITCHED BATTLE: TACTICS AND PRACTICE

ready to defend her cubs.[92] The most ferocious fighters were inhabited by some sort of insatiable destructive madness:

> He removes the head of this one with his sword, then throws the dart of the dying; he cuts this one from afar, pierces that one with a strong spear through the chest, threatening, he crosses with a trembling spear the shield of another as well as his hand and his side. This one, dying, watches his thigh partially cut by a wound fall, and still alive, he suffers because of his limbs. This one, wounded, is on the ground, broken by the fall of his horse and his pierced steed is above him, the foamy blood shines brightly and, as it flows, mixes with the warm sand.[93]

Corippus frequently depicted the cruel image of slaughtered horses crushing their riders and dying on the ground.[94] As for the men, they were killed by a fatal blow to the head, chest or by slow haemorrhage. Corippus described the fate of two mercenaries: 'The immense Ariarith falls, and not by a single stroke, and the magnanimous Ziper by 100 wounds.'[95] The figure of 100 was of course an exaggeration to say 'a lot', but more realistic were the 13 wounds that left Wisandus Vandalarius to bled out on the field.[96] Wounds and agony were depicted by Corippus in a clinical manner, like the nerves of a corpse still moving, the insides throbbing, the wounded man vomiting blood in spasms, the severed hand just hanging down by a flap of flesh.[97] These details, which were generally overlooked by ancient historians, give battle its real butchery taste.

Physical and nervous fatigue played its part after a while. The soldier was sweating under the weight of the shield and of javelins stuck in it. He was jostled by the pressure of the bodies pressed in a melee.[98] Men were so pressed against each other as to undoubtedly die by suffocation, as happened to the beaten Goths in March 538 at the engagement of the Porta Pinciana before Rome.[99] As the battles were fought in the summer on plains, mostly in the desert lands of Asia or Africa, a strong dust was raised by men and horses. As a result, field of vision and identification of friends or foes were both reduced, '…and no one recognises his brother covered with dust.'[100] In this bloody mess it was better to strike first. In 550 Persian General Chorianes was killed during an intense exchange of missiles: 'By

---

92 Corippus, *Joh*, VI, v. 625 and 650 (growling; teeth); v. 707 (tigress).
93 Corippus, *Joh*, VI, v. 715–729.
94 Corippus, *Joh*, VI, v. 722–723.
95 Corippus, *Joh*, VI, v. 665–666.
96 Procopius, *BG*, V, 18, 29–33.
97 Corippus, *Joh*, V, v. 124 (nerves); v. 256 (guts); 289 (blood); 324 (hanging hand).
98 Corippus, *Joh*, VI, v. 737–738.
99 Procopius, *BG*, VI, 10, 17.
100 Corippus, *Joh*, V, v. 355.

whom this man was injured is not clear to anyone. Some chance guided the missile out of a mass of huddled men and planted it in the man's neck, killing him dead.'[101] The infernal loudness of the fighting added to the overall fury: 'An enormous clamour was raised, and trumpets in each camp broadcast warlike music. The howling of the horses, the clash of the shields and the clash of the breastplates mingled into an enormous noise.'[102] Fury came also into sheer barbarity. To terrorise the Ostrogoths at the Battle of Mons Lactarius in late 552, some Romano-Byzantine soldiers put King Teias' head on the end of a pole after killing him with a javelin. This psychological gesture had the opposite effect and the infuriated and indignant Ostrogoths fought until nightfall.[103] Battle deeply shook the minds of combatants. Corippus was the only antico-medieval writer to describe the psychological trauma of fighters who, in their sleep, dreamt that they were still fighting and even killing friends in the confusion of the battle, yet another evocation of friendly losses.[104]

---

101 Procopius, *BG*, VIII, 8, 33.
102 Agathias, *Hist.*, III, 25, 7.
103 Procopius, *BG*, VIII, 35, 30.
104 Corippus, *Joh*, II, v. 459–469.

THE PITCHED BATTLE: TACTICS AND PRACTICE

Table 17, Manpower and Casualties during Battle (fifth to seventh centuries)

Battle	Victor	Strength	Cavalry	Losses	Loser	Strength	Cavalry	Losses
Tzurta 499	Bulgars	?	?	?	Byzantines	15,000	?	4,000
Martyropolis 530	Byzantines	?	?	?	Persians	6,000	?	2,000 + more drowned in a river
Dekimon 533	Byzantines	12,500	5,000	?	Vandals	+ 10,000?	?	nr >2,000
Trikamaron 533	Byzantines	- 15,000	- 5,000	50	Vandals	10,000?	?	+ 800
Mammes 534	Byzantines	18,000?	?	?	Moors	50,000	?	10,000
Mount Bourgaon 535	Byzantines	18,000?	?	0?	Maures	+ 50,000	?	50,000
Salarian Gate (Rome) 537	Byzantines	5,000	?	?	Ostrogoths	150,000	?	30,000 KIA Nr WIA
Faenza 542	Ostrogoths	5,000	?	?	Byzantines	- 12,000 (5,000?)	?	Few survivors
Taginae 552 Busta Gallorum	Byzantines	20,000-35,000?	1,500 Byzantines *Bucellarii?* 5,000 Lombards 3,000* Heruls** nr Huns Persians?	?	Ostrogoths	12,000?	?	6,000 KIA Nr prisoners
Casilinum 554	Byzantines	18,000	2/3	80	Franks	+ 30,000	a few	- 5 survivors
Phasis 556	Byzantines	?	5,000	200	Persians	- 60,000	?	- 12,000
Chettos 559	Byzantines	300	200	WIA	Huns	- 2,000	2,000	400 KIA
Scoltenna 643	Lombards	?	?	?	Byzantines	?	?	8,000 KIA

nr = 'numerous'
KIA = killed
WIA = wounded

* cavalry and infantry
** dismounted horsemen fighting on foot

The Bloody Fate of the Defeated

Examples of battle show that the principle of winning was to unbalance the adversary physically and morally. Firstly, the battle was indecisive for a long time before one side suddenly panicked when it lost any hope to win. The vanquished side did not lead a tactical fighting retreat like Wellington did at Quatre-Bras but simply fled, forgetting all discipline, abandoning weapons and wounded comrades – then the pursuit by the victor degenerated into a bloody massacre. When defeated, Romano-Byzantines soldiers behaved no differently to the barbarians, and a sudden panic led them to a rout. At Callinicum in 531, two-thirds of the day had passed before the Persians broke through the enemy's right wing and reached the centre behind the Romano-Byzantine cavalry and thereafter routing Belisarius's Army.[105]

Surprise was the key of victory as demonstrated in 539 by the unusual Battle of Ticinum (today Pavia). The Goths camped near the River Po and saw small groups of Frankish warriors arriving, who they initially mistook for friends. Taken aback when the Franks threw javelins and axes at them, the Goths fled in such panic that they broke through the Romano-Byzantine camp on the road to Ravenna. The Romano-Byzantines were themselves so surprised that they did nothing to stop the defenceless mass of their fleeing enemy; they thought that the Goths had been defeated by reinforcements led by Belisarius and went to meet them. They were surprised to find the aggressive Franks and fled south in a panic, abandoning their camp to these dubious allies. At Faenza in 542, Totila sent 300 men behind the Imperial lines which fled without fighting anymore offering their backs to the enemy's blows. There were few survivors and all the standards were taken by the Ostrogoths. Surprise could also be caused by a false rumour, such as the death of John the nephew of Vitalian during the cavalry charge at Mucellium. Totila did not pursue but many soldiers died during the rout, probably trampled underfoot by their fleeing comrades. The Romano-Byzantine Army was completely destroyed because of a lack of competent generals.[106]

A comparable fate struck their opponents when they were defeated. Some striking events like the death of the commander-in-chief or being caught in a pincer movement could cause an army to flee, as happened to the Persians at the Battle of Dara in 530. After a fierce battle, the disordered Persian infantry threw down their shields and fled.[107] The enemy rout was sometimes explained by a sudden drop in morale. Procopius stated that at Taginae in 552, the Ostrogoths fled as if an apparition had descended from the heavens. Consequently, in ancient and medieval battles, the defeated suffered most of their losses during the rout. Procopius described the

---

105 Procopius, *BP*, I, 18, 35 (long indecision); 36 (right wing broken); 37 (rout).
106 Procopius, *BG*, VI, 25, 12–16 (Pavia); VII, 4, 19–32 (Faenza); 5, 10–18 (Mugello).
107 Procopius, *BP*, I, 14, 51–53.

THE PITCHED BATTLE: TACTICS AND PRACTICE

final phase of the battle in this way: 'Meanwhile the Roman Army taking advantage of their panic continued to mercilessly kill all those in their path, while their victims offered no defence nor dared to look them in the eye, but indulged in the will of their enemies, so much terror and panic had seized them.' The Ostrogoths lost some 6,000 killed; many of them were first taken prisoners and then executed shortly after, including Roman deserters, while a multitude fled in rout. Their King Totila only had five horsemen left to accompany him.[108] Five was also the figure given by Agathias for the Franks surviving the Battle of Casilinum in 554, out of a force he had estimated at 30,000. Butilinus/Buccelinus general of the Franks was among those killed. Meanwhile the 18,000 Romano-Byzantines suffered only 80 killed.[109]

In most battles, the victor took the lion's share of the spoils and inflicted appalling losses on the enemy, while he himself suffered relatively few.[110] This huge difference can be explained because most of killed in action were killed when fleeing as suggested above at the Battle of Taginae and can be seen in later battles. Counting the losses of the vanquished has never been an easy task in a general rout, and some Byzantine historians' estimates are to be questioned. This is the case of the Battle of the Salarian Gate in Rome in 537, where Procopius asserted that 'according to their leaders' the Goths suffered 30,000 dead plus a large number of wounded, out of an army estimated at 150,000 warriors.[111] These losses would be proportionally greater than those that the French suffered at Waterloo: around 24,000 to 26,000 including 6,000 to 7,000 prisoners. It makes sense to reduce the Salarian Gate figures, since whatever the number of losses suffered in this engagement, the Goths were still able to continue the siege of Rome, probably because their entrenched camps saved them from total annihilation. The *sauve-qui-peut* attitude was not the ethos of Romano-Byzantine officers. During a retreat, they tried to take away comrades and relatives wounded from the enemy; this was the case when Tarnuntos was saved by his brother Ennes, and that of Bochas whose horse Martin and Valerian pulled away by the bridle.[112]

On rare occasions, the Romano-Byzantines showed relative mercy, not guided by any morale purpose but by pure strategy. This was the case after Trikamaron. The Vandals, civilians and warriors alike, took refuge in a church after having been defeated. Belisarius promised them their lives and had them escorted to Carthage. Other fugitives were killed while

---

108 Procopius, *BG*, VIII, 32, 14 (panic); 32, 19 (pursuit and massacre); 32, 20 (Totila last followers).
109 Agathias, *Hist.*, II, 4, 10 (respective strengths); 9, 11 (death of Butilin; less than five survivors); 9, 12 (80 Romano-Byzantines KIA). Marius Aventicensis, *Chr.*, a. 555 (death of Buccelin/Buccelin and its army).
110 Ph. Richardot, *Les erreurs stratégiques des Gaulois face à César* (Paris: Economica, 2006), pp.135–138. Ph. Richardot, 'La bataille antique: représentation et modèle', *Prétoriens*, 9, avril-juin (2009), pp.19–27 (a typical battle).
111 Procopius, *BG*, V, 23, 26 (losses); 24, 3 (numbers).
112 Procopius, *BG*, V, 29, 42 (Tarnuntos); VI, 2, 24 (Bochas).

women and children captured in the Vandal camp were doomed to slavery. Captured warriors were shipped to the East to be enlisted into five cavalry units, the 'Justinianic Vandals'.[113] The Romano-Byzantine military habits after a victory were similar to those of the Romans: massacre when the fight was difficult or moderate the killing when capturing slaves or enlisting prisoners were wanted. Eventually, the local population could take its share in the spoils: for instance, after the victory of Martyropolis in 530, the duke left the inhabitants of the city to plunder the corpses of the Persians.[114]

Then the victorious general-in-chief stopped the pursuit with a trumpet call and went amongst the soldiers to calm their raging bloodlust.[115] After the Persian rout at Dara, Belisarius halted the pursuit for fear of a counter-offensive, reminding the army that it could be dangerous to pursue a retreating enemy too far. Vegetius had written something similar saying that the enemy had to be given an escape to deprive him of the last energy of despair.[116] In 535, blinded by anger and sorrow the Master of the Soldiers Mundo, who had previously lost his son in a reconnaissance action, won the ensuing battle but pursued the fleeing enemy without any precautions and found himself ambushed and killed near Salona.[117] Victory was measured by a factor other than enemy losses and retreat and the enemy camp had to be taken. Losing the camp meant losing an army's train, rendering further action impossible. In 555 the defeated Romano-Byzantines lost their camp at Onoguris and had to take refuge as far away as Phasis.[118] Once victory was gained, the victor could scour the field, collect the spoils and celebrate the success, as in the aftermath of the Battle of Casilinum in 554:

> Then the Romans, after having buried their dead, as is the custom, and stripped the enemies, gathered a great quantity of weapons. Having again overthrown their fortifications and looted everything, they returned to Rome, laden with spoils, with songs of victory of the crowns, and gloriously preceding their general. Over a great distance, in the vicinity of Capua, one could see all the fields that flowed with blood and the rivers that overflowed, filled with corpses. One of the locals told me that someone had written an elegiac poem on a stone column near the banks of the river.[119]

This common practice of the victors only burying their own dead and stripping those of the enemy could be observed at Phasis two years later.[120]

---

113 Procopius, *BV*, IV, 4, 11–12 (churches); 4, 24 (slavery); 14, 17 (Justinianic Vandals).
114 John Malalas, *Chrgr.*, XVIII, 65.
115 Agathias, *Hist.*, II, 27, 9.
116 Vegetius, *DRM*, III, 21, 2.
117 Procopius, *BG*, V, 7, 5.
118 Agathias, *Hist.*, III, 7, 11 (Onoguris); 27, 10 (Phasis).
119 Agathias, *Hist.*, II, 10, 7–8.
120 Agathias, *Hist.*, III, 28, 4–5.

THE PITCHED BATTLE: TACTICS AND PRACTICE

Burial of the defeated was undoubtedly left to the inhabitants who wanted to cultivate their land and purify the air.

Care for the Wounded

'It is right to care about the injured. If we neglect them, the rest of the troops will work to fight poorly, and our negligence will cause us to lose what could have been saved.'[121]

The Imperial Army was followed by poorly trained 'first-aiders' called *depoutatoi* but also by more professional *iatroi* (medics). Procopius liked to specify the medical follow-up of some Belisarian *doryphoroi* with complex battle injuries. This was the case of Arzes who received an arrow between his nose and his right eye:

> Now in the case of Arzes, though the physicians wished to draw the weapon from his face, they were for some time reluctant to do so, not so much on account of the eye, which they supposed could not possibly be saved, but for fear lest, by the cutting of membranes and tissues such as are very numerous in that region, they should cause the death of a man who was one of the best of the household of Belisarius. But afterwards one of the physicians, Theoctistus by name, pressed on the back of his neck and asked whether he felt much pain. And when the man said that he did feel pain, he said, 'Then both you yourself will be saved and your sight will not be injured.' And he made this declaration because he inferred that the barb of the weapon had penetrated to a point not far from the skin. Accordingly, he cut off that part of the shaft which shewed outside and threw it away, and cutting open the skin at the back of the head, at the place where the man felt the most pain, he easily drew towards him the barb, which with its three sharp points now stuck out behind and brought with it the remaining portion of the weapon. Thus, Arzes remained entirely free from serious harm, and not even a trace of his wound was left on his face.[122]

So, Arzes survived against the odds. This was not unfortunately the case for Kutilas, who was wounded in the same fight by a javelin in his head. It was taken out too brutally and Kutilas died from a brain inflammation. Another *doryphoros* named Bochas bled to death within three days after a wound in the right thigh.[123] Tarnuntos was evacuated on a shield after multiple

---

121 Maurice, *Strategikon*, VII, 2, 41.
122 Procopius, *BG*, VI, 2, 26–29.
123 Procopius, *BG*, VI, 2, 30–33.

wounds and bled to death in two days.[124] This was the type of wound that Romano-Byzantine doctors did not know how to tend, simply because blood transfusion did not exist.

Sweet or Bitter Victory?

'Next to a battle lost, the greatest misery is a battle gained' said the Duke of Wellington.

In a Romano-Byzantine context, the bitter victory already existed, the type of victory that Procopius called 'Cadmean victory' probably referring to the two ill-fated Theban, or Cadmean, heroes Eteocles and Polynices, or perhaps to Epaminondas who perished during his last victory. Procopius used this expression for the battle near Salona in 535, when the master of the soldiers to Illyricum defeated the Ostrogoths but lost his life.[125] The historian Malchus put this expression in the speech of Theodoric Strabo to his enemy brothers, the Goths of Pannonia, who came to attack him: waging a war between them would amount to a 'Cadmean victory'.[126] It can be equated to what is today called a 'Pyrrhic victory' - a reference to the costly successes of the King of Epirus against the Romans in the third century BCE..

---

124 Procopius, *BG*, V, 29, 44.
125 Procopius, *BG*, V, 7, 3.
126 Malchus, *Fragm.*, 18, 2.

15

The Battle of the Yarmuk, the End of the Late Antique World

> Then God brought Islam: his religion prevailed over all others. The possessions of the Romans extended all around the sea, on both its shores. The Muslims first took away the whole of the southern shore, from Syria to Egypt, as far as Africa and the Maghreb. After crossing the Gulf of Tangiers, they took the whole of Spain from the Goths and the Galicians.
>
> Ibn Khaldun, *Ibar*, t.1, 1995, p.231.

Saracens were not newcomers to the Romano-Byzantine world. They had long been auxiliaries and plundering neighbours. One of them, known as Philip the Arab, was even a Roman Emperor. However, the Saracens were those who dealt the fatal blow to Mediterranean world unity. These men from the sandy desert, accustomed to mobile cavalry or meharist combat, also had a tradition of maritime trade in the Indian Ocean. They proved to be formidable enemies, both on land and at sea, and posed a lasting challenge to Byzantium's hegemony in the Mediterranean. The *Mare al-Rom* (Sea of the Romans) as the Arabs called it, no longer deserved the name.

The Arab conquest was rapid in historical terms: after the death of Muhammad in 632, the Arabs prepared to subjugate Palestine and Syria. Religious fanaticism, or perhaps simply a faith which turned warriors killed in battle into martyrs, motivated many Muslim fighters, but at the start of the conquest their leaders seemed more concerned with extracting tribute than converting the former subjects of the Romano-Byzantine Empire. Moreover, Islamism and Arabism were closely linked from this period on, and the idea of an Arab Empire professing Islam was then very much alive, giving them a moral superiority over their adversaries. Emperors of Byzantium saw them as nothing more than looters and had little understanding of the religious dimension of this enemy.[1] Nevertheless,

---

1   M. Canard, 'The Arab Expansion: The Military Problem' in F. M. Donner, *The*

why did the military art inherited from Rome proved so ineffective against these long-contained desert warriors?

Palestine and Syria: Keys to Arab Expansion

Thousands of civilians are screaming and running, blood is flowing in the streets: Islamic warriors have broken through the walls of their city. From Muhammad onwards, the Arabs attacked the provinces of Arabia Petraea, Palestine, Phoenicia and Syria, an area corresponding to today's Israel, Jordan and Syria, until they were subjugated.[2]

The strategic weakness of this region was due to several points. The first was the low number of troops to defend it. The second was the distance which separated it from Mesopotamia or Byzantium from where the elite troops would arrive, some 900km or 1,600km by road. The third was the eastwards orientation of the defence system designed to counter the Persians and their Lakhmid allies and not southwards against the Arabs coming from the peninsula. It was a house of cards that had already collapsed in *c.* 613 when the Persians arrived, after overrunning the defences of Mesopotamia and Osrhoene. The spine of the Desert watch was the 650km long military road connecting cities such as Emesa, Damascus, Bosra, Philadelphia and Petra of Arabia up to the Red Sea (respectively present-day Homs, Damascus, Busra al-Sham in Syria, Amman and Petra, the current archaeological site in Jordan). Midway, in the province of Arabia Petraea, the River Yarmuk, main tributary to the River Jordan was a barrier for an invader coming from the south. Draining much of the Hauran Plateau its narrow and shallow course lined with vegetation the river is enclosed in a canyon. Near to the Yarmuk is Bosra, then a prosperous caravan city, today its Roman Theatre and baths are still visible. It was no more a legionary city but remained a crossroads not only between Emesa and the Red Sea but also with the Sea of Galilee in Palestina II. The whole region was demographically weak before the Arab conquest and beforehand the Persian occupation had partly dismantled its defences. In the 16th year of the reign of Heraclius and the 6th of the *Hegira*, 627–628, a plague killed 'myriads of people in Palestine.'[3]

The Muslim invaders were nomadic Bedouins, hardened by the wars Muhammad had fought; accustomed to long-distance raiding warfare and skilful in their handling of swords, spears and bows. Depending on the situation, they went to war with or without their families and herds. They were cavalry or foot soldiers but were moved on horses and camels.

Expansion of the Early Islamic State (London: Routledge, 2007), pp.65–67.
2   H. Kennedy, *The Great Arab Conquests: how the spread of Islam changed the world we live in* (London: Weidenfeld & Nicholson; Philadelphia PA: Da Capo Press, 2007), pp.66–97 (Generally accepted version of the conquest of Palestine and Syria).
3   Michael the Syrian, *HU*, XI, 3, t. 2 (1963), p.412.

THE BATTLE OF THE YARMUK, THE END OF THE LATE ANTIQUE WORLD

In battle, the Arabs were classically arranged in three bodies: the centre, the left wing and the right wing.

Tribal divisions remained the basis of the organisation of the Muslim armies of the conquest era. Each tribe has his own square banner, *rāya*, with a distinctive design or *liwā*. Numerical superiority was not the cause of their successes, but rather their innate sense of manoeuvre. Arabic sources are abundant in anecdotes but explained the Muslim victories by the will of Allah, leaving little tactical information other than that from the centuries following the conquest, since it came from historians of the Umayyad and early Abbassid period.[4]

According to Theophanes Confessor, Muhammad first led his armies against the Ghassanids, the Christian Bedouin allies of the Romano-Byzantine Empire protecting Arabia Petraea and Palestine. He delegated this campaign to four generals who first suffered a failure at the Battle of Mothous where three perished except Khalid ibn al-Walid.[5] According to Tabari, 'the King of Rum' Heraclius was present with an army of 100,000 men, an inaccurate and highly exaggerated figure.[6] Theophanes Confessor says that the *vicarius* Theodore from the province of Arabia or Gaza led border guards to surprise the Saracens at the village of Mothous, thanks to information given by Koutabas from the tribe of Koraishites, from which the current Jordanian royal family descends.[7] The battle was rather a large skirmish, took place at today's Mu'tah in Jordan, around 20km east of the Dead Sea, and is dated to 629 or 630. The Muslim expeditionary force at Mothous numbered only 3,000 men.[8] Fighting in the Arabian Peninsula was still raging and Mecca had not yet been taken, so the Muslims' best troops were not yet engaged against the Empire. The elite troops of the Muslim Army then consisted of the 5,000 Companions of the Prophet, most of them sheiks and renowned warriors.[9] The Muslim conquest probably began with a financial dispute, which demonstrates that the security of the Empire's Arab frontier was guaranteed by tribute:

> At this time [around 630] some Arabs on our borders received small remuneration for guarding the approaches to the desert. It was then that a certain Eunuch arrived to distribute the soldiers' pay, and when the Arabs came to receive their due according to custom, the Eunuch chased them away saying: 'The Emperor has difficulty

---

4   H. Kennedy, *The Armies of the Caliphs. Military and Society in the Early Islamic State* (Abingdon: Routledge, 2006), pp.1–17.
5   Theophanes Confessor, *Chrgr.*, AM 6123, 336 (four emirs sent by Mohamed/Mahomet to fight the Christian Arabs; Mouthous; three emirs killed except Khalid).
6   Tabari, *Tarikh*, III, 30, t. 3 (1958), p.117.
7   Theophanes Confessor, *Chrgr.*, AM 6123, 336.
8   Tabari, *Tarikh*, III, 30, t. 3 (1958), p.117.
9   Tabari, *Tarikh*, IV, 62, t. 3 (1958), p.471.

paying the salaries of his soldiers, even more so for these dogs!' Distraught by these words, the Arabs went to find the people of their tribes and this is what led them to Gaza which is the gateway to the desert towards Mount Sinai.[10]

In 631, without a fight, Muhammad subdued the Christian and Arab cities of Tabuk, a large city without a Roman garrison, Djarba and Adsro'h, who all paid tribute to him.[11]

The Muslim Conquest Begins

Abu Bakr As-Siddiq, Aboubacharos in Greek, first Caliph of Muhammad, began the Muslim conquest. After his accession in 632, or the 23rd year of the reign of Heraclius according to Theophanes Confessor, Abu Bakr sent four generals as Muhammad had done. Michael the Syrian reported that their mission was to conquer Palestine, Egypt, Persia, and the Christian Taiyayē (Ghassanid Bedouins).[12] The area comprising Syria and Iraq that they were to conquer was named Sham in Arabic sources, and *Futuh al-Sham* was the common name for this conquest.[13] According to Tabari these generals mustered only 7,000 men and their names and objectives were: Abu Obaid ibn al-Jarrah to Emesa, Yazid ibn Abu-Sofian to Damascus, Amr ibn al-As to Palestine, Shurabil ibn Hassan to Ordûn (Jordan).[14] Al-Baladhuri stated that Abu Bakr issued only three banners for a holy war in Syria, to take the spoils of the Greeks. He dated this event from the first of the month of Safar in the thirteenth year of the *Hegira*, (6 April 634). The three generals were Khalid ibn Said ibn al-As, soon replaced with Yazid ibn abi-Sofian, Shrurabil and Amr ibn al-As; they had only two objectives: Palestine for the first and Tabuk for the other two, with a force of roughly 23,500 men in three bodies of 7,500.[15] Disentangling the truth is not easy as the sources do not agree on numbers and dates. The start of the campaign can be assumed to be in 634.

On the Romano-Byzantine side, Sergius, Governor of Palestine, left Caesarea with 300 soldiers who were soon annihilated with him. The Arabs returned home after taking many captives and a great deal of loot.

---

10 Theophanes Confessor, *Chrgr.*, AM 6123, 336.
11 Tabari, *Tarikh*, III, 34, t. 3 (1958), p.167 (Tabuk).
12 Theophanes Confessor, *Chrgr.*, AM 6124, 336 (four generals sent by Aboubacharos/Abu Bakr-not to be confounded with the previous four sent by Muhammad). Michael the Syrian, *HU*, XI, 4, t. 2 (1963), p.413 (objectives). *Chr. 1234*, t. 1 (1937), pp.180–190 (four generals).
13 M. J. De Goeje, *Mémoire sur le Fotouho's-Sham attribué à Abou Ismail al-Baçri* (Leiden: *Mémoires d'histoire et de géographie orientales*, 2, 1864).
14 Tabari, *Tarikh*, IV, 29, t. 3, (1958), p.349.
15 Al-Baladhuri, *Kitab*, II, 1, 1916, p.165 (appointment of generals on 1 Safar AH 13, 6 April 634); 166–167 (objectives given to three generals); 167 (strengths).

Nikephoros of Constantinople identified Sergius with the eunuch who had stopped paying the tribute, estimated at 30 pounds of gold. To punish him for that, his killing by the Arabs would have been cruel and he was suffocated in a dried camel skin.[16] This version of events was partially confirmed by Michael the Syrian, who granted the title of Patrician to Sergius, but accompanied by a contingent of 5,000 infantry, composed of Romans and Samaritans. He did not locate the battle. During the encounter, the Samaritans were slaughtered first and a few Romans managed to escape. The unfortunate Sergius was said to have fallen three times from his horse before being hacked to death. The name of the Muslim general responsible for conquering Palestine is not recorded, but after this victory he marched on Caesarea.[17] Bar Hebraeus gave a very similar account. Sergius was reportedly defeated in Palestine with an army of 5,000 men gathered from Shamrayē (Samaritans) and Rhomayē (Romans). He fell from his horse three times while trying to escape and the last time was killed by the Arabs.[18] This battle is identified as at Dâthín on 4 February 634 by today historiography.[19] A Syrian chronicle that has long been judged to be from the eighth century, but is now considered to be *c*. 640, reported the defeat and death of Sergius in a battle near Gaza:[20]

> In the year 945 [of the Seleucid Era], indiction VII, in the month of *Chebot*, on the fourth day [4 February 634], a Friday at the ninth hour, a battle began between the Romans and the Arabs of Muhammad, in Palestine, 12 miles east of Gaza. The Romans fled and abandoned the Patrician Ryrdn [presumably Sergius], whom the Arabs killed. There were killed 40,000 poor Palestinian peasants, Christians, Jews and Samaritans. The Arabs devastated the entire region.[21]

Al-Baladuhri gave a brief account of this battle, which he located in Dâthín, between the Muslim camp and the residence of the 'Patrician of Gaza', presumably the Vicar Theodore. According to him, no Romano-Byzantine leaders were killed. The General Khalid ibn al-Walid had not yet arrived from Iraq, where he was fighting the Lakhmids.[22] Al-Baladuhri was the only

---

16 Theophanes Confessor, *Chrgr.*, AM 6124, 336 (Sergius death with 300 soldiers). Nikephoros of Constantinople, *Brev.*, 20, 11–21 (Sergius death; cause of the war).
17 Michael the Syrian, *HU*, XI, 6, t. 2 (1963), p.413 (5,000-strong Roman force; Sergius death).
18 Bar Hebraeus, *Chr.*, 100, 1932, p.72.
19 W. E. Kaegi, W. E., *Byzantium and Early Islamic Conquests*, p.88.
20 A. Palmer, 'Une chronique syriaque contemporaine de la conquête arabe: essai d'interprétation théologique et politique' in P. Canivet (ed.), *La Syrie de Byzance à l'Islam (VIIe-VIIIe siècles)*, (Damascus: Institut français d'études arabes de Damas, 1992), p.31–46.
21 *Chronicon miscellaneum ad annum Domini 724 pertinens* (1904), p.11. A. Guillou, 'Prise de Gaza', p.403, n.1 and 2.
22 Al-Baladhuri, *Kitab*, II, 1 (1916), pp.167–168.

one to report another battle which ensued at al-Araba, a desert area south of the Dead Sea, where the Muslims defeated a contingent of 3,000 Greeks, killing one of their leaders, probably Sergius, then pursued them until ad-Dubbiyah where they won another action.[23] It appears that most sources have conflated Dâthín and al-Araba.

Oversimplifying the chronology, Theophanes Confessor wrote that in the first year the Arabs took Hera, or al-Hira, capital of the Lakhmids in Iraq, and Gaza in Byzantine territory.[24] Muslim sources do not mention any capture of Gaza, then an important caravan centre, but the region was undoubtedly pillaged. The episode of the 60 martyrs of Gaza evokes a prolonged resistance by Byzantine units until 637, after the Battle of the Yarmuk. Indeed, in parallel with the Palestine operation against Sergius, the Muslims under the leadership of Emir Khalid ibn al-Walid seized Hera, on the Arab-Persian border, that they turned into a province called Iraq. On this occasion, the Romano-Byzantines helped their former Persian enemies to contain the Muslim advance. According to Tabari, the Emperor sent 100,000 men from Byzantium, the Ghassanids mobilised 30,000 and the Persians brought the coalition to 180,000 men, figures that appear exaggerated. This improbable coalition was defeated by Khalid ibn al-Walid at Firaz, near the Euphrates. The conquest of Iraq ended late in the twelfth year of *Hegira*, (18 March 633 to 6 March 634). The Battle of Firaz may have been in January 634.[25]

Abu Bakr ordered Khalid to leave Iraq and join the fighting in Syria with reinforcements from Medina commanded by Muawiya. He justified his decision by the numerical strength of the enemy.[26] According to Tabari, Khalid ibn al-Walid left Iraq with 9,000 men, plus other reinforcements which brought the Muslim strength to 30,000–36,000 men.[27] He left Iraq in the month of Rabi al-thani, the thirteenth year of the *Hegira* (10 March 634 to 27 February 6350), probably in June.[28] Regrouping their forces the Muslims won new victories in 634. Khalid ibn al-Walid subjugated the Bedouin tribes from Arabia Petraea, took Palmyra, attacked the Ghassanids and got as far as Damascus. He was dissuaded from opening a siege by a generous tribute given by the Damascene bishops and moved south to Bosra. The Governor of Bosra was defeated trying to fight and then preferred to pay a tribute. Khalid subdued the region of Hauran and then the city of Areopolis (today Rabbat Moab) to the east of the Dead Sea.[29] It was probably at this

---

23 Al-Baladhuri, *Kitab*, II, 1 (1916), p.168.
24 Theophanes Confessor, *Chrgr.*, AM 6124, 336.
25 Tabari, *Tarikh*, IV, 27 (t. 3, 1958, pp.345 (battle), 347 (ending operations in Iraq).
26 Al-Baladhuri, *Kitab*, II, 1 (1916), p.167 (Roman strengths). Michael the Syrian, *HU*, XI, 4, t. 2 (1963), p.413 (four generals victorious in Iraq). Tabari, *Tarikh*, IV, 28, t. 3 (1958), p.348 (reinforcements from Medina).
27 Tabari, *Tarikh*, IV, 29, t. 3 (1958), p.349 (Tabari mixed the end of operations in Iraq with the Yarmuk campaign).
28 Al-Baladhuri, *Kitab*, II, 2 (1916), p.169.
29 Al-Baladhuri, *Kitab*, II, 2 (1916), pp.169–172 (Bedouins; Palmyra), 173 (Bosra;

point, after Vicar Theodore's defeat in the Gaza region and Sergius' defeat in al-Araba, that the Romano-Byzantine field troops arrived from the north to stem the Muslim advance.

Khalid ibn al-Walid won a major victory at Ajnadayn, dated to 30 July 634 by historiography, which conjecturally locates it in the Valley of the Terebinths, Hebrew for the Valley of Elah. This was a crossroads linking Judea to the coastal plains, 20km south-west of Bethlehem.[30] Al-Waqidi estimates the Muslim Army at 32,000 soldiers.[31] Al-Baladhuri unhesitatingly recorded that Khalid ibn al-Walid defeated a gigantic army of 100,000 Greeks while Emperor Heraclius cowardly remained in Emesa. According to Khalid ibn al-Walid, this victory took place in 13 AH, in the month of *Jumada al-'anwal or* at the beginning of *Jumada al-thani* (21 July or 2 August).[32] Theophanes Confessor dated this battle to the 24th year of the reign of Heraclius and the 3rd year of the Caliph Au Bakr (634), but did not locate it. According to him, Theodore the Kouropalates, Master of the Soldiers to the East and brother of the Emperor, was defeated by the Arabs and joined Heraclius back in Edessa.[33] Michael the Syrian also dated the battle to the 24th year of Heraclius' reign and even to 13 AH. He did not however locate it, only saying that Theodore the Kouropalates had to replace Sergius the Patrician at the request of his brother Heraclius. Theodore was arrogant and had to flee to escape the disaster he suffered at Gousit near Antioch, but this location seems doubtful because it does not fit with the geographical progression of the Muslims, at that time limited to Bosra.[34] According to al-Baladhuri, the Emperor Heraclius took refuge in Antioch and the Greeks were again defeated in the Yaqusah Valley on the Golan Heights. Shortly afterwards, on 22 August 634, the Caliph Abu Bakr died,[35] and operations ended until the end of the year. Damascus and Emesa still remained under Imperial control while Muslims held the Bosra region. The capture of Jerusalem and the coastal towns was not yet of interest to them.

Caliph Omar ibn al-Khattab, Oumaros in Greek, succeeded Abu Bakr and pursued the same strategy. Five months after his accession to the throne, in January 635, his General Abu Ubayda ibn al-Jarrâ won a victory at Fahl or Fih (formerly called Pella and Berenice, and now Tabaqat Fahil in the Jordan Valley). There a patrician trusted by the Emperor and not otherwise known was killed in action with 10,000 soldiers. The remnants of the Imperial Army took refuge in the cities of Syria and the inhabitants of Pella or Berenic after a short siege preferred to pay tribute to the Jizya.[36] Marching

---

  Hauran; Moab).
30 W. E. Kaegi, *Byzantium and Early Islamic Conquest*, p.96.
31 Al-Waqidi, *Futuh al-Sham*, 3, 54 (2012), p.341.
32 Al-Baladhuri, *Kitab*, II, 3 (1916), p.174 (12 days before the end of *Jumada* I or two days after the beginning of Jumada II).
33 Theophanes Confessor, *Chrgr.*, AM 6125, 337.
34 Michael the Syrian, *HU*, XI, 6, t. 2 (1963), p.418.
35 Al-Baladhuri, *Kitab*, II, 3 (1916), p.175.
36 Al-Baladhuri, *Kitab*, II, 5 (1916), pp.176–177.

on Damascus the Muslims had to fight their way at Marj as-Suffar during the first day of the Muharram month 14 AH (25 February 635). Although some 4,000 Muslims were wounded, the Romano-Byzantines troops retreated to Jerusalem and Damascus.[37] Damascus fell into Arab hands on 12 March because of the betrayal of a bishop who wanted to save the lives of the inhabitants.[38] When Emesa was reached the Arabs the city's Governor sallied out with a huge army, including 5,000 horsemen in coats of mail. The Arabs were put to flight but Khalid restored the balance by forcefully counter-attacking while the Byzantine troops plundered the Arab camp. He won the day and only 235 Arab horsemen were killed during the entire battle.[39] Thereafter the Muslims took Emesa.[40]

Faced with so many disasters, Heraclius dismissed his brother Theodore the Kouropalates, then placed command of the Eastern Army in the hands of Theodore Trithyrios the Sakellarios and the Armenian General Baanes. Unlike Michael the Syrian, Theophanes Confessor did not mention Shahrbaraz's son among the newly-appointed generals. By summer 635, the new commanders carried out a counter-offensive which defeated the Arabs in front of Emesa and forced them to retreat towards Damascus. Then they camped on the River Bardanēsios, called Farfar or Bardan by Michael the Syrian, current Barada where the Muslims had previously set up camp. According to Theophanes Confessor, at this Heraclius returned to Constantinople with the True Cross, but it was probably later. In 636, the Muslims returned to Damascus.[41] The new Romano-Byzantine military leaders pushed them back again and moved south to the River Yarmuk.

Locating and Dating the Battle of the River Yarmuk

The Battle of the Yarmuk, or al-Yarmuk, is generally dated to 20 August 636. The historiographical tradition locates it to the River Yarmuk, a tributary of the Jordan, to the east of Lake Tiberias and to the south of the Golan Heights. The river was called Hieromykes in Greek. It is a river that winds for 70m south of Syria, north of Jordan into Israel. The Yarmuk is deeply incised into the Hauran plateau and in places forms a canyon. Further west, its banks are covered with shrubs in the middle of a rocky area with dry grasses. The site controls the road from Damascus to Arabia. Location, dating and course of the battle are problematic, because the literary sources

---

37 Al-Baladhuri, *Kitab*, II, 7 (1916), pp.182–183.
38 Al-Baladhuri, *Kitab*, II, 8 (1916), p.187 (fall of Damascus).
39 Al-Waqidi, *Futuh al-Sham*, 2, 55–58 (2012), pp.243–247 (battle at Hims/Homs); 59, p.249 (losses).
40 Al-Baladhuri, *Kitab*, II, 9 (1916), pp.200–201 (Homs).
41 Theophanes Confessor, *Chrgr.*, AM 6125, 337 (new generals appointed by Heraclius; counter-offensive; Heraclius); AM 6126, 338 (Saracens at Damascus the following year).

offer modern historians a puzzle with missing pieces and accounts that do not fit together.[42]

The Battle as Seen by the Syrians

The nearest contemporary source of the battle is the few Syrian fragments written *c.* 647, on the margins of older Gospels:

> ...and in January they took an oath to stay alive. Emesa and many villages were ruined with massacre by Muhammad, and many people were killed and captured from Galilee to Beth [Sacharya?] .... and these Arabs set up a siege in front .... and we saw everywhere.... and brought them olive oil. On 26 May the S(akellarios) arrived .... from the neighbourhood of Emesa and the Romans pushed them back .... On 10 August, the Romans fled from the neighbourhood of Damascus and there many were killed, almost 10,000. In the middle of the year the Romans arrived. On 20 August, in the year 947 [636 in the Seleucid calendar] they gathered at Gabitha .... The Romans and many people perished. The Romans were about 50,000.[43]

This text provides the most precise location and dating but there is a problem, Gabitha is not on the Yarmuk. The capital of the Ghassanids, the city was located 60km to the north, on the Golan Heights, identified today with the archaeological site of Jabiyah, the 'Watering Place', crucial for armies in dry countries. These fragments suggest that a new Muslim invasion reached Emesa in January 636, but was repulsed around May. The Romano-Byzantine counter-attack reached Damascus, where it failed on 10 August. New Imperial reinforcements forced the Arabs to retreat southwards to Gabitha-Jabiyah. The River Yarmuk is not mentioned. The 50,000 Romans killed may not be a fanciful estimate of the casualties in the battle, the text being incomplete, but a possible estimate of the civilians slaughtered.

The Melkite historian from Northern Syria, Agapius of Hierapolis (died *c.* 942) wrote a universal history in Arabic with the title *Kitab al-Unwan*. He gave a concise account of the battle dated to 632 and located on the River Yarmuk:

---

42 L. Caetani, Annali dell'Islam (Hildesheim: G. Olms, 1972), vol. 3, pp.499–613.

43 Fragment n°1 edited and translated into English by A. Palmer in *The Seventh Century in the West-Syrian Chronicles* (Liverpool: Liverpool University Press, 1993), pp.1–4; R. G. Hoyland, *Seeing Islam as Others Saw It: A Survey and Evaluation of Christian, Jewish and Zoroastrian Writings on Early Islam* (Princeton NJ: Darwin Press, Studies in Late Antiquity and Early Islam series, 13, 1998), p.116.

> In the year 22 of Heraclius, the Greeks met the Arabs on the banks of the Yarmuk; and the Arabs killed so many Greeks that (their bodies) formed a bridge over which we could pass. This happened in the year 943 of Alexander.[44]

Michael the Syrian (1126–1199) mentioned two battles on the Yarmuk, the first of which was at Gabita, but over two years:

> In the year 5 of Omar, the Romans engaged the Arabs in the region of the town of Bostra, which they called Gabita, on the River Yarmuka. The Romans were cruelly torn to pieces and abandoned this region. The battle took place like this: General Baanes and the son of S(h)ahrbaraz the Persian united their troops and came in front of Damascus to guard this place. The King of the Taiyayē [the Muslim Bedouins] came to meet them and killed a good number. Having come to Damascus, they camped on the River Farfar, which the Arabs call Bardan.[45] The following year, the Taiyayē returned to the confines of Damascus, and the Patrician having learned of it, trembled and sent to warn the *Sakellarios* of the Emperor, who was in Edessa. He gathered an army of 10,000 men and came to Emesa to find the Patrician who had 60,000 with him. When the Romans met the Taiyayē, the first were defeated, 40,000 men of the Roman Army succumbed that day, with Baanes and the *Sakellarios*. A multitude of them drowned in the River Yarmuka. The son of S(h)ahrbaraz, having survived the battle, joined the Taiyayē and came to live in Emesa.[46]

Michael the Syrian actually made a geographical error by locating Gabita on the Yarmuk. There are two alternate theories for the so-called Battle of Gabita. The first one identifies it with the battle that Arab historians call Ajnadayn, in the Terebinth Valley, and which took place in July 634 and was lost by Theodore the Kouropalates. The second theory dates the battle to 636 and equates Gabita with the archaeological site of Jabiyah, and as the site of the preliminary engagement before the 'Battle of Jabiyah-Yarmuk'.[47] Michael the Syrian left a gap of one year between the Battles of Gabita and

---

44 Agapius of Hierapolis, *Kitāb al-'unwān* (1912), p.453.
45 *Bible, Kings*, 2, 5, 12 (Farfar ou Pharphar/Pharpar, current Barada).
46 Michael the Syrian, *HU*, XI, 5, t. 2 (1963), p.417 (troops sent to Bosra after the death of Abu Bakr in AG 946, 24th year of the reign of Heraclius, AH 13); *HU*, XI, 6, t. 2 (1963), p.420 (At the beginning of his reign, Omar had already sent a troop to take Bosra: literary confusion from the sources or military redundancy?).
47 W. E. Kaegi, *Byzantium and Early Islamic Conquests*, pp.112 & 141; W. E. Kaegi, *Heraclius, Emperor of Byzantium* (Cambridge: Cambridge University Press, 2003), p.239 (Battle of Jabiyah-Yarmuk in 636); J. F. Haldon, *The Byzantine Wars*, pp.58–66 (battlefield situated between Yarmuk and Jabiyah in 636).

THE BATTLE OF THE YARMUK, THE END OF THE LATE ANTIQUE WORLD

Yarmuk. At the Gabita preliminary battle, the Romano-Byzantines were defeated and allowed the Arabs to temporarily set-up camp in front of Damascus.

In the following year the Romans drove the Arabs back from Damascus and pursued them to the Yarmuk. They were nevertheless beaten and their command was destroyed: Theodore Trithyrios the Sakellarios, mentioned only by his function as treasurer, and Baanes were killed. Niketas the son of Shahrbaraz, who was previously unmentioned, defected to the enemy. After their victory at Yarmuk, the Arabs negotiated the surrender of Damascus.[48] Unlike Theophanes Confessor, who has Heraclius leave the East the year before Yarmuk, Michael the Syrian has him departing from Antioch after the Persians were defeated by the Arabs at al-Qadisiyah in November 636. Heraclius was in despair:

> Heraclius, Emperor of the Romans, seeing that the devastation was spreading, departed with sorrow from Antioch and went to Constantinople. It is reported that he had said goodbye as he left, shouting: 'sozou Syria', that is, 'Peace be on Syria.'[49]

According to Michael the Syrian Heraclius ordered his troops to sack Syria before withdrawing. He also ordered the provinces of Mesopotamia, Egypt and Armenia not to fight with the Arabs but to hold their positions.[50] To make the story short, the Imperial field army ran away letting the border troops to fend for themselves. This was the Yarmuk's grim result.

Although his name evokes some Jewish origins, Bar Hebraeus was a thirteenth-century Syrian cleric and author of a chronography. His version of the Battle of Yarmuk was largely inspired by Michael the Syrian:

> In the fourth year of Omar, Baanis [Baanes in Greek/Vahan in Armenian], commander of the Roman Army and also the son of Shahrbaraz the Persian who, on the death of his father had taken refuge among the Romans, the Emperor's treasurer who was also in Edessa gathered 60,000 horsemen. Then they faced the Arabs in the region of Emesa where the Romans were defeated and 40,000 of them perished, most of whom were drowned in the River Yarmuka.[51]

With more than 150km separating Emesa from the Yarmuk, Bar Hebraeus confused two battles: the Battle of Emesa in which the Romano-Byzantines drove back the Arabs, and the Battle of Yarmuk.

---

48 Michael the Syrian, *HU*, XI, 6, t. 2 (1963), p.421.
49 Michael the Syrian, *HU*, XI, 7, t. 2 (1963), p.424.
50 Michael the Syrian, *HU*, XI, 7, t. 2 (1963), p.425.
51 Bar Hebraeus, *Chronographia*, 101 (1932), p.72.

The Battle as Seen by the Greeks

The Greek historians who reported the battle were not contemporaries of it. Theophanes Confessor (died in 817) wrote a chronography in which he wanted precise dates based on all the calendars then known, including Muslim ones. The battle would have taken place during the 6,126th year of the world, the 25th year of the reign of Heraclius, year 636 of our calendar:

> That year a huge mass of Saracens (stormed) out of Arabia and launched a raid in the region of Damascus. When Baanes [Armenian General Vahan] learned of this, he sent a message to the Imperial *Sakellarios*, asking him to come to his aid with his army, noting that the Arabs were very numerous. The *Sakellarios* joined with Baanes. They left Emesa and engaged the Arabs. A battle took place on the first day, which was a Tuesday, the 23rd of the month of Loos [in the Macedonian calendar, i.e. July], where the men of the *Sakellarios* were defeated. The soldiers of Baanes then revolted, proclaiming him Emperor and abjuring Heraclius. Then the men of the *Sakellarios* retreated, and the Saracens, seizing the opportunity, engaged in battle. As a south wind blew in the direction of the Romans, they could not face the enemy because of the dust and were defeated. Massed in the defiles of the River Hieromouchtas [Yarmuk], they all perished, the army of the two generals amounting to 40,000. Having achieved this brilliant success, the Arabs came to Damascus which they took like the entire province of Phoenicia where they settled down to launch an expedition against Egypt.[52]

According to this account, the Imperial Army went from Emesa to the River Yarmuk, suggesting that it drove back the Arabs by around 140km. This move and the choice of a narrow valley as a stop line by the Arabs confirm the numerical superiority of the Romano-Byzantines over their opponents. Theophanes Confessor and, after him, the *Chronicle of 1234*, then spoke of two battles lost by the Roman Empire, the first of which, although not located, led to a mutiny by the Armenian contingent. Patriarch Eutychius of Alexandria, an Arab historian who died in 940, reported that some of Baanes's soldiers deserted or became angry when they learned that there was not enough money to pay them. The second battle was the result of a retreat by the Imperial Army after losing the first. With the road to Damascus probably cut by the Arabs, the men of the *Sakellarios*, separated from the mutineers of Baanes, fled along the Yarmuk towards their only route of retreat, Samaria, with the Arabs hot on their heels. Presumably stuck in a canyon, they were annihilated in an ambush battle which evokes

---

52 Theophanes Confessor, *Chrgr.*, AM 6126, 338. *Chr.1234*, t. 1(1937), pp.195–196.

the much later charges of Lawrence of Arabia against the retreating Turks. The Arabs then retook Damascus. Eutychius of Alexandria reported the defection of the Governor of Damascus, who he called by the Arabic name Mansur, stating that he sounded cymbals and drums to make believe the arrival of the Muslims and to divert the Imperial Army from his city.[53]

Nikephoros, Patriarch of Constantinople (died 828), did not date the events precisely but made a linear narrative according to what he knew. He reported Theodore the Kouropalates was dismissed from his command to the East for having mocked his Imperial brother. Instead, Theodore Trithyrios, the Imperial treasurer, was appointed as sole general, literally 'general of Anatolia'. After speaking of the ignominious death of Sergius, he came to a great battle that can be identified with the Yarmuk:

> On these facts [Heraclius] ordered Theodore to avoid battle with the Saracens. But this man did not comply with the Emperor's wishes because he had rebellion in mind and his men thought they would defeat the enemy by surprise. They thought that victory would be on the side of the rebels against the Emperor. So, they engaged the Saracens in battle at a place called Gabita. But they had long set up ambushes and advanced against the Romans with few men, skirmishing. The men in ambush fell on the latter and, having surrounded them, killed many men and officers.[54]

Nikephoros added a dramatic event with the disobedience of Theodore Trithyrios the Sakellarios, which is not attested elsewhere. He was very imprecise about dating. He also mentioned a battle that did not take place on the Yarmuk but at Gabita. In fact, he amalgamated all the battles of 634–636 into a single large one. Notwithstanding, his idea of an ambush battle was consistent with Theophanes Confessor. Like Michael the Syrian, Nikephoros said that Heraclius had evacuated Syria just as the Saracens were defeating reinforcements led by the Marinos Master of the Soldiers to the East in Egypt, the one to the Thracians and his successor.[55] Nikephoros was clumsily referring to the battles that followed Yarmuk.

The Battle as Seen by the Armenian Sebeos

A very different version of the battle was given by the Armenian Sebeos. He reported the mobilisation of a large Imperial force led by eunuchs, to whom Heraclius gave the order to reach Arabia, and not to give battle before they

---

53 Eutychius of Alexandria, *Annales*, 278–279.
54 Nikephoros of Constantinople, *Brev.*, 20, 21–31.
55 Nikephoros of Constantinople, *Brev.*, 20, 23, 1–8 (subsequent battles); 24, 1–2 (Heraclius).

received other reinforcements. The battle itself includes ethnic and tactical elements specific to Arabs warriors:

> [Heraclius] began to gather troops numbering 70,000 and appointed one of his trusted eunuchs to lead them and ordered them to go to Arabia [the Byzantine province]. He commanded them not to fight with them [Saracens] but to take care of their own defence until he had gathered enough troops to help them. But when they crossed the Jordan to go to Arabia, they left their camps on the banks of the river and went on foot to attack the Saracen army. They placed part of their forces in ambush on each side, and arranged the multitude of their tents around their camp. Bringing their herds of camels, they arranged them around their tents and tied their legs with ropes. Such was the fortification of their camp. The others, although tired from the march, were able to penetrate this fortification in certain places and began to massacre them. When suddenly, those who were placed in ambush appeared and attacked them. The Fear of God fell on the Greek army and they fled before them. But they could not escape because of the depth of the sand in which their feet sank up to their heels, and the heat of the sun produced great distress as the sword of the enemy pursued them. So, all the generals fell and were killed. The number of those killed was more than 2,000. Few escaped and were able to find refuge.[56]

Sebeos' narrative is the only one militarily constructed, but it is not without flaws. It placed the battle in a sandy area, which is neither the Yarmuk nor the River Jordan. It mentioned the River Jordan but not its tributary the Yarmuk. Nor did he speak about Gabitha. The battle did not end with the collective drowning of the fugitives, as in Michael the Syrian. The 'Fear of God' referred to by Sebeos is reminiscent of Fredegar's 'sword of God', the nickname of Khalid ibn al-Walid. Sebeos said nothing about the Roman command and did not mention Baanes, an Armenian like himself. There is an obvious contradiction between an army he estimated to be 70,000-strong and losses of 2,000 men presented as almost complete annihilation.

The Battle as Seen by the Latins

The encounter is also in a seventh-century Frankish compilation attributed to Fredegar, who made the Saracens a population of the Caucasus (*sic*):

---

56   Sebeos, *Hist.*, 42.

THE BATTLE OF THE YARMUK, THE END OF THE LATE ANTIQUE WORLD

A large crowd of soldiers was gathered from everywhere, from all the provinces of the Empire. Heraclius sent an embassy to the Caspian Gates [Serdere defile in the Elbrus range], the Bronze Gates that the Macedonian Alexander the Great had built on the Caspian Sea and which he had ordered closed due to the flood of nations full of barbarians who lived beyond the peaks of the Caucasus. Heraclius then ordered these same doors to be opened. He brings out 100 and 50,000 warriors, hired at a price of gold to help him fight the Saracens. The Saracens, who had two princes, numbered about 200,000. The two armies had established their camp not far from each other, so as to engage in combat the next day. The same night, the army of Heraclius was struck by the sword of God: in the camp, 52,000 soldiers of Heraclius found death in their beds. When they were to march into battle the next day, they realised that a very large part of the soldiers in their army had been killed by divine judgement, they did not dare to engage in combat against the Saracens. The entire army of Heraclius returned to his lands, while the Saracens, as they had become accustomed to, continued to ceaselessly devastate the provinces of Emperor Heraclius.[57]

This miraculous non-battle with exaggerated numbers has little historical value. The phrase 'sword of God' may be a reference to Khalid ibn al-Walid, probably nicknamed *Sayf Allah* (Sword of Allah) who according to Muslim sources was present at the battle. Fredegar's text referred indirectly to an epidemic that decimated the Imperial Army. Syrian and Muslim sources spoke of plague epidemics around 634 and 638–639, the last of which even killed Caliph Omar.[58] The term plague generically translated to any epidemic and it should probably not be seen as literal.

The *Chronicle of 754*, also called *Pseudo-Isidoriana*, written in Latin and Mozarabic, erroneously dated the battle between 618 and the death of the Prophet Muhammad in 632. In addition, it confused Theodore the Kouropalates, brother of the Emperor, and Theodore Trithyrios the Sakellarios the new appointed general to the East:

8. In the year 656 [618 of the Gregorian calendar] the seventh of the reign of Heraclius, they [the Saracens] invaded the Kingdom. 9. After having fought numerous battles against the Saracens, Theodore, brother of Emperor Heraclius, retreated to mobilise the populations for war, on the orders of his brother who had in mind the prophecy of the rats. But as their losses increased day by day

---

57 Fredegar, *Chr.*, IV, 66.
58 D. Woods, 'Jews, rats and the Battle of Yarmuk', in A. S. Lewin, P. Pellegrini, Z. T. Fiema, S. Janniard (eds), *The Late Roman Army in Near East*, pp.372–373, 374, n. 47.

the Roman legions were so afraid that, engaged in the Battle of Gabata, their army was completely defeated and Theodore having been killed left this world. The Saracens, fearless after the massacre of so many noble people, established their power over Damascus. 10. After the 10 years of the reign of Mamet [Muhammad] were completed, Abubaccar [Abu Bakr] who was from his tribe ascended the throne.[59]

The *Chronicle of 754* also said that Theodore Trithyrios the Sakellarios was ordered to retreat because his brother Emperor Heraclius was frightened by 'the prophecy of the rats', probably a reference to Isaiah 2:2 in *the Bible*. Losses that 'grew by the day' could be attributed to an epidemic. Fear reigned in Theodore Trithyrios the Sakellarios' troops, soon destroyed with him in Gabata, which opened Damascus to the Saracens.[60] Gabata was a confusion that was intended to refer Gabitha/Gabita, the Ghassanid capital (modern Jabiyah) between the Hawran Plain and the Golan Heights in Southern Syria. All in all, the *Chronicle of 754* amalgamated several battles into one event and did not mention the Yarmuk. Western sources are the only ones which refer to an epidemic during this campaign.

The Battle as Seen by Muslim Sources

While Christian sources were marked by Attic 'nothing too much' and Latin ones were concise, Muslim sources were loquacious in the manner of oriental storytellers, and some tended towards legend. They did not fail to report any battles, often victories, while Christian sources sought to conflate everything into a single battle. Unlike the Syrians or the Latins, Muslim sources never spoke of a battle at Gabitha or Gabata. They represented the Arab numbers realistically, but their evaluation of Romano-Byzantine numbers was more than greatly exaggerated, as were their losses.[61]

Al-Waqidi (died 823) was and remains a controversial historian. From the middle ages onwards, many of his compilers criticised him as well as praising him. Contemporary historiography has doubts, sometimes about the very origin of his writings and refer to pseudo-Waqidi. Given in to poetry, he liked to reconstruct dialogues about which Greek sources are silent. Al-Waqidi was to Yarmuk what Shakespeare was to Agincourt. He was more the author of a gesture than a story. Nevertheless, medieval Muslim sources refer to him for the Battle of Yarmuk, to which he devoted

---

59   *Chr. 754*, 8–10.
60   *Chr. 754*, 9.
61   A. Cameron & L. I. Conrad (eds), *The Byzantine and Early Islamic Near East*, vol. 1, *Problems in the Literary Source Materials* (Princeton NJ: The Darwin Press, 1992). R. Paret, 'The Legendary Futūḥ Literature' in F. M. Donner, *The Expansion of the Early Islamic State* (London: Routledge, 2007), pp.163–176.

a long section.⁶² He depicted the Yarmuk Campaign as the result of an Imperial counter-offensive. The capture of Emesa by the Arabs shocked Heraclius, who sent troops to defend Caesarea in Palestine, the Syrian coast and Tiberias and brought in reinforcements from Baanes, King of Armenia.⁶³ Al-Waqidi mentioned five other contingents each with the fabulous strength of 100,000 men commanded by generals to each of whom Heraclius is said to have given a flag embroidered with gold or pearls and gems with cross or sun motifs. The first was a King of Rusiyah named Canter, a Slav therefore, an anachronism and parallel with al-Waqidi's own era where the Byzantine Emperor employed Varangians from Kievan Rus. The second general was George, Governor of Amorium (today Hisarköy in Turkey), within the lands of Phrygia, and of Malūriyah (?). The third general was Trajan, Governor of Constantinople at the head of the Tartars, Franks and the Qaln (?). The fourth was Theodore, with Tartars and Armenians. The fifth was Bannes, so-called King of Armenia, a brave man who fought Persians and Turks.⁶⁴ Only Bannes is attested by other sources. He was the primary commander of the Romano-Byzantines, while his vanguard was made up of Christian Ghassanid, Lakhmid and Jutam Arabs, estimated at 60,000 men.⁶⁵ In fact, al-Waqidi describes the Battle of Yarmuk as a kind of Armageddon battle between Muslims and infidels of all kinds. He quoted ancient Muslim historians who fantastically put the number of troops in the Imperial Army at between 600,000 and 1,000,000.⁶⁶ He turned the campaign into a kind of duel between Abu Obaidah ibn al-Jarrah, his main subordinate Khalid ibn al-Walid, the hero of Islam, against Bannes, the champion of the Romano-Byzantine Empire, supported by the Ghassanid King Jabalah, who was presented as a deceiver.

It is unlikely that there is any credible military information from al-Waqidi among a lot of re-enacted dialogue full of faith and heroism. Propaganda or not, he claimed that Bannes' soldiers were pillaging the Syrian population,⁶⁷ and that this brutal behaviour had alienated the civilians they were supposed to defend. In the same passage, Abu Obaida ibn al-Jarrah was in Jabiyah (Gabitha in Christian sources) when he learned from his spies of the imminent arrival of the enemy. During a council of war he estimated his own forces at 30,000 cavalry.⁶⁸ Khalid advised his chief Abu Obaidah to leave Jabiyah for Yarmuk as in Caesarea was an enemy force of 40,000 cavalry, reinforced by Jordanians who had fled the Muslim

---

62 A. Matvieiev, 'Kitab Futuh el-Sham of (Pseudo-) Muhammad ibn Umar al-Waqidi as a Source for Studying the Battle on the Yarmuk River (636)', *Vox Patrum*, 77 (2021), pp.51–80.
63 Al-Waqidi, Waqidi, *Futuh al-Sham*, 3, 1 (2012), p.257.
64 Al-Waqidi, *Futuh al-Sham*, 3, 3 (2012), p.259.
65 Al-Waqidi, *Futuh al-Sham*, 3, 3 and 12 (2012), p.261 (Bannes), p.273 (strengths).
66 Al-Waqidi, *Futuh al-Sham*, 3, 3 (2012), p.260.
67 Al-Waqidi, *Futuh al-Sham*, 3, 3 and 12 (2012), p.261.
68 Al-Waqidi, *Futuh al-Sham*, 3, 7; 12 (2012), p.265 (Jabiyah), 273 (40,000-strong army).

advance. He explained the strategic choice of this position: 'You will be able to quickly receive reinforcements from the Commander of the Faithful Omar ibn al-Khattab. You will have a good position to obtain victory and a spacious country for horses.'[69] The army brought back from Iraq by Khalid was estimated at only 4,000 and formed the rearguard.[70] The Arabs retreated to the Yarmuk and set up camp near a hill.

The Imperial Army reached a distance of 3 *farsakhs* or 16.5km near a place called the Monastery of the Mountain near ar-Ramadah and al-Jula, probably in the Eastern Golan and the current Syrian village of Jamla.[71] The episode where Khalid put the vanguard of 60,000 horsemen from Jabalah to flight with only 60 volunteers is highly unlikely.[72] It was a reconnaissance skirmish. However, the situation was unsettling for the Muslims and Abu Obaida ibn al-Jarrah wrote to the caliph asking for reinforcements in the face of 'an enemy totalling 800,000 men without the non-combatants.'[73] Caliph Omar assembled 7,000 men in Medina, who defeated an blocking force of Christian Arabs from Amman.[74] Al-Waqidi, commenting on various sources, gave several controversial estimates of the Muslim strength at Yarmuk, from 25,000 to 41,000, letting the reader choose.[75]

Before the battle, negotiations with Armenian General Bannes broke down on the pretext of not fraternizing with Christians.[76] Apparently, Bannes launched a surprise attack.[77] The battle would have lasted several days, the third being the worst.[78] Muslim women stood out for their bravery at Yarmuk. At one point in the battle, the Muslim cavalry on the right wing gave up and took refuge in the camp. There, their wives did what every married man knows, they reprimanded them: 'You are no longer our husbands if you do not protect our children from Christians!' Later, they took up arms when the 'Romans' attacked the camp.[79] The involvement of women with arms in hand is highly unlikely in the Muslim tradition, but can be explained in the event of an attack on the Arab camp, a fact attested by the historian Armenian Sebeos. There was discord among the Romano-Byzantines, and George accused Canter of inertia. With his troops alone George pushed the Saracens between the centre and their left wing

---

69 Al-Waqidi, *Futuh al-Sham*, 3, 7 (2012), p.264.
70 Al-Waqidi, *Futuh al-Sham*, 3, 7 (2012), p.265 (army from Iraq and camp near theYarmuk).
71 Al-Waqidi, *Futuh al-Sham*, 3, 8 (2012), p.266.
72 Al-Waqidi, *Futuh al-Sham*, 3, 12-17 (2012), pp.273-281 (Jabalah routed by Khalid).
73 Al-Waqidi, *Futuh al-Sham*, 3, 18 (2012), p.282.
74 Al-Waqidi, *Futuh al-Sham*, 3, 22; 25 (2012), pp.289 (reinforcements), 293–295 (Governor of Amman).
75 Al-Waqidi, *Futuh al-Sham*, 3, 54 (2012), p.341.
76 Al-Waqidi, *Futuh al-Sham*, 3, 29–30 (2012), pp.300–304.
77 Al-Waqidi, *Futuh al-Sham*, 3, 45 (2012), p.324.
78 Al-Waqidi, *Futuh al-Sham*, 3, 55 (2012), p.341.
79 Al-Waqidi, *Futuh al-Sham*, 3, 49; 51; 60 (2012), pp.331 (1st alert), 368 (2nd alert), 352 (fight).

and reached the interior of their camp. Here again the wives reproached their husbands, brothers and fathers for abandoning them and the latter then repulsed the Romano-Byzantines.[80] The outcome of the battle was still uncertain. It was then that a notable from Emesa named Abu al-Jaid, whose young wife had been raped by the Emperor's soldiers, decided to take revenge. He went to find Khalid who promised him reward and tax exemption for bringing the Imperial forces to the River an-Naqusah, without telling them the depth. The Muslims pretended to camp opposite and simulated an attack with only 500 men. So, the overconfident Romano-Byzantines imprudently counter-attacked through the river and were drowned.[81] This fact was also mentioned by Michael the Syrian, no doubt influenced by Muslim sources. Eventually Bannes, after losing George and other officers, retreated, only to be killed later in a duel in Damascus.[82] Al-Waqidi's most interesting account was probably the report that Emir Abu Obaida ibn al-Jarrah wrote to Caliph Omar:

> Know, O Commander of the Faithful that I went to Yarmuk and that Bannes, leader of the Roman Army, encamped before us. The Muslims had never seen such a large army. God subdued them gracefully and helped us against them in His special favour. We killed nearly 105,000 of them and captured 40,000. God conferred martyrdom on 4,000 Muslims. I did not recognise some faces but I prayed for the dead and buried them. Asim ibn Khawwal killed Bannes [Baanes] in Damascus. Before the final battle, a local man, Abu al-Jaid, tricked them into sending them all to drown in the River Naqusah. Only God can estimate their number. I counted more than 1,000 fugitives killed in the mountains and valleys. We captured their wealth, their horses and their lands. We wrote this letter after the victory and entering Damascus.[83]

With much intellectual integrity, Al-Waqidi quoted previous Muslim historians who gave narratives and estimations different of him. Like this Abdullah ibn Awf al-Maliki who overestimated the Roman Army at 1,060,000![84] Al-Waqidi completed his bravado piece on the Yarmuk battle with the bitter loot-sharing dispute. He was the only one to mention this painful, but realistic, incident.[85]

Al-Baladhuri, although he lived later than these events (he died in 892), and was a critical compiler of al-Waqidi, was the Arab historian who gave the most chronologically structured and detailed account of the conquest of

---

80 Al-Waqidi, *Futuh al-Sham*, 3, 51 (2012), pp.334–335.
81 Al-Waqidi, *Futuh al-Sham*, 3, 63 (2012), p.358.
82 Al-Waqidi, *Futuh al-Sham*, 3, 66; 67 (2012), pp.365 (duel), 365–366 (victory).
83 Al-Waqidi, *Futuh al-Sham*, 3, 68 (2012), pp.367–368.
84 Al-Waqidi, *Futuh al-Sham*, 3, 68 (2012), p.368.
85 Al-Waqidi, *Futuh al-Sham*, 3, 69 (2012), pp.369–371.

Syria. He is not refering to Khalid in the chapter he devoted to the Yarmuk battle:

> Heraclius assembled numerous corps of Greeks, Syrians, Mesopotamians and Armenians, totalling nearly 200,000 men. He placed this army in the hands of a trusted man and sent in an advance guard Jabalah ibn al-Ayham the Ghassanid at the head of the Moustarabim [Arabised Jews of Syria, Palestine and Iraq], the tribes of the Lakhmids, of Judah and others determined to fight the Muslims to the point of having no choice but to conquer or go to live in the country of the Greeks in Constantinople. The Battle of the Yarmuk was of the fiercest and bloodiest kind. The Yarmuk is a river. In this battle, 24,000 Muslims took part. The Greeks and their allies had chained themselves so as not to have any hope of fleeing. With God's help, some 70,000 of them perished and the survivors fled as far as Palestine, Antioch, Aleppo, Mesopotamia and Armenia. In this battle some Muslim women participated violently. Among them, Hind daughter of Utbah and mother of Mouawiya ibn abi-Sofian, who constantly shouted: Cut the arms of these uncircumcised with your swords![86]

Al-Baladhuri dated the battle to the month of Rajab AH 15, August 636 in our calendar.[87] Unlike Greek sources, he did not mention any retreat of the Muslims before Yarmuk, although in his account he spoke of the previous capture of Damascus and Emesa. Al-Baladhuri reported the presence of the Arabs of Syria or Ghassanids commanded by their King Jabalah ibn al-Ayham, a fact confirmed by Eutychius of Alexandria.[88] They held the vanguard, which is consistent with their knowledge of the terrain and their probable armament as light cavalry. It is very unlikely that Romano-Byzantines and the Ghassanids were chained so as not to flee, and their losses of 70,000 killed are also overestimated. Al-Baladhuri added a picturesque element that he found in al-Waqidi's text.

After the victory, the Romano-Byzantine fugitives were pursued by horsemen led by Habib ibn-Maslamah.[89] Al-Baladhuri also reported the conversion of the Ghassanid King Jabalah, without specifying the date or occasion, but said that two years later (AH 17), after being punished for an act of violence, he renounced Islam and joined the Greeks with his 30,000 men.[90] According to him Heraclius, hearing of the disaster, bade farewell to Syria and left Antioch for Byzantium, turning to say, "Peace be upon you,

---

86　Al-Baladhuri, *Kitab*, II, 10 (1916), pp.207–208.
87　Al-Baladhuri, *Kitab*, II, 10 (1916), p.210.
88　Eutychius of Alexandria, *Annales*, 278–279 (Jabalah).
89　Al-Baladhuri, *Kitab*, II, 10 (1916), p.208.
90　Al-Baladhuri, *Kitab*, II, 10 (1916), pp.208–209.

THE BATTLE OF THE YARMUK, THE END OF THE LATE ANTIQUE WORLD

O Syria, what a country you make for the enemy!" The farewell episode was also reported in three Christian sources.[91] The Muslims reoccupied Emesa where Christians and Jews had said they preferred Muslim justice to the tyranny of Heraclius.[92] In November 636, the Muslims besieged Jerusalem, which the Caliph Omar ibn al-Khattab took in April of the following year.[93]

A later author, Tabari (who died in 923) gave a detailed account of the Battle of the Yarmuk in his *Chronicle* or *Tarikh*, although the account is much shorter than that of al-Waqidi.[94] For him the real hero of the Muslims was no other but Khalid ibn al-Walid who harangued his men in these terms before to join battle:

> Never since the existence of Islam has there been a day like today. Never has such a large army of infidels been found in the presence of Muslims. Do not give in to discouragement because of Abu Bakr's illness. Fight God's fight and fight for religion![95]

Warned of the arrival of the Romans coming out of their fortified camp, Khalid divided his army into 36 units, assembled into three corps. He lined up 36,000 men against no fewer than 250,000 Romans commanded personally by 'the King of Rum' Heraclius.[96] Of course, the numbers given for Roman Army are an epic exaggeration. Khalid held the centre, and before the battle, he had a *surat* recited and placed the Prophet's fellow fighters in first line. He asked the 100 veterans of the Battle of Badr not to fight but to bend over and pray. The battle was about to begin when a courier announced the death of the Caliph Abu-Bakeur, the advent of Omar and the dismissal of Khalid ibn al-Walid. He hid this bad news from the army and went into battle. The right and left wings charged simultaneously, respectively commanded by Amr ibn al-As and Yazid ibn Abu-Sofian. This big frontal shock pushed back the enemy. According to Tabari, who here was more of a storyteller than a historian, the leader of the Ghassanids Djaradja or Jabalah ibn al-Ayham came out of the ranks, approached Khalid, had talks with him, converted to Islam and then the final phase of the battle began:

> This desertion broke the courage of the Romans. Khalid threw himself on them with all his troops, and the Romans began to flee.

---

91 Al-Baladhuri, *Kitab*, II, 10 (1916), p.210. Theophanes Confessor, *Chrgr.*, AM 6125, 337 (this farewell dated one year before the Yarmuk); Michael the Syrian, *HU*, XI, 7, t. 2 (1963), p.424 and *Chr.1234*, t. 1 (1937), p.196 (after the Yarmuk).
92 Al-Baladhuri, *Kitab*, II, 10 (1916), p.211.
93 Al-Baladhuri, *Kitab*, II, 11 (1916), pp.213–214.
94 Tabari, *Tarikh*, IV, 29, t. 3 (1958), pp.349–352.
95 Tabari, *Tarikh*, IV, 29, t. 3 (1958), p.350.
96 Tabari, *Tarikh*, IV, 29, t. 3 (1958), p.350 (36,000 Muslims organised into 3 divisions with a total of 36 units versus 250,000 Romans).

The Muslims cut them to pieces and continued the massacre from sunrise to sunset. 120,000 enemies were killed. The Muslims had 3,000 men killed, in addition to the wounded among whom was Abu-Sofyan, the son of Harb, who lost an eye from an arrow. Khalid, leaving the banks of the Yarmuk, invaded the Roman camp. There we found 30 hangings of 1,000 Roum brocades. This victory took place on Saturday of the thirteenth year of the *Hegira* [28 of the month of Jumada I, 30 July 634].[97]

The estimated losses of the Romano-Byzantine Army are as fanciful as the whole narrative. Rather than a sudden conversion on the battlefield, Jabalah ibn al-Ayham's defection was probably as a result of bribery or a way to avoid oblivion on the battlefield. Al-Baladhuri took a different view suggesting that Jabalah fought afterwards but only temporarily.

Some Thoughts

The arrival of a large Romano-Byzantine Army compelled the Muslim warriors to evacuate Damascus and retreat south towards to Jabiyah, the Gabitha of Christian Sources. From there, they took refuge behind the Yarmuk no doubt at the suggestion of Khalid ibn al-Walid who fought a delaying battle to protect the retreat. The battle subsequently began on the Yarmuk, maybe like Adrianople in 378 when the Roman Army of the East had fallen on the camp of the Goths whose main forces had left to forage but suddenly returned afterwards.[98] In the case of the Muslims, it seems that their camp was endangered by the Romano-Byzantines who were attacked from behind by a returning body or caught in a tactical trap. The other hypothesis is that the Heraclius' generals were trapped by Muslims between ravines in a tactical situation where their numbers turned against them, and they were massacred.[99] The Romano-Byzantine defeat was due to a crisis in command, as Heraclius could not find a competent general to rely on.

Assessing the armies' strengths is quite difficult. The Romano-Byzantine Army was led by the Armenian Baanes (Vahan), by Theodore Trithyrios, known as the *Sakellarios* and *Stratēgos* of Anatolia, equivalent to the Master of the Soldiers to the East, by George leader of the Armenian troops and finally by Jabalah ibn al-Ayham King of the Ghassanids. Michael the Syrian was the only one to mention a Persian general officer who rallied to the Empire, the son of Shahrbaraz. All sources agree that the Romano-Byzantines were numerically superior. Theophanes estimated their army at 40,000 men, while Sebeos and Michael the Syrian put it at 70,000. According

---

97 Tabari, *Tarikh*, IV, 29, t. 3 (1958), p.352.
98 Ph. Richardot, *La fin de l'Armée Romaine*, pp.303–321.
99 H. Kennedy, (2006), p.6.

THE BATTLE OF THE YARMUK, THE END OF THE LATE ANTIQUE WORLD

to Tabari, the expeditionary army from Constantinople had reached 50,000 men, divided into 10,000 to 20,000-strong marching parties. In addition, 200,000 men joined them, commanded in person by the 'King of Rum', Heraclius. Al-Baladhuri counted 200,000 Greeks, Syrians, Armenians and Mesopotamians, plus the Syrian vanguard led by Jabalah ibn al-Ayham. The *Chronicle of 1234* went as high as 300,000, a victim of the epic inflation that spread to the later medieval sources! Servants-in-arms and soldiers' families could increase from a quarter to a double the number of rations being drawn in a Romano-Byzantine Army. Thus, an army of 40,000 soldiers consisted of 50,000 to 80,000 rations. Al-Baladhuri unexaggeratedly estimated the Arabs at 24,000.[100] The most realistic estimate, based on sources and what the Imperial Army could do, was 40,000 Romano-Byzantines against 24,000 Muslims. Numbers were probably not a cause of Byzantium's defeat, but the poor quality of troops. Heraclius military did not recover from his defeat by the Persians, and after Yarmuk, the Empire could no longer could mobilise a large army.

Yarmuk was the least clear and most decisive battle of the early middle ages. Strategically, this battle allowed the Arabs to establish themselves in the Mediterranean and deprived the Romano-Byzantine Empire of most of its resources. Three years later Syria was conquered, 10 years later Egypt fell. On a civilisational level, it drew up a religious map which remains generally in force today and affirmed the predominance of Islam in the region.

---

100 Nikephoros of Constantinople, *Brev.*, 2, 55–58 (Theodore Trithyrios *stratēgos* of Anatolia). Theophanes Confessor, *Chrgr.*, AM 6125 and 6126 (Baanes and Theodore the Sakellarios; 40,000 strong army the previous year), Eutychius of Alexandria, *Annales*, 278–279 (Jabalah); Sebeos, *Hist.*, 42 (trusted eunuchs; 70,000 strong army). Tabari, *Tarikh*, IV, 29, t. 3 (1958), p.349 (a 250,000-strong army). Al-Baladhuri, *Kitab*, II, 10 (1916), p.135 (an unnamed general promoted by Heraclius I; 200,000 Romans; 24,000 Muslims). Michael the Syrian, *HU*, XI, 6, t. 2 (1963), p.420 (2nd battle; Baanes, the Sakellarios and the son of Shahrbaraz; 70,000-strong army). *Chr. 1234*, t. 1 (1937), pp.195–196 (three generals; 300,000-strong army).

Conclusion

A New Model Army

> You know, don't you, that Roman troops have been able to defeat any people for centuries? We tamed the Parthian Kingdom, the Lazians, the Huns, the Franks, the Getes, and savage peoples scattered across the vast world serve in our courts under the ethereal sky.
>
> Corippus, *Johannis*, II, v. 383 and v. 385.

Through the sixth and seventh centuries, Byzantium's Army was still 'Roman' but without ethnic Romans. Heir to the troops of the later Roman Empire in terms of armaments and structures, it was a continuation albeit not a fixed copy. The maintenance in the Eastern Roman Empire of a solid tax administration plus a strong central power explain this historical continuity, whereas in the West the disintegration of the central power and tax administration led to the disappearance of the state army. Barbarian kingdoms' forces plus some surviving regular units were the new armies. The impecuniousness of the late Roman state was an endemic disease; however, Byzantium was rich enough to maintain a large standing professional army. So, the military genius of Byzantium was primarily an administrative one. It was an expensive army that chiefly protected the state and partly defended the civilian population. Its early army remained an Imperial force and thus multinational, with regular troops, foreign mercenaries (*foederati*) and private or semi-private soldiers (*bucellarii*). It was a two-tier professional army, with poorly-paid border guards and intervention troops commissioned to fight the battles, supplemented by 'barbarian' mercenaries when needed. As a consequence, military units from the Principate or Dominate periods persisted, at least in name, until the 630s. Some troops garrisoned in Italy and coastal Spain had been created in the sixth century with Latin names in the late Roman tradition, but their structure was no longer the same as before.

Military ranks mentioned in Vegetius by the 380s were still in use 100 years later. However, by the 580s, the military ranks given in the *Strategikon* reveal many changes. From the Roman military past a strong chain of command remained at tactical, administrative and logistical levels. Other characteristics also persisted: a good training and a solid tactical discipline with few exceptions. Early Byzantine officers were not aristocratic buffoons who paid with gold for their ranks; they were competent men who purchased any promotion by shedding their blood.

One point often neglected in studies on late antiquity was the high quality of the military staff. Ammianus Marcellinus in the fourth century, the last great Roman historian, and Procopius in the sixth century, the first great Greek Byzantine historian, were both staff officers, reflecting a solid amount of knowledge and a deep sense of operational analysis. As Général de Gaulle said centuries later, 'The real school of command is general culture.'

Nevertheless, things had changed between Ammianus Marcellinus and Procopius. Early Byzantines were no longer fully late Romans. Under Justinian, soldiers who sought to show themselves in preliminary duels had more in common with the Homeric Greek ethos, or with the early Roman Republic, than with the more disciplined ethos of the Imperial Army. No such thing is to be found in Ammianus Marcellinus, notwithstanding historian and military veteran of Greek culture who served during the 350–360s. By the later Roman Empire, the army's elite was made up of Germanic and Gallic palatine troops. In the middle of the sixth century, the cutting edge of Romano-Byzantine Army was formed by the senior officers and their bodyguards, most of Balkan origin and Latin speaking. They fought in the front line, leading by example and opening a bloody breach through the losses that they inflicted. Senior military leaders no longer believed in the dogma of the military invincibility of the Roman model and its legionary infantry, as Vegetius still did in the 380s. The classic legion of 4,000 to 6,000 men in 10 cohorts no longer existed, but the Empire did not return to it afterwards and was unwilling to do so. Nevertheless, Belisarius' soldiers were proudly convinced to be better equipped than Homeric heroes, feeling they lived in an age of technological progress. So, they did not look back to an ideal past with a tearful nostalgia. They had an undisguised contempt for barbarians who were too lightly armed and poorly protected, such as the Moors, the Sklavenes and even their Herulic *foederati*. But the facts also prove they were above all realistic and could appreciate barbarian armament. The rule from then on was adaptation through imitation. The eleventh, and penultimate, book of Maurice's *Strategikon* was a sound tactical study of the various barbarian peoples.

In the 580s and even before, Byzantine soldiers adopted the best equipment and weaponry from their barbarian opponents, who were highly inventive in this respect. The high quality of these weapons and variety of their tactical styles also explained the Empire's military difficulties. By this time, not only had the cavalry become the main branch of the Imperial Army, but its weaponry was largely inspired by a recent enemy, the Avars, not to mention the composite bow that had already been in use for two centuries by the Steppe nomads. The new Romano-Byzantine heavy cavalry replaced the heavy infantry as the picked troops. This cavalry had the shock power of the Alano-Gothic long spear with the full armour adopted from the Persians or the Avars, but also the shooting accuracy and penetration ability of the Hunnic bow. This efficient tactical mix had begun with the *scutarii*-archers in the fourth century. However, the average early Byzantine infantry was no longer the 'cattle' trapped and slaughtered by the Gothic cavalry at Adrianople in 378. The Eastern Army's infantry kept the helmets and body armour that the Western Army had abandoned during the reign of Gratian in the 380s. Shortly after, the Eastern Army had clearly shown its tactical superiority over their western colleagues at the Battle of the Frigidus in 394, where Emperor Theodosius I and Alaric, King of the Visigoths, defeated the usurper Eugenius backed by the Frankish Master of the Soldiers Flavius Arbogast. The undisputable victory of the Christian Emperor Theodosius I, 'the Great', over the pagans Eugenius and Arbogast certainly cemented Christianity into the Eastern Roman Empire.

The way to deal with barbarian *foederati* evolved very progressively during the fifth century. After the Frigidus battle, Alaric had been shown to be a treacherous ally. He failed to take Constantinople in 400 and was pushed to the West where he succeeded in taking Rome in 410. The Western Roman Empire never recovered from this Visigothic invasion and had also to accept its military colonisation by the Burgundians and by the Franks during the fifth century. In contrast the Eastern Roman Empire has better managed the problem of these long-staying barbarian guests. The sad experience of the overthrow of the West by barbarian mercenaries was a good lesson to the East who almost had a comparable situation with the Generalissimo and Patrician Flavius Ardabur Aspar – the Imperial puppet-master from the 420s until his death in 471. So informed by the experience by early Byzantine era the Emperors distrusted barbarian auxiliaries and *foederati*, even if they were unable to do without them. Unlike their western counterparts in the 400s, Eastern Emperors no longer gave them high command and rarely made them generals.

After nearly a century of Ostrogothic occupation, in 488 Emperor Zeno persuaded Theodoric Master of the Soldiers, Consul and, above all, King of the Ostrogoths, to go to free Italy from the usurper Odoacer. This cynical and selfish strategy has resulted in the Eastern Roman Empire's avoidance of long-term military colonisation by Germanic barbarians; it was an existential and historical chance for Byzantium. The Romano-Byzantine Emperors chose to control the migratory flow and restrain the hierarchical influence of their often-gifted barbarian mercenaries. They did not any longer want to settle barbarian *foederati* in Imperial lands, a risky measure that had dismembered the Western Empire. Justinian I's *foederati* resided outside the borders or were scattered in small units far from their homeland. Later, in the 650s/660s, a few groups of Sklavenes were allowed to settle in Imperial territory, but this was rare and not without misfortune. Barbarian mercenaries remained a necessary evil as Byzantium was unable to find enough recruits within the Empire. The absence of any military conscription no doubt explains this apparent lack of manpower. Although the Byzantine sources were nearly always contemptuous of the barbarians, some, even those who were previously enemies, could reach the highest ranks of the Eastern Imperial Army. The Emperor ensured that there were not too many of them, because recognition of their merit did not come without a necessary distrust.

A sense of loyalty had also changed. Quick to sedition, the early Byzantine Army was reminiscent of its Roman ancestor from the third and fourth centuries. But the propensity of deserters to make common cause with barbarians was a completely new aspect. For a Gallic deserter to act as a spy for the Persians was a rare occurrence in the 360s, but by Justinian's reign, Imperial defectors to the Ostrogoths could number in the hundreds or thousands, after the final defeat. This betrayal, which was a novelty for these so-called 'Romans', can be explained by the contempt of political authorities for soldiers often forced to obey without being paid and obliged to live on the land from rapine. Moreover, western barbarians had changed because they were now settled on formerly Roman land such as Africa and Italy, and had often now become Latin speakers and become Christianised. Although sometimes Arians, these barbarians no longer seemed a radical enemy to the local Roman populations and even for Eastern Roman Armies who deliberately recruited them. Nevertheless, un-Romanised barbarians from the outer lands were still always considered a danger.

Cosmopolitan professional armies were the military model under Justinian and his successors to the bitter end. These armies included old and new Roman units with barbarian mercenaries organised into permanent troops and occasional levies. Cultural changes were important too. Latin disappeared from both the military language and the law after Heraclius' reign with the loss of Illyricum. Christianity had been dominant since the later Roman Empire, but far from weakening mentalities, as Edward Gibbon claimed, to the contrary Eastern Christianity adopted a hagiography in which armed saints abounded. A general turned into a monk, and then a monk turned into a general again, such as Philippicus in the late seventh century, had not been seen in late Roman era. The army was clearly a more Christian army and the militarisation of Christianity was one of the keys to Byzantium's survival.

From a crude military point of view, Romano-Byzantine soldiers and generals were more capable than their predecessors of the fifth century who had lost the West. Making war against Byzantium could have proved fatal and the Vandals and the Ostrogoths completely disappeared from history – amalgamated into the Empire rather than suffering genocide from it. With the exception of Heraclius, the Emperor did not lead the armies in person and relied on the skill of his generals. The latter's role was much more important than it had been during the time of the Republic or the Principate, because there was no longer a national constantly victorious order of battle over any enemy. Although tactically flexible, early Byzantine commanders used the classical and reliable infantry phalanx. They also better knew how to deal with camel-mounted enemies as the *Strategikon* well demonstrated.

There were two types of general: the 'soldier-general' and the 'courtier-general'. The first, famously exemplified by Belisarius or John Troglita, had only a dedicated military career and came from the palatine troops or the *bucellarii*, but did not rise from the ranks. The courtier-general was a skilful high-ranking official or a relative of the Emperor, typically the Emperor's brother. Byzantium had a galaxy of good generals during Justinian's I reign and, oddly, two of the best were eunuchs, including Narses, a septuagenarian. Discretionary Imperial favours could lead to the promotion of a formidable strategist such Narses the Eunuch but also a mean general like Theodore the Kouropalates, Heraclius's own brother. This latter type of general was responsible for defeats in the face of the early Islamic wars of conquest, but the task was a tough one. A eunuch general would have been unimaginable in the classical Roman period, even in the late Empire when this oriental fashion first appeared although not in the military. A remarkable paradox was that these warlike eunuchs contributed to the virile warrior mentality: Solomon through his taste for front-line combat, which cost him his life, and Narses, who was infuriated to see himself compared to a woman by the Empress. Generals of the 530s–590s were good professionals. The only Soldier-Emperor was in the 630s – the well-named Heraclius (strong as Hercules) who defeated the Persians as no other had done since Alexander the Great. Nevertheless, he went too far in his waging war and, like his illustrious role model, left a fragile Empire. Finally exhausted and ill, he proved incapable of stemming the Muslim Arab threat. The era of great generals was over but Heraclius' successors were not unworthy of their task and kept a smaller Empire alive for another 800 years.

Surprisingly, strategic theory was rather weak in early Byzantine military treatises. The *Strategikon* did not mention strategy and the *Peri Strategikes* did not go beyond a simplistic definition: 'strategy teaches us how to defend what is ours and to threaten what belongs to the enemy.'[1] Of course, early Byzantines did not ignore what strategy was. Theirs consisted of holding the crossing points, incoming valleys and rivers, and by fortifying major ports or large cities on the road network. Even 2,000km away, the Emperor was well informed about the state of places and the work that needed to be carried out.

The principle of having second-rate border garrisons and elite troops assembled in rear areas persisted for a long time. There were only three major strategic projects during the sixth and seventh centuries: Justinian I's reconquest of Africa, then of Italy, and Heraclius' counter-attack on the heart of the Persian Empire. The battles for reconquering the West were not easy, as the swift conquest of Africa was followed by years of instability, and it took 27 years to conquer Italy. Nevertheless, Justinian's Army defeated the Vandals and Ostrogoths, who the late Roman Empire had proved unable to defeat. Byzantium's Empire had few military resources to conquer, and then to control the entire Italian peninsula. The full reconquest of Italy was short-lived: only five years separated the defeat of Teias the last Ostrogothic

---

1   *Peri Strategikes*, 5, 1–2.

King and the Lombard invasion of 568. The Byzantines did more harm to Italy than the Ostrogoths!

The so-called Gothic War was a disaster for Italy, with the utter destruction of Milan while Rome was partially ruined and depopulated after three sieges and three invasions without combat. The Justinianic reconquest was not a revival of the former Roman Empire as the link between Roman West and East has been broken for more than a century. It was factually pure conquest and a harsh task to carry out because the Ostrogoths had firmly held and administered Italy. The Eastern Roman Empire was in Italy at the very peak of its strategic possibilities. It then reached the 'climax of the attack' as Clausewitz put it. In geopolitical terms, the 'reconquest' of Italy was a grandiose idea, but in economic terms and military sustainability it was a different story. Justinian behaved like a predator and completed the economic fall of the Roman civilisation that Theodoric had tried to maintain. The Italian/Roman economy no longer provided enough military resources to sustain itself fully. The *Exarchate* of Ravenna, from which the Imperial power clung on after 573, was reduced by the Lombards to a strip of land stretching from Ravenna to Rome, plus a few places scattered like confetti in the south of the peninsula, in Sicily, Corsica and Sardinia. The reconquest of Italy permanently drained military resources in the East, weakening the Eastern regions of the Balkans, while the transfer of elite units from the East disrupted the equilibrium inherited from the later Roman Empire.

Thereafter, the strategic situation became increasingly unbalanced. From the 530s, Byzantium had to fend off the beginning of a second wave of great invasions with the coming of the Sklavenes, a persistent enemy. By 568, the Germanic Lombards invaded Italy then in the 580s the Avars joined the Sklavenes in the Balkan region, bringing a body of barbarians to the gates of Byzantium. From the reign of Tiberius II, the Byzantine Empire became militarily outnumbered having to pay the Franks for a proxy war in Italy just to slow down the Lombards. The Byzantine state could not sustain war on three, or sometimes four, fronts, as demonstrated by the collapse of the Danubian and Persian borders in the 610s and 620s. The strategic situation had then worsened: civil war against the *exarch* of Africa then against Sklavenes, Avars and Persians attacking in effectively a vast pincer movement. The Roman Empire had never suffered from such a joint attack and Byzantium's survival during the siege of 626 was nothing short of miraculous. However, with Heraclius' zeal the Romano-Byzantine Army recovered and defeated the Persians. Heraclius' strategic choice of a total and final war with the Persian Empire led to temporarily vassalising it rather than maintaining a more sustainable balance of power. In doing so, he weakened his own Empire to such an extent that, 15 years later, it had lost Syria, Palestine, Mesopotamia and Egypt, changing the geopolitical and religious map for 14 centuries – even up to today. As a new sword thrown into the balance of arms, the Arabs destroyed a balance that was uneasy to maintain: *Vae victis*!

Geography and distances, which had been fairly well mastered up until Justinian I, were now working against the Eastern Roman Empire. This discontinuous territorial mosaic was overstretched by Justinian as well as the military effort. Later, the loss of Illyricum to the Sklavenes broke the geographic continuity with Italy. It dried up a pool of Latin-speaking recruits and over-Hellenised the Eastern Roman Empire. The loss of Syria, Palestine and then Egypt severed the land link with Tripolitania and Libya, giving the opportunity for a Muslim thalassocracy to emerge – it was a new threat to the communications with Africa and Italy and, in 673, to Byzantium itself. Twenty-four years later, the Imperial Province of Africa fell to the Arabs. As the territorial base was reduced, the Imperial Treasury and Army lost a large part of their resources in terms of both money and men. By the standards of the former Eastern late Roman Army as it stood *c.* 400, almost 200 Roman units disappeared along with their territorial base, approximatively 40 percent of the total. The Empire was now left with only a Hellenic bastion corresponding to Byzantium, coastal Thrace, Greece, the islands of the Eastern Mediterranean plus Anatolia and a piece of Armenia. After Heraclius's reign, the loss of the richest provinces in the East meant that previous model of army could no longer be funded. The military therefore adopted a regional organisation with professional troops reinforced by reservists organised into militias. Only the theme of the *Opsikion* and its elite mobile troops maintained, under a different name, what had been the corps of palatine troops under the master of the soldiers present. This army ceased to be Romano-Byzantine and became truly Byzantine, but did not break up. In fact, the Byzantine Army between 476 and 641 simply evolved.

Colour Plate Commentaries

Plate A. The Theodosian Walls were built in the Fifth century to protect the northwestern approaches. They are the greatest achievement of military architecture, as they withstood all assaults for a thousand years until the city was taken in 1453, thanks to powerful artillery and negligence. The Crusaders' entry into Constantinople in 1204 was due to internal treachery and military errors. This defensive effectiveness was due to the general layout of these lines of fortification; a quadruple barrier, consisting of a water-filled moat, a low stopping wall, and a double stepped wall with square and some hemispherical towers, interspersed along the intermediary wall, the latter covering the other defences with their height and larger towers. Walls and towers are crenelated. The solidity of the construction should be noted, as it combines cut stone with layers of bricks, which allowed for shock absorption, as Vitruvius explained in his *De Architectura*. Today, the Theodosian Walls have been partially restored in the city now called Istanbul.

Plate B. Iustiniana Prima, today, the site of Caričin Grad is an archaeological site which is located in the south of Serbia, 30 km southwest of Leskovac at the confluence of two rivers. It was identified by John of Antioch as Bederiana, the birthplace of Justin I, renamed as Justinian and the archdiocese of all Illyricum was established there by April 535. Measuring only about 10 hectares, it was nevertheless the key fortress of Illyricum.

Plate C. Bochas a Hunnic *doryphoros* from the *bucellarii* of Belisarius. He was fighting with the bow during the siege of Rome in 537 and was an elite heavy cavalryman, with all the weaponry. After Procopius, *BP*, I, 1, 12–13. His helmet is a 450–480s Spangenhelm from Gültlingen, and is in the Landesmuseum Württemberg in Stuttgart, Germany. Umutkor collar, a Fifth-century Hunnic gold collar, Kyrgyzstan (auction). See Plate 33 for reconstructed lamellar armour.

Plate D. Late Sixth century cataphract. This heavy cavalryman wears a *zaba* (long hauberk) under an Avar kaftan, which is probably the origin of today's traditional Greek Sarakatsani shepherd's felt woollen cloak. After

Maurice's *Strategikon* and the Sassanid cataphract relief of Taq-e-Bostan, Iran. See Plate 37 for detailed description.

Plate E. Seventh century infantryman from Syria. A leather *subalare babylonicum* (Babylonian harness) keeps his chain mail stable on his white *subarmalis*, a sort of buff coat with pteruges/pteryges. There are no classicising or esthetical effects as in the silver Cyprus plates. After a lost Syrian mosaic showing the fight between David and Goliath, a recurrent theme in early Byzantine art. See Plate 42.

Plate F. Macrobius, who died in Florence in 547 was a *primicerius* or junior officer from the *Primi Theodosiani*, an elite *auxilium palatinum* unit created under Emperor Theodosius I (died in 395). Near 400 this unit served under the command of the first master of the soldiers in the Imperial Presence (*Magister Militum Praesentalis I*). Under Justinian, this unit simply called a *numerus* was sent to reconquer Italy. After *Notitia Dignitatum*, OR.V.64 and *CIL*, XI, 1693 = *ILCV*, I, 486; *ILS*, 2806. Macrobius is wearing a Spangenhelm-type helmet, also used by Western Germanic chiefs but Byzantine-made and often sold to them. The white sash around his chest identifies him as a junior officer, a distinctive mark often seen on later Byzantine mosaics for military Saints, like in the Tenth century mosaic of Saint Merkourios at Hosios Loukas in Greece or, also, in the Eleventh century Saint George icon, at Vatopedi Monastery, Mount Athos, Greece. He wears an iron scale armour as shown in the mosaic with Melchizedek offering Abraham bread and wine basilica Santa Maria Maggiore in Rome. It is a common mistake among reenactors of the late Roman army or its Byzantine successor, to depict two-tone shafts for spears. In the vignettes in the *Notitia Dignitatum*, spear shafts are monochrome, but some have grooves. This is a way of representing a crossed leather-covered shaft, a practice always found on some Renaissance or Seventeenth century halberds. The shaft is thus less slippery to handle, especially if there is flowing blood... The spearhead's shape allows for the cutting of hamstrings from behind during combat, making it an infantry weapon. Its shape is frequent in the 200–400s Nydam Mose bog deposits, suggesting a Germanic origin, but the reverse is still possible as many Roman weapons were found in this very place. Such spearheads are shown with Roman soldiers according to the manuscript Vaticanus Vergilius, fol 73v, depicting the Trojan Council. Spearhead from an auction R287 Time Vault Gallery.

Plate G. Byzantine footman in Lazica from the second half of the Sixth century. He is wearing a Batoumi-Staritsa hemispherical or conical type helmet, common in Russia, and Central Asia during this period. Most of these Asian or Slavic helmets have a mail aventail. The figure is from a find in Petra fortress. After the Byzantine Siverik mosaic in Turkey; A.L. Kubik, O.A. Radyuš, L.A. Vyazov, 'On one series of the VI century AD Iron One-Piece Asian Helmets', *Bulletin of the Institute of Oriental Studies*, 3(1) (2023), pp. 52–82. Many weapons were taken from Persians after the fall of Petra according to Procopius, probably including mercenaries like Huns, after Procopius, *BG*, VIII, 12, 17. The soldier is from the *Prima Armeniaca*, First Armenian, a *pseudocomitatensis* legion under the control of soldiers to the East. The blue symbol is a *peltè* (lunar shield), once used by Hellenistic light infantry called peltasts and linked to the Amazon in Classic artworks. He is wearing a Sassanid longsword and battleaxe. After *Notitia Dignitatum*, OR.VII.13=49.

Plate H. Sixth/Seventh century foot archer. This foot archer has a composite bow, no quiver, arrows in the belt, breeches tied above the knees and a *spatha* long sword.

Bibliography

Abbreviations

AE	Année épigraphie
Aed.	*Aedificiis* from Procopius
AFAM	Association française d'Archéologie Mérovingienne
AH	*Hijri* year (*Anno Hegirae*) which begins on 16 July 622 in the Gregorian calendar and is based on lunar months
AG	Year of the Greeks (*Annum Graecorum*) instituted by the Seleucids (1 October 312 BC)
AJA	*American Journal of Archaeology*
AM	Year of the World (*Annum Mundi*) since the creation of the World according to the Bible
Ant tard	*L'Antiquité tardive*
ARB-AFAM	M. Kazanski, F. Vallet F. (eds), *L'armée romaine et les Barbares du IIIe siècle au VIe siècle*, Colloque international organisé à Saint-Germain-en-Laye, 1990 (Association française d'Archéologie Mérovingienne et Société des Amis du Musée des Antiquités Nationales, t. 5 des Mémoires publiés par l'Association française d'Archéologie Mérovingienne: 1993)
BAR	British Archaeological Reports
BCH	Bulletin de Correspondance Hellénique
BG	*Bellum Gothicum* from Procopius of Caesarea, Books V to VIII of *The History of the Wars*
BGU	*Ægyptische Urkunden aus den königlichen Museen zu Berlin, Griesche Urkunden*, I-IV (Berlin: 1895-)
BIFAO	*Bulletin de l'Institut français d'archéologie orientale*
Brev.	*Breviarium* from Nikephoros of Constantinople
BP	*Bellum Persicum* from Procopius of Caesarea, Books I to II of *The History of the Wars*
BV	*Bellum Vandalum* from Procopius of Caesarea, Books III to IV of *The History of the Wars*
BZ	*Byzantinische Zeitschrift*
CCSL	*Corpus Christianorum Series Latina* (Turnhout: Brepols, 1945-)

ChLA	*Chartae Latinae antiquiores* A. Bruckner, R. Marichal (eds), papyrus and parchments before 800, 49 vols
Chr.	*Chronicle from* Fredegar, Joshua the Stylite, Count Marcellinus (Marcellinus Comes)
Chr. 754	Mozarabic Chronicle from 754
Chr.VT	*Chr. continuans Victorem Tunnunensem* from John of Biclaro.
Chrgr.	*Chronographia* from John Malalas or Theophanes Confessor.
CEFR	Collection de l'École Française de Rome
CFHB	*Corpus Fontium Historiae Byzantinae* (1967-)
CIG	*Corpus Inscriptionum Graecorum* (Berlin, 1828–1877)
CIL	*Corpus Inscriptionum Latinarum* (Berlin: 1863-)
CJ	*Codex Iustinianus* in *Corpus Iuris Civilis*, P. Krüger, Th. Mommsen (eds), (Berlin: Weidmann, reprint 1970–1973, 2 vols)
CNRS	Centre National de la Recherche Scientifique
CQ	Classical Quarterly
CR	Classical Review
CRAI	Comptes rendus des séances de l'année. Académie des Inscriptions et Belles-Lettres
CSEL	*Corpus Scriptorum Ecclesiasticorum Latinorum* (Vienna: 1866-)
CSCO	*Corpus Scriptorum Christianorum Orientalium* (Paris: 1903-)
CSHB	*Corpus Scriptorum Historiae Byzantinae*
CSM	*Corpus Scriptorum Muzarabicorum*, Insituto Antonio de Nebrija, Madrid
CTh	*Codex Theodosianus*, Th. Mommsen (ed.), (Berlin: 1904–1905).
CUF	*Collection des Universités de France*, associated to *LBL*
DBG	*De Bello Gallico* from Julius Caesar
DOP	*Dumbarton Oaks Papers*
DRM	*De Re Militari* from Vegetius
Ed. Anast.	Emperor Anastasius (edict on Libya Pentapolis), *Die vom Kaiser Anastasius fur Libya Pentapolis erlassenen Formae*, K. E. Zakariä von Lingenthal (ed.), (Berlin: *Monatsberichte der k. Akademie der Wissenschaften zu Berlin*, 1879), pp.134–158
EFR	École Française de Rome
EH	Hispanic era (38 years longer than the Julian Calendar).
Ep.H	*Epitome Historiarum* from Zonaras
Ep.	*Epistulae* (Letters) from Sidonius Apollinaris or Gregory the Great
Exc.	*Excerpta Valesiana*, extracts from Anonymus Valesianus, *pars posterior*
Fragm.	*Fragmenta* (fragments)
FHG	*Fragmenta Historicorum Graecorum*, 4, K. Müller (ed.), (Paris: Firmin Didot, 1848–1870)
GRBS	*Greek, Roman and Byzantine Studies*
HE	*Historia Ecclesiastica* from Evagrius Scholasticus, John of Ephesus, (Pseudo-)Zachariah Rhetor
HF	*Historia Francorum from* Gregory of Tours

Hist.	*Historiae* from Agathias, Isidore of Seville, Sebeos
HL	*Historia Langobardorum* from Paul the Deacon
HU	*Historia Universalis* from Theophylact Simocatta
IBLA	*Institut des Belles Lettres Arabes*
IGLS	*Inscriptions grecques et latines de la Syrie*, Paris, Librairie Orientaliste Paul Geuthner, Bibliothèque archéologique et historique, 1929–2009
I Prusias	Inscriptions from Prusias
Joh	*Johannis* (*Johannide* in French) *from* Corippus
JRS	*Journal of Roman Studies*
Kitab	*Futuh al-Bouldan* from al-Baladhur
LBL	*Les Belles Lettres*, Paris
LPR	*Liber Pontificalis sive vitae Pontificum Ravennatum* from Andreas Agnellus of Ravenna (also known as *Breviarium Ecclesiae Ravennatis*).
MAMA	*Monumenta Asiae Minoris Antiqua* (Oxford: 1928–2014, 11 vols)
MEFR	*Mélanges de l'École Française de Rome*
MGH	*Monumenta Germaniae Historica*, G. H. Pertz et al (eds), (Berlin/ Munich/ Hanover: 1823–1874)
	Online version in digitalen *Monumenta Germaniae Historica* (dMGH):
	https://www.dmgh.de
MIFAO	Mémoire de l'Institut Français d'archéologie orientale
Nov. J.	*Novellae Justiniani* in *Corpus Iuris Civilis*, t. 3, R. Schoell, G. Kroll (eds), (Berlin: 1895)
Op.Chr.	Elias of Nisibis, *Opus Chronologicum*
O&M	*Orient & Méditerranée*
P. Brit.	*Greek papyri in the British Museum*, F. G. Kenyon (ed.), (London: British Museum, Dept. of Manuscripts, 1893)
P. Caire	*Papyrus grecs d'époque Byzantine*, J. Maspéro (ed.), I and II (Cairo: Catalogue général des antiquités égyptiennes du Musée du Caire, n°67 001–67 187, 1910–1912)
P. Ital.	*Die nichtliterarischen lateinischen Papyri Italiens aus der Zeit 445–700*, J. O. Tjäder (ed.), (Lund: *Papyri* 1–28, 1955, tome I; Stokholm: *Papyri* 29–59, 1982, tome II)
P. Monac	*Byzantinische Papyri in der Königlichen Hof und Staatsbibliothek zu München*, A. Heisenberg., L. Wenger (eds), (Leipzig-Berlin: 1914)
PL	*Patrologia Latina*, J. P. Migne (ed.), (Paris: Jacques-Paul Migne Imprimerie catholique, 1841–1865, 221 vols)
	Online version in *Documenta Catholica Omnia*:
	http://www.documentacatholicaomnia.eu/25_10_MPL.html
PEFR	Publications de l'École Française de Rome.
PG	*Patrologia graeca*, J. P. Migne (ed.), (Paris: Jacques-Paul Migne Imprimerie catholique, 1857–1866, 161 vols)
	Online version in *Patrologia Graeca*:
	https://patrologia.graeca.org/phd/apix/jsasync/pg_https.html

	http://patristica.net/graeca/
PLRE	A. H. M. Jones, J. R. Martindale, J. Morris, *The Prosopography of the Later Roman Empire* (Cambridge: Cambridge University Press (years 260–395) tome 1, 1971, tome 2 (395–527) 1980, tome 3 (526–641) 1992)
	Online version in Internet Archive archive.org:
	Vol. 1 https://archive.org/details/prosopography-later-roman-empire/PLRE-I/.
	Vol. 2 https://archive.org/details/prosopography-later-roman-empire/PLRE-II/.
	Vol. 3 a https://archive.org/details/prosopography-later-roman-empire/PLRE-III-A/.
	Vol. 3 b https://archive.org/details/prosopography-later-roman-empire/PLRE-III-B/.
PO	*Patrologia Orientalis*, R., Graffin, F. Nau (eds), (Paris: Firmin Didot; Turnhout: Brepols, 1899-)
	Online version in Tertullian.org:
	https://www.tertullian.org/fathers/patrologia_orientalis_toc.htm.
P. Oxy.	*The Oxyrhynchus Papyri* published by the Egypt Exploration Society in *Graeco-Roman Memoirs* (London: 1898–2020, 85 vols. The vol. quoted in this book is B. P. Grenfell, A. S. Hunt, H. I. Bell (eds), *The Oxyrhynchus papyri*, XVI, 1924)
REA	Revue des Études Anciennes
REB	Revue des Études Byzantines
REG	Revue des Études grecques
REL	Revue des Études Latines
REMA	Revue des Études militaires anciennes
RG	*Res Gestae* from Ammianus Marcellinus.
RH	*Revue Historique*
SC	*Sources Chrétiennes*, Le Cerf
Tarikh	*al-Rusul wa al-Muluk* from Tabari
TTH	*Translated Texts for Historians* (Liverpool University Press).
VE	*Variae Epistulae from* Cassiodorus

Note regarding Sources

Most ancient authors have digital original versions or translations available in the public domain: Internet Archive, archive.org, Academia.edu, Dokumen, The Online Books Page, Perseus Digital Library, The Internet Classic Archive, The Project Gutenberg eBook, The Latin Library, Corpus Scriptorum Latinorum forumromanorum.org, Digital Fragmenta Historicarum Graecorum.

1, Latin and Greek sources

Acta Sancti Anastasii Persae (B. Flusin, ed.), *Saint Anastase le Perse et l'histoire de la Palestine au début du VIIe siècle, Le texte*, vol. 1 (Paris: édition du *CNRS*, 1992)

Agathias (R. Keydell, ed.), *Agathiæ Myrinæi Historiarum libri quinque* (Berlin: De Gruyter, *CFHB*, 2, 1967)

Agathias (S. Costanza, ed.), *Agathiæ Myrinæi Historiarum libri quinque* (Messina: Biblioteca di Helikon, Testi e Studi, 7, Università degli Studi, 1969)

Agathias (translated into English by J. D. C. Frendo), *The Histories* (Berlin, New York: De Gruyter, 1975)

Agathias (translated into French by P. Maraval), *Histoires. Guerres et malheurs du temps de Justinien* (Paris: *LBL*, La Roue à Livres, 2007)

Andreas Agnellus of Ravenna (G. Rabotti, C. Curradi, A. Vasina, eds), *Breviarium Ecclesiae Ravennatis (Codice Bavaro) secoli 7–10* (Rome: Istituto Storico Italiano per il Medioevo, Nella sede dell'Istituto, 1985)

Andreas Agnellus of Ravenna (translated into English by D. Mauskopf Deliyannis), *The Book of Pontiffs of the Church of Ravenna* (Washington: Catholic University of America Press, 2004)

Anonymus Valesianus (Th. Mommsen, ed.), *Origo Constantini imperatoris sive Anonymi Valesiani pars prior; Anonymi Valesiani pars posterior*, (Berlin: Weidmann, *MGH*, 9.1, Auctores Antiquissimi, Chronica minora Sæc. IV.V.VI.VII, 1961), pars prior, pp.7–11, pars posterior, pp.306–328

Anonymus Valesianus (translated into English by J. C. Rolfe), *The Excerpts of Valesius*, in *Ammianus Marcellinus*, 3rd edition (London: Heinemann, Loeb Classical Library; Cambridge (Massachusetts): Harvard University Press, 1986), pp.506–569

Anonymus Valesianus (I. König, ed.), *Excerpta Valesiana, pars posterior* in *Aus der Zeit Theoderichs der Grossen. Einleitung, Text, Übersetzung und Kommentar einer anonymen Quelle* (Darmstadt: Wissenschaftliche Buchgesellschaft, 1997)

Arrian (R. Hercher A. Eberhard, eds), *Arriani Nicomediensis Scripta Minora* (Leipzig: Teubner, 2008)

Athenaeus Mechanicus (R. Schneider, ed.), *Griechische Poliorketiker*, vol. III (Berlin: Weidmann, 1912)

Athenaeus Mechanicus (translated into French by M. de Rochas d'Aiglun), *Traduction du traité des machines* (Paris: Ernest Thorin, 1884)

Athenaeus Mechanicus (translated into English by D. Whitehead & P. H. Blyth), *On Machines*, (Stuttgart: Franz Steiner Verlag *Historia-Einzelschrift*, 182, 2004).

(Saint) Augustine of Hippo (J. P. Migne, ed.), *Opera omnia*, (Paris: Jacques-Paul Migne Imprimerie catholique, *PL*, 32–47, 1841–1849).

(Saint) Augustine of Hippo (translated into French by J. B. F. Poujoulat & Abbot Raulx), *Oeuvres complètes de Saint Augustin* (Bar-le-Duc:1864–1872)

BIBLIOGRAPHY

Cassiodorus (Th. Mommsen, L. Traube, eds), *Cassiodori Senatoris Variæ* (Berlin: Weidmann, *MGH* 12, *Auctores Antiquissimi*, 1898)

Cassiodorus (Th. Mommsen, ed.), *Cassiodori Senatoris Chronica* (Berlin: Weidmann, *MGH*, 11, *Auctores Antiquissimi, Chronica minora sæcula* IV, V, VI, VII, 1961), pp.109–161

Cassiodorus (A. J., Fridh, ed.), *Magni Aurelii Cassiodori Variarum Libri XII* (Turnhout: Brepols, *CCSL*, 96, 1973)

Cassiodorus (S. J. B. Barnish, ed.), *The Variæ of Magnus Aurelius Cassiodorus Senator* (Liverpool: Liverpool University Press, *TTH*, 12, 1992)

Caesar (translated into French and commented by L. A. Constans), *La guerre des Gaules* (Paris: *LBL*, *CUF*, 1967)

Caesar (translated into English by C. Hammond), *Caesar: The Gallic War* (Oxford: Oxford University Press, 1996)

(Mommsen, Th., ed.), *Chronica Gallica of 452* and *Chronica Gallica of 511* [Anonymous Latin chronicle written in Gaul *c.* 452 and 511], *Chronica Gallica a. CCCCLII et DXI* (Berlin: Weidmann, *MGH*, 9.1, *Auctores Antiquissimi, Chronica minora sæcula IV, V, VI, VII*, 1961), pp.615–666

(Burgess, R., ed.), *Chronica Gallica of 452* [Anonymous Latin chronicle written in Gaul from 379 to 452], *The Gallic Chronicle of 452 A New Critical Edition with a Brief Introduction*, in R.W. Mathisen, D. Shanzer (eds), *Society and Culture in Late Antique Gaul. Revisiting the Sources* (Aldershot: Ahsgate, 2001), pp.52 seq

(Burgess, R., ed.), *Chronica Gallica of 511* [Anonymous Latin chronicle written in Gaul *c.* 452 and 511], *The Gallic Chronicle of 511: A New Critical Edition with a Brief Introduction*, in Mathisen R.W., Shantzer D. (eds), *Society and Culture in Late Antique Gaul: Revisiting the Sources*, (Aldershot: Ahsgate, 2001), pp.85–100

(Batista Rodríguez, J. J., Blanco Silva, R., eds), 'Un cronica mozarabe a la que se dado en llamar Arabigo-bizantina y una traduccion', (*Rivista de Filología de la Universidad de la Laguna* 17, 1999), pp.153–167

(Mommsen, Th., ed.), *Chronicle of 754* [Anonymous Mozarabic Latin chronicle from 610 to 754], *Continuatio Isidoriana Hispana a. DCCLIV* (Munich: Weidmann, *MGH*, *Auctores Antiquissimi*, 11.2, 1981), pp.323–368

(Gil, J., ed.), *Chronicle of 754* [Anonymous Mozarabic Latin chronicle from 610 to 754], *Chronica Muzarabica* (Madrid: Instituto Antonio de Nebrija, *CSM*, 1, 1973)

(Lopez Pereira, J. E., ed.), *Chronicle of 754* [Anonymous Mozarabic Latin chronicle from 610 to 754], *Cronica mozarabe de 754: edicion crítica y traduccion*, (Zaragoza: Anúbar, 1980)

Chronicle of 754 [Anonymous Mozarabic Latin chronicle from 610 to 754] (translated into English by K. B. Wolf), in *Conquerors and Chroniclers of Early Medieval Spain* (Liverpool, Liverpool University Press, *TTH*, 9, 1999), pp.111–160

(Mommsen, Th., ed.), *Chronicle of 741* [Anonymous Latin chronicle written in Spain *c.* 741], *Continuatio Byzantina-Arabica a DDCXLI* (Berlin: Weidmann, *MGH*, *Auctores Antiquissimi*, 11.2, 1981), pp.323–359

Chronicon Paschale (translated into Latin by J. P. Migne), *Paschalion, seu, Chronicon Paschale* (Paris: Jacques-Paul Migne Imprimerie catholique, PG, 92, 1860)

Chronicon Paschale (translated into English by M. Whitby), *Chronicon Paschale. 284–628 AD*, (Liverpool: Liverpool University Press, TTH, 7, 2007)

Claudius Ptolemy (translated into German by Stückelberger A. et al), *Klaudios Ptolémaios Handbuch der Geographie* (Basel: Schwabe Verlag, 2006), 2 vols

Constantine VII Porphyrogenitus (translated into French by A. Vogt), *Livre des cérémonies*, Books 1–2 (Paris: *LBL*, Collection Byzantine, 2006)

Constantine VII Porphyrogenitus (translated into English by A. Moffatt & M. Tall), *The Book of Ceremonies in 2 volumes,* from *CSHB*, J. J. Reiske Bonn, Weber, 1829–1830 edition (Canberra: Australian Association for Byzantine Studies, *Byzantina Australiensia*, 18, 2012).

Corippus (I. Diggle, F. R. D. Goodyear, eds), Flavii Cresconi Corippi Iohannidos seu de bellis libycis libri VIII (Cambridge: Cambridge, University Press, 1970)

Corippus (translated into English by A. Cameron), *In laudem Iustini Augusti minoris libri IV* (London: University of London, The Athlone Press, 1976)

Corippus (translated into French by S. Antès), *Éloge de l'empereur Justin II* (Paris: *LBL, CUF*, 2002)

Corippus (translated into French by S. Antès), *Panégyrique d'Anastasius. Éloge de Justin II* (Paris: *LBL, CUF*, 1981)

Corippus (M. A. Vinchesi, ed.), *Flavii Cresconi Corippi Iohannidos liber primus* (Naples: M. d'Auria editore, 1983)

Corippus (translated into French by J. C. Didderen), *La Johannide ou sur les guerres de Libye* (Paris: Errances, 2007)

Cyril of Scythopolis (E. Schwartz, ed.), *Cyrilli Vita S. Sabae* (Leipzig: J. C. Hinrich Verlag, 1939)

(Delehaye, H., ed.), Synaxarium Ecclesiae Constantinopolitanae (Brussels: Propylaeum ad Acta Sanctorum, 1902)

Diocletian (Emperor) (translated into English by A. Kropff), *An English Translation of the Edict on Maximum Prices, also known as the Price Edict of Diocletian (Edictum de pretiis rerum venalium)* (Published at Academia.edu April 27, 2016)

Elias of Nisibis (translated into Latin by E.W. Brooks), *Eliæ Metropolitæ Nisibeni Opus Chronologicum, pars prior* (Rome, Paris, Leipzig: *CSCO, Scriptores Syri*, 3, 7, 1910)

Ennodius of Pavia (W. A. Hartel, ed.), *Opera Omnia* (Vienna: C. Gerold, 1882)

Eugippius (Ph. Régérat, ed.), *Vie de Saint Séverin* (Paris: Le Cerf, SC, 374, 1991)

Evagrius Scholasticus (J. Bidez, L. Parmentier, eds), *The Ecclesiastical History of Evagrius* (London: Methuen, 1898)

Evagrius Scholasticus (translated into French by A. J. Festugière), *Histoire ecclésiastique* (*Byzantium*, 45, 1975), pp.187–488

Fredegar (B. Krusch, ed.), *Fredegarii Scholastici libri IV cum Continuationibus* (Berlin: Weidmann, *MGH, Scriptores Rerum Merovingicarum, Fredegarii et aliorum Chronica. Vitæ Sanctorum*, 2, 1888), pp.1–193

Fredegar (translated into English by J. M. Wallace-Hadrill), *The Fourth Book of the Chronicle of Fredegar with its Continuations* (London: Greenwood Press, 1981)

Fredegar (translated into French by O. Devillers & J. Meyers), *Frédégaire, Chronique des temps mérovingiens* (Turnhout: Brepols, 2001)

George Kedrenos/Cedrenus (I. Becker, ed.), *Compendium Historiarum*, vol. 1 (Bonn: Weber, *CSHB*, 4, 1838–1839), 2 vols

George of Pisidia (translated into Latin by J. P. Migne, ed.), *Georgius Pisida, Diaconus Constantinopolitanus, opera omnia* (Paris: Jacques-Paul Migne Imprimerie catholique, *PG*, 92, 1860), *De Heraclii Expeditione Persica*, col. 1198–1262, *Bellum Avaricum*, col. 1263–1297, *Heraclias*, col. 1298–1334

George of Pisidia (A. Pertusi, ed.), *Giorgio di Pisidia. Poemi. I. Panegirici epici* (Ettal: Buch-Kunst-Verlag, *Studia Patristica et Byzantina*, 7, 1959)

Gregory I the Great (L. M. Hartmann, ed.), *Gregorii I Papæ Registrum Epistolarum* (Berlin: Weidmann, *MGH, Epistolæ*, 2.34, 1899)

Gregory I the Great (translated into French by P. Minard), *Registre des lettres (livres I et II)* (Paris: Le Cerf, 1991)

Gregory of Tours (B. Krusch, W. Levison, eds), *Gregori Turonensis Opera. Teil 1. Libri Historiarum X*, 3 t. (Hanover: Hahn, *MGH, Scriptores rerum Merovingicarum* 1.1, 1993)

Gregory of Tours (translated into French by H. Latouche), *Histoire des Francs* (Paris: *LBL*, Les Classiques de l'Histoire de France au Moyen Âge, 1995)

Gregory of Tours (Dom Bouquet, ed., translated into French by F. Guizot), *Histoire des Francs, Œuvres complètes*, tome 1, Livres I à V, tome 2, Livres VI à X (Clermont-Ferrand: Paléo, L'Encyclopédie médiévale, 2001)

Gregory of Tours (translated into French by J. J. E. Roy), *L'Histoire des rois Francs par Gregory of Tours*, Paris: Gallimard, *NRF*, L'Aube des peuples, 2006)

Hierocles (E. Honigmann, ed.), *Le Synecdèmos d'Hiéroclès et l'opuscule géographique de George de Cyprus* (Brussells: Éditions de l'Institut de Philologie et d'Histoire orientales et Slaves, 1939)

Hydatius (translated into English by R. Burgess), *The Chronicle of Hydatius and the Chronica Constantinopolitana: Two Contemporary Accounts of the Final Years of the Roman Empire* (Oxford: Oxford University Press, 1999)

Isidore of Seville (translated into English by St. A. Barney, W. J. Lewis, J. A. Beach & O. Berghof), *The Etymologies of Isidore of Seville* (Cambridge: Cambridge University Press, 2006).

Isidore of Seville (translated into Spanish by J. Oroz Reta, M. A. Marcos Casquero), *Etimologías* (Madrid: Biblioteca de Autores Cristianos, 2009)

Isidore of Seville (J. P. Migne ed.), *Historia de regibus Gothorum, Wandalorum et Suevorum* (Paris: Jacques-Paul Migne Imprimerie catholique, *PL*, 83, 1862), col. 1057–1082

Isidore of Seville (Th. Mommsen, ed.), *Historia Gothorum, Wandalorum et Sueborum* (Berlin: Weidmann, *MGH, Auctores Antiquissimi, Chronica minora sæc. IV. V. VI. VII.*, 11, 1894), pp.241–390

Isidore of Seville (translated into French by N. Desgrugillers), *Chronique Universelle. Histoire de l'Espagne wisigothique*, tomes 1 and 2 (Clermont-Ferrand: Paléo, L'Encyclopédie médiévale, 2009)

Isidore of Seville (translated into French by N. Desgrugillers), *Le Livre des Hommes Illustres. Histoire de l'Espagne wisigothique*, tome 3 (Clermont-Ferrand: Paléo, L'Encyclopédie médiévale, 2009)

Jean de Joinville (J. Martin, ed.), *Vie de Saint Louis* (Paris: Le Livre de Poche, Lettres Gothiques, 1995)

(Saint) Jerome of Stridon (translated into French by J. Labourt), *Correspondance* (Paris: *LBL, CUF*, 2002), 8 vols.

John of Antioch (K. Müller, ed.), *Fragmenta* (Paris: Firmin Didot, *FHG*, 4, 1851), pp.535–662; 5 (1870), pp.27–38

John of Antioch (translated into English by S. Mariev, ed.), *Ioannis Antiocheni fragmenta quae supersunt omnia* (Berlin, New York: De Gruyter, *CFHB – Series Berolinensis*, 47, 2008)

John of Biclaro (Th. Mommsen, ed.), *Chr. continuans Victorem Tunnunensem* (Berlin: Weidmann, *MGH, Auctores Antiquissimi*, 11.1, 1961), pp.211–220

John of Biclaro (translated into English by K. B. Wolf, ed.), *Conquerors and Chroniclers of Early Medieval Spain* (Liverpool: Liverpool University Press, *TTH*, 9, 1991)

John of Epiphania (C. Müller, ed.), *Fragmenta* (Paris: Firmin Didot, *FHG*, 4, 1851), pp.272–276

John the Lydian (R. Wünsch, ed.), *De Magistratibus* (Leipzig: Teubner, 1963)

John the Lydian (translated into English by T. F. Carney), *John the Lydian. On the Magistracies of the Roman Constitution (De Magistratibus)*, (Sydney: Coronado Press, 1971)

John the Lydian (translated into English by A. C. Bandy), *Joannes Lydus. On Powers or The Magistracies of the Roman State* (Philadelphia: American Philosophical Society, 1983)

John Malalas (L. Dindorf, ed.), *Ioannis Malalae Chronographia* (Bonn: Weber, *CSHB*, 32, 1831)

John Malalas (E. Jeffreys, R. Scott, eds), *The Chronicle of John Malalas* (Melbourne: Australian Association for Byzantine Studies, *Byzantina Australiensa*, 4, 1986)

Jordanes (Th. Mommsen, ed.), *Iordanis Romana et Getica* (Berlin: Weidmann, *MGH, Auctores Antiquissimi*, 5.1, 1882)

Jordanes (translated into French by O. Devillers), *Histoire des Goths* (Paris: *LBL*, La Roue à Livres, 1995)

(Kenyon, F. G., ed.), *Greek papyri in the British Museum* (London: British Museum, Dept. of Manuscripts, 1893)

(Kraemer, G. J., ed.), *Excavations at Nessana, III, Non-literary papyri* (Princeton: Princeton University Press, 2016)

(Krueger, P., ed.), *Justinian Code, Codex Justinianus* (Berlin: Weidmann, 1877)

Leo VI the Wise, the Tactician (translated into Latin by J. P. Migne) *Taktika* (Paris: Jacques-Paul Migne Imprimerie catholique, *PG*, 107, 1863), col. 669–1116

Leo VI the Wise (translated into English by G. T. Dennis), *The Taktika of Leo VI, Text, Translation and Commentary*, *CFHB*, 49 (Washington: John Duffy, 2010)

Liudprand of Cremona (E. Dümmler, ed.), *Relatio de legatione constantinopolitana* (Hanover: Hahn, *MGH*, *Scriptores rerum Germanicarum*, 41, 1877), pp.124–136.

Liudprand of Cremona (translated into English by J. J. Norwich), *Liudprand of Cremona: The Embassy to Constantinople and Other Writings* (London: Rutland, 1993), pp.177–210.

Malchus of Philadelphia (K. Müller, ed.), *Fragmenta* (Paris: Firmin Didot, *FHG*, 4, 1851), pp.111–132

Malchus of Philadelphia (translated into English by R. C. Blockley), *The Fragmentary Classicising Historians of the Later Roman Empire: Eunapius, Olympiodorus, Priscus and Malchus*, 2 (Cambridge: Francis Cairns Publications, ARCA Classical and Medieval Texts, Papers and Monographs, 10, 2007)

Marcellinus Comes (Th. Mommsen, ed.), *Chr.* (Berlin: Weidmann, *MGH*, *Auctores Antiquissimi*, 11.2, 1961), pp.37–108

Marcellinus Comes (Th. Mommsen, ed., translated into English by B. Croke), *The Chronicle of Marcellinus: A Translation and Commentary (with a reproduction of Mommsen's edition of the Text) by Comes Marcellinus* (Sydney: Australian Association for Byzantine Studies, 1995)

Marius Aventicensis (translated into French by N. Desgrugillers), *Chronique 455–581 suivie de sa Continuation jusqu'à l'année 615* (Clermont-Ferrand: Paléo, L'Encyclopédie médiévale, 2007)

(Maspéro, J., ed.), *Papyrus grecs d'époque Byzantine*, I and II (Cairo: Catalogue général des antiquités égyptiennes du Musée du Caire, no. 67 001–67 187, 1910–1912)

Maurice (translated into English by G. T. Dennis), *Maurice's Strategikon* (Philadelphia: University of Pennsylvania Press, 1984)

Maurice (G. T. Dennis, ed., translated into German by E. Gamillscheg), *Das Strategikon des Maurikios* (Vienna: Verlag der Österreichischen Akademie der Wissenschaften, 2021)

Menander Protector (translated into English by R. C. Blockley), *The History of Menander the Guardsman* (Liverpool: Francis Cains, ARCA, Classical and Medieval Texts, Papers and Monographs, 17, 2006)

(Lemerle, P., ed.), *Miracula Sancti Demetrii*, Les *plus anciens recueils des miracles de Saint Démétrius et la pénétration des Slaves dans les Balkans, I – Le texte, II – Commentaire* (Paris: Éditions du *CNRS*, 1979–1981)

Nikephoros (translated into English by C. Mango), *Nikephoros, Patriarch of Constantinople. Short History* (Dumbarton Oaks: Trustees for Harvard University, *CFHB*, 13, 1990)

Olympiodorus (translated into English by R. C. Blockley), *The Fragmentary Classicising Historians of the Later Roman Empire: Eunapius, Olympiodorus, Priscus and Malchus* (Cambridge: Francis Cairns Publications, ARCA Classical and Medieval Texts, Papers and Monographs, 10, 2007)

Paul the Deacon (translated into English by W. D. Foulke), *History of Langobards* (Philadelphia: Department of History, University of Pennsylvania; New York: Longmann, Green and Co, 1907)

Paul the Deacon (L. Bethmann, G. Waitz, eds), *Pauli Historia Langobardorum* (Hanover: Hahn, *MGH*, Scriptores rerum Langobardicarum et Italicarum sæc. VI-IX, 1964), pp.12–188

Paul the Deacon (translated into French by F. Bougard) *Histoire des Lombards* (Turnhout: Brepols, Miroir du Moyen Âge, 1994)

Paul the Deacon (H. Droysen, ed.), *Historia Romana* (Berlin: Weidmann, *MGH, Auctores Antiquissimi*, 2, 1882)

Peri Strategikes (translated into English by G. T. Dennis), *Three Byzantine Military Treatises*, (Dumbarton Oaks: Trustees for Harvard University, *CFHB*, 25, 1985), pp.1–136

Polybius (translated into English by William R. Paton), *Polybius: The Histories* (London: Heinemann, Loeb Classical Library, 1922–1927)

Polybius (translated into French by D. Roussel), *Histoire* (Paris: Éditions Gallimard, coll. Quarto, 2003)

Pomponius Mela (translated into French by A. Silbermann), *Pomponius Mela. Chorographie* (Paris: *LBL, CUF*, 1988)

Priscus of Panium (Priscos Panita) (K. Müller, ed.), *Fragmenta* (Paris: Firmin Didot, *FHG*, 4, 1851), pp.69–110

Priscus of Panium (Priscos Panita) (translated into English by R. C. Blockley), *The Fragmentary Classicising Historians of the Later Roman Empire: Eunapius, Olympiodorus, Priscus and Malchus*, 2 (Cambridge: Francis Cairns Publications, ARCA Classical and Medieval Texts, Papers and Monographs, 10, 2007)

Procopius of Caesarea (translated into English by H. B. Dewing et al), *History of the Wars*, 6 vols (London: Heinemann, Loeb Classical Library, 1979)

Procopius of Caesarea (translated into English by H. B. Dewing, revised and modernized, with an introduction and notes by A. Kaldellis, maps and genealogies by I. Mladjov), *Prokopios. The Wars of Justinian* (Indianapolis: Hackett Publishing Company, Inc., 2014)

Procopius of Caesarea (translated into English by E. H. Warmington), *The Anecdota* (London: Heinemann, Loeb Classical Library, 1979)

Procopius of Caesarea (translated into English by H. B. Dewing), *Buildings* (London: Heinemann, Loeb Classical Library, 1979)

Procopius of Caesarea (translated into French by D. Roques), *La guerre contre les Vandales* (Paris: *LBL*, La Roue à Livre, 1990)

Procopius of Caesarea (translated into French by P. Maraval), *Histoire secrete* (Paris: *LBL*, La Roue à Livres, 2004)

Procopius of Caesarea (translated into French by D. Roques), *Constructions de Justinien Ier* (Alexandria: Edizioni dell'Orso, 2011)

Procopius of Caesarea (translated into French by D. Roques & J. Auberger), *Histoire des Goths* (Paris: *LBL*, La Roue à livres, 2015)

Procopius of Gaza (J. P. Migne, ed.), *Panegyric of the Emperor. Anastasius I* (Paris: Jacques-Paul Migne Imprimerie catholique, *PG*, 87, 1865)

Prosper of Aquitaine and his continuor (Th. Mommsen, ed.), *Prosperi Tironis Epitoma Chr. ed. primum a. CCCCXXXIII (433), continuata ad a. CCCCLV (455)* (Berlin: Weidmann, *MGH, Auctores Antiquissimi, Chronica minora sæcula IV, V, VI, VII*, 9, 1961), pp.341–501

Sidonius Apollinaris (translated into French by A. Loyen), *Tome II: Correspondance. Livres I-V, Tome III: Correspondance. Livres VI-IX* (Paris: *LBL, CUF*, 1970)

Socrates of Constantinople (Scholasticus) (translated into English by A. C. Zenos), *The Ecclesiastical History of Socrates Scholasticus*, in Ph. Schaff and H. Wallace (eds), *Nicene and Post-Nicene Fathers*, Second Series, vol. 2 (New York: Christian Literature Publishing Co., 1890), pp.1–178

Socrates of Constantinople (G. Hansen, ed., translated into French by P. Maraval), *Histoire ecclésiastique* (Paris: Le Cerf, *SC*, 477, 493, 505, 506, 2004–2007)

Synesius of Cyrene (translated into English by A. Fitzgerald), The letters of Synesius of Cyrene (London: A., Oxford University Press, 1926)

Synesius of Cyrene (A. Garzya, ed., translated into French by D. Roques), *Lettres*, 2 vols (Paris: *LBL, CUF*, 2003)

Theodore Synkellos (translated into French by F. Makk), *Traduction et Commentaire de l'homélie écrite probablement par Théodore le Syncelle sur le siège de Constantinople en 626* (Szeged: Acta Universitatis de Attila Jozsef Nominatae, *Acta antiqua et archaeologica*, 19, 1975)

Theodore Synkellos (S. Szadeczky-Kardoss and Th. Olejos, eds), Breviarium homiliae Theodorei Syncelli de obsidione avarica Constantinopolis (Turnhout: Brepols, Analecta Bollandiana, Revue critique d'hagiographie, 108, 1, 1990)

Theodoret of Cyrus (Y. Azéma, ed.), Correspondance (Paris: Le Cerf, 1964)

Theophanes Confessor (J. P. Migne, ed.), *Theophanis Abbatis Agri et Confessoris Chronographia* (Paris: Jacques-Paul Migne Imprimerie catholique, PG, 108, 1863), col. 55–1009

Theophanes Confessor (C. de Boor, ed.), *Theophanis Chronographia*, 2 vols (Leipzig: Teubner, 1883)

Theophanes Confessor (translated into English by C. Mango & R. Scott), *The Chronicle of Theophanes Confessor. Byzantine and Near Eastern History AD 284–813* (Oxford: Clarendon Press, 1997)

Theophylact Simocatta (Simokatès), *Histoire de Constantinople depuis le règne de Justin jusqu'à la fin de l'Empire traduite sur les originaux grecs par Mr Cousin* (Paris: Damien Foucault, 1685)

Theophylact Simocatta (C. de Boor, ed.), *Theophylacti Simocattæ Historiæ* (Leipzig: Nabu Press, 2014)

Theophylact Simocatta (translated into German by P. Schreiner), *Theopylaktes Simokates: Geschichte* (Stuttgart: Hiersemann, 1985)

Theophylact Simocatta (translated into English by M. and M. Whitby), *The History of Theophylact Simocatta: An English Translation with Introduction* (Oxford: Oxford University Press, 1986)

Vegetius (Flavius Vegetius Renatus) (K. Lang, ed.), *Flavii Vegetii Renati Epitoma Rei Militaris* (Leipzig: Teubner, 1967)

Vegetius (translated into English by N. P. Milner), *Vegetius: Epitome of Military Science* (Liverpool: Liverpool University Press, *TTH*, 16, 1993)

VEGETIUS (TRANSLATED BY M. D. REEVE), EPITOMA REI MILITARIS (OXFORD: CLARENDON PRESS, 2017)

Virgil, Vergilius Vaticanus facsimile edition (Graz: Akademische Druck-u. Verlagsanstalt (ADEVA), 1980)

Virgil, Vergilius Romanus facsimile edition (Zurich: Belser Verlag, 1985)

Victor of Tunnuna (Tonnena) (C. Cardelle de Hartmann, ed.), Victor Tunnunensis, Iohannes Biclarensis. Chronicon cum reliquiis ex Consularibus Caesaraugustanis (Turnhout: Brepols, CCSL, 173 A, 2001)

Victor of Tunnuna (translated into English by J. R. C. Martin), *Arians and Vandals of the 4th–6th Centuries: Annotated translations of the historical works by Bishops Victor of Vita (Historia Persecutionis Africanae Provinciae) and Victor of Tonnena (Chronicon), and of the religious works by Bishop Victor of Cartenna* (Newcastle: Cambridge Scholars Publishing, 2008)

Vitelli, G., Norsa M., et al (eds), *Papiri greci e latini*, III (Florence: Felice Le Monnier, 1914)

Wessely, C., 'Griechische Papyri des British Museum' (Vienna: Universität Wien, *Wiener Studien. Zeitschrift für classische Philologie*, 9, 1887), pp.235–278

(Wessely C., ed.), *Studien zur Palaeographie und Papyruskunde*, XX (Leipzig: Verlag von E. Avenarius, 1921)

Xenophon (translated into English by C. L. Brownson), Anabasis. Books I-VII (London: Heinemann, Loeb Classical Library, 1989)

(Pseudo-)Zachariah Rhetor (translated into English by G. Greatrex), *The Chronicle of Pseudo-Zachariah Rhetor: Church and War in Late Antiquity* (Liverpool: Liverpool University Press, 2011)

(John) Zonaras (L. Dindorf, ed.), *Epitome Historiarum Ioannis Zonarae Epitome Historiarum*, 6 vols (Leipzig: 1868–1875)

(John) Zonaras (translated into English by T. Banchich & E. Lane), *The History of Zonaras: from Alexander Severus to the Death of Theodosius the Great* (London: Routledge, Routledge Classical Translations, 2009).

Zosimus, *Histoire Nouvelle* (translated into French by F. Paschoud, ed.), *Histoire Nouvelle*, 5 vols (Paris: LBL, CUF, 1971–1989)

Zosimus (translated into English by J. J. Buchanan & H. T. Davis, eds), *Historia Nova; the Decline of Rome* (San Antonio: Trinity University Press, 1967)

2, Middle-Eastern Sources

Agapius of Hierapolis (Agapios Manbidj or Maḥbūb ibn Qusṭanṭīn) (translated into French by A. A. Vasiliev), *Kitāb al-'Unvan*, 2nd part (Paris: Firmin Didot, *PO*, 8, 1912), pp.399–554

Al-Azdi (translated into English by H. Hamada & J. Scheiner), *The Early Muslim Conquest of Syria: An English Translation of al-Azdi's Futüh al-Sham* (London: Routledge, 2019)

Al-Baladhuri (translated into English by Ph. Hitti), *The Origins of the Islamic State*, Studies in History, Economics and Public Law 163 (London: P. S. King and Son, 1916)

Al-Hakam (Ch. C. Torrey, ed.), *The History of the Conquest of Egypt, North Africa and Spain: known as Futuh Misr by Ibn Abd al-akam* (New York: Cosimo Classics, 2010)

Al-Hakam (translated into English by Y. Hilloowla), *The History of the Conquest of Egypt, being a partial Translation of Ibn'Abd al-Hakam Futuh Misr and an Analysis of this Translation. A Dissertation Submitted to the Faculty of the Department Near Eastern Studies* (Tucson: The University of Arizona Press, 1998)

Al-Mo'izz Mohammad ibn Mohammad (*Futuh al-Bahnasâ*) (translated into French by É. Galtier). *Foutouh al-Bahnasâ* (Cairo: Imprimerie de l'Institut français d'archéologie orientale, *MIFAO*, 22, 1909)

Bar Hebraeus (translated into English by E. A. Wallis Budge), *The Chronography of Gregory Abû'l Faraj, commonly known as Bar Hebraeus* (London: Oxford University Press, 1932)

Bar Hebraeus (translated into French by Ph. Talon), *La Chronographie de Bar Hebraeus* (Brussels: EME éditions, Nouvelles Études Orientales, 3 vols, 2013)

(Chabot, J. B. ed.), *Chronicle of 1234* [Anonymous Syrian chronicle of 1203–1204], *Anonymi auctoris chronicon ad annum 1234 pertinens* (Paris: *CSCO*, 14–15, *Scriptores Syri*, 3, t. 1, 1937), pp.118–126

Chronicle of Zuqnin (Chabot J. B., ed.), *Incerti auctoris chronicon Pseudo-Dionysianum vulgo dictum*, II (Leuven: *CSCO*, 104, *Scriptores Syri* 53, 1933)

Chronicle of Zuqnin (translated into English by A. Harrak), *The Chronicle of Zuqnîn, parts III and IV (A.D. 488–775)*, (Toronto: Pontifical Institute of Medieval Studies, *CSCO*, 507, *Scriptores Syri* 213, 1999)

Chronicle of Zuqnin (translated into French by R. Hespel), *La Chronique du Pseudo-Denys de Tell-Mahré* (Leuven: Durbecq, 1989).

Eutychius of Alexandria (translated into German by M. Breydy), *Das Annalenwerk des Eutychios von Alexandrien* (Leuven: Peeters, 1985) 471–472

Ibn Khaldun (translated by F. Rosenthal), *The Muqaddimah: An introduction to History*, 3 vols (New York: Pantheon Books, Bollingen Series, 1958)

Ibn Khaldun (extracts translated into French by A. Cheddadi), *Peuples et nations du monde. Extraits des Ibar*, 2 vols (Paris: Sinbad, La Bibliothèque arabe, 1995)

John of Nikiu (translated into French by H. Zotenberg), *Chronique de Jean, évêque de Nikiou*, Notices et extraits des manuscrits de la bibliothèque Nationale, 24 (Paris: Imprimerie nationale, 1883)

John of Nikiu (translated into English by R. H. Charles), *The Chronicle of John Bishop of Nikiu* (London: Text and Translation Society, 1916)

John of Ephesus (translated into English by E. W. Brooks), *Ecclesiastical History* (Leuven: *CSCO*, 106, *Scriptores Syri*, 55, 1952).

Joshua the Stylite (translated into English by F. R. Trombley and J. W. Wat), *The Chronicle of Pseudo-Joshua the Stylite* (Liverpool: Liverpool University Press, 2000)

Juansher Juansheriani (translated into English by D. Gamq'relidze), 'The Life of Vakhtang Gorgasali' in *Kartlis Tskhovreba. A History of Georgia* (Tbilissi: Artanuji Publishing, Oxford Oriental Monographs, 2014), pp.77–134

Michael the Syrian (translated into French by J. B. Chabot), *Chronique de Michel le Syrien*, vol. 2 (Brussels: Culture et civilisation, 1963)

Michael the Syrian (Michael the Great) (G. Yuhanna Ibrahim, ed.), *Text and Translations of the Chronicle of Michæl the Great*, *The Edessa-Aleppo Syriac Codex of the Chronicle of Michæl the Great*, vol. 1 (Piscataway: Gorgias Press, 2009)

Movses Dasxuranci (translated into English by C. F. J. Dowsett), *The History of the Caucasian Albanians by Movses Dasxuranci*, London Oriental Series 8 (London: Oxford University Press, 1961)

Strategius (Antiochus Strategos) (F. C. Conybeare, ed.), The Capture of Jerusalem by the Persians in 614,' *English Historical Review*, 25, 1910, pp.502–517

Strategius (translated into French by G. Garitte). *La prise de Jérusalem par les Perses en* 614 (Leuven: *CSCO*, 202–203, *Scriptores Iberici* 11–12 1960)

Tabari (translated into French by H. Zotenberg), *Chronique de Abou-Djafar-Mo' hammed-Ben-Djarir-Ben-Yezid-Tabari, traduite sur la version persane d'Abou-'Ali Mo' hammed Bel'Ami d'après les manuscrits de Paris, de Gotha, de Londres et de Canterbury*, 4 vols (Paris: Librairie G. P. Maisonneuve, Éditions Besson et Chantemerle, 1958)

Tabari (translated into English by F. Rosenthal), *The History of al-Tabari*, 5 vols (Albany: State University of New York, 1989)

Thomas the Presbyter (translated into Latin by J. B. Chabot), *Chronicon miscellaneum ad annum Domini 724 pertinens* or *Liber Calipharum* (Paris: *CSCO*, 4, *Scriptores Syri*, 4, 1904), pp.61–119

Al-Waqidi (translated into English by W. N. Lees), *The Conquest of Syria, commonly Acribed to Aboo Abdallah Mohammad B. Omar Al-Waqidi*, Bibliotheca Indica 66 (Calcutta: F. Carbery, 1854).

Al-Waqidi (translated into English by Mawlana Sulayman al-Kindi), *The Islamic Conquest of Syria. A Translation of Futuhusham by al-Imam al-Waqidi* (London: Ta-Ha Publishers, 2012)

3, Scholarly Works

Abadie-Reynal, C., 'Séleucie-Zeugma et Apamée sur l'Euphrate: étude d'un cas de villes jumelles dans l'Antiquité' *Histoire urbaine*, 1/3 (2001), pp.7–24

Ager, B., 'West Wight, Isle of Wight: Anglo-Saxon Grave Assemblages (2004 T187)' in *Treasure Annual Report 2004* (London: Department for Culture, Media and Sport, 2006), pp.68–71

Akram, A. I., *The Sword of Allah: Khalid bin al-Waleed – His Life and Campaigns* (Oxford: Oxford University Press, 2004)

Al-Shbib, Sh., 'La défense des villes à l'époque Byzantine: alternance entre les tours et les bastions, tradition ou innovation?' *Syria*, 95 (2018), pp.413–430

Anson, E. M., 'Alexander's Hypaspists and the Argyraspids', *Historia*, 30 (1981), pp.117–120

Arce, I., Feissel, D., Weber-Karyotaki, Th. M., 'The Anastasius Edict Project: A Preliminary Report. Part 1 – The Epigraphic Evidence' in C. Sebastian Sommer & S. Matešic (eds), *Limes*, XXIII, Sonderband 4 / II, *Proceedings of the 23rd International Congress of Roman Frontier Studies, Ingolstadt, 2015, Akten des 23. Internationalen Limeskongresses in Ingolstadt 2015* (Mainz: Nünnerich-Asmus Verlag, 2018), pp.673–681

Aussaresses, F., *L'Armée Byzantine à la fin du VIe siècle d'après le Strategicon de l'empereur Maurice* (Bordeaux: Féret et Fils, Bibliothèque Universitaire du Midi, 1909)

Asufay-Effenberger, N., *Die Landmauer von Konstantinopel-Istanbul: Historisch-topographische und baugeschichtliche Untersuchungen* (Berlin: De Gruyter, 2007)

Bachrach, B. S., 'On Roman Ramparts 300–1300' in G. Parker (ed.), *The Cambridge illustrated History of Warfare: The Triumph of the West* (Cambridge, Cambridge University Press, 1995), pp.64–91

Badel, Ch., 'Un chef germain entre Byzance et l'Italie. L'épitaphe d'Asbadus à Pavie (*Suppl. It.* 9, 15)' in M. Ghilardi, Chr. J. Goddard and P. Porena (eds), *Les cités de l'Italie tardo-antique (IVe-VIe siècle). Institutions, économie, société, culture et religion* (Rome, CEFR, 2006), pp.91–100.

Baldwin, B., 'The Career of Corippus' *CQ*, 28 (1978), pp.195–212.

Barnea, I., 'Dinogetia – ville Byzantine du Bas-Danube, sec. IV-XII', *Byzantina*, 10 (1980), pp.237–287

Bass, G. F. & Doorninck, F. H. van Jr., *Yassi Ada I: A Seventh Century Byzantine Shipwreck* (College Station: Texas A & M University Press, 1982)

Bataille, A., 'Un inventaire de vêtements inédit', *Eos*, 48, fasc. 2 (1956), pp.83–88

Bavant, B., 'Le duché Byzantin de Rome. Origine, durée et extension géographique', *MEFR, Moyen Âge, Temps modernes*, 91, n° 91–1 (1979), pp.41–88

Bavant, B., 'La ville dans le Nord de l'Illyricum (Pannonie, Mésie I, Dacie et Dardanie)', *PEFR*, 77 (1984), pp.245–288

Baynes, N. H., 'The Supranatural Defenders of Constantinople' in *Byzantine Studies and Other Essays* (London: The University of London, Athlone Press, 1955), pp.248–260

Bellen, H., 'Der Primicerius Mauricius. Ein Beitrag zum Thebäerproblem', *Historia*, X, 2 (1961), pp.238–247

Benaissa, A., 'The Size of the Numerus Transtigritanorum in the Fifth Century', *Zeitschrift für Papyrologie und Epigraphik*, 175 (2010), p 224–226

Bénazeth, D., 'Calques de Baouit archivés à l'Ifao', *BIFAO*, 105 (2005), pp.1–12

Boespflug, F., *La Crucifixion dans l'art: Un sujet planétaire* (Montrouge, Bayard Éditions, 2019)

Bohlendorf-Arslan, B. & Ricci, A. (eds), 'Early Byzantine Iron Helmets from Novae (the Diocese of Thrace)', DAI Istanbul, *BYZAS*, 15, *Byzantine Small Finds in Archaeological Contexts* (2012), pp.91–104

Boozer, A. L., 'Frontiers and Borderlands in Imperial Perspectives: Exploring Rome's Egyptian Frontier', *AJA*, 117/2 (2013), pp.275–292

Borel, C., 'Spangenhelm' in M. Martiniani-Reber (ed.), *Byzance en Suisse, catalogue d'exposition* (Genève: Musées d'art et d'Histoire, 2015), pp.400–405

Börm, H., *Westrom. Von Honorius bis Justinian* (Stuttgart: Kohlhammer, 2013)

Bréhier, L., *Les institutions de l'Empire Byzantin*, L'Évolution de l'humanité (Paris, Albin Michel, 1970)

Brodka, D., *Die Geschichtesphilosophie in der spätantiken Historiographie. Studien zu Prokopios, Agathias von Myrina und Theophylaktos Simokates* (Frankfurt am Main: Peter Lang, Studien und Texte zur Byzantinistik, 5 2004)

Brown, T. S., *Gentlemen and Officers: Imperial Administration and Aristocratic Power in Byzantine Italy, AD 554–800* (London: British School at Rome, 1984)

Bugarski, I., 'A Contribution to the Study of Lamellar Armours', *Starinar*, 55 (2005), pp.161–180

Bugarski, I. & Ivanišević, V., 'Sixth century Foederati from the Upper Moesian Limes: Weapons in a Social Context' in S. Golubović, N. Mrđić (eds), Vivere militare est, vol. I (Belgrade: Institute of Archaelogy, Monographies, 68/1, 2018), pp.291–332.

Burck, E., 'The Die Iohannis des Corippus' in E. Burck (ed.), *Das römische Epos* (Darmstadt: Buchgesellschaft, 1979), pp.379–399

Bury, J. B., A History of the Later Roman Empire from the Death of Theodosius I to the Death of Justinian (AD 395 to AD 565), (New York: Dover Publications, 1958), 2 vols

Butler, A., *The Arab Conquest of Egypt and the Last Thirty Years of the Roman Dominion* (Oxford: Clarendon Press, 1902)

Caetani, L., *Annali dell'Islam* (Hildesheim: G. Olms, 1972), 10 vols

Cagnat, R., 'strator' in Ch. Daremberg & E. Saglio, *Dictionnaire des Antiquités*, tome IV (Paris: Hachette, 1900), p.1530.

Calament, Fl., 'L'apport historique des découvertes d'Antinoé au costume dit de cavalier sassanide' in C. Flück & G. Vogelsang-Eastwood, *Riding Costume in Egypt: Origin and Appearance* (Leiden, Boston: Brill, 2004), pp.37–72

Cambeda, A. Ceccherelli, *Le Mura di Aureliano, itinerari d'arte e di cultura* (Rome: Fratelli Palombi Editor, 1990)

Cameron, A., *Agathias* (Oxford: Oxford University Press, 1970)

Cameron, A., 'Agathias on Sassanians', *DOP*, 23, 1969–1970), pp.78–176

Cameron, A., *Circus Factions. Blues and Greens at Rome and Byzantium* (Oxford: Oxford University Press, 1976)

Cameron, A., 'The Virgin's Robe: An Episode in the History of Seventh Century Constantinople', *REB*, 49 (1979), pp.42–56

Cameron, A. & Conrad, L. I. (eds), *The Byzantine and Early Islamic Near East*, vol. 1, *Problems in the Literary Source Materials* (Princeton NJ: The Darwin Press, 1992)

Cameron, A., *The Mediterranean World in Late Antiquity AD 395–600* (London: Routledge, 1993)

Cameron, A. & Conrad, L. I. (eds), *The Byzantine and Early Islamic Near East*, vol. 3, *States, Resources and Armies* (Princeton NJ: Darwin Press, 1995).

Cameron, A., Ward-Perkins, B., Whitby, M. (eds), *Late Antiquity: Empire and Successors, AD 425–600* (Cambridge, Cambridge University Press, The Cambridge Ancient History, 14, 2008).

Canard, M., 'The Arab Expansion: The Military Problem' in F. M. Donner, *The Expansion of the Early Islamic State* (London: Routledge, 2007) pp.63–80

Caprioli, M., '… *a parte Romanonum octo milia numerus*. Considerazioni sulla batalla dello Scultenna (643) e sull' esercito esarcale (VI-VIII secolo)', *Nueva Antologia Militare*, 3, fasc. 9, *Storia Militare Medievale* (2022), pp.7–19

Casson, L., *Ships and Seafaring in ancient Times* (London: British Museum Press, 1994)

Chabot, G., 'La vitesse des navires anciens', *Annales de Géographie*, 288 (1942), pp.284

Chadburn, C., 'Les guerriers berbères dans l'Antiquité', *Prétorien*, 15 (2010), pp.21–28

Chagnon, L., *La conquête musulmane de l'Égypte* (Paris: Economica, 2008)

Chamoux, F., 'Une nouvelle copie de l'édit d'Anastasius Ier sur la Cyrénaïque', *Comptes rendus des séances de l'Académie des Inscriptions et Belles-Lettres*, 99–3 (1955), pp.333–334

Chapot V., 'Resapha-Sergiopolis' *Bulletin de Correspondance Hellénique*, 27, 2903, p.280-291

Charles, M. B., 'Vegetius on Liburnae: Naval Terminology in the Late Roman', *Scripta classica Israelica*, 24 (2005), pp.181–194

Chatzidakis, M., *Byzantine Art in Greece, Mosaics – Wall Paintings. Hosios Loukas* (Athens: Melissa, 1997)

Chauvot, A., 'Figure du cercle et représentation des Goths chez Ammien Marcellin', *Ktèma*, 35 (2010), pp.231–241

Chevedden, P. E., 'Artillery in Late Antiquity: Prelude to the Middle Ages' in J. F. Haldon (ed.), *Byzantine Warfare* (Aldershot: Ashgate Publishing, 2007), pp.453–496

Christie, N., *The Lombards. The Ancient Langobards* (Oxford: Blackwell, 1995)

A. Claridge, *Rome: An Oxford Archaeological Guide* (Oxford: Oxford University Press, 1998)

Clédat, J., *Le monastère et la nécropole de Baouît* (Cairo: Imprimerie de l'Institut français d'archéologie orientale, MIFAO 12, 1 and 2, 1904)

Colin, F., *Les peuples libyens de la Cyrénaique à l'Égypte d'après les sources de l'Antiquité* (Brussels: Académie Royale de Belgique, 2000)

Comfort, A. M., 'Roman Bridges of South-East Anatolia' in H. Bru & G. Labarre, *L'Anatolie des peuples, des cités et des cultures (IIe millénaire av. J.-C.-Ve siècle ap. J.-C.). Colloque international de Besançon – 26-27 novembre 2010*, vol. 2 (Besançon: Institut des Sciences et Techniques de l'Antiquité (ISTA), 1277-2, 2013), pp.315–342

Conant, J., *Staying Roman. Conquest and Identity in Africa and the Mediterranean, 439–700* (Cambridge: Cambridge University Press, 2012)

Cosentino, S., 'Gaudiosus Draconarius: la Sardegna bizantina attraverso un epitafio del secolo 6', *Quaderni della Rivista di bizantinistica*, 13 (1994)

Courtois, C., *Les Vandales et l'Afrique* (Paris: Arts et Métiers Graphiques, 1955)

Croke, B., 'Two Early Byzantine Earthquakes and Their Liturgical Commemoration', *Byzantion*, 51 (1981), pp.122–147

Croke, B., 'The Date of the 'Anastasian Long Wall' of Thrace', *GRBS*, 23 (1982), pp.59–78

Croke, B., *Count Marcellinus and His Chronicle* (Oxford: Oxford University Press, 2001)

Croke, B., 'Leo I and the Palace Guard', *REB*, 75 (2005), pp.117–151

Crow, J. & Ricci, A., 'Investigating the Hinterland of Constantinople: Interim Report on the Anastasian Long Wall,' *Journal of Roman Archaeology*, 10 (1997), pp.235–262

Curta, F., *The Making of the Slavs. History and Archælogy of the Lower Danube c.500–700* (Cambridge: Cambridge University Press, 2001)

Curta, F. & Kovalev, R., (eds), *The Other Europe in the Middle Ages. Avars, Bulgars, Khazars and Cumans, East Central and Eastern Europe in the Middle Ages, 450–1450*, vol. 2 (Leiden: Brill, 2009)

Curta, F., 'Chronology: what is the date of the earliest stirrups in Europe?' in F. Curta & R. Kovalev (eds), *The Other Europe in the Middle Ages. Avars, Bulgars, Khazars and Cumans* (Leiden: Brill, 2009), pp.297–326

Curta F., (ed.) *Neglected barbarians* (Turnhout: Brepols, 2011)

Dagron, G., 'Modèles de combattants et technologie militaire dans le *Strategikon* de Maurice' in *ARB-AFAM* (1990), pp.279–284

Dain, A., 'Les stratégistes byzantins', Collège de France, Centre de recherche d'histoire et civilisation de Byzance, *Travaux et Mémoires*, 2 (1967), pp.317–392

Dain, A., 'Urbicius ou Maurice', *REB*, 26 (1968), pp.123–136

D'Amato, Raffaele, *Roman military Clothing (3): AD 400–640* (Oxford: Osprey Publishing, Men-At-Arms series, 42, 2005)

D'Amato, Raffaele, 'A Sixth or Early Seventh Century AD. Iconography of Roman Military Equipment in Egypt: The Deir Abou Hennis Frescoes' in G. Theotokis, A. Yıldız, *A Military History of the Mediterranean Sea* (Leiden: Brill, *History of Warfare*, 118, 2018), pp.105–152

D'Amato, Raffaele & Pflaum, V., 'Two Suites of Lamellar Armour from Kranj (Carnium), Slovenia, in the light of Archaeological Analogies, Written Sources and Contemporary Iconography', *Acta Militaria Medievalia*, 15 (2019), pp.7–50

D'Amato, Raffaele *Roman Heavy Cavalry (2) AD 500–1450* (Oxford: Osprey Publishing, Elite series, 235, 2019)

Dana, D., 'Onomastique et recrutement de l'armée Byzantine d'Afrique, l'épitaphe du soldat Buraido révisée (ILAlg, I, 81)', *Antiquités Africaines*, 49 (2014), pp.151–160

Delehaye, H., *Les légendes grecques des Saints militaires* (Paris: Picard et Fils, 1909)

Dennis, G. T., 'Flies, Mice, and the Byzantine Crossbow', *Byzantine and Modern Greek Studies*, 7 (1981), pp.1–5

Dennis, G. T., 'Byzantine Battle Flags', *Byzantinische Forschungen*, 8 (1982), pp.51–59

Dey, H., 'Verso una storia edilizia delle Mura Aureliane, da Aureliano a Onorio (271–403 d.C.)' in R. Rita Volpe, R. Santangeli Valenzani, D. Esposito et al (eds), *Le Mura Aureliane nella storia di Roma, 1, Da Aureliano a Onorio, Atti Primo Convegno, 25 Marzo 2015* (Rome: TrE-Press, 2017), pp.13–28

Diehl, Ch., *Études sur l'administration Byzantine dans l'exarchat de Ravenne (568–751)* (Paris: Ernest Thorin, Bibliothèque des Écoles Françaises d'Athènes et de Rome, 53, 1888).

Diehl, Ch., *L'Afrique Byzantine. Histoire de la domination Byzantine en Afrique (533–709)* (Paris: Ernest Leroux, 1896)

Diesner, H. H. 'Das Bucellariertum von Stilicho und Sarus bis auf Ætius (454–455)', *Klio*, 54 (1972), pp.321–350.

Diethart, J. M. & Dintsis, P., 'Die Leontoklibanarier. Versuch einer archäologisch-papyrologischen Zusammenschau', Βυζάντιος. *Festschrift für Herbert Hunger zum 70. Geburtstag* (Vienna: E. Becvar, 1984), pp.67–84

Dillemann, L. *Haute Mésopotamie et pays adjacents: contribution à la géographie historique de la région du Ve s. avant l'ère chrétienne au VIe s. de cette ère* (Paris: Geuthner, Bibliothèque archéologique et historique, 72, 1962)

Dimitrova, E., *The Ceramic Relief Plaques from Vinica. The most significant values of the cultural and natural heritage* (Skopje: Directorate for protection of cultural heritage, 2017)

Dixon, K. R. & Southern P., *The Roman Cavalry* (London: Batsford, 1992)

Domínguez, J. F. & Manchon Gomez, R., 'Recherches sur les mots campidoctor et campiductor: de l'Antiquité au Moyen Âge tardif', *Bulletin Du Cange*, 58 (2000), pp.5–44

Donner, F. M. *The Expansion of the Early Islamic State* (London: Routledge, 2007)

Doorninck F. H. van Jr, 'The Seventh Century Byzantine Ship at Yass1ada and Her Final Voyage: Present Thoughts', in D. N. Carlson, J. Leidwanger, S. M. Kampbell (eds), *Maritime Studies in the Wake of the Byzantine Shipwreck at Yassiada, Turkey*, (College Station: Texas A & M University Press, 2015), pp.205–216

Drapeyron, L., *L'Empereur Héraclius et l'Empire Byzantin au VIIe siècle* (Paris: Ernest Thorin, 1869)

Duncan-Jones, R. P., 'Pay and Numbers in Diocletian's Army', *Chiron*, 8 (1978), pp.541–560

Durand, M., Guelton, M. H., et al, 'Les costumes des élégants d'Antinoé conservés au Musée des Tissus de Lyon: approche historique, analyses techniques et analyses de colorants', *Techne*, 41 (2015), pp.32–45

Durliat, J., *Les dédicaces d'ouvrages de défense dans l'Afrique Byzantine* (Rome: PEFR, 49, 1981).

Durliat, J., *De la ville antique à la ville Byzantine: le problème des subsistances* (Rome: CEFR, 136, 1990)

Dussaud, R., *Topographie historique de la Syrie antique et médiévale* (Paris: OpenEdition Books, 2015)

Eastmond, A., *The Glory of Byzantium and Early Christendom* (London: Phaidon, 2013).

Elsig, P. and Morand M. Cl. (eds), *Le Musée d'histoire du Valais, Sion. Collectionner au cœur des Alpes* (Sion, Paris: Somogy Édition d'Art, Musée d'histoire, 2013)

Emion, M., '*Christum in scutis notat*: le bouclier au chrisme des gardes impériaux dans l'Antiquité tardive', *Journée des doctorants du GRHis*, Université de Rouen-Normandie, 7 mai 2014

Esposito, G., 'The Isola Rizza Dish', *Medieval Warfare*, 4/6 (2014), p.58

Faider-Feytmans, G. & France-Lanord, A., 'Le casque mérovingien de Trivières', *Revue Belge d'archéologie et d'Histoire de l'Art*, t. 20, fasc. 4 (1951), pp.265–272

Fasano Guarini, F., 'Au XVIe siècle: comment naviguent les galères', *Annales*, 16-2 (1961), pp.279–296

Feissel, D., 'Les itinéraires de Procope et la métrologie de l'antiquité tardive', *AnTard*, 10 (2002), pp.383–400

Ferjančić, B., 'Invasions et installation des Slaves dans les Balkans' in *Villes et peuplement dans l'Illyricum protobyzantin. Actes du colloque de Rome (12–14 mai 1982)*, (Rome: PEFR, 1984), pp.85–109

Fleschenberg, O. Schissel von, 'Spätantike Anleitung zum Bogenschiessen', *Wiener Studien*, 59 (1941), pp.10–24, 60; (1942), pp.43–70

Fleury, Ph., 'Vitruve et la nomenclature des machines de jet romaines', *REL*, 59 (1981), pp.216–234

Fossella, J., 'Waiting Only for a Pretext: A New Chronology for the Sixth Century Byzantine Invasion of Spain', *Estudios bizantinos*, 1 (2013), pp.31–38

Fotiou, A., 'Recruitment Shortages in Sixth Century Byzantium', *Byzantion*, 58 (1988), pp.65–77.

Foulon, E., 'Hypaspistes, peltastes, chrysaspides, argyraspides, chalcaspides', *REA*, 98 (1996), pp.53–63

Frank, R. I., *Scholae Palatinae: The Palace Guards of the Later Roman Empire* (Rome: American Academy, Papers and Monographs of the American Academy in Rome, 23, 1969)

Freshfield, E. H., 'Notes on a Vellum Album Containing Some Original Sketches of Public Buildings and Monuments, drawn by a German Artist Who Visited Constantinople in 1574', *Archaeologia*, 72 (1921/1922), pp.87–104

Frendo, J. D. C., *History and Panegyric in the Age of Heraclius: The Literary Background to the Composition of the Histories of Theophylact Simocatta*, *DOP*, 42 (1988), pp.143–156

Fresne du Cange, Ch. du, et al, *Glossarium mediæ et infimæ latinitatis* (Niort: L. Favre, 1883–1887)

Galland-Hallyn, P., 'La *Johannide* (*De Bellis Libycis*). Corippus et le sublime dans la 'dernière' épopée romaine' in Droin J. & Roth A. (eds), *La croisée des études libyco-berbères: mélanges offerts à Paulette Galand-Pernet et Lionel Galand* (Paris: Geuthner, 1993), pp.73–87

Gascou, J., 'Militaires étrangers en Égypte Byzantine', *BIFAO*, 75 (1975), pp.203–206

Gascou, J., 'L'institution des bucellaires', *BIFAO*, 76 (1976), pp.143–156

Gascou, J., 'Deux Inscriptions Byzantines de Haute-Égypte (reedition from I. Thebes-Syène 196 r° and v°)', Collège de France, Centre de recherche d'histoire et civilisation de Byzance, *Travaux et Mémoires*, 12 (1994), pp.323–342

Ghilardi, M., Goddard, Ch. J., Porena, P. (eds), *Les cités de l'Italie tardo-antique (IVe-VIe siècle). Institutions, économie, société, culture et religion* (Rome: *CEFR*, 2006)

Gibbons, A., 'Why 536 was the "worst year to be alive"', *Science Magazine*, 362 (2018), pp.733–734

R. Ginouvès, 'La mosaïque des mois à Argos', *Bulletin de Correspondance Hellénique*, 81 (1957), pp.216–268

Glad, D., 'The Empire's Influence on Barbarian Elites from the Pontus to the Rhine (Fifth-Seventh Centuries): A Case Study of Lamellar Weapons and Segmental Helmets' in S. Ivanišević, M. Kazanski, *The Pontic Danubian in the Period of the Great Migration*, Centre de Recherche d'Histoire et Civilisation de Byzance (Paris-Belgrade: Collège de France/ CNRS,

Monographies 36-Arheološki Institute Beograd, *Posebna Izdanja, Knijiga*, 51, 2012), pp.349–362

Goddard, Chr. J. et al, 'D'Ulpiana à Iustiniana Secunda, d'une cité à l'autre dans l'Antiquité tardive (prospection géophysique 2019–2020)', *Revue archéologique. Bulletin de la Société française d'Archéologie classique*, 73 (2022), pp.153–162

Goeje, M. J. De, *Mémoire sur le Fotouho's-Sham attribué à Abou Ismail al-Baçri* (Leiden: *Mémoires d'histoire et de géographie orientales*, 2, 1864)

Goffart, W. A., *Barbarians and Romans AD 418–584: The Techniques of Accommodation*, (Princeton NJ: Princeton University Press, 1980)

Goffart, W. A., *The Narrators of Barbarian History AD 550–800. Jordanes, Gregory of Tours, Bede and Paul the Deacon* (Princeton NJ: Princeton University Press, 1988)

M. P. S. Gomez, 'The Byzantine Balkan Path in the Gothic Campaigns of 536 and 551', (Murcia: Universidad Catolica San Antonio-Online edition Academia.edu., 2014)

Gonis N., 'Payments to Bucellarii in Seventh Century Oxyrhynchus' in J. L. Fournet & A. Papaconstantinou, *Mélanges Jean Gascou* (Paris: Collège de France, Centre de recherche d'histoire et civilisation de Byzance, Travaux et Mémoires, 20/1, 2016), pp.175–192

Gračanin, H., 'The Gepids and Southern Pannonia in the Age of Justinian I' in T. Vida, D. Quast, Z. Racz, I. Koncz (eds), *Kollaps – Neuordnung – Kontinuität. Gepiden nach dem Ungtergang des Hunnenreiches. Tagung der Internationalen Konferenz and der Eötvös Lorand Universität, Budapest, 14–15 Dezember 2015*, (Mainz, Budapest: Institut für Archäologiewissenschaften, Eötvös Lorand Universität, Budapest Institut für Archäologie des Forschungszentrums für Humanwissenschaftender Ungarischen Akademie der Wissenschaften, Leibniz-Forschungsinstitut für Archäologie, Römisch-Germanisches Zentralmuseum, 2019), pp.185–274

Graf, D. F., 'The *Via Militaris* and the *Limes Arabicus*' in W. Groenman-van Waateringe, B. L. van Beek, W. J. H. Willems, S. L. Wynia (eds), *Roman Frontier Studies 1995, Proceedings of the XVI International Congress of Roman Frontier Studies* (Oxford: Oxbow, 1997), pp.123–133

Greatrex, G., *Rome and Persia at War, 502–532* (Cambridge: Francis Cairns, 2006)

Greatrex, G., Lieu, S. N. C. (eds), The Roman Eastern Frontier and the Persian Wars, Part II, AD 363–630. A Narrative Sourcebook (London: Routledge, 2002)

Greatrex, G., 'Moines, militaires et défense de la frontière orientale au VIe s.' in Lewin, A. S., Pellegrini, P., Fiema, Z. T., Janniard, S. (eds), *The Late Roman Army in Near East from Diocletian to the Arab Conquest*. Proceedings of a colloquium held at Potenza, Acerenza and Matera, Italy, May 2005 (Oxford: *BAR, BAR* International Series, 1717, 2007), pp.285–297

Greatrex, G., 'Perceptions of Procopius in Recent Scholarship' in Histos, 8 (2014), pp.76–121

Grotowski, P. L., Arms and Armour of the Warrior Saints. Tradition and Innovation in Byzantine Iconography (843-1261), (Leiden: BRILL, THE MEDIEVAL MEDITERRANEAN, 87, 2010)

Guilland, R., 'Les Logothètes: Études sur l'histoire administrative de l'Empire byzantin', *REB*, 29 (1971), pp.5–115

Guillou, A., 'Prise de Gaza par les Arabes au VIIe siècle', *BCH*, 81 (1957), pp.396–404

Hahn, W., *Moneta Imperii Byzantini*, vol.1, *Von Anastasius I. bis Justinianus I. (491–565)*, vol.2, *Von Justinus II bis Phocas (565–610)*, vol. 3, *Von Heraclius bis Leo III (610–720)*, (Vienna: Veröffentlichungen der Numismatischen Kommission X = Österr. Akad. der Wiss., phil.-hist. Kl., Denkschriften 148, 1973, 1975 and 1981)

Haldon, J. F., 'Solenarion-The Byzantine Crossbow', *Historical Journal of the University of Birgminham*, 12 (1970), pp.155–157

Haldon, J. F., *Byzantine Praetorians: an administrative, institutional and social survey of the Opsikion and tagmata, c. 580–900* (Bonn: Dr. Rudolf Habelt, Freie Universität Berlin, Byzantinisch-neugriegechischtes Seminar, Poikila Byzantina, 3, 1984)

Haldon, J. F., *Byzantium in the Seventh Century: The Transformation of a Culture* (Cambridge: Cambridge University Press, 1997)

Haldon, J. F., 'Some Aspects of Early Byzantine Arms and Armour' in D. Nicolle (ed.), *A Companion to Medieval Arms and Armour* (Woodbridge: The Boydell Press, 2002), pp.65–86.

Haldon, J. F., *Warfare, State and Society in the Byzantine world, 565–1204* (London: UCL Press, Warfare and History, 2003)

Haldon J. F. (ed.), *Byzantine Warfare* (Aldershot: Ashgate Publishing, 2007)

Haldon, J. F., *The Byzantine Wars* (Brimscombe Port Stroud: The History Press, 2008)

Haldon, J. F., 'The Army and Military Logistics' in I. P. Stephenson (ed.), *The Byzantine World* (London: Routledge, 2010), pp.47–60

Halifeoglu, F. M., 'Castle Architecture in Anatolia: Fortifications of Diyarbakir', *Frontiers of Architectural Research*, vol. 2/2 (2013), pp.209–221

Hallot-Charmasson, M., 'Saints guerriers ou guerriers saints? Les saints militaires à Byzance des origines à 1204' in M. Hallot-Charmasson (ed.), *Médiation, paix et guerre au Moyen Âge. Actes du 136e Congrès national des sociétés historiques et scientifiques, 'Faire la guerre, faire la paix', Perpignan, 2011* (Paris: Éditions du CTHS, Actes des congrès nationaux des sociétés historiques et scientifiques, 136–3, 2012), pp.51–62

Harl, K. W., *Coinage in the Roman Economy, 300 B.C. to AD 700* (Baltimore: The John Hopkins University Press, 1996)

Harris, W. V., *Roman Power: A Thousand Years of Empire* (Cambridge: Cambridge University Press, 2016)

Heather, P. J., *Empires and Barbarians. Migration, Development and the Birth of Europe*, (London: Macmillan, 2009)

Herrmann, P., *Itinéraires des voies romaines de l'Antiquité au Moyen Âge* (Paris: Errances 2007)

Hoffmann, D., *Das Spätrömische Bewegungsheer und die Notitia Dignitatum*, vol. 1 (Düsseldorf: Rheinland-Verlag, 1968)

Hombert, M., 'Bulletin papyrologique, XXVIII (1954 to 1959), 2ème partie', *REG*, t. 79, fasc. 374–375, January-June (1966), pp.99–278

Howard-Johnston, J., 'Heraclius' Persian Campaigns and the Revival of the East Roman Empire 622–630', *War in History*, 6 (1999), pp.1–44

Hoyland, R. G., *Seeing Islam as Others Saw It: A Survey and Evaluation of Christian, Jewish and Zoroastrian Writings on Early Islam*, Studies in Late Antiquity and Early Islam series 13 (Princeton NJ: Darwin Press, 1998)

Hoyland, R. G., *In God's Path: The Arab Conquests and the Creation of an Islamic Empire* (Oxford: Oxford University Press, 2015)

Iorga, N., *Histoire de la vie Byzantine, tome 1, l'Empire œcuménique (527–641)*, (Bucarest: Privately Published by the Author, 1934)

Ivanišević, V., Kazanski, M., Mastykova, A. (eds), *Les nécropoles de Viminacium à l'époque des Grandes Migrations*, Centre de Recherche d'Histoire et Civilisation de Byzance, Monographies, 22, Association des Amis du Centre d'histoire et civilisation de Byzance, (Paris: Collège de France-CNRS, 2006)

Ivanišević, V. & Kazanski, M., 'Illyricum du Nord et les Barbares à l'époque des Grandes Migrations (V^e-VIe siècles)', *Starinar*, 64 (2014), pp.131–160

Ivanišević, V., 'Une capitale revisitée: Caričin Grad (Justiniana Prima)', *Comptes rendus des séances de l'Académie des Inscriptions et Belles-Lettres*, 161-1 (2017), pp.93–115

James, S., 'The *Fabricae*: State Arms Factories of the Later Roman Empire' in J. C. Coulston, *Military Equipment and the Identity of Roman Soldiers. Proceedings of the Fourth Roman Military Equipment Conference* (Oxford: BAR, *BAR* International Series, 394, 1988), pp.257–331

Janin, R., 'Citharizum' in A. Baudrillart, A. De Meyer, É. Van Cauwenbergh (eds), *Dictionnaire d'Histoire et de Géographie ecclésiastiques*, vol. XII, fasc. 67–72 (Paris: Letouzey et Ané, 1953), col. 997

Janin, R., *Constantinople Byzantine. Développement urbaine et répertoire topographique* (Paris: Institut français d'Études Byzantines, 1964)

Janniard, S., 'Procope, les Huns et les transformations tactiques de la cavalerie romaine au VIe siècle' in G. Greatrex & S. Janniard (eds), *Le monde de Procope/ The World of Procopius*, (Paris: O&M, 28, 2018), pp.205–214

Jarry, J., 'La conquête du Fayoum par les Musulmans d'après le Futūḥ Al-Bahnasa', *Annales Islamologiques*, 9 (1970), pp.9–20

Jones, A. H. M., *The Later Roman Empire, 284–602. A Social, Economic and Administrative Survey*, 3 vols (Oxford: Blackwell, 1964). Abridged version in French, *Le déclin du monde antique, 284–610* (Paris: Sirey, 1970)

Jones, A. H. M., Martindale, J. R. and Morris, J., *The Prosopography of the Later Roman Empire* (Cambridge: Cambridge University Press, vol.1 [A.D. 260–395], 1971; vol. 2 [A.D. 395–527] 1980; vol. 3 [A.D. 526–641], 1992.)

Kaegi, W. E., *Byzantium and Early Islamic Conquests* (Cambridge: Cambridge University Press, 1992)

Kaegi, W. E., *Heraclius, Emperor of Byzantium* (Cambridge: Cambridge University Press, 2003)

Kaplan, M., *Byzance. Villes et campagnes* (Paris: Picard, 2006)

Karelin, D. A., 'Imaging of the Late Roman Castrum. Hypothetical Computer Reconstruction of Nag el-Hagar Fortress in Egypt', *AMIT*, 2/15, (2011) pp.1–20

Karelin, D. A., 'The Reconstruction of the Diocletianic Fortress in Babylon of Egypt: Architectural Decorations and Details' in A. V. Zakharova., S. V. Maltseva, E. I. Staniukovich-Denisova (eds), *Actual Problems of Theory and History of Art: Collection of articles*, 9, Lomonosov Moscow State University (St Petersburg: NP-Print, 2019) pp.180–188

Kawar, I., 'Procopius on the Ghassanids', *Journal of the American Oriental Society*, 77, 2 (1957), pp.79–87

Kazanski, M., Vallet, F., (eds), *L'armée romaine et les Barbares du IIIe au VIIe siècle*, Colloque international organisé à Saint-Germain-en-Laye, 1990 (Chelles: Association française d'Archéologie Mérovingienne et la Société des Amis du Musée des Antiquités Nationales, t. 5 des Mémoires publiés par l'Association française d'Archéologie Mérovingienne, 1993)

Kazanski, M., 'La cavalerie slave à l'époque de Justinien', *Archaeologia Baltica*, 11 (2009), pp.229–239, Russian version, 'О раннеславянской коннице', *Stratum Plus*, 5 (2009), pp.457–471

Kazanski, M., 'Les casques du type Baldenheim en Europe orientale: les origines' in M. Kazanski & P. Perin (eds), *Autour du règne de Clovis, Les grands dans l'Europe du Haut Moyen Âge, Histoire et archéologie* (Leuven: AFAM, 31, 2021), pp.230–229

Kazhdan, A. P., Talbot, A. M., Cutler, A., Gregory, T. E., Ševčenko, N. P. (eds), *The Oxford Dictionary of Byzantium*, 3 vols (Oxford: Oxford University Press, 1991)

Keating, P. *Belisarius Military Master of the West, Book One: Nika* (London: Vanguard Press, 2021)

Kennedy, H., *The Armies of the Caliphs. Military and Society in the Early Islamic State* (Abingdon: Routledge, 2006)

Kennedy, H., *The Great Arab Conquests: how the spread of Islam changed the world we live in* (London: Weidenfeld & Nicholson, 2007)

Kern, E. '*Non ignota cano:* histoire et mémoire dans 'la dernière épopée romaine', la *Johannide* de Corippe', *Schedæ*, fasc.1 (2007), pp.97–106

Keser-Kayaalp, E., Erdogan, N., 'Recent research on Dara/Anastasiopolis' in E. Rizos (ed.), *New Cities in Late Antiquity: Documents and Archaeology* (Turnhout: Brepols, 2017), pp.153–175

Khalidi, T., *Arabic historical though in the Classical Period*, Cambridge Studies in Islamic Civilisation (Cambridge: Cambridge University Press, 2004)

Khoperia, N., 'The Byzantine Lazic Phalanx at the Battle of the Hippis River (550 CE)', *The Journal of Politics and Democratisation-Online Publication*, 4/2, January (2020), pp.17–24

Kislinger, E., 'Ein Angriff zu viel: zur Verteidigung der Thermopylen in Justinianischen Zeit', *BZ*, 91 (1998), pp.45–58

Kiss, P. A., 'Huns, Germans, Byzantines? The origins of the narrow bladed long seaxes', *Acta Archaeologica Carpathica*, 49 (2014), pp.131–164

Kolias, T. G., *Byzantinische Waffen. Ein Beitrag zur byzantinischen Waffenkunde von den Anfängen bis zur lateinischen Eroberung* (Vienna: Verlag der Österreichischen Akademie der Wissenschaften, *Byzantina Vindobonensia* 17, 1988)

Kondić, Vl., 'Les formes des fortifications protobyzantines dans la région des Portes de Fer' in Collectif, *Villes et peuplement dans l'Illyricum protobyzantin. Actes du colloque de Rome (12–14 mai 1982)*, (Rome: *PEFR*, 77, 1984), pp.131–161

Konrad, M., *Der spätrömische Limes in Syrien. Archäologische Untersuchungen an den Grenzkastellen von Sura, Tetrapyrgium, Cholle und in Resafa* (Mainz: Verlag Philipp von Zabern, Deutsches Archäologisches Institut, *Resafa* 5, 2001)

Kraemer, C. J., *Excavations at Nessana, III, Non-literary papyri* (Princeton NJ: Princeton University Press, 1958)

Krischen, F., *Die Landmauer von Konstantinopel*, t. 1. Zeichnerische Wiederherstellung mit begleitendem Text (Berlin: De Gruyter, 1938)

Lassus, J., *La forteresse Byzantine de Thamugadi, fouilles à Timgad 1938–1956* (Paris: Éditions du CNRS, Études d'Antiquités africaines, 1981)

Kubik, A. L., 'Introduction to Studies on Late Sasanian Protective Armour. The Yarysh-Mardy1 Helmet', *Historia I Świat*, 5 (2016), pp.77–105

Kubik, A. L., Radyuš, O. A., Vyazov, L. A., 'On one series of the VI Century AD Iron One-Piece Asian Helmets', *Bulletin of the Institute of Oriental Studies*, 3 (1) (2023), pp.52–82

Lécrivain, Ch., 'Les soldats privés au Bas-Empire', *MEFR*, 10 (1890), pp.267–283

Lebedynsky, I., *Les Scythes. La Civilisation des steppes (VIIe-IIIe siècles av. J.-C.)*, (Paris: Errances 2001)

Lebedynsky, I., *De l'épée scythe au sabre mongol: Les armes blanches des Steppes* (Paris: Errances-Actes Sud, 2021)

Le Bohec, Y., 'Écuyers et marins militaires sous le Haut-Empire romain', *Ktèma*, 21 (1996), pp.313–320

Lehmann, Ph. W., 'Theodosius or Justinian? A Renaissance Drawing of a Byzantine Rider', *The Art Bulletin*, vol. 41, no. 1 (March, 1959), pp.39–57

Lendon, J. E., *Soldiers and Ghosts: A History of Battle in Classical Antiquity* (New Haven: Yale University Press, 2005)

Lendon, J. E., *Soldats et fantômes. Combattre pendant l'Antiquité*, translated into French by Villeneuve G. (Paris: Tallandier, 2009)

Lepie, H., Münchow, A., *Elfenbeinkunst aus dem Aachener Domschatz* (Pandersberg: Imhof Verlag, 2006)

Lewin, A. S., Pellegrini, P., Fiema, Z. T., Janniard, S. (eds), *The Late Roman Army in Near East from Diocletian to the Arab Conquest: Proceedings of a colloquium held at Potenza, Acerenza and Matera, Italy, May 2005* (Oxford: *BAR*, *BAR* International Series, 1717, 2007)

Llewellyn, P., *Rome in the Dark Ages* (London: Constable and Company Ltd, 1993)

Lo Jacono, Cl., 'La bataille d'Aǧnadain selon Ibn A'ṯam al-Kūfī's Kitab al-futūḥ' in R. Traini (ed.), *Études en l'honneur de Francesco Gabrieli à l'occasion de son quatre-vingtième anniversaire*, vol. 2 (Rome: 1984), pp.447–457

Lombardi, F. V., 'Lo scontro franco-bizantino fra Pesaro nel 554 d.C. (Agatia II, 2–3)', *Studia Oliveriana*, 12 (1992), pp.55–62

Lot, F., 'La *Notitia Dignitatum utriusque imperii* ses tares, sa date de composition, sa valeur', *REA* (1936), pp.285–338

Luchitskaya, S., 'L'Empereur Héraclius vu par les chroniqueurs occidentaux du XIIe siècle', *Cahiers de Recherches Médiévales et Humanistes*, 37 (2019), pp.75–96

Maas, M., *John Lydus and the Roman Past. Antiquarianism and Politics in the Age of Justinian* (London: Routledge, 1992)

Maas M. (ed.), *The Cambridge Companion to the Age of Justinian* (Cambridge: Cambridge University Press, 2005)

Macdowall, S., *Late Roman Infantryman, 236–565* (London: Osprey Publishing, Warrior Series, 9, 1994)

Macdowall, S., *Late Roman Cavalryman, 236–565* (London: Osprey Publishing, Warrior Series, 15, 1995)

Marciak, M., *Sophene, Gordyene, and Adiabene: Three Regna Minora of Northern Mesopotamia Between East and West* (Leiden: Brill, 2017)

Marciniak, M., *Draco – historia smoczego sztandaru – History of the Dragon standard, University of Varsaw*, Master's Degree in archaeology in the field of general anthropology n° 209 672 (Uniwersytet Warszawski Instytut Archeologii, 2010)

Maiuri, M., 'L'assedio di Narsete a Cuma nel racconto dello storico Agathias', *La Parola del Passato*, 4 (1949), pp.41–46

Maksimović, L., 'L'administration de l'Illyricum septentrional à l'époque de Justinien', in H. Ahrweiler, *Philadelphie et autres études* (Paris: Éditions de la Sorbonne, *Byzantina Sorboniensa*, 1984), pp.143–157

Maksymiuk, K., *Geography of Roman-Iranian Wars: Military operations of Rome and Sasanian Iran* (Siedlce: Uniwersytet Przyrodniczo-Humanistyczny w Siedlcach, 2015)

Maneva, E., 'Le casque à fermoir d'Héraclée', *Archaeologia Iugoslavica*, 24 (1987), pp.101–111

Mason, H. J., *Greek Terms for Roman Institutions. A Lexicon and Analysis* (Toronto: Hakkert, *American studies in papyrology*, 13, 1971)

Maspéro, J., *Organisation militaire de l'Égypte Byzantine* (Paris: Champion, 1912)

Matvieiev, A., 'Kitab Futuh el-Sham of (Pseudo-)Muhammad ibn Umar al-Waqidi as a Source for Studying the Battle on the River Yarmuk (636)', *Vox Patrum*, 77 (2021), pp.51–80

Meier, M., 'Prokop, Agathias, die Pest und das Ende der antiken Historiographie', *Historiche Zeitschrift*, 278 (2004), pp.281–310

Merrills, A., 'Understanding Late Antique North Africa' in A. Merrills (ed.), *Vandals, Romans and Berbers. New Perspectives on Late Antique North Africa* (London: Routledge, 2006), pp.1–28

Merrills, A., *War, Rebellion, Epic in Byzantine Africa. A Historical Study of Corippus' Iohannis* (Cambridge: Cambridge University Press, 2023)

(Michele Daviau, M. P., Chadwick, J. R., Steiner, M., eds), 'Excavation and Survey at Khirbat al-Mudayna and Its Surroundings: Preliminary Report of the 2001, 2004 and 2005 Seasons', in *Annual of the Department of Antiquities of Jordan* 50 (2006), pp.249–283

Mihaescu, H., '*Torna, torna, fratre*', *Byzantina*, 8 (1976), pp.21–35

Mitchell, S., *A History of the Later Roman Empire, AD 284-641* (Oxford: Blackwell, 2007)

Milligen, A. van, *Byzantine Constantinople. The Walls of the City and adjoining Historical Sites* (London: John Murray, 1899)

Modéran, Y., 'Corippe et l'occupation Byzantine de l'Afrique: Pour une nouvelle lecture de la Johannide', *Antiquités Africaines*, XXII (1986), pp.195–212

Modéran, Y., 'Koutzinas-Cusina. Recherche sur un Maure du VIe siècle' in A. Mastino (ed.), *L'Africa romana 7. Atto del VII convegno di studio, Sassari, 1989* (Sassari: Edizioni Galizzi, 1990), pp.393–407

Modéran, Y., 'Cusina', *Encyclopédie Berbère*, 14 (Aix-en-Provence: 1994), pp.2158–2159

Modéran, Y., 'Les frontières mouvantes du royaume Vandale' in Cl. Lepelley, X. Dupuis (eds), *Frontières et limites géographiques de l'Afrique du Nord antique, Hommage à Pierre Salama* (Paris: 1999), pp.241–264

Modéran, Y., *Encyclopédie berbère*, 23 (Aix-en-Provence: 2000), pp.3565–3567

Modéran, Y., *Les Maures et l'Afrique romaine (IVe-VIIe siècle)*, (Rome: PEFR, 2003)

Mollat, M., 'Problèmes maritimes de l'histoire des croisades', *Cahiers de Civilisation Médiévale*, 10–39–40 (1967), pp.345–359

Moorhead, J., 'Italian Loyalties During Justinian's Gothic War', *REB*, 53 (1983), pp.575–596.

Morizot, P., 'Aurès' in *Encyclopédie berbère*, 7 (Aix-en-Provence: 1990), pp.1103–1113

Morizot, P., 'Recherches sur les campagnes de Solomon en Numidie méridionale', *CRAI*, January-February (1993), pp.83–106

Morizot, P., 'Timgad et son territoire' in *L'Afrique, la Gaule et son territoire à l'époque romaine, Mélanges à la mémoire de Marcel Le Glay* (Brussels: Latomus, 226, 1994), pp.220–243

Morizot, P., *Romains et Berbères face à face* (Arles: Errances, Les Hesperides, 2015).

Morrisson, C. (ed.), *Le monde Byzantin. L'Empire romain d'Orient (330-641)* (Paris: PUF, Nouvelle Clio, 2006)

Mrav, Z., 'Maniakon. The Golden Torc in Late Roman and Early Byzantine Army' in T. Vida, Ph. Rance et al, *The Frontier World. Roman, barbarians and Military Culture* (Budapest: Eötvös Lorand University, Martin Optiz Kiado, 2015), pp.287–303

Nagy, K., 'Notes on the Arms of the Avar Heavy Cavalry' in *Proceedings of the First International Conference on the Medieval History of the Eurasian Steppe*, Szeged, May 11—16, 2004, Part II, (Szeged: Akadémiai Kiado, *Acta Orientalia Academiae Scientiarum Hungaricae*, 58, 2, 2005), pp.135–148

Narkiss, B., 'Scribes and Artists of the Ashburnham Pentateuch' in *Tributes to Jonathan J. G. Alexander. The Making and Meaning of Illuminated Medieval & Renaissance Manuscripts, Art & Architecture* (London: H. Miller, 2006)

Nelis-Clément, J., *Les Beneficiarii: militaires et administrateurs au service de l'empire: Ier s. a.C.-VIe s. p.C.* (Bordeaux: Ausonius-De Boccard, 2000)

(Nicholson, O., ed.), *The Oxford Dictionary of Late Antiquity*, 2 vols (Oxford: Oxford University Press, 2018)

Nicolle, David, *Yarmuk 636 AD: The Muslim Conquest of Syria* (Oxford: Osprey Publishing, Campaign Series, 31, 1994)

O'Donnell, J. J. 'Liberius the Patrician', *Tradition*, 31 (1981), pp.31–72

Oikonomidès, N., 'Les premières mentions des thèmes dans la chronique de Théophane', *Zbornik radova Vizantološkog Instituta*, 16 (1975), pp.1–8

Onur, F., 'The Anastasian Military Decree from Perge in Pamphylia: Revised 2nd Edition', *Gephyra*, 14 (2017), pp.133–212

Pacha Miran, F., *Le décor de la Bible syriaque de Paris (BnF syr. 341) et son rôle dans l'histoire du livre chrétien* (Paris: Geuthner, 2020)

Palmer, A., 'Une chronique syriaque contemporaine de la conquête arabe: essai d'interprétation théologique et politique' in P. Canivet (ed.), *La Syrie de Byzance à l'Islam (VIIe-VIIIe siècles)*, (Damascus: Institut français d'études Arabes de Damas, 1992), pp.31–46

Palmer, A., *The Seventh Century in the West-Syrian Chronicles* (Liverpool: Liverpool University Press, 1993)

Parani, M., *Reconstructing the Reality of Images: Byzantine Material Culture and Religious Iconography (11th–15th centuries)*, (Leiden: Brill, 2003).

Paret, R., 'The Legendary Futūḥ Litterature' in F. M. Donner, *The Expansion of the Early Islamic State* (London: Routledge, 2007), pp.163–176

Pargoire, J., 'Les LX soldats martyrs de Gaza', *REB*, 50 (1905), pp.40–43

Parnell, D. A., 'A Prosopographical Approach to Justinian's Army', *Medieval Prosopography*, 27, 1 (2012), pp.1–75

Parnell, D. A., 'Barbarians and Brothers-in-Arms. Byzantines on Barbarian Soldiers in the Sixth Century', *BZ*, 108, 2 (2015), pp.809–826

Parnell, D. A., *Justinian's Men: Careers and Relationships of Byzantine Army Officers, c. 518–610*, New Approaches to Byzantine History and Culture (London: Palgrave Macmillan, 2017).

Parnell, D. A., 'Procopius on Romans, non-Romans, and battle casualties' in G. Greatrex & S. Janniard (eds), *Le monde de Procope/ The World of Procopius,* (Paris: O&M, 28, 2018), pp.249–262

Paulsen, P., *Alamannische Adelsgräber von Niederstotzingen (Kreis Heindeinheim)*, (Stuttgart: Müller & Gräff, Kommissions Verlag, 1967)

Pietri, Ch., 'Le serment du soldat chrétien. Les épisodes de la Militia Christi sur les sarcophages', *MEFR*, 74–2 (1962), pp.649–664.

Pillon, M., 'Armée et défense de l'Illyricum Byzantin de Justinien à Héraclius (527–641). De la réorganisation justinienne à l'émergence des 'armées de cité'', *Erytheia*, 26 (2005), pp.7–85.

Polh, W. *Die Avaren. Ein Steppenwolk im Mitteleuropa 567–822 n. Chr* (Munich: C.H. Beck, 1988)

Pomey, P., 'À propos de la voile latine: la mosaïque de Kelenderis et les *Stereometrica* (II, 48–49) d'Héron d'Alexandrie', *Archeonautica*, 19 (2017), pp.9–25

Popović, Vl., 'Les témoins archéologiques des invasions avaro-slaves dans l'Illyricum byzantin', *MEFR*, 87–1 (1975), pp.445–504

Popović, Vl., 'La descente des Koutrigurs, des Slaves et des Avars vers la mer Égée: le témoignage de l'archéologie', *Comptes rendus des séances de l'Académie des Inscriptions et Belles-Lettres*, 122–3 (1978), pp.596–648

Poulter, A., 'The Use and Abuse of Urbanism in the Danubian Provinces During the Later Roman Empire' in J. Rich (ed.), *The City in Late Antiquity* (London, New York: Routledge, 2002), pp.106–109

Pralong, A., 'Remarques sur les fortifications Byzantines de Thrace orientale' in H. Ahrweiler, *Géographie historique du monde méditerranéen* (Paris: Éditions de la Sorbonne, 1988), pp.179–200

Pringle, D., *The Defence of Byzantine Africa from Justinian to The Arab Conquest. An account of the military history and archaeology of the African provinces in the sixth and seventh centuries* (Oxford: BAR, BAR International Series, 99, 2001)

Pryor, J. H. & Jeffrey, H., *The Age of the Dromōn: The Byzantine Navy Ca 500–1204*, The Medieval Mediterranean, Peoples, Economies and Cultures 400–1500, 62, (Leiden-Boston: Brill, 2006).

Puech, V., 'Les officiers de l'armée d'Afrique sous Justinien', *RM2E – Revue de la Méditerranée, édition électronique*, t. II.2 (2015), pp.57–82

Rance, Ph., 'The *Fulcum*, the Late Roman and Byzantine Testudo: The Germanisation of Roman Infantry Tactics', *Greek, Roman and Byzantine Studies*, 44 (2004), pp.265–326

Rance, Ph., 'Drungus, Δροῦγγος and Δρουγγιστί – a Gallicism and Continuity in Roman Cavalry Tactics', *Phoenix*, 58 (2004), pp.96–130

Rance, Ph., 'Narses and the Battle of Taginæ (Busta Gallorum) 552: Procopius and Sixth Century Warfare', *Historia*, 54 (2005), pp.424–472

Rance, Ph., 'Campidoctores Vicarii vel Tribuni: The Senior Regimental Officers of the Late Roman Army and Rise of the Campidoctor' in A. S Lewin, P. Pellegrini, Z. T. Fiema, S. Janniard (eds), *The Late Roman Army in Near East from Diocletian to the Arab Conquest: Proceedings of a colloquium held at Potenza, Acerenza and Matera, Italy, May 2005* (Oxford: BAR, BAR International Series, 1717, 2007), pp.395–409.

Rance, Ph., '*sculca, sculcator, exculcator* and *proculator*: The Scouts of the late Roman Army and a Disputed Etymology', *Latomus*, 73 (2014), pp.474–501.

Rapport, M., *Nationality and Citizenship in Revolutionary France* (Oxford: Oxford University Press, 2000)

Ravegnani, G., *Soldati di Bisanzio in Età Giustinianea* (Rome: Jouvence, 1998)

Ravegnani, G., *I bizantini e la guerra. L'età di Giustiniano* (Rome: Jouvence, Storia, 51, 2004)

Ravegnani, G., 'Le unità dell'esercito bizantino nel VI secolo tra continuità e innovazione' in S. Gaspari (ed.), *Alto Medioevo Mediterraneo* (Florence: Firenze University Press, 2005), pp.185–205

Ravegnani, G., 'Soldati di Bisanzio in Italia nelle epigrafi del VI secolo in G. Cresci Marrone', A. Pistellato, *Studi in ricordo di Fulviomario Broilo* (Padova, S.A.R.G.O.N., vol. 2, 2007), pp.523–530

Reichenkron, G., 'Zur romischen Kommando-sprache bei byzantinischen Schriftstellern', *BZ*, 54 (1961), pp.18–27

(Reinink, G. J. & Stolte, B. H., eds), *The Reign of Heraclius (610–641), Crisis and Confrontation* (Leuven: Paris; Dudley MA: Peeters, 2002)

Rémondon, R., 'Soldats de Byzance d'après un papyrus trouvé à Edfou', *Recherches de Papyrologie*, I (1961), pp.41–93

Rich, J., *The City in Late Antiquity* (London: Routledge, 1996).

Richardot, Ph., 'Du Ve au XVIe siècle: un millénaire stratégique' in *Méditerranée, Les constantes géostratégiques*, Actes du Colloque du Groupe des Écoles du Commissariat de la Marine et Fondation Méditerranéenne pour les Études Stratégiques, Toulon, 25–26 avril 1996, (Paris: Publisud, 1997), pp.87–143

Richardot, Ph., 'Le plus vieux limes: la défense de l'Afrique romaine', *Revue Internationale d'Histoire Militaire*, 76 (1997), pp.15–37

Richardot, Ph., *La fin de l'Armée romaine 284–476*, 3e édition revue et augmentée avec une traduction de la Notitia Dignitatum (Paris: Economica, 2005)

Richardot, Ph., *Les erreurs stratégiques des Gaulois face à César* (Paris, Economica, 2006)

Richardot, Ph., 'La bataille antique: représentation et modèle', *Prétorien*, 9, avril-juin (2009), pp. 19–27

Richardot, Ph., 'La pacification de l'Afrique Byzantine, 534–546' in Coutau-Bégarie (ed.), *Stratégies irrégulières* (*Stratégique*, 93–96, 1, 2009), pp. 129–158.

Richardot, Ph., *L'Âge des guerriers ou l'aube du Moyen Âge 476–711* (Le Rove: Centre Littéraire d'Impression Provençal, 2016).

Rodgers, W. L., *Naval Warfare under Oars 4th to 16th Centuries* (Annapolis: Naval Institute Press, 1990)

Roisl, H. N., 'Totila und die Schlacht bei den Busta Gallorum, Ende Juni/Anfang Juli 552', *Jahrbuch der Österreichischen Byzantinistk*, 30 (1981), pp.25–50

Rougé, J., 'Sur un mot de Cassiodore: Exculcatoriae-Sculcatoriae-Sulcatoriae' in *Latomus*, 21 (1962), pp.384–390

Ruysschaert, J., 'Lectures des illustrations du Virgile Vatican et du Virgile romain', *Monuments et Mémoires de la Fondation Eugène Piot*, 73 (1991), pp.25–51

Sahas, D. J., 'Face to Face Encounter Between Patriarch Sophronius of Jerusalem and the Caliph 'Umar Ibn al-Khattab: Friends or Foes?' in E. Grypeou, M. N. Swanson, D. R. Thomas (eds), *The Encounter of Eastern Christianity with Early Islam* (Leiden: Brill, 2006), pp.33–44

Sarantis, A., 'War and Diplomacy in Pannonia and the North-West Balkans During the Reign of Justinian: The Gepid Threat and Imperial Responses', *DOP*, 63 (2009), pp.15–40

Sarantis, A., 'The Justinianic Heruli: from allied barbarians to Roman provincials' in F. Curta (ed.) *Neglected barbarians* (Turnhout: Brepols, 2011), pp.361–402

Schlumberger, G., 'L'ivoire Barberini' in *Monuments et Mémoires de la Fondation Eugène Piot*, 7–1 (1900), pp.79–94

Scott, S., *The Response of the Royal Army to the French Revolution: The Role and Development of the Line Army 1787–93* (Oxford: Clarendon Press, 1978).

Shahid, I. *Byzantium and the Arabs in the Sixth century*, vol.1, part 1, *Political and Military History* (Washington: Dumbarton Oaks Research Library and Collection, 1995)

Speidel, M. P., 'Raising New Units for the Late Roman Army: Auxilia Palatina', *DOP*, 50 (1996), pp.163–170

Speidel, M. P., 'Who fought in the Front' in G. Alföldy, B. Dobson, W. Eck (eds), *Kaiser Heer und Gesellschaft in der Romischen Kaiserzeit. Gedenkschrift für Eric Birley* (Stuttgart: Franz Steiner Verlag, 2000), pp.473–482

Stadler, P., 'Avar Chronology Revisited, and the Question of Ethnicity in the Avar Qaganate' in F. Curta, R. Kovalev (eds), *The Other Europe in the Middle Ages. Avars, Bulgars, Khazars and Cumans* (Leiden: Brill, 2009), pp.47–82

Stein, E., '*Ordinarii* et *Campidoctores*', *REB*, 8 (1933), pp.379–387

Stephenson, I. P., (ed.), *The Byzantine World* (London: Routledge, 2010).

Stephenson, I. P., *Romano-Byzantine Infantry Equipment* (Stroud: Tempus, 2006)

Stewart, M. E., 'Contest of Andreia in Procopius' Gothic Wars', *Parekbolai*, 4 (2014), pp.21–54

Stewart, M. E., 'The Danger of the Soft Life: Manly and Unmanly Romans in Procopius' Gothic War', *Journal of Late Antiquity*, 10.2 (2017), pp.473–502

Stiebel, G. D., 'A Spangenhelm-type helmet' in E. Mazar, *The Temple Mount Excavations in Jerusalem 1968–1978. Directed by B. Mazar. Final Report II. The Byzantine Period*, (Jerusalem: The Hebrew University of Jerusalem, Qedem, Monographs of the Institute of Archaeology, The Institute of Archaeology 2003), pp.43–46

Stiernon, D., 'Bulletin de théologie mariale Byzantine', *REB*, 17 (1959), pp.201–250

Stratos, A., 'Byzance et la Perse', *La Nouvelle Revue des Deux Mondes*, April (1981), pp.32–46

Tarver, W. T. S., 'The Traction Trebuchet: A Reconstruction of *an Early Medieval Siege Engine*', Technology and Culture, 36, 1 (1995), pp.136–167

Torallas-Tovar, S., 'Los *Riparii* en los papiros del Egipto tardoantiquo', *Aquila Legionis*, 1 (2001), pp.123–149

Treadgold, W., *Byzantium and its Army, 284–1081* (Stanford: Stanford University Press, 1995)

Treadgold, W., *The Early Byzantine Historians* (Basingstoke, New York: Palgrave Macmillan, 2007)

Trombley, F. R., 'The Operational Methods of the Late Roman Army in the Persian War of 572–591' in Lewin, A. S., Pellegrini, P., Fiema, Z. T., Janniard, S. (eds), *The Late Roman Army in Near East from Diocletian to the Arab Conquest: Proceedings of a colloquium held at Potenza, Acerenza and Matera, Italy, May 2005* (Oxford: BAR, BAR International Series, 1717, 2007), pp.321–356

Trousset, P. 'Les limites Sud de la réoccupation Byzantine', *Ant tard*, 10 (2003), pp.143–150

Tsangadas, B. *The Fortifications and Defense of Constantinople* (New York: Columbia University Press, 1980)

Turnbull, S., *The Walls of Constantinople, AD 324–1453* (London: Osprey Publishing, Fortress Series, 25, 2004)

Vagalanski, L., 'Ein neuer spätantiker Segmenthelm aus Voivoda, Schumen Gebiet (Nordost)', *Archaelogica Bulgarica*, 2 (1998), pp.96–106

Valensi, L., 'La réorganisation de l'Égypte Byzantine au temps de Justinien Ier', *Bulletin de l'Association Guillaume Budé*, LH–11 (1952), pp.55–71

Amela Valverde, L., *Varia Historicorum*, I (Seville: Punto Rojo Libros, 2021)

Weitzmann, K., 'Prolegomena to a Study of the Cyprus Plates', *Metropolitan Museum Journal*, vol. 3 (1970), pp.97–111

Van Berchem D., 'Recherches sur la chronologie des enceintes de Syrie et de Mésopotamie', *Syria, Archéologie, Art et Histoire*, 31 3-4, 1954, pp.254-270

Viscidi, F., *I prestiti latini nel greco antico e bizantino* (Padua: Olschki, Università di Padova. Pubblicazioni della Facoltà di lettere e filosofia, 22, 1944).

Vogt, M., *Spangenhelme: Baldenheim und verwandte Typen* (Mainz: Verlag des Römisch-Germanischen Zentralmuseums, Kataloge vor – und frühgeschichtlicher Altertümer, 39, 2006).

Whately, C., 'Some Observations on Procopius' Use of Numbers in Descriptions of Combat in Wars Books 1–7', *Phoenix*, 69, 3/4 (2015), pp.394–411

Whately, C. *Battles and Generals: Combat, Culture, and Didacticism in Procopius' Wars* (Leiden: Brill, History of Warfare Series, 111, 2016)

Whately, C. *Procopius on Soldiers and Military Institutions in the Sixth-Century Roman Empire* (Leiden: Brill, 2021)

Wheeler, E. L., 'The legion as phalanx in the Late Empire, Part 2', *REMA*, 1 (2004), pp.147–175

Wiewiorowski, J., 'The Defence of the Long Walls of Thrace (Μακρά Τείχη τῆς Θράκης) under Justinian the Great (527–565 AD)', *Studia Ceranea*, 2 (2012), pp.181–194

Whitby, M., 'The Long Walls of Constantinople', *REB*, 55 (1985), pp.560–583

Whitby, M., *The Emperor Maurice and his Historian: Theophylact Simocatta on Balkan and Persian Warfare* (Oxford: Oxford University Press, 1988)

Whitby, M., 'Recruitment in Roman Armies from Justinian to Heraclius (ca. 565–615)' in A. Cameron & L. I. Conrad. (eds), (1995), pp.61–124

Wiesehöfer, J. 'CIRCESIUM' in *Encyclopaedia Iranica*, vol. V, fasc. 6 (1991), pp.595–596.

Williams, S. and Friell, G., *The Rome That Did Not Fall: The Survival of the East in the Fifth Century* (London: Routledge, 1999)

Woods, D., 'The 60 Martyrs of Gaza and the Martyrdom of Bishop Sophronius of Jerusalem', *ARAM*, 15 (2003), pp.129–150

Woods, D., 'Jews, rats and the Battle of Yarmuk' in Lewin, A. S., Pellegrini, P., Fiema, Z. T., Janniard, S. (eds), *The Late Roman Army in Near East from Diocletian to the Arab Conquest: Proceedings of a colloquium held at Potenza, Acerenza and Matera, Italy, May 2005* (Oxford: BAR, BAR International Series, 1717, 2007), pp.372–373, 374, n. 47

Vryonis, S. Jr. (ed.), 'The evolution of Slavic society and the Slavic invasions in Greece: the first major Slavic attack on Thessaloniki, AD 597', *Hesperia. Journal of the American School of Classical Studies at Athens*, 50 (1981), pp.378–390

Zarini, Z., *Berbères ou barbares? Recherches sur le livre second de la Johannide de Corippe*, Nancy (Paris: de Boccard, 1997)

Zarini, V., 'Images de guerre dans la poésie officielle de l'Antiquité tardive: l'exemple de la Johannide de Corippe', *Images romaines*, Études de littérature ancienne, IX (1998), pp.161–173

Zeller, A., *Soldats perdus. Des armées de Napoléon aux garnisons de Louis XVIII* (Paris: Perrin, 1977)

Zinski, Z., 'Ein völkerwanderungszeitlicher Helm aus Sinj', *Starohrvatska prosvjeta* 3712 (1982), pp.7–34

Zuckerman, C., 'The early Byzantine strongholds in eastern Pontus', Centre de recherche d' histoire et civilisation de Byzance, *Travaux et Mémoires*, 11 (1991), pp.473–486

Zuckerman, C., 'Le δευτερόν βάνδον Κωνσταντινιακῶν dans une épitaphe de Pylai', *Tyche*, 10 (1995), pp.233–235

Zuckerman, C., *Du village à l'Empire: autour du Registre fiscal d'Aphroditô (525/526)*, (Paris: Association des Amis du Centre d'Histoire et de Civilisation de Byzance, Monographies, 16, 2004)

Zuckerman, C., 'L'armée' in C. Morrisson (ed.), *Le monde Byzantin. L'Empire romain d'Orient (330–641)* (Paris: PUF, Nouvelle Clio, 2006), pp.143–182

Zuckerman C. (ed.), *Constructing the Seventh Century* (Paris: Collège de France, CNRS, Centre de recherche d'histoire et civilisation de Byzance, 2013)